The Drama of the Gifted Child

THE DRAMA

OF THE

GIFTED CHILD

Alice Miller

TRANSLATED FROM THE GERMAN BY

Ruth Ward

Basic Books, Inc., Publishers

NEW YORK

A previous version of chapter 1 appeared in the *International Journal of Psycho-analysis* 60 (1979):47; a previous version of chapter 2 appeared in the *International Review of Psychoanalysis* 6 (1979):61.

Grateful acknowledgment is made to the following for permission to reprint excerpts from the following: Herman Hesse, "A Child's Heart," from *Kling-sor's Last Summer*, translated by Richard and Clara Winston (New York: Farrar, Straus and Giroux, 1970) and *Demian*, translated by Michael Roloff and Michael Lebeck (New York: Harper & Row, 1965).

ORIGINALLY PUBLISHED AS

PRISONERS OF CHILDHOOD

Library of Congress Cataloging in Publication Data

Miller, Alice.
   Prisoners of childhood.

   Translation of Das Drama des begabten Kindes.
   Bibliography: p. 115
   Includes index.
   1. Narcissism.   2. Psychology, Pathological.
3. Self-respect.   I. Title.
RC553.N36M5413   616.89'17   80-50535
ISBN: 0-465-06347-0 (cloth)
ISBN: 0-465-01691-X (paper)

Contents

Preface

We live in a culture that encourages us not to take our own suffering seriously, but rather to make light of it or even to laugh about it. What is more, this attitude is regarded as a virtue, and many people—of whom I used to be one—are proud of their lack of sensitivity toward their own fate and particularly toward their fate as a child. I have tried to demonstrate in my books why the disastrous belief that this attitude is a desirable one has been held so tenaciously and to point out the tragic conditions it helps to conceal.

Again and again, readers from a number of countries have told me with great relief that after reading *The Drama of the Gifted Child*, they felt for the first time in their life something approaching sympathy for the neglected, abused, or even battered child they had been once. They say they now have more self-respect than before and are better able to recognize their needs and feelings. "It was *my* life you were describing in your book; how could you have known?" I am often asked.

How could I have known? Today I do not find it hard to answer this question. Today I know that it was not the books I read, it was not my teachers or my study of philosophy, nor was it my training to become a psychoanalyst that provided me with this knowledge. On the contrary, all of these together, with their mystifying conceptualization and their rejection of reality prevented me from recognizing the truth for years. Surprisingly, it was the child in me, condemned to silence long ago— abused, exploited, and turned to stone—who finally found her feelings and along with them her speech, and then told me, in pain, her story. Thus, it was *my* story I was telling in *The Drama*, and many people saw their own mirrored in it.

In my fourth book, *Pictures of a Childhood*, I describe in greater detail how my encounter with this child came about once she had reappeared after long banishment and how it happened that I was able to offer her the protection she needed in order to feel her pain and speak about it.

I was amazed to discover that I had been an abused child, that from the very beginning of my life I had no choice but to comply totally with the needs and feelings of my mother and to ignore my own. My discovery also showed me the power of repression, which had kept me from learning the truth all my life, and the inadequacy of psychoanalysis, which even reinforced my repression by means of its deceptive theories. For I had completed two analyses as part of my psychoanalytic training, but both analysts had been unable to question my version of the happy childhood I supposedly had enjoyed.

It was not until I started to experiment with spontaneous painting in 1973 that I first was able to gain access to the undistorted reality of my childhood. In the pictures I painted I was confronted with the terror that my mother, a brilliant pedagogue, had inflicted on me in my upbringing. I had been subjected to this terror for years because no one close to me, not even my kind and wise father, was capable of noticing or challenging this form of child abuse. Had just one person understood what was happening and come to my defense, it might have changed my entire life. That person could have helped me to recognize my mother's cruelty for what it was instead of accepting it for decades, to my great detriment, as something normal and necessary.

This part of my story—this lack of enlightened witnesses—may have been responsible for the attempts I have made in my books to provide information that would reach potential witnesses who could be of help to the suffering child. By witnesses I mean people who are not afraid to stand up for children assertively and protect them from adults' abuse of power. In our society, with its hostility toward children, such people are still hard to find, but their number is growing daily.

The spontaneous painting I began to do helped me not only to discover my personal story, but also to free myself from the intellectual constraints and concepts of my upbringing and my professional training, which I now recognized to be false, deceptive, and disastrous in its impact. The more I learned to follow my impulses in a playful way with colors and forms, the weaker became my allegiance to conventions of an aesthetic or any other nature. I did not want to paint beautiful pictures; it was not even my goal to paint good pictures. All I wanted was to help the truth to break through. In this way, when I finally confronted my own truth and was strengthened by it, I found the courage to see with ever-growing clarity how the conventional methods of psychoanalysis block the creativity of patients as well as analysts. This is what I have tried to portray in my books for the sake of helping the victims of this process to become aware of what has been done to them and of sparing them the arduous path of my search. For doing this I have been the recipient of much gratitude but I have also encountered much hostility.

In the meantime I had come to understand that I was abused as a child because my parents had experienced something similar in their childhood but had learned, as had my analysts and teachers, to regard this abuse as upbringing or treatment or training for their own good. Because they were not allowed to feel or, consequently, understand what had once been done to them, they were unable to recognize the abuse as such and passed it on to me in turn, without even the trace of a bad conscience. I realized that I could not change in the slightest my parents' and teachers' past, which had made them blind. But at the same time I felt that I could and must attempt to point out to today's young parents—and especially to future parents—the danger of misusing their power, that I must sensitize them to this danger and make it easier for them to hear the signals of the child inside them as well as of children everywhere.

This is something I can do if I help children—victims who have been condemned to silence and who have no rights—to speak; if I describe their suffering from *their* perspective and not from that of adults. For after all, it was from a child that I myself received crucial information, answers to questions which had gone unanswered throughout my study of philosophy and psychoanalysis and which did not cease to preoccupy me in the years that followed. It was thanks to the pain of the child in me that I fully grasped what so many adults must ward off all their life, and I also realized why they fail to confront their truth, preferring instead to plan self-destruction on a gigantic atomic scale, without even recognizing the absurdity of what they are doing. These are the same people who, like all of us, entered the world as innocent infants, with the primary goals of growing, living in peace, and loving—never of destroying life. I recognized the compelling logic of this absurdity after I found the missing piece of the *puzzle*: the secret of childhood, till then closely guarded. This discovery convinced me that if we are willing to open our eyes to the suffering of the child, we will soon realize that it lies within us as adults either to turn the newborn into monsters by the way we treat them or to let them grow up into feeling—and therefore responsible—human beings.

ALICE MILLER
Zollikerberg, Switzerland
1986

Foreword

"If a fool throws a stone into the water," goes an old saying, "even a hundred sages can't bring it back." Here we have a perfect reflection of the despair of the bright in the face of stupidity. But an ingenuous child, who still thinks in pictures, might ask: "Isn't the world full of stones—so why should a hundred clever people try so hard to get back this one? Why don't they look around? If they do, they might find all kinds of new treasures they can't see because they are so busy searching in vain in the water!"

This may well be the case with the word "narcissism." The word has become part of everyday speech to such an extent, and perhaps more than any other scientific term, that it is difficult today to rescue it for scientific use. The more sincerely the psychoanalytic profession toils for a deeper understanding of the concept of "narcissism," and to elucidate and define it for scientific use, the more the word attracts people to use it in everyday speech. The result of all this is such multiplicity of meanings that it is difficult to use the word now to define a precise psychoanalytic concept.

Now narcissism, the ambiguous noun, can be used, according to one's preference and need, to project a variety of meanings: a condition, a stage of development, a character trait, an illness. Yet, when used in its adverbial and adjectival forms, the word becomes more precise; for then it is possible to achieve some degree of complementary clar-

ification. On top of all this, the ambiguity that character-
izes the word narcissism, even in professional literature, is
further complicated by the derogatory emotional overtone
it receives in everyday use. For there such meanings as "in
love with oneself," "always thinking of oneself," "egocentric," "incapable of object-love" have become attached to
it. Even psychoanalysts are not always free of such judgmental, emotional use of the word—although they try for
neutrality.

Let us now examine some of these derogatory, judgmental words. What exactly, for instance, is egoism? The
fifteen-year-old schoolboy Sigmund Freud wrote in his
notebook of aphorisms that the worst egoist is the person
to whom the thought has never occurred that he might be
one. Many people, even in old age, do not reach the wisdom of the fifteen-year-old Freud but truly believe they
have no such needs of their own, simply because they are
not aware of them.

Our contempt for "egoists" begins very early in life.
Children who fulfill their parents' conscious or unconscious
wishes are "good," but if they ever refuse to do so or express
wishes of their own that go against those of their parents,
they are called egoistic and inconsiderate. It usually does
not occur to the parents that they might need and use the
child to fulfill their own egoistic wishes. They often are
convinced that they must teach their child how to behave
because it is their duty to help him along on the road to
socialization. If a child brought up this way does not wish
to lose his parents' love (And what child can risk that?), he
must learn very early to share, to give, to make sacrifices,
and to be willing to "do without" and forgo gratification
—long before he is capable of true sharing or of the real
willingness to "do without."

A child who has been breast-fed for nine months and no longer wants to drink from the breast does not have to be taught to give it up. And a child who has been allowed to be egoistic, greedy, and asocial long enough will develop spontaneous pleasure in sharing and giving. But a child trained in accordance with his parents' needs may never experience this pleasure, even while he gives and shares in a dutiful and exemplary way, and suffers because others are not as "good" as he is. Adults who were so brought up will try to teach their children this same altruism as early as possible. With gifted children this is an easy task; but at what cost!

Taking a closer look, we no longer find the meaning of the word "egoism" so clear-cut and unequivocal. It will be much the same when we examine "respect for others," which is often said to be missing in self-centered people. If a mother respects both herself and her child from his very first day onward, she will never need to teach him respect for others. He will, of course, take both himself and others seriously—he couldn't do otherwise. But a mother who, as a child, was herself not taken seriously by her mother as the person she really was will crave this respect from her child as a substitute; and she will try to get it by training him to give it to her. The tragic fate that is the result of such training and such "respect" is described in this book.

As soon as we look more closely and examine their origins, we shall see that other moralizing, derogatory words also will lose their popular clear-cut character.

The usually accepted judgmental contrast between self-love and object-love, and their portrayal as opposites, springs from naive and uncritical usage in our everyday language. Yet, a little reflection soon shows how inconceivable it is really to love others (not merely to need them), if one cannot love oneself as one really is. And how could a person do that if, from the very beginning, he has had no chance to experience his true feelings and to learn to know himself?

For the majority of sensitive people, the true self remains deeply and thoroughly hidden. But how can you love something you do not know, something that has never been loved? So it is that many a gifted person lives without any notion of his or her true self. Such people are enamored of an idealized, conforming, false self. They will shun their hidden and lost true self, unless depression makes them aware of its loss or psychosis confronts them harshly with that true self, whom they now have to face and to whom they are delivered up, helplessly, as to a threatening stranger.

In the following pages I am trying to come closer to the origins of this loss of the self. While doing so, I shall not use the term "narcissism." However, in my clinical descriptions, I shall speak occasionally of a healthy narcissism and depict the ideal case of a person who is genuinely alive, with free access to the true self and his authentic feelings. I shall contrast this with narcissistic disorders, with the true self's "solitary confinement" within the prison of the false self. This I see less as an illness than as a tragedy, and it is my aim in this book to break away from judgmental, isolating, and therefore discriminating terminology.

In order to avoid major misunderstandings, let me make clear that my thoughts on the genesis and treatment of narcissistic disorders in no way conflict with the concepts of drive theory.[1] Yet, all the work in the area of the patient's instinctual conflicts depends on the existence of an alive, true self that in the end is and must be the subject of those instinctual drives. This is what seems to be missing in our patients. As I think back over my last twenty years' work, in the light of my present understanding, I can find no patient whose ability to experience his true feelings was not seriously impaired. Yet, without this basic ability, all our work with the patient's instinctual conflicts is illusory: we might increase his intellectual knowledge, and in some circumstances strengthen his resistance, but we shall not touch the world of his feelings.

If, however, we now take the path that was opened up by D. W. Winnicott, for instance, then the patient will reach a new sense of being really alive and regain his capacity to open up to full experience. Then he will be able to face his repressed instinctual conflicts, which are sure to manifest themselves of their own accord, and he will experience them intensely.

So when in the following three essays I try, among other things, to show my way of treating narcissistic disorders, it is not my intention to present an alternative to classical psychoanalysis. On the contrary, I am looking for a way, within the framework of psychoanalysis, by which the patient can regain his long-lost authentic sense of being truly alive.

NOTE

1. See A. Miller, *Du Sollst Nicht Merken: Variationen Über das Paradies Thema* (Frankfurt: Suhrkamp Verlag, 1981), p.66, which has appeared since the first printing of this book: "When I wrote *The Drama* I still thought I could reconcile my own findings with Freud's drive theory. I considered my approach to the treatment of narcissistic disorders as preliminary work that had to be performed with many patients before 'conflict neuroses' could be addressed. But the more thought I give now to the theoretical consequences of my findings and the more carefully and impartially I test the empirical content of the traditional theories, the more clearly their function in the total structure of social repression emerges for me. As a result, I have become more and more suspicious of the validity of Freudian drive theory and have experienced a growing need to distinguish between it and my own views."
See also my book *Am Anfang war Erziehung* (Frankfurt: Suhrkamp Verlag, 1980) for further remarks on this subject.

The Drama of
the Gifted Child

Chapter 1

The Drama of
the Gifted Child
and the Psychoanalyst's
Narcissistic Disturbance

Introduction

EXPERIENCE has taught us that we have only one enduring weapon in our struggle against mental illness: the emotional discovery and emotional acceptance of the truth in the individual and unique history of our childhood. Is it possible then, with the help of psychoanalysis, to free ourselves altogether from illusions? History demonstrates that they sneak in everywhere, that every life is full of them—perhaps because the truth often would be unbearable. And yet, for many people the truth is so essential that they must pay dearly for its loss with grave illness. On the path of analysis we try, in a long process, to discover our own personal truth. This truth always causes much pain before giving us a new sphere of freedom—unless we content ourselves with already conceptualized, intellectual wisdom based on other people's painful experiences, for example that of Sigmund Freud. But then we shall remain in the sphere of illusion and self-deception.

There is one taboo that has withstood all the recent efforts at demystification: the idealization of mother love. The usual run of biographies illustrates this very clearly. In reading the biographies of famous artists, for example, one gains the impression that their lives began at puberty. Before that, we are told, they had a "happy," "contented," or "untroubled" childhood, or one that was "full of deprivation" or "very stimulating." But what a particular childhood really was like does not seem to interest these biographers—as if the roots of a whole life were not hidden and entwined in its childhood. I should like to illustrate this with a simple example.

Henry Moore describes in his memoirs how, as a small boy, he massaged his mother's back with an oil to soothe her rheumatism. Reading this suddenly threw light for me on Moore's sculptures: the great, reclining women with the tiny heads—I now could see in them the mother through the small boy's eyes, with the head high above, in diminishing perspective, and the back close before him and enormously enlarged. This may be irrelevant for many art critics, but for me it demonstrates how strongly a child's experiences may endure in his unconscious and what possibilities of expression they may awaken in the adult who is free to give them rein. Now, Moore's memory was not harmful and so could survive intact. But every childhood's conflictual experiences remain hidden and locked in darkness, and the key to our understanding of the life that follows is hidden away with them.

The Poor Rich Child

Sometimes I ask myself whether it will ever be possible for us to grasp the extent of the loneliness and desertion to which we were exposed as children, and hence intrapsychically still are exposed as adults. Here I do not mean to speak, primarily, of cases of obvious desertion by, or separation from, the parents, though this, of course, can have traumatic results. Nor am I thinking of children who were obviously uncared for or totally neglected, and who were always aware of this or at least grew up with the knowledge that it was so.

Apart from these extreme cases, there are large numbers of people who suffer from narcissistic disorders, who often had sensitive and caring parents from whom they received much encouragement; yet, these people are suffering from severe depressions. They enter analysis in the belief, with which they grew up, that their childhood was happy and protected.

Quite often we are faced here with gifted patients who have been praised and admired for their talents and their achievements. Almost all of these analysands were toilet-trained in the first year of their infancy, and many of them, at the age of one and a half to five, had helped capably to take care of their younger siblings. According to prevailing, general attitudes, these people—the pride of their parents—should have had a strong and stable sense of self-assurance. But exactly the opposite is the case. In everything they undertake they do well and often excellently; they are admired and envied; they are successful whenever they care to be—but all to no avail. Behind all this lurks depression, the feeling of emptiness and self-alienation, and a sense that their life has no meaning. These dark feelings will come to the fore as soon as the drug of grandiosity fails, as soon as they are not "on top," not definitely the "superstar," or whenever they suddenly get the feeling they failed to live up to some ideal image and measure they feel they must adhere to. Then they are plagued by anxiety or deep feelings of guilt and shame. What are the reasons for such narcissistic disturbances in these gifted people?

In the very first interview they will let the listener know that they have had understanding parents, or at least one such, and if they ever lacked understanding, they felt that the fault lay with them and with their inability to express themselves appropriately. They recount their earliest memories without any sympathy for the child they once were, and this is the more striking since these patients not only have a pronounced introspective ability, but are also able to empathize well with other people. Their relationship to their own childhood's emotional world, however, is characterized by lack of respect, compulsion to control, manipulation, and a demand for achievement. Very often they show disdain and irony, even derision and cynicism. In general, there is a complete absence of real emotional understanding or serious appreciation of their own childhood vicissitudes, and no conception of their true needs—beyond the need for achievement. The internalization of the original drama has been so complete that the illusion of a good childhood can be maintained.

In order to lay the groundwork for a description of these patients' psychic climate, I first will formulate some basic assumptions, which will provide us with a starting point and are close to the work of D. W. Winnicott, Margaret Mahler, and Heinz Kohut.

- The child has a primary need to be regarded and respected as the person he really is at any given time, and as the center—the central actor—in his own activity. In contradistinction to drive wishes, we are speaking here of a need that is narcissistic, but nevertheless legitimate, and whose fulfillment is essential for the development of a healthy self-esteem.

- When we speak here of "the person he really is at any given time," we mean emotions, sensations, and their expression from the first day onward. Mahler (1968) writes: "The infant's inner sensations form the core of the self. They appear to remain the central, the crystallization point of the 'feeling of self' around which a 'sense of identity' will become established." (p. 11)

- In an atmosphere of respect and tolerance for his feelings, the child, in the phase of separation, will be able to give up symbiosis with the mother and accomplish the steps toward individuation and autonomy.

- If they are to furnish these prerequisites for a healthy narcissism, the parents themselves ought to have grown up in such an atmosphere.

- Parents who did not experience this climate as children are themselves narcissistically deprived; throughout their lives they are looking for what their own parents could not give them at the correct time—the presence of a person who is completely aware of them and takes them seriously, who admires and follows them.

- This search, of course, can never succeed fully since it relates to a situation that belongs irrevocably to the past, namely to the time when the self was first being formed.

- Nevertheless, a person with this unsatisfied and unconscious (because repressed) need is compelled to attempt its gratification through substitute means.

- The most appropriate objects for gratification are a parent's *own children*. A newborn baby is completely dependent on his parents, and since their caring is essential for his existence, he does all he can to avoid losing them. From the very first day onward, he will muster all his resources to this end, like a small plant that turns toward the sun in order to survive. (Miller, 1971)

So far, I have stayed in the realm of more or less well-known facts. The following thoughts are derived more from observations made in the course of analyses I have conducted or supervised and also from interviews with candidates for the psychoanalytic profession. In my work with all these people, I found that every one of them has a childhood history that seems significant to me.

- There was a *mother** who at the core was emotionally insecure, and who depended for her narcissistic equilibrium on the child behaving, or acting, in a particular way. This mother was able to hide her insecurity from the child and from everyone else behind a hard, authoritarian, and even totalitarian façade.
- This child had an amazing ability to perceive and respond intuitively, that is, unconsciously, to this need of the mother, or of both parents, for him to take on the role that had unconsciously been assigned to him.
- This role secured "love" for the child—that is, his parents' narcissistic cathexis. He could sense that he was needed and this, he felt, guaranteed him a measure of existential security.

This ability is then extended and perfected. Later, these children not only become mothers (confidantes, comfort-

---

* By "mother" I here understand the person closest to the child during the first years of life. This need not be the biological mother nor even a woman. In the course of the past twenty years, quite often the fathers have assumed this mothering function (Mütterlichkeit).

ers, advisers, supporters) of their own mothers, but also take over the responsibility for their siblings and eventually develop a special sensitivity to unconscious signals manifesting the needs of others. No wonder that they often choose the psychoanalytic profession later on. Who else, without this previous history, would muster sufficient interest to spend the whole day trying to discover what is happening in the other person's unconscious? But the development and perfecting of this differentiated sensorium—which once assisted the child in surviving and now enables the adult to pursue his strange profession—also contains the roots of his narcissistic disturbance.

The Lost World of Feelings

The phenomenology of narcissistic disturbance is well-known today. On the basis of my experience, I would think that its etiology is to be found in the infant's early emotional adaptation. In any case, the child's narcissistic needs for respect, echoing, understanding, sympathy, and mirroring suffer a very special fate, as a result of this early adaptation.

1. One serious consequence of this early adaptation is the impossibility of consciously experiencing certain feelings of his own (such as jealousy, envy, anger, loneliness, impotence, anxiety) either in childhood or later in adulthood. This is all the more tragic since we are here concerned with lively people who are especially capable of differentiated feelings. This is noticeable at those times in their analyses when they describe childhood experiences

that were free of conflict. Usually these concern experiences with nature, which they could enjoy without hurting the mother or making her feel insecure, without reducing her power or endangering her equilibrium. But it is remarkable how these attentive, lively, and sensitive children who can, for example, remember exactly how they discovered the sunlight in bright grass at the age of four, yet at eight might be unable to "notice anything" or to show any curiosity about the pregnant mother or, similarly, were "not at all" jealous at the birth of a sibling. Again, at the age of two, one of them could be left alone while soldiers forced their way into the house and searched it, and she had "been good," suffering this quietly and without crying. They have all developed the art of not experiencing feelings, for a child can only experience his feelings when there is somebody there who accepts him fully, understands and supports him. If that is missing, if the child must risk losing the mother's love, or that of her substitute, then he cannot experience these feelings secretly "just for himself" but fails to experience them at all. But nevertheless . . . something remains.

Throughout their later life, these people unconsciously create situations in which these rudimentary feelings may awaken but without the original connection ever becoming clear. The point of this "play," as Jurgen Habermas (1970) called it, can only be deciphered in analysis, when the analyst joins the cast and the intense emotions experienced in the analysis are successfully related to their original situation. Freud described this in 1914 in his work "Recollection, Repetition, and Working Through."

Take, for an example, the feeling of being abandoned—not that of the adult, who feels lonely and therefore takes tablets or drugs, goes to the movies, visits friends, or telephones "unnecessarily," in order to bridge the gap some-how. No, I mean the original feeling in the small infant, who had none of these chances of distraction and whose communication, verbal or preverbal, did not reach the mother. This was not the case because his mother was bad, but because she herself was narcissistically deprived, de-pendent on a specific echo from the child that was so es-sential to her, for she herself was a child in search of an object that could be available to her. However paradoxical this may seem, a child is at the mother's disposal. A child cannot run away from her as her own mother once did. A child can be so brought up that it becomes what she wants it to be. A child can be made to show respect, she can impose her own feelings on him, see herself mirrored in his love and admiration, and feel strong in his presence, but when he becomes too much she can abandon that child to a stranger. The mother can feel herself the center of at-tention, for her child's eyes follow her everywhere. When a woman had to suppress and repress all these needs in re-lation to her own mother, they rise from the depth of her unconscious and seek gratification through her own child, however well-educated and well-intentioned she may be, and however much she is aware of what a child needs. The child feels this clearly and very soon forgoes the expres-sion of his own distress. Later, when these feelings of being deserted begin to emerge in the analysis of the adult, they are accompanied by such intensity of pain and despair that it is quite clear that these people could not have survived so much pain. That would only have been possible in an empathic, attentive environment, and this they lacked. The same holds true for emotions connected with the Oedipal drama and the entire drive development of the child. All this had to be warded off. But to say that it was absent would be a denial of the empirical evidence we have gained in analysis.

Several sorts of mechanisms can be recognized in the defense against early feelings of abandonment. In addition to simple denial there is reversal ("I am breaking down under the constant responsibility because the others need me ceaselessly"), changing passive suffering into active behavior ("I must quit women as soon as I feel that I am essential to them"), projection onto other objects, and introjection of the threat of loss of love ("I must always be good and measure up to the norm, then there is no risk; I constantly feel that the demands are too great, but I cannot change that, I must always achieve more than others."). Intellectualization is very commonly met, since it is a defense mechanism of great reliability.

All these defense mechanisms are accompanied by repression of the original situation and the emotions belonging to it, which can only come to the surface after years of analysis.

2. Accommodation to parental needs often (but not always) leads to the "as-if personality" (Winnicott has described it as the "false self"). This person develops in such a way that he reveals only what is expected of him, and fuses so completely with what he reveals that—until he comes to analysis—one could scarcely have guessed how much more there is to him, behind this "masked view of himself" (Habermas, 1970). He cannot develop and differentiate his "true self," because he is unable to live it. It remains in a "state of noncommunication," as Winnicott has expressed it. Understandably, these patients complain of a sense of emptiness, futility, or homelessness, for the emptiness is real. A process of emptying, impoverishment, and partial killing of his potential actually took place when all

that was alive and spontaneous in him was cut off. In child-hood these people have often had dreams in which they experienced themselves as partly dead. I should like to give three examples:

My younger siblings are standing on a bridge and throw a box into the river. I know that I am lying in it, dead, and yet I hear my heart beating; at this moment I always wake. [A recurrent dream.]

This dream combines her unconscious aggression (envy and jealousy) against the younger siblings, for whom the patient was always a caring "mother," with "killing" her own feelings, wishes, and demands, by means of reaction formation. Another patient dreamed:

I see a green meadow, on which there is a white coffin. I am afraid that my mother is in it, but I open the lid and, luckily, it is not my mother but me.

If this patient had been able as a child to express his disappointment with his mother—to experience his rage and anger—he could have stayed alive. But that would have led to the loss of his mother's love, and that, for a child, is the same as object loss and death. So he "killed" his anger and with it a part of himself in order to preserve his self-object, the mother. A young girl used to dream:

I am lying on my bed. I am dead. My parents are talking and looking at me but they don't realize that I am dead.

3. The difficulties inherent in experiencing and developing one's own emotions lead to bond permanence, which prevents individuation, in which both parties have an in-

terest. The parents have found in their child's "false self" the confirmation they were looking for, a substitute for their own missing structures; the child, who has been unable to build up his own structures, is first consciously and then unconsciously (through the introject) dependent on his parents. He cannot rely on his own emotions, has not come to experience them through trial and error, has no sense of his own real needs, and is alienated from himself to the highest degree. Under these circumstances he cannot separate from his parents, and even as an adult he is still dependent on affirmation from his partner, from groups, or especially from his own children. The heirs of the parents are the introjects, from whom the "true self" must remain concealed, and so loneliness in the parental home is later followed by isolation within the self. Narcissistic cathexis of her child by the mother does not exclude emotional devotion. On the contrary, she loves the child, as her self-object, excessively, though not in the manner that he needs, and always on the condition that he presents his "false self." This is no obstacle to the development of intellectual abilities, but it is one to the unfolding of an authentic emotional life.

In Search of the True Self

How can psychoanalysis be of help here? The harmony depicted in Käthchen von Heilbronn (Heinrich von Kleist's romantic heroine, in the drama of the same name, 1810) is probably only possible in fantasy, and particularly understandable arising from the longing of such a narcissistically tormented person as Kleist. The simplicity of Shakespeare's Falstaff—of whom Freud is reported to have said that he embodied the sadness of healthy narcissism—is neither possible nor desirable for these patients. The paradise of pre-ambivalent harmony, for which so many patients hope, is unattainable. But the experience of one's own truth, and the postambivalent knowledge of it, makes it possible to return to one's own world of feelings at an adult level—without paradise, but with the ability to mourn.

It is one of the turning points in analysis when the narcissistically disturbed patient comes to the emotional insight that all the love he has captured with so much effort and self-denial was not meant for him as he really was, that the admiration for his beauty and achievements was aimed at this beauty and these achievements, and not at the child himself. In analysis, the small and lonely child that is hidden behind his achievements wakes up and asks: "What would have happened if I had appeared before you, bad, ugly, angry, jealous, lazy, dirty, smelly? Where would your love have been then? And I was all these things as well. Does this mean that it was not really me whom you loved, but only what I pretended to be? The well-behaved, reliable, empathic, understanding, and convenient child, who in fact was never a child at all? What became of my childhood? Have I not been cheated out of it? I can never return to it. I can never make up for it. From the beginning I have been a little adult. My abilities—were they simply misused?"

These questions are accompanied by much grief and pain, but the result always is a new authority that is being established in the analysand (like a heritage of the mother who never existed)—a new empathy with his own fate, born out of mourning. At this point one patient dreamed that he killed a child thirty years ago and no one had helped him to save it. (Thirty years earlier, precisely in the Oedipal phase, those around him had noticed that this child became totally reserved, polite, and good, and no longer showed any emotional reactions.).

Now the patient does not make light of manifestations of his self any more, does not laugh or jeer at them, even if he still unconsiously passes them over or ignores them, in the same subtle way that his parents dealt with the child before he had any words to express his needs. Then fantasies of grandeur will be revived, too, which had been deprecated, and so split off. And now we can see their relation to the frustrated and repressed needs for attention, respect, understanding, for echoing and mirroring. At the center of these fantasies there is always a wish that the patient could never have accepted before. For example: I am in the center, my parents are taking notice of me and are ignoring their own wishes (fantasy: I am the princess attended by my servants); my parents understand when I try to express my feelings and do not laugh at me; (fantasy: I am a famous artist, and everyone takes me seriously, even those who don't understand me); my parents are rich in talents and courage and not dependent on my achievements; they do not need my comfort nor my smile (they are king and queen). This would mean for the child: I can be sad or happy whenever anything makes me sad or happy; I don't have to look cheerful for someone else, and I don't have to suppress my distress or anxiety to fit other people's needs. I can be angry and no one will die or get a headache because of it. I can rage and smash things without losing my parents. In D. W. Winnicott's words: "I can destroy the object and it will still survive." (1969)

Once these grandiose fantasies (often accompanied by

obsessional or perverse phenomena) have been experienced and understood as the alienated form of these real and legitimate needs, the split can be overcome and integration can follow. What is the chronological course?

1. In the majority of cases, it is not difficult to point out to the patient early in his analysis the way he has dealt with his feelings and needs, and that this was a question of survival for him. It is a great relief to him that things he was accustomed to choke off can be recognized and taken seriously. The psychoanalyst can use the material the patient presents to show him how he treats his feelings with ridicule and irony, tries to persuade himself they do not exist, belittles them, and either does not become aware of them at all or only after several days when they have already passed. Gradually, the patient himself realizes how he is forced to look for distraction when he is moved, upset, or sad. (When a six-year-old's mother died, his aunt told him: "You must be brave; don't cry; now go to your room and play nicely."). There are still many situations where he sees himself as other people see him, constantly asking himself what impression he is making, and how he ought to be reacting or what feelings he ought to have. But on the whole he feels much freer in this initial period and, thanks to the analyst as his auxiliary ego, he can be more aware of himself when his immediate feelings are experienced within the session and taken seriously. He is very grateful for this possibility, too.

2. This will, of course, change. In addition to this first function, which will continue for a long time, the analyst must take on a second as soon as the transference neurosis has developed: that of being the transference figure. Feelings out of various periods of childhood come to the surface then. This is the most difficult stage in analysis, when

there is most acting out. The patient begins to be articulate and breaks with his former compliant attitudes, but because of his early experience he cannot believe this is possible without mortal danger. The compulsion to repeat leads him to provoke situations where his fear of object loss, rejection, and isolation has a basis in present reality, situations into which he drags the analyst with him (as a rejecting or demanding mother, for example), so that afterward he can enjoy the relief of having taken the risk and been true to himself. This can begin quite harmlessly. The patient is surprised by feelings that he would rather not have recognized, but now it is too late, awareness of his own impulses has already been aroused and there is no going back. Now the analysand must (and also is allowed to!) experience himself in a way he had never before thought possible.

Whereas this patient had always despised miserliness, he suddenly catches himself reckoning up the two minutes lost to his session through a telephone call. Whereas he had previously never made demands himself and had always been tireless in fulfilling the demands of others, now he is suddenly furious that his analyst again is going on vacation. Or he is annoyed to see other people waiting outside the consulting room. What can this be? Surely not jealousy. That is an emotion he does not recognize! and yet. . . . "What are they doing here? Do others besides me come here?" He had never realized that before. At first it is mortifying to see that he is not only good, understanding, tolerant, controlled and, above all, adult, for this was always the basis of his self-respect. But another, weightier mortification is added to the first when this analysand discovers the introjects within himself, and that he has been their prisoner. For his anger, demands, and avarice do not at first appear in a tamed adult form, but in the childish-archaic one in which they were repressed. The patient is horrified when he realizes that he is capable of screaming with rage in the same way that he so hated in his father, or that, only yesterday, he has checked and controlled his child, "practically," he says, "in my mother's clothes!" This revival of the introjects, and learning to come to terms with them, with the help of the transference, forms the major part of the analysis. What cannot be recalled is unconsciously reenacted and thus indirectly discovered. The more he is able to admit and experience these early feelings, the stronger and more coherent the patient will feel. This in turn enables him to expose himself to emotions that well up out of his earliest childhood and to experience the helplessness and ambivalence of that period.

There is a big difference between having ambivalent feelings toward someone as an adult and, after working back through much of one's previous history, suddenly experiencing one's self as a two-year-old who is being fed by the maid in the kitchen and thinking in despair: "Why does mother go out every evening? Why does she not take pleasure in me? What is wrong with me that she prefers to go to other people? What can I do to make her stay at home? Just don't cry, just don't cry." The child could not have thought in these words at the time, but in the session on the couch, this man was both an adult and a two-year-old child, and could cry bitterly. It was not only a cathartic crying, but rather the integration of his earlier longing for his mother, which until now he had always denied. In the following weeks the patient went through all the torments of his ambivalence toward his mother, who was a successful pediatrician. Her previously "frozen" portrait melted into the picture of a woman with lovable aspects but who had not been able to give her child any continuity in their relationship. "I hated these beasts who were constantly sick and always taking my mother away from me. I hated my mother because she preferred being with them to being with me." In the transference, clinging tendencies and feelings of helplessness were mingled with long dammed-up rage against the love object who had not been available to him. As a result, the patient could rid himself of a perversion that had tormented him for a long time; its point was now easy to understand. His relationships to women lost their marked characteristics of narcissistic cathexis, and his compulsion first to conquer and then to desert them disappeared completely.

At this stage in the analysis the patient experienced his early feelings of helplessness, of anger, and of being at the mercy of the loved object in a manner that he could not previously have remembered. One can only remember what has been consciously experienced. But the emotional world of a child with a narcissistic disturbance is itself the result of a selection, which has eliminated the most important elements. These early feelings, joined with the pain of not being able to understand what is going on that is part of the earliest period of childhood, are then consciously experienced for the first time during analysis.

The true self has been in "a state of noncommunication," as Winnicott said, because it had to be protected. The patient never needs to hide anything else so thoroughly, so deeply, and for so long a time as he has hidden his true self. Thus it is like a miracle each time to see how much individuality has survived behind such dissimulation, denial, and self-alienation, and can reappear as soon as the work of mourning brings freedom from the introjects. Nevertheless, it would be wrong to understand Winnicott's words to mean that there is a fully developed true self hidden behind the false self. If that were so, there would be no narcissistic disturbance but a conscious self-protection. The important point is that the child does not know what he is hiding. A patient expressed this in the following way:

> I lived in a glass house into which my mother could look at any time. In a glass house, however, you cannot conceal anything without giving yourself away, except by hiding it under the ground. And then you cannot see it yourself either.

An adult can only be fully aware of his feelings if he has internalized an affectionate and empathic self-object. People with narcissistic disturbances are missing out on this. Therefore they are never overtaken by unexpected emotions, and will only admit those feelings that are accepted and approved by their inner censor, which is their parents' heir. Depression and a sense of inner emptiness is the price they must pay for this control. To return to Winnicott's concept, the true self cannot communicate because it has remained unconscious, and therefore undeveloped, in its inner prison. The company of prison warders does not encourage lively development. It is only after it is liberated in analysis that the self begins to be articulate, to grow, and to develop its creativity. Where there had only been fearful emptiness or equally frightening grandiose fantasies, there now is unfolding an unexpected wealth of vitality. This is not a homecoming since this home had never before existed. It is the discovery of home.

3. The phase of separation begins when the analysand has reliably acquired the ability to mourn and can face feelings from his childhood, without the constant need for the analyst.

The Psychoanalyst's Situation

It is often said that psychoanalysts suffer from a narcissistic disturbance. The purpose of my presentation so far has been to clarify the extent to which this can be confirmed, not only inductively based on experience, but also deductively from the type of talent that is needed by an analyst. His sensibility, his empathy, his intense and differentiated emotional responsiveness, and his unusually powerful "antennae" seem to predestine him as a child to be used—if not misused—by people with intense narcissistic needs.

Of course, there is the theoretical possibility that a child who was gifted in this way could have had parents who did not need to misuse him—parents who saw him as he really was, understood him, and tolerated and respected his feelings. Such a child would develop a healthy narcissism. One could hardly expect, however—(1) that he would later take up the profession of psychoanalysis; (2) that he would cultivate and develop his sensorium for others to the same extent as those who were "narcissistically used"; (3) that he would ever be able to understand sufficiently—on the basis of experience—what it means to "have killed" one's self.

I believe then, that it is no less our fate than our talent that enables us to exercise the profession of psychoanalyst, after being given the chance, through our training analysis, to live with the reality of our past and to give up the most flagrant of our illusions. This means tolerating the knowledge that, to avoid losing the object-love (the love of the first object), we were compelled to gratify our parents' unconscious needs at the cost of our own self-realization. It also means being able to experience the rebellion and mourning aroused by the fact that our parents were not available to fulfill our primary narcissistic needs. If we have never lived through this despair and the resulting narcissistic rage, and have therefore never been able to work through it, we can be in danger of transferring this situation, which then would have had remained unconscious, onto our patients. It would not be surprising if our unconscious anger should find no better way than once more to make use of a weaker person and to make him take the unavailable parents' place. This can be done most easily with one's own children, or with patients, who at times are as dependent on their analysts as children are on their parents. An analytically talented patient, one with "antennae" for his analyst's unconscious, reacts promptly. He will present the analyst with a complete picture of his "Oedipus complex," with all the affects and insights are required. The only disadvantage is that we then have to deal with an "as-if" Oedipus complex, a defense against the patient's real feelings. Not until he has been given time and space to develop his "true self," to let it speak and to listen to it, can the unknown, unique history of his Oedipal vicissitudes be unfolded, affecting both patient and analyst, because it is the painfully discovered truth.

This is true not only for the Oedipus complex, but for everything. Such an analysand will quickly "feel" himself autonomous, and he will react accordingly if he senses that it is important to his analyst to have analysands who soon become autonomous and behave with self-confidence. He can do that, he can do anything that is expected of him. But as this "autonomy" is not genuine, it soon ends in depression. True autonomy is preceded by the experience of being dependent, first on partners, then on the analyst, and finally on the primary objects. True liberation can only be found beyond the deep ambivalence of infantile dependence.*

The patient satisfies his analyst's narcissistic wish for approval, echo, understanding, and for being taken seriously when he presents material that fits his analyst's knowledge, concepts, and skills, and therefore also his expectations. In this way the analyst exercises the same sort of unconscious manipulation as that to which he was exposed as a child. He has, of course, long since seen through conscious manipulation and freed himself from it. He has also learned to say no and to stand up for his own opinions and carry them through. But a child can never see through *unconscious manipulation*. It is like the air he breathes; he knows no other, and it appears to him to be the only normal possibility.

One analysand, for example, could never be sad nor cry as a child, without being aware that he was making his beloved mother unhappy and very unsure of herself, for "cheerfulness" was the trait that had saved her life in her own childhood. Her children's tears threatened her equilibrium. The extremely sensitive child felt within himself a whole abyss warded off by his mother, who had been in a concentration camp as a child, but had never spoken about it. Not until her son was grown up and could ask her questions did she tell him that she was one of eighty children who had to watch their parents going into the gas chambers, and not one child had cried. Throughout his childhood this son had tried to be cheerful and could express his "true self," his feelings, and inklings only in obsessive perversions, which seemed alien, shameful, and incomprehensible to him until he came into analysis.

---

* The theses formulated here are based on my own experience, but they can also be illustrated by the experiences of other analysts; cf. case material presented by M. Stern, 1972 and Masud Khan, 1974.

The shaming nature of perversions and obsessional behavior can often be understood as the introjection of the parents' shocked reaction to their child's natural, instinctual behavior. "Normal" sexual fulfillment no longer evokes horror in the introjected mother as it formerly did in the real one, but perverted behavior is sure to do so.

One is totally defenseless against this sort of manipulation in childhood. The tragedy is that the parents too have no defense against it, since they do not know what is happening, and even if they have some inkling can do nothing to change it. Their conscious aims are genuinely quite different, even giving every possible support; but unconsciously the parents' childhood tragedy is continued in their children.*

Another example may illustrate this more clearly: a father, who as a child had often been frightened by the anxiety attacks of his periodically schizophrenic mother, without ever receiving an explanation, enjoyed telling his beloved small daughter gruesome stories. He laughed at her fears and afterward always comforted her with the words: "But it is only a made-up story. You don't need to be scared, you are here with me." In this way he could manipulate his child's fear and have the feeling of being strong. His conscious wish was to give the child something valuable that he himself had been deprived of, namely protection, comfort, and explanations. But what he unconsciously handed on was his own childhood fear, the expectation of disaster, and the unanswered question (also from his childhood): Why does the person whom I love and who loves me frighten me so much?

Probably everybody has a more or less concealed inner chamber that he hides even from himself and in which the props of his childhood drama are to be found. These props

* For the tragic aspects of psychoanalysis see Roy Schafer, 1972.

may be his secret delusion, a secret perversion, or quite simply the unmastered aspects of his childhood suffering. The only ones who will certainly gain entrance to this hidden chamber are his children. With them new life comes into it, and the drama is continued. All the same, when he was a child he hardly had a chance to play freely with these props, his role merged into his life. And so he could not take any memories of such playing with him for later, except through unconscious repetition in analysis, when he might begin to ask questions about his role. The props may well have frightened him at times. Understandably, he could not connect them with the familiar figures of father or mother, for, after all, they represented the split-off, unintegrated part of the parents. But the child cannot experience this contradiction consciously; he simply accepts everything and, at the most, develops symptoms. Then, in analysis, the feelings emerge: feelings of terror, of despair and rebellion, of mistrust but—if it is possible to reconstruct the parents' vicissitudes—also of compassion and reconciliation.

Can it be an accident that Heinrich Pestalozzi—who was fatherless from his sixth year onward and emotionally neglected despite the presence of his mother and of a nurse —had the idea of bringing up his only son according to Rousseau's methods, although he was capable, on the other hand, of giving orphan children genuine warmth and "fatherliness?" This son finally grew up neglected, as a ten-year-old was considered to be mentally defective, caused Pestalozzi much pain and guilt feelings, and then died at the age of thirty. (H. Ganz, 1966; M. Lavater-Sloman, 1977.*) It was also Pestalozzi who is reputed to have said:

* In H. Ganz (1966) we can read: "Jakobli is to have a garden of his own to look after, set plants in, 'collecting chrysalis and beetles in an

"You can drive the devil out of your garden but you will find him again in the garden of your son." In psychoanalytic terms, one could say that it is the split-off and unintegrated parts of his parents that have been introjected by the child.

Concluding Remarks

The more insight one gains into the unintentional and unconscious manipulation of children by their parents, the fewer illusions one has about the possibility of changing the world or of prophylaxis against neurosis. It seems to me that if we can do anything at all, it is to work through our narcissistic problems and reintegrate our split-off aspects to such an extent that we no longer have any need to manipulate our patients according to our theories but can allow them to become what they really are. Only after painfully experiencing and accepting our own truth can we be relatively free from the hope that we might still find an understanding, empathic mother—perhaps in a patient—who then would be at our disposal.

This temptation should not be underestimated; our own mother seldom or never listened to us with such rapt at-

orderly, exact, and industrious manner . . . what a bridle for indolence and wildness.' Jakobli is now three and a half.

It would be about a year later, on the occasion of his father's name-day; that Jakobli, who could not write, 'half singing half murmuring', gaily dictated to his mother: 'I wish my dear Papa . . . that you should see a lot more and I thank you a hundred thousand times for your goodness. . . . that you have brought me up so joyfully and lovingly. Now I shall speak from my heart. . . . it makes me terribly happy, if you can say I have brought my son up to happiness. . . . I am his joy and his happiness, then shall I first give thanks for what you have done in my life'. . . ." (p. 53) tention as our patients usually do, and she never revealed her inner world to us so clearly and honestly as our patients do at times. However, the never-ending work of mourning can help us not to lapse into this illusion. A mother such as we once urgently needed—empathic and open, understanding and understandable, available and usable, transparent, clear, without unintelligible contradictions—such a mother was never ours, indeed she could not exist; for every mother carries with her a bit of her "unmastered past," which she unconsciously hands on to her child. Each mother can only react empathically to the extent that she has become free of her own childhood, and she is forced to react without empathy to the extent that, by denying the vicissitudes of her early life, she wears invisible chains.

But what does exist are children like this: intelligent, alert, attentive, extremely sensitive, and (because they are completely attuned to her well-being) entirely at the mother's disposal and ready for her use. Above all, they are transparent, clear, reliable, and easy to manipulate—as long as their true self (their emotional world) remains in the cellar of the transparent house in which they have to live —sometimes until puberty or until they come to analysis, and very often until they have become parents themselves.

In Alphonse Daudet's *Lettres de mon moulin* I have found a story that may sound rather bizarre, but nevertheless has much in common with what I have presented here. I shall summarize the story briefly.

Once upon a time there was a child who had a golden brain. His parents only discovered this by chance when he injured his head and gold instead of blood flowed out. They then began to look after him carefully and would not let him play with other children for fear of being robbed. When the boy was grown up and wanted to go out into the world, his mother said: "We have done so much for you, we ought to be able to share your wealth." Then her son took a large piece of gold out of his brain and gave it to his mother. He lived in great style with a friend who, however, robbed him one night and ran away. After that the man resolved to guard his secret and to go out to work, because his reserves were visibly dwindling. One day he fell in love with a beautiful girl who loved him too, but no more than the beautiful clothes he gave her so lavishly. He married her and was very happy, but after two years she died and he spent the rest of his wealth on her funeral, which had to be splendid. Once, as he was creeping through the streets, weak, poor, and unhappy, he saw a beautiful little pair of boots that would just have done for his wife. He forgot that she was dead—perhaps because his emptied brain no longer worked—and entered the shop to buy the boots. But in that very moment he fell, and the shopkeeper saw a dead man lying on the ground.

Daudet, who was to die from an illness of the spinal cord, wrote below the end of this story:

This story sounds as though it were invented, but it is true from beginning to end. There are people who have to pay for the smallest things in life with their very substance and their spinal cord. That is a constantly recurring pain, and then when they are tired of suffering . . . .

Does not mother love belong to the "smallest," but also indispensable, things in life, for which many people paradoxically have to pay by giving up their living selves?

Chapter 2

Depression and Grandiosity

as Related Forms of

Narcissistic Disturbance

OVER THE YEARS, my analytic work has included many initial consultations with people seeking advice in looking for an analyst, whom I saw for one or two sessions. In these short encounters, the tragedy of an individual destiny can often be seen with moving clarity and intensity. What is described as depression and experienced as emptiness, futility, fear of impoverishment, and loneliness can often be recognized as the tragedy of the loss of the self, or alienation from the self, from which many suffer in our generation and society. Through the years of reconstructive work with my analysands, I think I have come closer to the childhood origins of this alienation from the self.

The observations of early mother-child interaction, recorded by Mahler, Spitz, and Robertson, confirm my suppositions. On reading Winnicott, I felt on familiar ground and encouraged to continue along this path. Finally, Kohut's studies on narcissism, especially his concept of narcissistic cathexis, helped me to conceptualize the relationships I had discovered.

I shall dispense here with the metapsychological language of structure theory and try to develop the connections I want to show on the basis of the mother-child relationship. Obviously, a large part of the events I shall describe take place intrapsychically, but every internalization is preceded by an object relationship and its language seems to me emotionally more true and, for some analysts, easier to understand.

The Vicissitudes of Narcissistic Needs

We cathect an object narcissistically, according to Kohut (1971), when we experience it not as the center of its own activity but as a part of ourselves. If the object does not behave as we expect or wish, we may at times be immeasurably disappointed or offended, almost as if an arm ceased to obey us or a function that we take for granted (such as memory) lets us down. This sudden loss of control may also lead to an intense narcissistic rage.

This sort of attitude is met far more frequently in adults than one might imagine, however much we like to regard it as pathological, unrealistic, or egocentric. Yet, in the earliest stage of our life, this is the only attitude possible. Not only during the phase of primary narcissism (the symbiotic phase) but also after the gradual separation between self- and object-representations does the mother normally remain a narcissistically cathected object, a function of the developing individual.

Every child has a legitimate narcissistic need to be noticed, understood, taken seriously, and respected by his mother. In the first weeks and months of life he needs to have the mother at his disposal, must be able to use her and to be mirrored by her. This is beautifully illustrated in one of Winnicott's images: the mother gazes at the baby in her arms, and baby gazes at his mother's face and finds himself therein . . . provided that the mother is really looking at the unique, small, helpless being and not projecting her own introjects onto the child, nor her own expectations, fears, and plans for the child. In that case, the child would not find himself in his mother's face but rather the mother's own predicaments. This child would remain without a mirror, and for the rest of his life would be seeking this mirror in vain.

HEALTHY NARCISSISM

If a child is lucky enough to grow up with a mirroring mother, who allows herself to be cathected narcissistically, who is at the child's disposal—that is, a mother who allows herself to be "made use of" as a function of the child's narcissistic development, as Mahler (1968) says—then a healthy self-feeling can gradually develop in the growing child. Ideally, this mother should also provide the necessary emotional climate and understanding for the child's needs. But even a mother who is not especially warmhearted can make this development possible, if she only refrains from preventing it. This enables the child to acquire from other people what the mother lacks. Various investigations have shown the incredible ability that a healthy child displays in making use of the smallest affec- tive "nourishment" (stimulation) to be found in his surroundings.

I understand a healthy self-feeling to mean the unquestioned certainty that the feelings and wishes one experiences are a part of one's self. This certainty is not something one can gain upon reflection; it is there like one's own pulse, which one does not notice as long as it functions normally.

This automatic, natural contact with his own emotions and wishes gives an individual strength and *self-esteem*. He may live out his feelings, be sad, despairing, or in need of help, without fear of making the introjected mother insecure. He can allow himself to be afraid when he is threatened, or angry when his wishes are not fulfilled. He knows not only what he does not want but also what he wants and is able to express this, irrespective of whether he will be loved or hated for it.

I will now enumerate some characteristics of a successful narcissistic development but would like to make it clear that here, as also later on, I am describing constructions of phenomena that are only approximated in reality. Instead of "healthy narcissism," it would also be possible to speak of inner freedom and vitality.

- Aggressive impulses could be neutralized because they did not upset the confidence and self-esteem of the parents.
- Strivings toward autonomy were not experienced as an attack.
- The child was allowed to experience and express "ordinary" impulses (such as jealousy, rage, defiance) because his parents did not require him to be "special," for instance, to represent their own ethical attitudes.
- There was no need to please anybody (under optimal

conditions), and the child could develop and exhibit whatever was active in him during each developmental phase.

- He could use his parents because they were independent of him.
- These preconditions enabled him to separate successfully self- and object-representations.
- Because the child was able to display ambivalent feelings, he could learn to regard both his self and the object as "both good and bad," and did not need to split off the "good" from the "bad" object.
- Object love was made possible because the parents also loved the child as a separate object.
- Provided there were phase-appropriate and nontraumatic frustrations, the child was able to integrate his narcissistic needs and did not have to resort to repression or splitting.
- This integration made their transformation possible, as well as the development of a drive-regulating matrix, based on the child's own trial-and-error experiences.

NARCISSISTIC DISTURBANCE

What happens if the mother not only is unable to take over the narcissistic functions for the child but also, as very often happens, is herself in need of narcissistic supplies? Quite unconsciously, and despite her own good intentions, the mother then tries to assuage her own narcissistic needs through her child, that is, she cathects him narcissistically. This does not rule out strong affection. On the contrary, the mother often loves her child as her self-object, passionately, but not in the way he needs to be loved. Therefore, the continuity and constancy that would be so important for the child are missing, among other things, from this love. Yet, what is missing above all is the framework within which the child could experience his feelings and his emotions. Instead, he develops something the mother needs, and this certainly saves his life (the mother's or the father's love) at the time, but it nevertheless may prevent him, throughout his life, from being himself.

In such cases the natural narcissistic needs appropriate to the child's age that are here described cannot be integrated into the developing personality. They are split off, partially repressed, and retain their early, archaic form, which makes their later integration still more difficult.

"It is the specific unconscious need of the mother," writes Mahler (1968), "that activates, out of the infant's infinite potentialities, those in particular that create for each mother 'the child' who reflects her own unique and individual needs." In other words, the mother communicates a "mirrored framework" in infinitely varied ways to which the infant's primitive self accommodates itself. If the mother's "primary occupation with her child—her mirroring function during the period of early childhood—is unpredictable, insecure, anxiety-ridden, or hostile, or if her confidence in herself as a mother is shaken, then the child has to face the period of individuation without having a reliable framework for emotional checking to his symbiotic partner. The result is a disturbance in his primitive self-feeling."

With two exceptions, the mothers of all my patients had a narcissistic disturbance, were extremely insecure, and often suffered from depression. The child, an only one or often the first-born, was the narcissistically cathected object. What these mothers had once failed to find in their own mothers they were able to find in their children: someone at their disposal who can be used as an echo, who can be controlled, is completely centered on them, will never desert them, and offers full attention and admiration.

If the child's demands become too great (as once did those of her own mother), she is no longer so defenseless and will not allow herself to be tyrannized: she can bring the child up in such a way that he neither cries nor disturbs her. At last she can make sure that she receives consideration and respect.

Let me illustrate this with an example. A patient who was the mother of four children had only scanty memories of her own mother. At the beginning of the treatment, she described her as an affectionate, warm-hearted woman who spoke to her "openly about her own troubles" at an early age, who was very concerned for her own children, and sacrificed herself for her family. She must have had the ability to empathize with other people, for she was often asked for advice by others within the sect to which the family belonged. The patient reported that her mother had always been especially proud of her. The mother was now old and an invalid, and the patient was very concerned about her health. She often dreamed that something had happened to her mother and woke up with great anxiety.

During the further course of the analysis and as a consequence of the emotions that arose in the transference, this picture of her mother changed. Above all, when the period of toilet-training entered the analysis, she experienced her mother in me as domineering, demanding, controlling, manipulative, bad, cold, stupid, petty, obsessional, touchy, easily offended, overwrought, false, and hard to please. Even if this picture contained the projection of her long dammed-up anger, many childhood memories of her mother did in fact include these characteristics.

It was only in the course of the analysis, during which she reenacted a great deal from her childhood, that this patient could discover what her mother was really like, through observing her own relationship to her children. Toward the end, she felt that when her mother had felt insecure in relation to her, she had in fact often been cold and had treated her badly. Her mother's anxious concern for the child had been a reaction formation to ward off her aggression and envy. Since the mother had often been humiliated as a child, she needed to be valued by her daughter. Gradually, the two pictures of the loving mother and of the wicked witch were united into that of a single human being whose weakness, insecurity, and oversensitivity made it necessary for her to have her child at her disposal. The mother, who apparently functioned well, was herself basically still a child in her relationship to her own child. The daughter, on the other hand, took over the understanding and caring role until she discovered, with her own children, the demanding child within herself who seemed compelled to press others into her service.

Not all children of narcissistically deprived mothers have to suffer from such a disturbance. The siblings can usually obtain a certain freedom when one child has already accepted this role. Children who have a nurse or another stranger caring for them from the beginning are usually freer to develop in their own way because they are less often the object of narcissistic cathexis.

In his novel *Le Lys dans la vallée*, Honoré de Balzac described his childhood. His mother preferred his brother, gave Honoré first into the care of a nurse and then sent him away to school. He suffered greatly and all his life courted his mother in the guise of different women. But perhaps he was fortunate that this mother did not use him as a glorification of herself. The very hopelessness of his wooing gave him the possibility of developing his own emotional wealth and the ability to freely develop his exceptional capacity for suffering. Perhaps the same is true of Vincent van Gogh, whose mother, throughout her life, mourned and idealized the first Vincent who had died very young. (Humberto Nagera, 1967).

The narcissistically cathected child has the chance to develop his intellectual capacities undisturbed, but not the world of his emotions, and this will have far-reaching consequences for his well-being. Now his intellect will assume a supportive function of enormous value in strengthening his defense mechanism, but hidden behind that, his narcissistic disturbance may grow deeper.

We may, in fact, find various mixtures and nuances of narcissistic disturbances. For the sake of clarity, I shall try to describe two extreme forms, of which I consider one to be the reverse of the other—grandiosity and depression. Behind manifest grandiosity, there constantly lurks depression, and behind a depressive mood there often hide unconscious (or conscious but split off) fantasies of grandiosity. In fact, grandiosity is the defense against depression, and depression is the defense against the deep pain over the loss of the self.

Grandiosity.   The person who is "grandiose" is admired everywhere and needs this admiration; indeed, he cannot live without it. He must excel brilliantly in everything he undertakes, which he surely is capable of doing (otherwise he just does not attempt it). He, too, admires himself—for his qualities: his beauty, cleverness, talents—and for his success and achievements. Woe betide if one of these fails him, for then the catastrophe of a severe depression is imminent. It is usually considered normal that sick or aged people who have suffered the loss of much of their health and vitality, or, for example, women at the time of the menopause, should become depressive. There are, however, other personalities who can tolerate the loss of beauty, health, youth, or loved ones, and although they mourn them they do so without depression. In contrast, there are those with great gifts, often precisely the most gifted, who suffer from severe depression. One is free from depression when self-esteem is based on the authenticity of one's own feelings and not on the possession of certain qualities.

The collapse of self-esteem in a "grandiose" person will show clearly how precariously that self-esteem had been hanging in the air—"hanging from a balloon," a female patient once dreamed. That balloon flew up very high in a good wind but then suddenly got a hole and soon lay like a little rag on the ground. . . . For nothing genuine that could have given strength and support later on had even been developed.

The "grandiose" person's partners (including sexual partners) are also narcissistically cathected. Others are there to admire him, and he himself is constantly occupied, body and soul, with gaining that admiration. This is how his torturing dependence shows itself. The childhood trauma is repeated: he is always the child whom his mother admires, but at the same time he senses that so long as it is his qualities that are being admired, he is not loved for the person he really is at any given time. In the parents' feelings, dangerously close to pride in their child, shame is concealed—lest he should fail to fulfill their expectations.

In a field study conducted at Chestnut Lodge, Maryland, in 1954, the family backgrounds of twelve patients suffering from manic-depressive psychoses were examined. The results strongly confirm the conclusions I have reached, by other means, about the etiology of depression, and, I believe, of narcissistic disturbances as a whole.

All the patients came from families who were socially isolated and felt themselves to be too little respected in their neighborhood. They therefore made special efforts to increase their prestige with their neighbors through conformity and outstanding achievements. The child who later became ill had been assigned a special role in this effort. He was supposed to guarantee the family honor, and was loved only in proportion to the degree to which he was able to fulfill the demands of this family ideal by *means of his special abilities, talents, his beauty, etc.** If he failed, he was punished by being cold-shouldered or thrown out of the family group, and by the knowledge that he had brought great shame on his people. (M. Eicke-Spengler, 1977, p. 1104)

I have found a similar social isolation in the families of my patients but saw this as the result rather than the cause of the parents' narcissistic disturbance.

It is thus impossible for the grandiose person to cut the tragic link between admiration and love. In his compulsion to repeat he seeks insatiably for admiration, of which he never gets enough because admiration is not the same thing as love. It is only a substitute gratification of the primary needs for respect, understanding, and being taken seriously —needs that have remained unconscious.

When Kernberg (1974) spoke of the remarkably strong envy shown by narcissistically disturbed patients in a discussion group at the Paris Congress in 1973, he remarked, almost as an aside: "These people are envious of everything, even of other people's object relations." Do we not have to assume that it is precisely there that the unconscious roots of their excessive envy are to be found? A patient once spoke of the feeling of always having to walk on stilts. Is somebody who always has to walk on stilts not bound to be constantly envious of those who can walk on their own legs, even if they seem to him to be smaller and

* Italics mine.

more "ordinary" than he is himself? And is he not bound to carry pent-up rage within himself, against those who have made him afraid to walk without stilts? Thus envy of other things can come about as the result of the defense mechanism of displacement. Basically, he is envious of healthy people because they do not have to make a constant effort to earn admiration, and because they do not have to do something in order to impress, one way or the other, but are free to be "average."

Manifest grandiosity, especially in the erotic sphere, is often described as "phallic narcissism." The women with the structure and pathogenesis described here usually attained their "special position" in the sexual sphere during the Oedipal phase or even earlier (in cases where the mother was emotionally replaced by the father). They had been specially predestined to this by their development during the pre-Oedipal period as narcissistic showpieces of the mother. If seductive behavior on the father's part is added, then the woman is forced, by the compulsion to repeat, to go on looking for a special position in her relationships to men. She also has to repress the painful rivalry of the Oedipal triangle in order to maintain the fantasy of her favored position with her father. The inability to develop genuine object love is also narcissistically mortifying, since it is part of her ambition to be a complete woman— that is, capable of loving. Paradoxically, she owes this to her introjected and subsequently transformed mother as well.

Things may be simpler for the so-called phallic man. He is his mother's special son and, in the seduction situation, her preferred sexual object. The "phallic man" must be a really splendid fellow if he wants to feel like a man at all. However, as soon as he has to be something specific and is not allowed to be what he really is, he loses, understandably, his sense of self. He then tries all the more to blow up his self-esteem, which again leads to narcissistic weakening, and so on, ad infinitum. Fellini's *Casanova* portrayed this person and his anguish most impressively.

The grandiose person is never really free, first, because he is excessively dependent on admiration from the object, and second, because his self-respect is dependent on qualities, functions, and achievements that can suddenly fail.

Depression as the Reverse of Grandiosity. Among the patients I have known, depression was coupled with grandiosity in many ways.

1. Depression sometimes appeared when grandiosity broke down as a result of sickness, disablement, or aging. The source of external narcissistic supplies, for example, gradually dried up in the case of an unmarried woman as she grew older. She no longer received, from men, constant confirmation of her attractiveness, which earlier had a directly supportive function as a substitute for the missing mirroring by her mother. Superficially, her despair about getting old seemed to be due to the absence of sexual contacts but, at a deeper level, early pre-Oedipal fears of being abandoned (stemming from the symbiotic phase) were now aroused, and this woman had no new conquests with which to counteract them. All her substitute mirrors were broken, and she again stood helpless and confused, as the small girl once did before her mother's face in which she did not find herself but her mother's confusion.

The so-called phallic, narcissistic men can experience their aging in a similar way, even if a new love affair may seem to create the illusion of their youth for a time and in this way may introduce brief manic phases into the early stages of the depression caused by their aging.

2. This combination of alternating phases of grandiosity and depression can be seen in many other people. They are the two sides of the medal that could be described as the "false self," a medal that was actually once given for achievements.

An actor, for example, at the height of his success, can play before an enthusiastic audience and experience feelings of heavenly greatness and almightiness. Nevertheless, his sense of emptiness and futility, even of shame and anger, can return the next morning if his happiness the previous night was due not only to his creative activity in playing and expressing the part but also, and above all, was rooted in the substitute satisfaction of old needs for echoing, mirroring, and being seen and understood. If his success the previous night only serves as the denial of childhood frustrations, then, like every substitute, it can only bring momentary satiation. In fact, true satiation is no longer possible, since the right time for that now lies irrevocably in the past. The former child no longer exists, nor do the former parents. The present parents—if they are still alive—are now old and dependent, have no longer any power over their son, are delighted with his success and with his infrequent visits. In the present, the son enjoys success and recognition, but these things cannot offer him more than they are, they cannot fill the old gap. Again, as long as he can deny this with the help of illusion, that is, the intoxication of success, the old wound cannot heal. Depression leads him close to his wounds, but only the mourning for what he has missed, *missed at the crucial time,* can lead to real healing.*

* Let me cite a remark by Igor Stravinsky as an example of successful mourning: "I am convinced that it was my misfortune that my father was spiritually very distant from me and that even my mother had no love for me. When my oldest brother died unexpectedly (without my

3. Continuous performance of outstanding achievements may sometimes enable an individual to maintain the illusion of constant attention and availability of his self-object(whose absence, in his early childhood, he must now deny just as much as his own emotional reactions). Such a person is usually able to ward off threatening depression with increased displays of brilliance, thereby deceiving both himself and those around him. However, he quite often chooses a marriage partner who either already has strong depressive traits or at least, within their marriage, unconsciously takes over and enacts the depressive components of the grandiose partner. This means that the depression is outside. The grandiose one can look after his "poor" partner, protect him like a child, feel himself to be strong and indispensable, and thus gain another supporting pillar for the building of his own personality, which actually has no secure foundations and is dependent on the supporting pillars of success, achievement, "strength," and, above all, of denying the emotional world of his childhood.

4. Finally, depression can be experienced as a constant and overt dejection that appears to be unrelated to grandiosity. However, the repressed or split-off fantasies of grandiosity of the depressive are easily discovered, for example, in his moral masochism. He has especially severe standards that apply only to himself. In other people he ac-

---

mother transferring her feelings from him onto me, and my father, also, remaining as reserved as ever), I resolved that one day I would show them. Now this day has come and gone. No one remembers this day but me, who am its only remaining witness." This is in marked contrast to the statement by Samuel Beckett: "One could say that I had a happy childhood, although I showed little talent for being happy. My parents did all that can be done to make a child happy, but I often felt very lonely." Here the childhood drama has been fully introjected, and idealization of the parents was maintained with the help of denial, yet the boundless isolation of his childhood found expression in Beckett's plays. (For both quotations see H. Mueller-Braunschweig, 1974.)

cepts without question thoughts and actions that, in himself, he would consider mean or bad when measured against his high ego ideal. Others are allowed to be "ordinary," but that he can never be.

Although the outward picture of depression is quite the opposite of that of grandiosity and has a quality that expresses the tragedy of the loss of self to a great extent, they have the same roots in the narcissistic disturbance. Both are indications of an inner prison, because the grandiose and the depressive individuals are compelled to fulfill the introjected mother's expectations: whereas the grandiose person is her successful child, the depressive sees himself as a failure.

They have many points in common:

- A "false self" that has led to the loss of the potential "true self"
- A fragility of self-esteem that is based on the possibility of realizing the "false self" because of lack of confidence in one's own feelings and wishes
- Perfectionism, a very high ego ideal
- Denial of the rejected feelings (the missing of a shadow in the reflected image of Narcissus)
- A preponderance of narcissistic cathexes of objects
- An enormous fear of loss of love and therefore a great readiness to conform
- Envy of the healthy
- Strong aggression that is split off and therefore not neutralized
- Oversensitivity
- A readiness to feel shame and guilt
- Restlessness

Thus depression can be understood as a sign of the loss of the self and consists of a denial of one's own emotional reactions and feelings. This denial begins in the service of an absolutely essential adaptation during childhood, to avoid losing the object's love. Subsequently, it continues under the influence of the introjects. For this reason depression indicates a very early disturbance. Right at the beginning, in infancy, such persons have suffered from a deficiency in certain affective areas that are necessary for stable self-confidence. From the reconstructions available through analyses, I have gained the impression that there are children who have not been free to experience the very earliest feelings, such as discontent, anger, rage, pain, even hunger and, of course, enjoyment of their own bodies.

Discontent and anger had aroused uncertainty in the mother over her maternal role, pain had made her anxious. Her children's enjoyment of their bodies sometimes aroused her envy, sometimes her shame about "what other people would think," or it disturbed the mother's reaction formations (A. Miller, 1971). Thus, under certain circumstances, a child may learn very early what he is not allowed to feel, lest he run the risk of losing his mother's love.

A patient in her fourth year of analysis came to a session several weeks after the birth of her third child and told me how free and alive she felt with this baby, quite in contrast to the way she had felt with the two earlier ones. With them she had constantly felt that excessive demands were being made upon her, that she was a prisoner, and that the baby was taking advantage of and "exploiting" her. Thus she rebelled against his justified demands and, at the same time, felt that this was very bad of her: as in depression, she was separated from her true self. She thought these earlier reactions might have been rebellion against her mother's demands, for this time she was experiencing nothing of this sort. The love she had then struggled to

Dear Ellen,   1-28-91

So how are U doing in these rough global times? It's helping me appreciate one day at a time, God, the simple life -- breathe in breathe out. Wow is this shit around us weird.

I made an appt. to see a therapist here for this week, however, I think I'm going to cancel it. I'd like to get out of my head + more into my body. Think I'm gonna do some regular bodywork sessions. Connie + I still see our couples counseler 2x/month. Things are going very well. Did I tell you she got a new job? Helps her self esteem + brings in bux. I'm still doing the $\frac{1}{2}$ way attempt at a "real" job; otherwise enjoying simple jobs + lots of hikes in the redwoods + on the beach. Lots of magical places to explore.

I hope you + Joe are doing well + feel happy. Lots of love to both of you,

♡ Tammy

T. Pallington
513 1So. Quarry Rd
Bayside, CA 95524

America the Beautiful   USA 15

EUREKA · CA
PM
28 JAN
1991
955

ELLEN HULME-POHH
306 RARITAN AVE
HIGHLAND PARK, NJ
08904

feel now came of its own accord. She could enjoy her unity with this child and with herself. Then she spoke of her mother in the following words:

I was the jewel in my mother's crown. She often said: "Maja can be relied upon, she will cope." And I did cope, I brought up the smaller children for her so that she could get on with her professional career. She became more and more famous, but I never saw her happy. How often I longed for her in the evenings. The little ones cried and I comforted them but I myself never cried. Who would have wanted a crying child? I could only win my mother's love if I was competent, understanding, and controlled, if I never questioned her actions nor showed her how much I missed her; that would have limited her freedom, which she needed so much. It would have turned her against me. At that time, nobody ever would have thought that this quiet, competent, useful Maja could be so lonely and have suffered so much. What could I do but be proud of my mother and help her? The deeper the hole in my mother's heart was, the bigger the jewels in her crown needed to be. My poor mother needed these jewels because, at bottom, all her activity served only to suppress something in herself, perhaps a longing, I don't know . . . . Perhaps *she* would have discovered it if she had been fortunate enough to be a mother in more than a biological sense. It is not her fault. She tried so hard. But she had not been given the gift.

And how all of this repeated itself with Peter! How many empty hours my child had to spend with the maids so that I could get my diploma, which only took me further away from him and from myself. How often I deserted him without seeing what I was doing to him, because I had never been able to experience my own sense of being deserted? Only now do I begin to realize what motherhood without crown or jewels or a halo can be like.

A German women's magazine (which tries to speak openly of truths that have been tabooed) published a reader's letter in which the tragic story of her experience of motherhood was told without camouflage. It is in the nature of the problem that she could not really experience either her own tragedy or that of her child, since her own emotionally inaccessible childhood was the real beginning of the story. Her report ends with the following passage:

And then the breast-feeding! The baby was put to the breast all wrong and soon my nipples were all bitten. God, how that hurt. Just two hours and then it was back: another one . . . the same . . . while it was sucking there, I was crying and swearing above it. It was so terrible that soon I couldn't eat any more and had a temperature of 40° [Celsius]. Then I was allowed to wean and suddenly felt better. It was a long time before I noticed any maternal feelings. I wouldn't have minded if the baby had died. And everybody expected me to be happy. In despair I telephoned a friend who said that I'd get fond of him in time through being busy with him and having him around all the time. But that did not happen either. I only *began to be fond* of him when I could go back to work and only saw him when I came home, as a *distraction and toy*, so to speak. But quite honestly, a little dog would have done just as well. Now that he is gradually getting bigger and I see that *I can train him and that he is devoted to me and trusts me*, I am beginning to develop *tender feelings* for him and am glad that he is there.*

I have written all this because I think it is a good thing that someone should, at last, say that there is no such thing as mother love—not to speak of a maternal instinct. [*Emma*, July 1977.]

* Italics added.

The Legend of Narcissus

The legend of Narcissus actually tells us the tragedy of the narcissistic disturbance. Narcissus sees his reflection in the water and falls in love with his own beautiful face, of which his mother was surely proud. The nymph Echo answers the young man's calls because she is in love with his beauty, just as their mothers are with our patients. Echo's answering calls deceive Narcissus. His reflection deceives him as well, since it shows only his perfect, wonderful side and not his other parts. His back view, for instance, and his shadow remain hidden from him; they do not belong to and are cut off from his beloved reflection.

This stage of rapture can be compared with grandiosity, just as the next (the consuming longing for himself) can be likened to depression. Narcissus wanted to be nothing but the beautiful youth. He denied his true self, wanted to be at one with the beautiful picture. This leads to a giving up of himself, to death or, in Ovid's version, to being changed into a flower. This death is the logical consequence of the fixation on the false self. It is not only the "beautiful," "good," and pleasant feelings that make us really alive, deepen our existence, and give us crucial insight—but often precisely the unacceptable and unadapted ones from which we would prefer to escape: impotence, shame, envy, jealousy, confusion, and mourning. These feelings can be experienced in the analyst's consulting room and grow beyond their archaic form. In this way this room is also a mirror of the analysand's inner world, which is much richer than the "beautiful countenance!"

Narcissus was in love with his idealized picture, but

neither the grandiose nor the depressive "Narcissus" can really love himself. His passion for his false self not only makes object love impossible but also love for the one person who is fully entrusted to his care: he, himself.

Depressive Phases During Analysis

A grandiose person will only look for an analyst if depressive episodes come to his aid and force him to do so. As long as the grandiose defense is effective, this form of narcissistic disturbance exerts no pressure through visible suffering, except when other members of the family (spouse or children) have to seek psychotherapeutic help for depression or psychosomatic disorders. In our analytic work, we encounter grandiosity that is coupled with depression. On the other hand, we see depression in almost all our patients, either in the form of a manifest illness or in distinct phases of depressive moods. These phases can have different functions.

SIGNAL FUNCTION

Every analyst is familiar with sessions when the patient arrives complaining of depression and later leaves the consulting room in tears but much relieved and free from depression. Perhaps this patient now has been able to experience a long-pent-up rage against his mother; or he has been able to express his mistrust of the analyst's superiority, or to feel for the first time his sadness over the many lost years of his life during which he did not really live; or he has vented his anger over the impending holidays and separation from his analyst. It is irrelevant which of these feelings are coming to the fore; the important thing is that they could be experienced. The depression had signaled their proximity but also their denial. The analytic session enabled the feelings to break through and then the depression disappeared. Such a mood can be an indication that parts of the self that had been rejected (feelings, fantasies, wishes, fears) have become stronger without finding discharge in grandiosity.

DENIAL OF SELF

Some patients, while feeling content and understood after having come close to the core of their selves in a session, will organize a party or something else equally unimportant to them at that moment, which will make them feel lonely and inadequate again. After a few days they will complain of self-alienation and emptiness, of again having lost the way to themselves. Here the patient has actively, though unconsciously, provoked a situation that could demonstrate the repetition of what used to happen to him as a child: when he really got a sense of himself in "play"—feeling creative in Winnicott's sense—he would be asked to do something "more sensible," to achieve something, and his world, which was just beginning to unfold, would be overthrown. These patients, even as children, probably reacted to this by withdrawing their feelings and by becoming depressed.

THE ACCUMULATION OF STRONG, HIDDEN FEELINGS

Patients who are no longer depressive sometimes still have depressive phases that may last several weeks before strong emotions from their childhood break through. It is as though the depression had held back the effect. When it can be experienced, insight and associations related to the primary objects follow, often accompanied by significant dreams. The patient feels fully alive again until a new depressive phase signals something new. This may be expressed in the following fashion: "I no longer have a feeling of myself. How could it happen that I should lose myself again? I have no connection with what is within me. It is all hopeless. . . . It will never be any better. Everything is pointless. I am longing for my former sense of being alive." An aggressive outbreak may follow, with reproaches against the analyst, and only after this outbreak will a new link become clear and new vitality be felt.

THE STRUGGLE WITH THE INTROJECTS

During an analysis, there will also be times of depressive moods even after the patient has started to resist the demands of his introjects. He may, for example, resist their demands for achievement, although he has not yet fully freed himself from them. Then he lands again in the cul-de-sac of making pointlessly excessive demands upon himself and he will only become aware of this when a depressive mood rises. This, for instance, may find expression in the following way:"The day before yesterday I was so happy, my work went easily. I was able to do more work for the exam than I had planned for the whole week. Then I thought I must take advantage of this good mood and do another chapter in the evening. I worked all evening but without any enthusiasm and the next day I couldn't do any more. I felt like such an idiot, nothing stayed in my head. I didn't want to see anyone either, it felt like the depressions I used to have. Then I 'turned the pages back' and found where it had begun. I had spoiled my pleasure as soon as I made myself do more and more—but why? Then I remembered

how my mother used to say: 'You have done that beautifully, now you could surely do this, too. . . .' I got angry
and left the books alone. Then, suddenly, I trusted myself
to know when I was ready to work again. And, of course,
I did, too. But the depression went away sooner—at the
point when I realized that I had once again exceeded my
limits."

The Inner Prison and Analytic Work

Everyone probably knows from his own experience about
depressive moods; they may be expressed as well as hidden
by psychosomatic suffering. It is easy to notice, if we pay
attention, that they hit a person almost with regularity—
whenever he suppresses an impulse or an unwanted emotion. And then, at once, such depressive moods will stifle
all spontaneity. If an adult, for example, cannot experience
mourning when he loses somebody dear to him but tries
to distract himself from his sadness, or if he suppresses and
hides from himself his indignation over an idealized friend's
behavior out of fear of losing his friendship, he must reckon
with the probability of depression (unless his grandiose
defense is constantly at his disposal). When he begins to
pay attention to these connections in his analysis, he can
benefit from his depression and use it to learn the truth
about himself.

A child does not yet have this possibility. He cannot yet
see through his mechanism of self-deception and, on the
other hand, he is far more threatened than an adult by the
intensity of his feelings if he does not have a supportive

(holding) empathic environment. Winnicott (1969) compared the infant's emotional world with that of a psychotic, and there is something convincing about this comparison. What these two worlds have in common, in addition to the lack of structuring, is the extreme intensity of feeling that is otherwise only to be found in puberty. Yet, the recollection of the pains of puberty, of not being able to understand or to place our own impulses is usually more accessible than the earliest narcissistic traumata that are often hidden behind the picture of an idyllic childhood or even behind an almost complete amnesia. This is perhaps one reason why adults less often look back nostalgically to the time of their puberty than to that of their childhood. The mixture of longing, expectation, and fear of disappointment, which for most people accompanies the remembrance of the festivities they have known in their childhood, can perhaps be explained by their search for the intensity of feeling they knew in childhood, and cannot regain.

It is precisely because a child's feelings are so strong that they cannot be repressed without serious consequences. The stronger a prisoner is, the thicker the prison walls have to be, which impede or completely prevent later emotional growth.

Once a patient has experienced a few times in the course of his analysis that the breakthrough of intense early-childhood feelings (characterized by the specific quality of noncomprehension) can relieve a long period of depression, this experience will bring about a gradual change in his way of approaching "undesired" feelings, above all, those of pain. He discovers that he is no longer compelled to follow the former pattern of disappointment, suppression of pain, and depression, since he now has another possibility of dealing with disappointment, namely, that of experiencing pain. In this way he at least gains access to his earlier experiences—to the parts of himself and of his fate that were previously hidden from him.

A patient, in the closing phase of his analysis, expressed it thus:

> It was not the beautiful or pleasant feelings that gave me new insight but the ones against which I had fought most strongly: feelings that made me experience myself as shabby, petty, mean, helpless, humiliated, demanding, resentful, or confused; and, above all, sad and lonely. It was precisely through these experiences, which I had shunned for so long, that I became certain that I now understand something about my life, stemming from the core of my being, something that I could not have learned from any book!

This patient was describing the process of creative insight in psychoanalysis. Interpretations play an important part in this process. They can accompany it, support ("hold"), and encourage, but they can also disturb, hamper, and delay, or even prevent it or reduce it to mere intellectual insight. A patient with narcissistic problems is all too ready to give up his own pleasure in discovery and self-expression and accommodate himself to his analyst's concepts—out of fear of losing the latter's affection, understanding, and empathy, for which he has been waiting all his life. Because of his early experiences with his mother, he cannot believe that this need not necessarily be so. If he gives way to this fear and adapts himself, the analysis slides over into the sphere of the "false self," and the true self remains hidden and undeveloped. It is therefore extremely important that the analyst does not cathect the patient narcissistically, that is, his own needs should not impel him to formulate connections that the patient himself is discovering with the help of his own feelings. Otherwise he is in danger of behaving like a friend who brings some good food to a prisoner in his cell, at the precise moment when that prisoner has the chance to escape, perhaps spending his first night without shelter and hungry, but nevertheless in freedom. Since this step into unknown territory requires a great deal of courage in the first instance, it can happen that the prisoner, comforting himself with his food and shelter, misses his chance and stays in prison.

Recognizing the fragility of a creative process obviously does not mean that the analyst must adopt a mostly silent and hurtful attitude but merely that he must exercise care in this respect. It is possible, for example—provided the analyst respects the analysand's need to discover things for himself—that his compulsion to repeat can be of good service to his creative self-discovery, especially if its indirect communications are understood. This will come about through producing a variety of new situations through which an old, unremembered situation can, for the first time, be consciously experienced in its full tragedy and then finally be mourned. It is part of the dialectic of the mourning process that such experiences both encourage and are dependent on self-discovery. (Cf. p. 18–20.)

Grandiosity is the counterpart of depression *within* the narcissistic disturbance. The patient can therefore be freed from his depression for a while if the psychotherapist knows how to let the patient share in his own grandeur— that is, when he can enable the patient to feel big and strong as a part of the idealized therapist. The narcissistic disturbance then appears in a different guise for a while, even though it still exists. The achievement of freedom from both forms of narcissistic disturbance in analysis is hardly possible without deeply felt mourning. This ability to mourn, that is, to give up the illusion of his "happy" childhood, can restore the depressive's vitality and creativity, and (if he comes to analysis at all) free the grandiose person from the exertions of and dependence on his Sisyphean task. If a person is able, during this long process, to experience that he was never "loved" as a child for what he was but for his achievements, success, and good qualities, and that he sacrificed his childhood for this "love," this will shake him very deeply but one day he will feel the desire to end this courtship. He will discover in himself a need to live according to his "true self" and no longer be forced to earn love, a love that at root, still leaves him empty-handed since it is given to the "false self," which he has begun to relinquish.

The true opposite of depression is not gaiety or absence of pain, but vitality: the freedom to experience spontaneous feelings. It is part of the kaleidoscope of life that these feelings are not only cheerful, "beautiful," and "good;" they also can display the whole scale of human experience, including envy, jealousy, rage, disgust, greed, despair, and mourning. But this freedom cannot be achieved if the childhood roots are cut off. For a person with narcissistic problems access to the "true self" is thus only possible when he no longer has to be afraid of the intense "psychotic" emotional world of his early childhood. Once he has experienced this during the analytic process, it is no longer strange and threatening and need no longer be hidden behind the prison walls of illusion.

A good deal of advice for dealing with the depressive patient (for example, turning his aggression from the inner to the outer world) has a clearly manipulative character. S. Levin,* for instance, suggested that one should demon-

* S. Levin: "Some Suggestions for Treating the Depressed Patient," *Psychoanalytic Quarterly* (1965) *34*, p. 37–65.

strate to the patient that "his hopelessness is not rational," or make him aware of his "oversensitivity" (R. Fischer, 1976). I think that such procedures will only strengthen the "false self" and emotional conformity—will reinforce the depression, too. If we want to avoid this, we must take *all* the patient's feelings seriously. It is precisely his oversensitivity, shame, and self-reproach (how often a depressive patient knows that he reacts oversensitively and how much he will reproach himself for it), which form a continuous thread throughout his analysis, even before we understand what these feelings really relate to. The more unrealistic such feelings are and the less they fit present reality, the more clearly they show that they are concerned with unremembered situations from the past that are still to be discovered. If, however, the feeling concerned is not experienced but reasoned away, the discovery cannot take place, and depression will be triumphant.

After a long depressive phase, accompanied by suicidal thoughts, a forty-year-old patient was at last able to experience her violent, very early ambivalence in the transference. This was not immediately followed by visible relief but by a period full of mourning and tears. At the end of this period she said:

> The world has not changed, there is so much evil and meanness all around me, and I see it even more clearly than before. Nevertheless, for the first time I find life really worth living. Perhaps this is because, for the first time, I have the feeling that I am really living my own life. And that is an exciting adventure. On the other hand, I can understand my suicidal ideas better now, especially those I had in my youth—it seemed pointless to carry on—because in a way I had always been living a life that wasn't mine, that I didn't want, and that I was ready to throw away.

A Social Aspect of Depression

One might ask whether adaptation must necessarily lead to depression. Is it not possible, and are there not examples, that emotionally conforming individuals may live quite happily? There are indeed such examples, and above all there were more in the past, for depression is a disease of our time. Within a culture that was shielded from other value systems, such as that of orthodox Jewry in the ghetto, or of Negro families in the Southern states a hundred years ago, an adapted individual was not autonomous and did not have his own individual sense of identity (in our sense) that could have given him support; but he did feel supported by the group. The sense of being a "devout Jew" or a "loyal slave" gave individuals a measure of security in this world. Of course, there were some exceptions, people for whom that was not sufficient and who were strong enough to break away. Today it is hardly possible for any group to remain so isolated from others who have different values. Therefore it is necessary today for the individual to find his support within himself, if he is not to become the victim of various interests and ideologies. This strength within himself—through access to his own real needs and feelings and the possibility of expressing them—thus becomes crucially important for him on the one hand, and on the other is made enormously more difficult through living in contact with various different value systems. These factors can probably explain the rapid increase of depression in our time and also the general fascination with various groups.

Within the partially adapted child there are latent powers

that resist this adaptation. In older children, particularly as they reach puberty, these powers attach themselves to new values, which are often opposed to those of the parents. Thus the youths will create new ideals and will try to put them into practice. Since this attempt is nevertheless not rooted in awareness of his own true needs and feelings, the individual adolescent accepts and conforms to the new ideals in a similar way to that which he previously adopted in relation to his parents. He again gives up and denies his true self in order to be accepted and loved by the heirs of the primary objects (whether in his ego-ideal or in the group). But all that is of little avail against depression. This person is not really himself, nor does he know or love himself: he does everything to make a narcissistically cathected object love him in the way he once, as a child, so urgently needed it. But whatever could not be experienced at the right time in the past can never be attained later on.

There are innumerable examples of this dilemma and I would like to include two of them:

1. A young woman wants to free herself from her patriarchal family in which her mother was completely subjected by the father. She marries a submissive man and seems to behave quite differently from her mother. Her husband allows her to bring her lovers into the house. She does not permit herself any feelings of jealousy or tenderness and wants to have relations with a number of men without any emotional ties, so that she can feel as autonomous as a man. Her need to be "progressive" goes so far that she allows her partners to abuse and humiliate her as they wish, and she suppresses all her feelings of mortification and anger in the belief that this makes her modern and free from prejudice. In this way she carries over both her

childhood obedience and her mother's submissiveness into these relationships. At times she suffers from severe depression.

2. A patient from an African family grew up alone with his mother after his father had died while he was still a very small boy. His mother insists on certain conventions and does not allow the child to be aware of his narcissistic and libidinal needs in any way, let alone express them. On the other hand, she regularly massages his penis until puberty, ostensibly on medical advice. As an adult her son leaves his mother and her world and marries an attractive European with quite a different background. Is it due to chance or to his unerring instinct that this woman not only torments and humiliates him but also undermines his confidence to an extreme degree, and that he is quite unable to stand up to her or leave her? This sadomasochistic marriage, like the other example, represents an attempt to break away from the parents' social system with the help of another one. The patient was certainly able to free himself from the mother of his adolescence, but he remained emotionally tied to the Oedipal and pre-Oedipal mother whose role was taken over by his wife as long as he was not able to experience the feelings from that period. In his analysis he encountered his original ambivalence. It was terribly painful for him to realize the extent to which he had needed his mother as a child and at the same time had felt abused in his helplessness; how much he had loved her, hated her, and been entirely at her mercy. The patient experienced these feelings after four years of analysis, with the result that he no longer needed his wife's perversions and could separate from her. At the same time he was able to see her far more realistically, including her positive sides.

Points of Contact with Some Theories of Depression

When we conceptualize depression as giving up one's real self in order to preserve the object, we can find within this view the main elements of theories of depression:

1. Freud's factor of *impoverishment* of the ego is, of course, centrally contained in this concept, allowing for the fact that, at the time of writing "Mourning and Melancholy" (1917), he used the term "ego" in the sense in which we now use the term "self."

2. What Karl Abraham (1912) described as turning aggression against the self also is closely related to the idea of the loss of the self, which I have tried to describe here. The "destruction" of one's own feelings, needs, and fantasies that are unwelcome to the primary object is an aggressive act against the self. The feelings that are thus "killed" by the depressive may vary according to the child's specific situation—they are not merely linked to aggressive impulses.

3. W. Joffe and J. Sandler (1965a and 1965b) define depression as a possible *reaction to psychic pain* caused by the discrepancy between the actual and the ideal self-representation. Congruity of these two leads to a feeling of well-being. In the language of object relations, that would mean: the ideal self-representation is the heritage of the primary objects whose approval and love ensure a sense of well-being, just as their discrepancy brings the danger of loss of love. If this pain could be risked and experienced, there would be no depression, but for that a supportive ("holding") environment would have been necessary at the crucial time.

4. Finally, according to Edith Jacobson (1971), the

conditions for a depressive development arise when loss of the ideal object is denied. Loss here does not merely mean real separation from the self-object, or disappointment that will be traumatic if it is not phase-appropriate, but also the unavailability of the self-object.

The narcissistically disturbed patient did not have a self-object at his disposal during the symbiotic phase, nor a "usable" object, in Winnicott's sense (1971)—one that would have survived its own destruction. Both the depressive and the grandiose person *deny this reality completely* by living as though the availability of the self-object could still be salvaged: the grandiose person through the illusion of achievement, and the depressive through his constant fear of losing the self-object. Neither of them can accept the truth that this loss or this unavailability has *already happened* in the past, and that *no effort* whatsoever *can ever change this fact.*

Chapter 3

The Vicious Circle

of Contempt

Would not God find a way out, some superior deception such as the grownups and the powerful always contrived, producing one more trump card at the last moment, shaming me after all, not taking me seriously, humiliating me under the damnable mask of kindness?

Herman Hesse
"A Child's Heart"

Humiliation for the Child, Contempt for the Weak, and Where It Goes from There

EVERYDAY EXAMPLES

While away on a vacation, I was sorting out my thoughts on the subject of "contempt" and reading various notes on this theme that I had made about individual analytic sessions. Probably sensitized by this preoccupation, I was more than usually affected by an ordinary scene, in no way spectacular or rare. I shall describe it to introduce my observations, for it illustrates some of the insights I have gained in the course of my analytic work, without any danger of indiscretion.

I was out for a walk and noticed a young couple a few steps ahead, both tall; they had a litttle boy with them, about two years old, who was running alongside and whining. (We are accustomed to seeing such situations from the adult point of view, but here I want to describe it as it was experienced by the child.) The two had just bought themselves ice-cream bars on sticks from the kiosk and were licking them with enjoyment. The little boy wanted one, too. His mother said affectionately, "Look, you can have a bite of mine, a whole one is too cold for you." The child did not want just one bite but held out his hand for the whole ice, which his mother took out of his reach again. He cried in despair, and soon exactly the same thing was repeated with his father: "There you are, my pet," said his father affectionately, "you can have a bite of mine." "No, no," cried the child and ran ahead again, trying to distract himself. Soon he came back again and gazed enviously and sadly up at the two grown-ups, who were enjoying their ice creams contentedly and at one. Time and again he held out his little hand for the whole ice-cream bar, but the adult hand with its treasure was withdrawn again.

The more the child cried, the more it amused his parents. It made them laugh a lot and they hoped to humor him along with their laughter, too: "Look, it isn't so important, what a fuss you are making." Once the child sat down on the ground and began to throw little stones over his shoulder in his mother's direction, but then he suddenly got up again and looked around anxiously, making sure that his parents were still there. When his father had completely finished his ice cream, he gave the stick to the child and walked on. The little boy licked the bit of wood expectantly, looked at it, threw it away, wanted to pick it up again but did not do so, and a deep sob of loneliness and disappointment shook his small body. Then he trotted obediently after his parents.

It seemed clear to me that this little boy was not being frustrated in his "oral drives," for he was given ample opportunity to take a bite; it was his narcissistic needs that were constantly being wounded and frustrated. His wish to hold the ice-cream stick in his hand like the others was not understood, worse still, it was laughed at: they made fun of his needs. He was faced with two giants who were proud of being consistent and also supported each other, while he, quite alone in his distress, obviously could say nothing beyond "no," nor could he make himself clear to his parents with his gestures (which were very expressive). He had no advocate.*

Why, indeed, did these parents behave with so litttle empathy? Why didn't one of them think of eating a little quicker or even of throwing away half his ice cream and giving the child his stick with a bit of edible substance? Why did they both stand there laughing, eating so slowly and showing so little concern about the child's obvious distress? They were not unkind or cold parents, the father spoke to his child very tenderly. Nevertheless, at least at this moment, they displayed a lack of empathy. We can only solve this riddle if we manage to see the parents, too, as insecure children—children who have at last found a weaker creature, and in comparison with him they now

* What an unfair situation it is, by the way, when a child is opposed by two big, strong adults, as by a wall; we call it "consistency in upbringing" when we refuse to let the child complain about one parent to the other.

can feel very strong. What child has never been laughed at for his fears and been told, "You don't need to be afraid of a thing like that." And what child will then not feel shamed and despised because he could not assess the danger correctly, and will that little person not take the next opportunity to pass on these feelings to a still smaller child. Such experiences come in all shades and varieties. Common to them all is the sense of strength that it gives the adult to face the weak and helpless child's fear and to have the possibility of controlling fear in another person, while he cannot control his own. (Cf. p. 25.)

No doubt, in twenty years' time, or perhaps earlier, if he has younger siblings, our little boy will replay this scene with the ice cream, but then *he* will be in possession and the other one will be the helpless, envious, weak little creature, whom he then no longer has to carry within himself, but now can split off and project outside himself.

Contempt for those who are smaller and weaker thus is the best defense against a breakthrough of one's own feelings of helplessness: it is an expression of this split-off weakness. The strong person who knows that he, too, carries this weakness within himself, because he has experienced it, does not need to demonstrate his strength through such contempt.

Many adults first become aware of their Oedipal feelings of helplessness, jealousy, and loneliness through their own children, since they had no chance to acknowledge and experience these feelings consciously in their childhood. (Cf. pp. 25–26.) I spoke of the patient who was obsessively forced to make conquests with women, to seduce and then to abandon them, until he was at last able to experience in his analysis how he himself had repeatedly been abandoned by his mother. Now he remembered how he had been caught at night outside the locked door of his parents' bedroom and laughed at. Now in the analytic session, is the first time that he consciously experiences the feelings of humiliation and mortification that were then aroused.

The Oedipal suffering that was not lived out can be got rid of by delegating it to one's own children—in much the same way as in the ice cream scene I have just described: "You see, we are big, we may do as we like, but for you it is 'too cold.' You may only enjoy yourself as we do when you get to be big enough." So, in the Oedipal area, too, it is not the instinctual frustration that is humiliating for the child, but the contempt shown for his instinctual wishes. It may well be that the narcissistic component of Oedipal suffering is commonly accentuated when the parents demonstrate their "grown-upness" to revenge themselves unconsciously on their child for their own earlier humiliation. In the child's eyes they encounter their own humiliating past, and they must ward it off with the power they now have achieved.

In many societies, little girls suffer additional discrimination because they are girls. Since women, however, have control of the new-born and the infants, these erstwhile little girls can pass on to their children at the most tender age the contempt from which they once had suffered. Later, the adult man will idealize his mother, since every human being needs the feeling that he was really loved; but he will despise other women, upon whom he thus revenges himself in place of his mother. And these humiliated adult women, in turn, if they have no other means of ridding themselves of their burden, will revenge themselves upon their own children. This indeed can be done secretly and without fear of reprisals, for the child has no way of telling anyone, except perhaps in the form of a perversion or obsessional neurosis, whose language is sufficiently veiled not to betray the mother.

Contempt is the weapon of the weak and a defense against one's own despised and unwanted feelings. And the fountainhead of all contempt, all discrimination, is the more or less conscious, uncontrolled, and secret exercise of power over the child by the adult, which is tolerated by society (except in the case of murder or serious bodily harm). What adults do to their child's spirit is entirely their own affair. For the child is regarded as the parents' property, in the same way as the citizens of a totalitarian state are the property of its government. Until we become sensitized to the small child's suffering, this wielding of power by adults will continue to be a normal aspect of the human condition, for no one pays attention to or takes seriously what is regarded as trivial, since the victims are "only children." But in twenty years' time these children will be adults who will have to pay it all back to their own children. They may then fight vigorously against cruelty "in the world"—and yet they will carry within themselves an experience of cruelty to which they have no access and which remains hidden behind their idealized picture of a happy childhood.

Let us hope that the degree to which this discrimination is persistently transmitted from one generation to the next might be reduced by education and increasing awareness—especially in its more subtle manifestations. Someone who slaps or hits another or knowingly insults him is aware of hurting him. He has some sense of what he is doing. But how often were our parents, and we ourselves toward our own children, unconscious of how painfully, deeply, and lastingly we injured a child's tender, budding self. It is very fortunate when our children are aware of this situation and are able to tell us about it, for this may enable them to throw off the chains of power, discrimination, and scorn that have been handed on for generations. When our children can consciously experience their early helplessness and narcissistic rage they will no longer need to ward off their helplessness, in turn, with exercise of power over others. In most cases, however, one's own childhood suffering remains affectively inaccessible and thus forms the hidden source of new and sometimes very subtle humiliation for the next generation. Various defense mechanisms will help to justify this: denial of one's own suffering, rationalization (I owe it to my child to bring him up properly), displacement (it is not my father but my son who is hurting me), idealization (my father's beatings were good for me), and more. And, above all, there is the mechanism of turning passive suffering into active behavior. The following examples may illustrate how astonishingly similar the ways are in which people protect themselves against their childhood experiences, despite great differences in personality structure and in education.

A thirty-year-old Greek, the son of a peasant and owner of a small restaurant in Western Europe, proudly described how he drinks no alcohol and has his father to thank for this abstinence. Once, at the age of fifteen, he came home drunk and was so severely beaten by his father that he could not move for a week. From that time on he was so averse to alcohol that he could not taste so much as a drop, although his work brought him into constant contact with it. When I heard that he was soon to be married, I asked whether he, too, would beat his children. "Of course," he answered, "beatings are necessary in bringing up a child properly: they are the best way to make him respect you.

I would never smoke in my father's presence, for example —and that is a sign of my respect for him." This man was neither stupid nor uncongenial, but he had little schooling. We might therefore nurse the illusion that education could counteract this process of destroying the spirit.

But how does this illusion stand up to the next example, which concerns an educated man?

A talented Czech author is reading from his own works in a town in Western Germany. After the reading there follows a discussion with the audience, during which he is asked questions about his life, which he answers ingenuously. He reports that despite his former support of the Prague Spring he now has plenty of freedom and can frequently travel in the West. He goes on to describe his country's development in recent years. When he is asked about his childhood, his eyes shine with enthusiasm as he talks about his gifted and many-sided father who encouraged his spiritual development and was a true friend. It was only to his father that he could show his first stories. His father was very proud of him, and even when he beat him as punishment for some misdemeanor reported by the mother, he was proud that his son did not cry. Since tears brought extra blows, the child learned to suppress them and was himself proud that he could make his admired father such a great present with his bravery. This man spoke of these regular beatings as though they were the most normal things in the world (as for him, of course, they were), and then he said: "It did me no harm, it prepared me for life, made me hard, taught me to grit my teeth. And that's why I could get on so well in my profession."

Contrasting with this Czech author, the film director Ingmar Bergman spoke on a television program with great awareness and far more understanding of the implications about his own childhood, which he described as one long story of humiliation. He related, for example, that if he wet his trousers he had to wear a red dress all day so that everybody would know what he had done and he would have to be ashamed of himself. Ingmar Bergman was the younger son of a Protestant pastor. In this television interview he described a scene that often occurred during his childhood. His older brother has just been beaten by the father. Now their mother is dabbing his brother's bleeding back with cotton wool. He himself sits watching. Bergman described this scene without apparent agitation, almost coldly. One can see him as a child, quietly sitting and watching. He surely did not run away, nor close his eyes, nor cry. One has the impression that this scene did take place in reality, but at the same time is a covering memory for what *he himself* went through. It is unlikely that only his brother was beaten by their father.

It sometimes happens that patients in analysis are convinced that only their siblings suffered humiliation. Only after years of analysis can they remember, with feelings of rage and helplessness, of anger and indignation, how humiliated and deserted they felt when they were beaten by their beloved father.

Ingmar Bergman, however, had other possibilities, apart from projection and denial, for dealing with his suffering— he could make films. It is conceivable that we, as the movie audience, have to endure those feelings that he, the son of such a father, could not experience overtly but nevertheless carried within himself. We sit before the screen confronted, the way that small boy once was, with all the cruelty "our brother" has to endure, and hardly feel able or willing to take in all this brutality with authentic feelings; we ward them off. When Bergman speaks regretfully of his failure to see through Nazism before 1945, although as an adolescent he often visited Germany during the Hitler period, we may see it as a consequence of his childhood. Cruelty was the familiar air that he had breathed from early on—and so, why should cruelty have caught his attention?

And why did I describe these three examples of men who had been beaten in their childhood? Are these not borderline cases? Do I want to consider the effects of beatings? By no means. We may believe that these three cases are crass exceptions. However, I chose these examples partly because they had not been entrusted to me as secrets but had already been made public, but, above all, I meant to show how even the most severe ill-treatment can remain hidden, because of the child's strong tendency to idealization. There is no trial, no advocate, no verdict; everything remains hidden in the darkness of the past, and should the facts become known, then they appear in the name of blessings. If this is so with the crassest examples of physical ill-treatment, then how is mental torment ever to be exposed, when it is less visible and more easily disputed anyway? Who is likely to take serious notice of subtle discrimination, as in the example of the small boy and the ice cream?

Metapsychology has no model for these processes. It is concerned with cathexis, with intrapsychic dynamics, object- and self-representations, but not with facts that at most are taken into account as the patient's fantasies. Its concern is the meaning attached to experiences and not the reality behind them. Nevertheless, we do analyze parents, too, and we hear about their feelings toward their children and about their narcissistic needs, and we have to ask ourselves what the consequences of all this are for the development of their children. What are we to do with this information? Can we ignore its implications? Can we blind ourselves with the argument that an analyst is only concerned with intrapsychic processes? It is as if we did not dare to take a single step in order to acknowledge the child's reality, since Freud recognized the conjecture of sexual seduction as the patient's fantasy. Since the patient also has an interest in keeping this reality hidden from us, and still more from himself, it can happen that we share his ignorance for a long time. Nevertheless, the patient never stops telling us about part of his reality in the language of his symptoms.

Possibly, the child's actual seduction did not take place the way Freud's hysterical patients related it. Yet, the parents' narcissistic cathexis of their child leads to a long series of sexual and nonsexual seductions, which the child will only be able to discover with difficulty, as an adult in his analysis (and often not before he himself is a parent).

A father who grew up in surroundings inimical to instinctual drives may well be inhibited in his sexual relationships in marriage. He may even remain polymorphous perverse and first dare to look properly at a female genital, play with it, and feel aroused while he is bathing his small daughter. A mother may perhaps have been shocked as a small girl by the unexpected sight of an erect penis and so developed fear of the male genital, or she may have experienced it as a symbol of violence in the primal scene without being able to confide in anyone. Such a mother may now be able to gain control over her fear in relationship to her tiny son. She may, for example, dry him after his bath in such a manner that he has an erection, which is not dangerous or threatening for her. She may massage her son's penis, right up to puberty, in order "to treat his phimosis" without having to be afraid. Protected by the unquestioning love that every child has for his mother she can carry on with her genuine, hesitating sexual exploration that had been broken off too soon.

What does it mean to the child, though, when his sexually inhibited parents make narcissistic use of him in their loneliness and need? Every child seeks loving contact and is happy to get it. At the same time, however, he feels insecure when desires are aroused that do not appear spontaneously at this stage in his development. This insecurity is further increased by the fact that his own autoerotic activity is punished by the parents' prohibitions or scorn.

There are other ways of seducing the child, apart from the sexual, for instance, with the aid of indoctrination, which underlies both the "antiauthoritarian" and the "strict" upbringing. Neither form of rearing takes account of the child's needs at his particular stage of development. As soon as the child is regarded as a possession for which one has a particular goal, as soon as one exerts control over him, his vital growth will be violently interrupted.

It is among the commonplaces of education that we often first cut off the living root and then try to replace its natural functions by artificial means. Thus we suppress the child's curiosity, for example (there are questions one should not ask), and then when he lacks a natural interest in learning he is offered special coaching for his scholastic difficulties.

We find a similar example in the behavior of addicts, in whom the object relationship has already been internalized. People who as children successfully repressed their intense feelings often try to regain—at least for a short time—their lost intensity of experience with the help of drugs or alcohol.

If we want to avoid the unconscious seduction and discrimination against the child, we must first gain a conscious awareness of these dangers. Only if we become sensitive to the fine and subtle ways in which a child may suffer humiliation can we hope to develop the respect for him that a child needs from the very first day of his life onward, if he is to develop emotionally. There are various ways to reach this sensitivity. We may, for instance, observe children who are strangers to us and attempt to feel empathy for them in their situation—or we might try to develop empathy for our own fate. For us as analysts, there is also the possibility of following our analysand into his past—if we accept that his feelings will tell us a true story that so far no one else knows.

Introjected Contempt in the Mirror of Psychoanalysis

DAMAGED SELF-ARTICULATION IN
THE COMPULSION TO REPEAT

If we want to do more than provide patients with intellectual insight, or—as may be necessary in some psychotherapies—merely to strengthen their defense mechanisms —then we shall have to embark on a new voyage of discovery with each patient. What we so discover will not be a distant land but one that does not yet exist and will only begin to do so in the course of its discovery and settlement. It is a fascinating experience to accompany a patient on this journey—so long as we do not try to enter this new land with concepts that are familiar to us, perhaps in order to avoid our own fear of what is unknown and not yet understood. The patient discovers his true self little by little through experiencing his own feelings and needs, because the analyst is able to accept and respect these even when he does not yet understand them.

I am sometimes asked in seminars or supervisors sessions how one should deal with "undesirable" feelings such as the irritation that patients sometimes arouse in their analyst. A sensitive analyst will of course feel this irritation. Should he suppress it to avoid rejecting the patient? But then the patient, too, will sense this suppressed anger, without being able to comprehend it, and will be confused. Should the analyst express it? If he does, this may offend the patient and undermine his confidence. I have found that when I do not attempt to respond to such questions and remarks with advice, the discussion among colleagues reaches a much deeper and more personal dimension. The question of how to deal with anger and other feelings in the countertransference no longer needs to be asked if we begin with the assumption that *all* the feelings that the patient arouses in his analyst, during his analysis, are part of his unconscious attempt to tell the analyst his story and at the same time to hide it from him—that is, to protect himself from the renewed manipulation he unconsciously expects. I always assume that the patient has no other way of telling me his story than the one he actually uses. Seen thus, all feelings arising in me, including irritation, belong to his coded language and are of great heuristic value. At times they may help to find the lost key to still invisible doors.

At one time there was discussion in the literature about how to recognize whether countertransference feelings are an expression of the analyst's transference. If the analyst has gained emotional access to his own childhood, then he should easily be able to distinguish between countertrans-

ference feelings and his own childish ones (his own transference). Feelings that belong to the countertransference
are like a quick flash, a signal, and clearly related to the
analysand's person. When they are intense, tormenting, and
continuous, they have to do with oneself. The countertransference indicates either the former attitudes of the patient's primary objects (or the analyst's unconscious rejection of this role), or the child's feelings, split-off and never
experienced, which the patient in the course of his analysis
has delegated to his analyst.

Can one portray a story that one does not know? This
sounds impossible—but it happens in every analysis. The
patient needs the analytic situation as a framework for the
development of his transference before he can stage his
story and make it understood. He needs somebody who
does not need him to behave in a particular manner, but
can let him be as he is at the moment, and who at the same
time is willing to accept any of the roles with which he
may be charged for as long as the analytic process requires.

The compulsion to repeat plays a prominent role in an
analysis conceived in this way. Much has been written
about the negative aspect of the compulsion to repeat: the
uncanny tendency to reenact a trauma, which itself is not
remembered, at times has something cruel and self-destructive about it and understandably suggests associations with
the death instinct. Nevertheless, the need to repeat also
has a positive side. Repetition is the language used by a child
who has remained dumb, his only means of expressing himself. A dumb child needs a particularly emphatic partner if
he is to be understood at all. Speech, on the other hand, is
often used less to express genuine feelings and thoughts
than to hide, veil, or deny them, and thus to express the
false self. And so there often are long periods in our work
with our patients during which we are dependent on their

compulsion to repeat—for this repetition is then the only manifestation of their true self. It lays the basis for the transference, and also for the whole mise en scène of the patient's field of interaction, which in the literature is described as acting out and is often met with mistrust.

Take an example. In many analyses the patient's wish to have a child is expressed during the first weeks or months. For a long time this wish was traced back to Oedipal wishes. This may well be correct. Nevertheless, the patient's associations often show the narcissistic background to this wish very clearly.

For the patient this means: "I want to have somebody whom I can completely possess, and whom I can control (my mother always withdrew from me); somebody who will stay with me all the time and not only for four hours in the week. Right now I am nobody, but as a mother or a father I should be somebody, and others would value me more than they do now that I have no children." Or it may mean: "I want to give a child everything that I had to do without, he should be free, not have to deny himself, be able to develop freely. I want to give this chance to another human being."

This second variation looks as though it were based on object relationships. But if that were so the patient would be able to take his time in fulfilling this wish—and to wait until he would be able to give from his abundance toward the end of his analysis. If, however, this wish for a child at the beginning of the analysis cannot be delayed but shows such urgency, then it is rather an expression of the patient's own great need.

Various aspects come together:

· The wish to have a mother who is available (the child as a new chance to achieve the good symbiosis, which the patient still seeks since he has never experienced it).

- The hope that with this birth the patient may become truly alive (the child as symbol for the patient's true self).
- Unconscious communication about the patient's own fate as a child, with the aid of compulsive repetition (the child as rival sibling, and abandoned hope); the sibling's birth had increased the patient's loss of self, and with the birth of his child the patient would give up (for the time being) his hope of realizing his true self.

To interpret this questionable wish to have a child as acting-out is not usually successful, since the compulsion to repeat is too strong. The analyst is then experienced as a strict mother, against whom the patient would like to rebel. At present, however, the patient can do so only in this self-destructive way, since he is not yet free from introjects. So the analyst is forced to be a spectator while the patient gives life to a new human being, apparently in order to destroy his own chance, but also thereby to rediscover his formerly only half-experienced life and to experience it consciously now with his newly awakened feelings. Just as a child uses the Sceno test figures to represent his family, so the patient unconsciously uses his new-born child to lay out for himself the tragedy of his own fate.

This is the double function of the compulsion to repeat. The patient senses that here for the first time he is really involved, that it is his own self that is being born. The wish to have a child expresses this desire, but it has to be expressed through another person. For the patient now will devote himself not to the baby he once was, but to an actual baby in the present. However, since this new-born baby also stands for his own childhood self, the patient can emotionally discover his own warded off childhood story, piece by piece, partly through identification and partly in the guise of his own parents, whom he gradually discovers within himself.

The compulsion to repeat is, in fact, more or less powerful even outside analysis. It is, for example, well-known that partner choice is closely related to the primary object's character. In analysis, however, this tendency is particularly strong—above all because the staging here includes the analyst, and the patient feels that a solution can be found. A detour by way of secondary transference figures is nevertheless often unavoidable, since fear of object-loss becomes intolerable as soon as ambivalent feelings develop. It is still necessary to separate the "mother as environment" from the "mother as object." The patient has learned very early in life that he must not show any dissatisfaction or disappointment with the object, since this would lead to the beloved father or mother withdrawing himself and his love. In the analysis a stage must certainly be reached, when even this risk can be endured and survived. Before that time, however, there is a long period when the analyst is needed as a companion, while early experiences with the primary objects which hitherto were inaccessible to memory, are rediscovered in a trial run with secondary transference figures.

The newly won capacity to accept his feelings frees the way for the patient's long-repressed needs and wishes, which nevertheless cannot yet be satisfied without self-punishment, or even cannot in reality be satisfied at all, since they are related to past situations. The latter is clearly seen in the example of the urgent and not to be postponed wish for a child, which, as I have tried to describe, expresses among other things the wish to have a mother constantly available.

All the same, there are needs that can and should be satisfied in the present and that regularly come up in the analyses of narcissistically disturbed individuals. Among these is every human being's central need to express himself—to show himself to the world as he really is—in word, in gesture, in behavior, in every genuine utterance from the baby's cry to the artist's creation.

For those people who, as children, had to hide their true selves from themselves and others, this first step into the open produces much anxiety. Yet, these people, especially, feel a great need to throw over their former restraints within the protection of their analysis. These first steps do not lead to freedom but to a compulsive repetition of the patient's childhood constellation, and so he will experience those feelings of agonizing shame and painful nakedness that accompany self-display. With the infallibility of a sleepwalker, the analysand seeks out those who, like his parents (though for different reasons), certainly cannot understand him. Through his compulsive need to repeat, he will try to make himself understandable to precisely these people—trying to make possible what cannot be.

At a particular stage in her analysis, a young woman fell in love with an older, intelligent, and sensitive man, who nevertheless, apart from eroticism, had to ward off and reject everything he could not understand intellectually, including psychoanalysis. Precisely this person was the one to whom she wrote long letters trying to explain the path she had taken in her analysis up to this point. She succeeded in overlooking all his signals of incomprehension and increased her efforts even more, until at last she was forced to recognize that she had again found a father substitute, and that this was the reason why she had been unable to give up her hopes of at last being understood. This awakening brought her agonizingly sharp feelings of shame that lasted for a long time. One day she was able to experience this during a session and said: "I feel so ridiculous, as if I had been talking to a wall and expecting it to answer, like a silly child." I asked: "Would you think it ridiculous if you saw a child who had to tell his troubles to a wall because there was no one else available?" The despairing sobbing that followed my question gave the patient access to a part of her former reality that was pervaded by boundless loneliness. It freed her at the same time from her agonizing, destructive, and compulsively repeated feelings of shame. The following day this patient brought her first poem, which she had written that night.

Only much later could she risk repeating this experience with "a wall" with me and not only with subsidiary transference figures. For a time this woman, who was normally capable of expressing herself so clearly, described everything in such an extraordinarily complicated and precipitate way that I had no chance of understanding it all, probably much like her parents earlier. She went through moments of sudden hate and narcissistic rage, reproaching me with indifference and lack of understanding. My patient now could hardly recognize me any more, although I had not changed. In this way she rediscovered with me her own childhood. A child, too, can never grasp the fact that the same mother who cooks so well, is so concerned about his cough, and helps so kindly with his homework, in some circumstances has no more feeling than a wall for his hidden inner world. This young woman's vehement reproaches that now were directed against me finally released her from her compulsion to repeat, which had consisted of constantly seeking a partner who had no understanding for her or of arranging such a constellation, so that she would then feel helplessly dependent on him. The fascination of such tormenting relationships is part of the compulsion constantly to reenact one's earliest disappointments with the parents.

PERPETUATION OF CONTEMPT IN PERVERSION
AND OBSESSIONAL NEUROSIS

If we start from the premise that a person's whole development (and his narcissistic balance that is based upon it) is dependent on the way *his mother* experienced his *expression of needs and sensations* during his first days and weeks of life, then we must assume that here the *valuation* of *feelings* and *impulses* is set. If a mother cannot take pleasure in her child as he is but must have him behave in a particular way, then the first value selection takes place for the child. Now "good" is differentiated from "bad," "nice" from "nasty," and "right" from "wrong," and this differentiation is introjected by the child. Against this background will follow all his further introjections of the parents' more differentiated valuations.

Since every mother has her own "roomful of props," virtually every infant must learn that there are things about him for which the mother has "no use." She will expect her child to control his bodily functions as early as possible. On the conscious level his parents want him to do this so that he will not offend against society, but unconsciously they are protecting their own reaction formation dating from the time when they were themselves small children afraid of "offending."

Marie Hesse, the mother of the poet and novelist Hermann Hesse, undoubtedly a sensitive woman, describes in her diaries how her own will was broken at the age of four. When her son was four years old, she suffered greatly under his defiant behavior, and battled against it with varying degrees of success. At the age of fifteen, Hermann Hesse was sent to an institution for the care of epileptics and defectives in Stetten, "to put an end to his defiance once and for all." In an affecting and angry letter from Stetten, Hesse wrote to his parents: "If I were a bigot, and not a human being, I could perhaps hope for your understanding." All the same, his release from the home was made conditional upon his "improvement," and so the boy "improved." In a later poem dedicated to his parents, denial and idealization are restored: he reproaches himself that it had been "his character" that had made life so difficult for his parents. Many people suffer all their lives from this oppressive feeling of guilt, the sense of not having lived up to their parents' expectations. This feeling is stronger than any intellectual insight that it is not a child's task or duty to satisfy his parent's narcissistic needs. No argument can overcome these guilt feelings, for they have their beginnings in life's earliest period, and from that they derive their intensity and obduracy.

That probably greatest of narcissistic wounds—not to have been loved just as one truly was—cannot heal without the work of mourning. It can either be more or less successfully resisted and covered up (as in grandiosity and depression), or constantly torn open again in the compulsion to repeat. We encounter this last possibility in obsessional neurosis and in perversion. The mother's (or father's) scornful reactions have been introjected. The mother often reacted with surprise and horror, aversion and disgust, shock and indignation, or with fear and panic to the child's most natural impulses. And so these have been the mother's reactions to such natural impulses as the child's autoerotic behavior, investigating and discovering his own body, oral greed, urination and defecation, touching and playing with his own excrement, or to his curiosity or rage in response to failure or disappointment. Later, all these experiences remain closely linked to the mother's horrified eyes, and this clearly emerges in the analytic transference.

The patient goes through torment when he reveals to the analyst his hitherto secret sexual and autoerotic behavior. He may, of course, also relate all this quite unemotionally, merely giving information, as if he were speaking of some other person. Such a report, however, will not help him to break out of his loneliness nor lead him back to the reality of his childhood. It is only when he is encouraged in the analysis not to fend off his feelings of shame and fear, but rather to accept and experience them, that he can discover what he has felt as a child. His most harmless behavior will cause him to feel mean, dirty, or completely annihilated. He himself indeed is surprised when he realizes how long this repressed feeling of shame has survived, and how it has found a place alongside his tolerant and advanced views of sexuality. These experiences first show the patient that his early adaptation by means of splitting was not an expression of cowardice, but that it was really his only chance to escape this sense of impending destruction.

What else can one expect of a mother who was always proud of being her mother's dear good daughter, who was dry at the age of six months, clean at a year, at three could "mother" her younger siblings, and so forth. In her own baby, such a mother sees the split-off and never-experienced part of her self, of whose breakthrough into consciousness she is afraid, and she sees also the uninhibited sibling baby, whom she mothered at such an early age and only now envies and perhaps hates in the person of her own child. So she trains her child with looks, despite her greater wisdom—for she can do nothing else. As the child grows up, he cannot cease living his own truth, and expressing it somewhere, perhaps in complete secrecy. In this way a person can have adapted completely to the demands of his surroundings and can have developed a false self, but in his perversion or his obsessional neurosis he still allows a portion of his true self to survive—in torment. And so the true self lives on, under the same conditions as the child once did with his disgusted mother, whom in the meantime he has introjected. In his perversion and obsessions he constantly reenacts the same drama: a horrified mother is necessary before drive-satisfaction is possible: orgasm (for instance, with a fetish) can only be achieved in a climate of self-contempt; criticism can only be expressed in (seemingly) absurd, unaccountable (frightening), obsessional fantasies.

Nothing will serve better to acquaint us with the hidden tragedy of certain unconscious mother-child relationships than the analysis of a perversion or an obsessional neurosis. For in such an analysis we witness the destructive power of the compulsion to repeat, and that compulsion's dumb, unconscious communication in the shaping of its drama.

It is of eminent importance that, although the patient has the possibility to *experience* the analyst as hostile to his drives, critical and contemptuous, yet the analyst should in fact never really be so. This may sound obvious but it is not always in practice.

Sometimes the analyst does just the opposite, quite unconsciously and with the best intentions. It may be that he can hardly bear being turned into a figure so hostile to instinctual drives, and so must demonstrate his tolerance by persuading the patient, for example, to describe his masterbatory practice fearlessly. In doing so he will prevent the patient from experiencing his mother in the transference. At the same time this analyst repeats, in reality, the mother's rejection of the patient's childish instinctual impulses, for he does not allow the childish fear and confusion to come out as they were originally felt and will only speak to his patient on an adult level.

One might, in fact, think of it as discrimination, as a devaluation of the childlike, when an analyst emphasizes that, for him, of course, his patients are always adults and not children—as if being a child were something to be ashamed of, and not something valuable that we lose later on. Occasionally one hears similar remarks about sickness, when an analyst is eager to consider his patients as healthy as possible, or warns them against "dangerous regression"— as if sickness were not sometimes the only possible way of expressing the true self. The people who come to us have, after all, been trying all their lives to be as adult and healthy (normal) as possible. They experience it as a great, inner liberation when they discover this socially conditioned straitjacket of child-rejection and "normalcy"-worship within themselves and can give it up.

A person who suffers under his perversion bears within himself his mother's rejection, and thus he flaunts his perversion, in order to get others to reject him, too, all the time—so reexternalizing the rejecting mother. For this reason he feels compelled to do things that his circle and society disapprove of and despise. If society were suddenly to honor his form of perversion (as may happen in certain circles), he would have to change his compulsion, but it would not free him. What he needs is not permission to use one or another fetish, but the disgusted and horrified eyes. If he comes to analysis he will look for this in his analyst, too, and will have to use all possible means to provoke him to disgust, horror, and aversion. This provocation is of course a part of the transference, and from the incipient countertransference reactions one can surmise what happened at the beginning of this life.

If the analyst can see through to the goals and compulsions behind this provocation, then the whole decayed building collapses and gives way to true, deep, and defenseless mourning. When finally the narcissistic wound itself can be felt, there is no more necessity for all the distortions. This is a clear demonstration of how mistaken the attempt is to show a patient his instinctual conflicts, if he has been trained from earliest childhood on to *feel nothing*. How can instinctual wishes and conflicts be experienced without feelings? What can orality mean without greed, what anality without defiance and envy, what is the Oedipus complex without feelings of rage, abandonment, jealousy, loneliness, love? It is very striking to see how often pseudo-instinctual acting-out ceases when the patient begins to experience *his own* feelings and can recognize his *true* instinctual wishes.

The following citation is taken from a report about St. Pauli, Hamburg's red-light district, that appeared in the German magazine *Stern* (June 8, 1978): "You experience the masculine dream, as seductive as it is absurd, of being coddled by women like a baby and at the same time commanding them like a pascha." This "masculine dream," indeed is not absurd; it arises from the infant's most genuine and legitimate needs. Our world would be very different if the majority of babies had the chance to rule over their mothers like paschas and to be coddled by them, without having to concern themselves with their mothers' needs too early.

The reporter asked some of the regular clients what gave them most pleasure in these establishments and summarized their answers as follows:

> . . . that the girls are available and completely at the customer's disposal, they do *not require protestations of love like girlfriends*. There are *no obligations, psychological*

dramas, nor *pangs of conscience* when desire has passed: *"You pay and are free!"* Even (and especially) the *humiliation* that such an encounter also involves for the client can *increase stimulation*—but that is less willingly mentioned.*

The humiliation, self-disgust, and self-contempt are intrapsychic reflections of the primary objects' contempt and, through the compulsion to repeat, they produce the same tragic conditions for pleasure.

Perversion is a borderline case, but gives us an understanding that is valid for the treatment of other disorders, namely, understanding of the great importance to be attached to unconscious, introjected contempt.

What is unconscious cannot be abolished by proclamation or prohibition. One can, however, develop sensitivity toward recognizing it and can experience it consciously, and thus gain control over it. A mother can have the best intentions to respect her child and yet be unable to do so, so long as she does not realize what deep shame she causes him with an ironic remark, intended only to cover her own uncertainty. Indeed, she cannot be aware of how deeply humiliated, despised, and devalued her child feels, if she herself has never consciously suffered these feelings, and if she tries to fend them off with irony.

It can be the same for us in our analytic work. Certainly, we do not use words like bad, dirty, naughty, egoistic, rotten—but among ourselves we speak of "narcissistic," "exhibitionistic," "destructive," and "regressive" patients, without noticing that we (unconsciously) give these words a pejorative meaning. It may be that in our abstract vocabulary, in our objective attitudes, even in the way we formulate our theories, we have something in common with a mother's contemptuous looks, which we can trace

* Italics added.

90

to the accommodating three-year-old little girl within her. It is understandable that a patient's scornful attitude should induce an analyst to protect his superiority with the help of theory. But in such a dugout the patient's true self will not pay us a visit. It will hide from us just as it did from the mother's disgusted eyes. However, we make good use of our sensitivity. We can detect the successive installments in the story of a despised child, that lies behind all the analysand's expressions of contempt. When that happens, it is easier for the analyst not to feel he is being attacked and to drop his inner need to hide behind his theories. The knowledge of theory is surely helpful, but only when it has lost its defensive function—when it no longer is the successor of a strict, controlling mother, forcing the analyst to accommodate himself, and narrowing his possibilities. Then the knowledge of theory is like Winnicott's "teddy bear, lying about"—simply within reach when it is needed.

"DEPRAVITY" IN HERMANN HESSE'S CHILDHOOD WORLD AS AN EXAMPLE OF CONCRETE "EVIL"

It is very difficult to describe how a person has dealt with the contempt under which he had suffered as a child —especially the contempt for all his sensual enjoyment and pleasure in living, without giving concrete examples. With the aid of various metapsychological models one could certainly portray the intrapsychic dynamics, shifts in cathexis, structural changes and various defense mechanisms, especially the defense against affect. None of this, however, would communicate the emotional climate, which alone evokes a person's suffering, and so will make identification and empathy possible for the reader. With purely theoretical representations we remain "outside," can talk about "the others," classify, group, and label them, and discuss them in a language that only we understand.

There is, of course, an inequality in the analytic setting (between the analysand on his couch and the analyst in his chair), which has both point and validity. But there is no essential reason to extend it to other situations, such as discussions, lectures, and articles. Thus I must reduce the inequality and distance between couch and chair in myself, if I want to avoid degrading patients to scientific specimens for my study.

How is this to be put into practice if one feels called upon not only to accompany the patient but also to pass on the experience one has gained? Metapsychological concepts alone do not make it clear how far we all as human beings (as small children and as analysands) have need of our common sensitivity. If, however, I describe examples in detail, then I am in danger of revealing a person's secret and hidden tragedy to the world. I thereby should (in effect though not by intention) be repeating the mother's lack of respect, for instance, when she discovered the child's masturbation and shamed him for it. Yet, it is only through the concrete example of a specific life that we can show how a person has experienced the concrete "naughtiness" of his childhood as "wickedness itself." Only the history of an individual life will make us realize how impossible it is for an individual to recognize his parents' compulsion as such, once they have become part of himself—although he may try all his life to break out of this inner prison.

In this dilemma between metapsychology and indiscretion I have decided to use the example of the poet and novelist Hermann Hesse to demonstrate the very complicated situation. This eliminates from the beginning any moral evaluation, and although it does not concern a perversion, it does seem to me to have something in common with the early history of a perversion, namely, the introjection of parental contempt for the child's instinctual needs. This example also has the advantage that it has been published, and published by the person himself, so that the connections that I shall postulate can be clarified with concrete examples from his life.

At the beginning of his novel *Demian*, Hermann Hesse describes the goodness and purity of a parental home that gave neither a place nor a hearing to a child's fibs. (It is not difficult to recognize the author's own parental home in this novel, and he confirms this indirectly.) Thus the child is left alone with his sin and feels that he is depraved, wicked, and outcast, though nobody scolds him (since nobody knows the "terrible facts") and everyone shows him kindness and friendliness.

Many people recognize this situation. The idealizing way of describing such a "pure" household is not strange to us either, and it reflects both the child's point of view and the hidden cruelty of educational methods that we know well.

> Like most parents [writes Hesse], mine were no help with the new problems of puberty, to which no reference was ever made. All they did was take *endless trouble* in supporting my hopeless attempts to *deny reality* and to continue dwelling in a childhood world that was becoming *more and more unreal*. I have no idea whether parents can be of help, and I do not blame mine. It was my own affair to come to terms with myself and to find my own way, and like most well-brought-up children, I managed it badly. (p. 49) *

To a child his parents seem to be free of instinctual wishes, for they have means and possibilities of hiding their

---

* Italics added.

sexual satisfactions, whereas the child is always under surveillance.*

The first part of *Demian*, it seems to me, is very evocative and easy to appreciate, even for people from quite different milieu. What makes the later parts of the novel so peculiarly difficult must be in some way related to Hesse's introjection of his parents' and grandparents' emotional values (they were missionary families), which is to be felt in many of his stories, but can perhaps most easily be shown in *Demian*.

Although Sinclair has already had his own experience of cruelty (blackmail by an older boy), this has had no effect and gives him no key to a better understanding of the world. "Wickedness" for him is "depravity" (here is the missionaries' language). It is neither the hate, nor the ambivalence, nor the cruelty that are present in every human being and that Sinclair himself has already experienced, but such trivialities as drinking in a tavern.

The little boy Hermann Hesse took over from his parents this particular concept of wickedness as "depravity": it is not rooted in his personality but is like a foreign body. This is why everything in *Demian* that happens after the appearance of the god Abraxas, who is to "unite the godly and the devilish," is so curiously removed, it no longer touches us. Wickedness here is supposed to be artfully united with goodness. One has the impression that, for the boy, this is something strange, threatening, and above all

---

* In his story "A Child's Heart" Hesse writes: "The adults acted as if the world were perfect and as if they themselves were demigods, we children were nothing but scum. . . . Again and again, after a few days, even after a few hours, something happened that should not have been allowed, something wretched, depressing, and shaming. Again and again, in the midst of the noblest and staunchest decisions and vows, I fell abruptly, inescapably, into sin and wickedness, into ordinary bad habits. Why was it this way? (pp. 7, 8)

unknown, from which he nevertheless cannot free himself, because of his emotional cathexis of "depravity," which is already joined to fear and guilt.

> Once more I was trying most strenuously to construct an intimate "world of light" for myself out of the shambles of a period of devastation; once more I sacrificed everything within me to the aim of banishing darkness and evil from myself. (pp. 81–82)

In the Zürich exhibition (1977) to commemorate the centenary of Hesse's birth, there was a picture with which the little Hermann grew up, since it hung above his bed. In this picture, on the right, we see the "good" road to heaven, full of thorns, difficulties, and suffering. On the left, we see the easy pleasurable road that inevitably leads to hell. Taverns play a prominent part on this road—the devout women probably hoped to keep their husbands and sons away from these wicked places with this threatening representation. These taverns play an important role in *Demian*, too. This is particularly grotesque because Hesse had no urge at all to get drunk in such taverns, though he certainly did wish to break out of the narrowness of his parental system of values.

Every child forms his first image of what is "bad," quite concretely, by what is forbidden—by his parents' prohibitions, taboos and fears. He will have a long way to go until he can free himself from these parental values and discover his own "badness" in himself. He then will no longer regard it as "depraved" and "wicked," because it is instinctual, but as an aspect of life from which no human being can be free at bottom—although the strength of their disavowal may be sufficient for some people to convince themselves that they are. Possibly, Hermann Hesse in his puberty also had to live out his father's split-off and denied "depravity," and this he tried to portray in his books. Perhaps this is why there is so much in his novels that is not easy to empathize with, though it communicates the atmosphere under which Hesse suffered as a child, and from which he could not free himself, because he had been compelled to introject it so very early.

The following passage from *Demian* shows how deeply the loss of the loved objects threatened Hesse's search for his true self:

> But where we have given of our love and respect not from habit but of our own free will, where we have been disciples and friends out of our inmost hearts, it is a bitter and horrible moment when we suddenly recognize that the current within us wants to pull us away from what is dearest to us. Then every thought that rejects the friend and mentor turns on our own hearts like *a poisoned barb*, then each blow struck in defense *flies back into one's own face*, the words "disloyalty" and "ingratitude" strike the person who feels he was morally sound *like catcalls and stigma*, and the *frightened heart flees timidly back* to the *charmed valleys of childhood* virtues, unable to believe that this break, too, must be made, this bond also broken. (p. 127) *

And in "A Child's Heart" we read:

> If I were to reduce all my feelings and their painful conflicts to a single name, I can think of no other word but: dread. It was dread, dread and uncertainty, that I felt in all those hours of shattered childhood felicity: dread of punishment, dread of my own conscience, dread of stirrings in my soul which I considered forbidden and criminal. (p. 10)

In his story "A Child's Heart" Hesse portrays with great tenderness and understanding the feelings of an eleven-year-old boy, who had stolen some dried figs from his

---

* Italics added.

beloved father's room so that he could have in his possession something that belonged to his father. Guilt feelings, fear, and despair torment him in his loneliness and are replaced at last by the deepest humiliation and shame when his "wicked deed" is discovered. The strength of this portrayal leads us to surmise that it concerns a real episode from Hesse's own childhood. This surmise becomes certainty, thanks to a note made by his mother on November 11, 1889: "Hermann's theft of figs discovered."

From the entries in his mother's diary and from the extensive exchange of letters between both parents and various members of the family, which have been available since 1966, it is possible to guess at the small boy's painful path. Hesse, like so many gifted children, was so difficult for his parents to bear, not despite but *because* of his inner riches. Often a child's very gifts (his great intensity of feeling, depth of experience, curiosity, intelligence, quickness—and his ability to be critical) will confront his parents with conflicts that they have long sought to keep at bay with rules and regulations. These regulations must then be rescued at the cost of the child's development. All this can lead to the apparently paradoxical situation when parents who are proud of their gifted child and who even admire him are forced by their own distress to reject, suppress, or even destroy what is *best,* because truest, in that child. Two of Hesse's mother's observations may illustrate how this work of destruction can be combined with loving care:

1. (1881): "Hermann is going to nursery school, his violent temperament causes us much distress." (1966, p. 10) The child was three years old.

2. (1884): "Things are going better with Hermann, whose education causes us so much distress and trouble. From

the 21st of January to the 5th of June he lived wholly in the boys' house and only spent Sundays with us. He behaved well there but came home pale, thin and *depressed*. The *effects are decidedly good and salutary*. He is much *easier to manage now*." (1966, pp. 13–14) The child now was seven years old.*

On November 14, 1883, his father, Johannes Hesse, writes:

Hermann, who was considered almost a model of good behavior in the boys' house is sometimes *hardly to be borne*. Though it would be very humiliating *for us*[!], I am earnestly considering whether we should not place him in an *institution* or *another household*. We are too nervous and weak for him, and the whole household [is] too undisciplined and irregular. He seems to be gifted for everything: he observes the moon and the clouds, extemporizes for long periods on the harmonium, draws wonderful pictures with pencil or pen, can sing quite well when he wants to, and is never at a loss for a rhyme.† (1966, p. 13)

In the strongly idealized picture of his childhood and his parents, which we encounter in *Hermann Lauscher*,‡ Hesse has completely abandoned the original, rebellious, "difficult," and for his parents troublesome, child he once was. He had no way to accommodate this important part of his self and so was forced to expel it. Perhaps this is why his

* Italics added.
† Italics added.
‡ When my childhood at times stirs my heart, it is like a gold-framed, deep-toned picture in which predominates a wealth of chestnuts and alders, an indescribably delightful morning light and a background of splendid mountains. All the hours in my life, in which I was allowed a short period of peace, forgetful of the world; all the lonely walks, which I took over beautiful mountains; all the moments in which an unexpected happiness, or love without desire, carried me away from yesterday and tomorrow; all these can be given no more precious name than when I compare them with this green picture of my earliest life. (*Gesammelte Werke*, vol. I, Frankfurt: M. Suhrkamp, 1970, p. 218.)

great and genuine longing for his true self remained unfulfilled.

That Hermann Hesse was not deficient in courage, talent, or depth of feeling is, of course, evident in his works and in many of his letters, especially the unforgettable letter from Stetten. But his father's answer to this letter (cf. 1966), his mother's notes, and the passages from *Demian* and "Kinderseele" quoted above show us clearly how the crushing weight of his introjects became his fate. Despite his enormous acclaim and success, and despite the Nobel prize, Hesse in his mature years suffered from the tragic and painful feeling of being separated from his true self, which doctors refer to curtly as depression.

THE MOTHER DURING THE FIRST YEARS OF LIFE AS SOCIETY'S AGENT*

If we were to tell a patient that in other societies his perversion would not be a problem, that it is a problem here sheerly because it is our society that is sick and produces constrictions and constraints. this would certainly be partially true, but it would be of little help to him. He would feel, rather, that, as an individual, with his own individual history, he was being passed over and misunderstood; for this interpretation makes too little of his own very real tragedy. What most needs to be understood is his compulsion to repeat, and the state of affairs behind it to which this compulsion bears witness. All this no doubt is the result of social pressures, and these do not have their effect on his psyche through abstract knowledge but are anchored in his earliest affective experience with his mother. His problems cannot be solved with *words*, but only

* See footnote on p. 8 herein.

through *experience*, not merely corrective experience as an adult but, above all, through a reliving of his early fear of his beloved mother's contempt and his subsequent feelings of indignation and sadness. Mere words, however skilled the interpretation, will leave the split from which he suffers unchanged or even deepened.

One can therefore hardly free a patient from the cruelty of his introjects by showing him how the absurdity, exploitation, and perversity of society causes our neuroses and perversions, however true this may be. Freud's patient Dora became sick because of society's sexual hypocrisy, which she was unable to see through. Things we can see through do not make us sick; they may arouse our indignation, anger, sadness, or feelings of impotence. What makes us sick are those things we cannot see through, society's constraints that we have absorbed through our mother's eyes —eyes and an attitude from which no reading or learning can free us. To put it another way: our patients are intelligent, they read in newspapers and books about the absurdity of the armaments race, about exploitation through capitalism, diplomatic insincerity, the arrogance and manipulation of power, submission of the weak and the impotence of individuals—and they have thought about these subjects. What they do not see, because they cannot see it, is the absurdities of their own mothers at the time when they still were tiny children. One cannot remember one's parents' attitudes then, because one was a part of them, but in analysis this early interaction can be recalled and parental constraints are thus more easily disclosed.

Political action can be fed by the unconscious anger of children who have been so misused, imprisoned, exploited, cramped, and drilled. This anger can be partially discharged in fighting our institutions, without having to give up the idealization of one's own mother, as one knew her in one's childhood. The old dependency can then be shifted to a new object. If, however, disillusionment and the resultant mourning can be lived through in analysis, then social and political disengagement do not usually follow, but the patient's actions are freed from the compulsion to repeat.

The inner necessity to constantly build up new illusions and denials, in order to avoid the experience of our own reality, disappears once this reality has been faced and experienced. We then realize that all our lives we have feared and struggled to ward off something that really cannot happen any longer: it has already happened, happened at the very beginning of our lives while we were completely dependent. The situation is similar in regard to creativity. Here the prerequisite is the work of mourning—not a neurosis, although people often think it is the latter—and many artists believe that analysis (the mother?) would "take away" their creativity.

Let us assume that an analyst tries to talk a patient out of his guilt feelings by tracing his strict superego back to those of society's norms that serve particular capitalist interests. This interpretation is not false. "Society" not only suppresses instinctual wishes but also (and above all) it suppresses particular feelings (for instance, anger) and narcissistic needs (for esteem, mirroring, respect), whose admissibility in adults and fulfillment in children would lead to individual autonomy and emotional strength, and thus would not be consonant with the interests of those in power. However, this oppression and this forcing of submission do not only begin in the office, factory, or political party; they begin in the very first weeks of an infant's life. Afterward they are internalized and repressed and are then, because of their very nature, inaccessible to argument. Nothing is changed in the character of submission or dependency, when it is only their object that is changed.

Therapeutic effects (in the form of temporary improvement) may be achieved if a strict superego can be replaced by the analyst's more tolerant one. The aim of analysis, however, is not to correct the patient's fate, but to enable him to confront both his own fate and his mourning over it. The patient has to discover the parents of his early years in the transference, and within himself, and must become consciously aware of his parents' unconscious manipulation and unintended contempt, so that he can free himself from them. So long as he has to make do with a tolerant substitute superego, borrowed from his analyst, his contemptuous introject will remain unchanged, and hidden in his unconscious, despite all his better conscious knowledge and intentions. Although this contemptuous introject will show itself in the patient's human relationships and will torment him, it will be inaccessible to any working through. The contents of the unconscious, as Freud said, remain unchanged and timeless. Change can only begin as these contents become conscious.

THE LONELINESS OF THE CONTEMPTUOUS

The contempt shown by narcissistically disturbed patients (to which Kernberg points with much emphasis, 1970) may have various forerunners in their life history. These may have been, for instance, "the stupid little brothers and sisters," or the uneducated parents who don't understand anything—but the function all these expressions of contempt have in common is the defense against unwanted feelings. Contempt for younger siblings often hides envy of them, just as contempt for the parents often helps to ward off the pain of being unable to idealize them. Contempt also may serve as a defense against other feelings, and it will lose its point when it fails as a shield—for instance, against shame over one's unsuccessful courting of the parent of the opposite sex; or against the feeling of inadequacy in rivalry with the same-sex parent; and above all against narcissistic rage that the object is not completely available. So long as one despises the other person and overvalues one's own achievements ("he can't do what I can do"), one does not have to mourn the fact that love is not forthcoming without achievement. Nevertheless, avoiding this mourning means that one remains at bottom the one who is despised. For I have to despise everything in myself that is not wonderful, good, and clever. Thus I perpetuate intrapsychically the loneliness of childhood: I despise weakness, impotence, uncertainty—in short, the child in myself and in others.

The patient seldom directly expresses his contempt for the analyst at the beginning of treatment. At first his scorn is consciously directed at other people. He thinks, for example: "I don't need any childish feelings, they are alright for my younger brothers and sisters, who do not have my judgment. Anyway, it is only sentimental stuff, ridiculous. I am grown-up, I can think and act, I can make changes in things around me, I don't need to feel helpless any more, or dependent. If I am afraid, I can do something about it or try to understand it intellectually. My intelligence is my most reliable companion."

Well, all that sounds pretty good. But the analysand comes to analysis because he feels lonely, despite or even because of his clear superiority, and because he suffers from difficulties in making contacts, or perhaps he comes because he suffers from compulsions or perversions. In the course of analysis it can then be seen how far this contempt has protected him from his own feelings.

Sometimes contemptuous feelings toward the analyst will show up very early in the analysis. But this can only be worked through when the analysand has found the broader basis for his whole world of feeling on which he can then play out and work through his ambivalence. It is then decisive that the analyst should not let himself be provoked into demonstrating his own superiority to the patient. The contempt that Kernberg describes as ubiquitous in grandiose, successful people always includes contempt for their own true selves. For their scorn implies: without these qualities, which I have, a person is completely worthless. That means further: without these achievements, these gifts, I could never be loved, would never have been loved. Thus the small, powerless child, who is helplessly dependent on others, and also the awkward or difficult child will have to suffer contempt. Grandiosity guarantees that the illusion continues: I was loved.

Those whose grandiose, false self needs to act out this certainty are often envied or admired by those whose narcissistic disturbance has a primarily depressive structure, whereas the grandiose will despise the depressives. Nevertheless, this is no basis for a typology, since grandiosity and depression express the same underlying problem.

Contempt as a rule will cease with the beginning of mourning for the irreversible that cannot be changed. For contempt, too, had in its own way served to deny the reality of the past. It is, after all, less painful to think that the others do not understand because they are too stupid. Then one can make efforts to explain things to them. This is the process, described by Kohut, that takes place when idealization of the self-object fails and the grandiose self has to be cathected. There seems to be a way out, in fantasy at least. Through (one's own) grandiosity, power as such can be salvaged, and so the illusion of being understood ("if only I can express myself properly") can be maintained.* If however this effort is relaxed, one is forced to see how little there was on the other side and how much one had invested oneself. (Cf. p. 82.)

One must come to realize that here a general understanding as such is not possible, since each person is individually stamped by his own fate and his own childhood. Many parents, even with the best intentions, cannot always understand their child, since they, too, have been stamped by their experience with their own parents and have grown up in a different generation. It is indeed a great deal when parents can respect their children's feelings even when they cannot understand them. There is no contempt in saying, "it was not possible"—it is a reconciliatory recognition that is hard to achieve. A detailed example may illustrate this.

A patient who had sought a second analysis because of tormenting obsessions repeatedly dreamed that he was on a lookout tower that stood in a swampy area, at the edge of a town dear to him. From there he had a lovely view, but he felt sad and deserted. There was an elevator in the tower, and in the dream there were all kinds of difficulties over entrance tickets and obstacles on the way to this tower. In reality, the town had no such tower, but it belonged unequivocally to the patient's dream landscape, and he knew it well. The phallic meaning of this dream had been considered in his previous analysis, and it was certainly not wrong to see this aspect, though it was obviously not sufficient, since the dream recurred later with the same feelings of being deserted. Interpretation of instinctual con-

---

* Devastating examples of this process are the works of Van Gogh and of the Swiss painter Max Gubler, who so wonderfully and so unsuccessfully courted the favor of their mothers with all the means at their disposal.

flicts had absolutely no effect, the obsessional symptoms remained unchanged.

Only after much had changed in the course of analysis were there new variations in the dream, too, and at last it changed in a decisive way. The patient first was surprised to dream that he already had entrance tickets, but the tower had been demolished and there was no longer a view. Instead, he saw a bridge that joined the swampy district to the town. He could thus go on foot into the town and saw "not everything" but "some things close up." The patient, who suffered from an elevator phobia, was somehow relieved, for riding in this elevator had caused him considerable anxiety. Speaking of the dream, he said he was perhaps no longer dependent on always having a complete view, on always seeing everything, being on top, and cleverer than other people. He now could go on foot like everyone else.

The patient was the more astonished when, toward the end of his analysis, he dreamed that he was suddenly sitting in this elevator in the tower again and was drawn upward as in a chair lift without feeling any fear. He enjoyed the ride, got out at the top and, strange to say, there was colorful life all about him. It was a plateau, and from it he had a view of the valleys. There was also a town up there, with a bazaar full of colorful wares; a school where children were practicing ballet and he could join in (this had been a childhood wish); and groups of people holding discussions with whom he sat and talked. He felt integrated into this society, just as he was. This dream impressed him deeply and made him happy, and he said:

My earlier dreams of the tower showed my isolation and loneliness. At home, as the eldest, I was always ahead of my siblings, my parents could not match my intelligence, and in all intellectual matters I was alone [the town he loved was a European center of culture]. On the one hand, I had to demonstrate my knowledge, in order to be taken seriously, and on the other, I had to hide it or my parents would say: "Your studies are going to your head! Do you think you are better than everyone else, just because you had the chance to study? Without your mother's sacrifice and your father's hard work you would never have been able to do it." That made me feel guilty and I tried to hide my difference, my interests, and my gifts. I wanted to be like the others. But that would have meant being untrue to myself.

So the patient had searched for his tower and had struggled with obstacles (on the way, with entrance tickets, his fears, and more), and when he got to the top—that is, was cleverer than the others—he felt lonely and deserted.

It is a well-known and common paradox that parents take up this grudging and competitive attitude toward their child (understandable in view of their envy), and at the same time urge him on to the greatest achievement and (in identification) are proud of his success. Thus the patient *had to* look for his tower and had to encounter obstacles, too. In his analysis he went through a revolt against this pressure toward achievement, and so the tower disappeared in the first of the dreams I have described here. He could give up his grandiose fantasy of seeing *everything* from above and could look at things in his beloved town (into his self) from close-by. The second dream came at a time when he first succeeded in expressing and experiencing himself in an artistic profession, and was receiving a lively echo. This time he did not meet the proud and envious parent figures whom he feared, but true partners in a group. Thus ended not only his "tower" existence, but almost at the same time his contempt for others who were not so clever and quick (for instance, in his first, highly specialized profession).

Only now did it become clear to him that he had felt compelled to isolate himself from others by means of his contempt and at the same time was isolated and separated from his true self (at least from its helpless, uncertain part). The integration of this side of his personality put him in the way of a daring and very successful change of profession that gave him much happiness. And now, after five years of analysis, this patient could become aware of his Oedipal fate with an intensity and richness of feeling perhaps no one could have suspected earlier in this scornful, distant, and intellectualizing man.

ACHIEVING FREEDOM FROM THE CONTEMPTUOUS INTROJECTS

Sexual perversions and obsessional neuroses are not the only possibilities of perpetuating the tragedy of early suffering from contempt. There are countless forms in which we may observe the fine nuances of this tragedy. The child in the adult is full of narcissistic rage against his mother because she was not available to him and because she rejected some parts of his self, and in the analysis, for instance, this rage at first finds expression in the same form as that in which he felt rejected by his mother.

There are many ways in which one may transmit the discrimination under which one has suffered as a child. There are people, for example, who never say a loud or angry word, who seem to be only good and noble, and who still give others the palpable feeling of being ridiculous or stupid or too noisy, at any rate too common compared with themselves. They do not know it and surely do not intend it, but this is what they radiate. They have introjected a parental attitude of which they have never been aware. The children of such parents find it particularly difficult to formulate any reproach in their analysis.

Then there are the people who can be very friendly, perhaps a shade patronizing, but in whose presence one feels as if one were nothing. They convey the feeling that they are the only ones who exist, the only ones who have anything interesting or relevant to say. The others can only stand there and admire them in fascination, or turn away in disappointment and sorrow about their own lack of worth, unable to express themselves in these persons' presence. These people might be the children of grandiose parents, with whom these children had no hope of rivalry, and so later, as adults, they unconsciously pass on this atmosphere to those around them.

Now those people who, as children, were intellectually far beyond their parents and therefore admired by them, but so also had to solve their own problems alone, will give us quite a different impression. These people will give us a feeling of their intellectual strength and will power, and they also seem to demand that we, too, ought to fight off any feeling of weakness with intellectual means. In their presence one feels one can't be recognized as a person with problems—just as they and their problems had not been recognized by their parents, for whom they always had to be strong.

Keeping these examples in mind, it is easy to see why some professors, who are quite capable of expressing themselves clearly, will use such complicated and convoluted language when they present their ideas that the students can only acquire them in a fog of anger and diligence—without being able to make much use of them. These students then may well have the same sorts of feelings that their teacher once had and was forced to suppress in relation to his parents. If the students themselves become teachers one day, they will have the opportunity of handing on this unusable knowledge, like a pearl of great price (because it had cost them so much).

It greatly aids the success of analytic work when the patient can become aware of the inner objects that work within him. Here is an example: at a certain point in her analysis a patient suddenly began to help her very intelligent ten-year-old daughter with her schoolwork, although the girl never had any difficulty in doing it alone. The patient's conscious motive was a bit of general advice from the teacher at a parent-teacher meeting. The child soon lost her spontaneity in learning, became unsure of herself, and actually began to have difficulty with her schoolwork. Now the patient's continued supervision of her daughter's homework was fully justified. The patient's own mother, a teacher, had been very proud of her pedagogic talent. She could, as she put it, "make something out of any child." She was one of those unsure mothers who would even teach their children to walk and talk, if they could. By then both the patient and I knew this, for the patient had repeatedly experienced her mother in me in the transference, and she had fantasized that I was less concerned with her than with my own success and the confirmation of my own value in wanting her analysis to turn out well. Thereafter, she had remembered and experienced in her dreams scenes with her mother that confirmed these feelings. But that did not suffice. The patient also needed to discover her mother in *herself*, had to see how she had become so afraid—quite unrealistically—that her daughter would compromise her, in her ability as a mother, before the teacher. She hated her own compulsion to meddle in her daughter's life, and experienced it as something foreign to her nature, but she could not give up this need to supervise the child. At last she found help through her dreams, in which she felt that she herself was in her mother's situation during the postwar period. Now she was able to imagine how it had been for her mother, who had been widowed early and had to make her own way, for herself and her daughter, and apparently also had to contend with "public opinion," which had it that because she went out to work she was neglecting her daughter. Her only child, my patient, had therefore to be the more perfect. The family constellation in the daughter's case was quite different, however, and the need to supervise her child disappeared when my patient realized this difference. "I am a different person and my fate is different from that of my mother," she once said. As a result, not only the teacher, but also her husband and neighbors "spontaneously" stopped giving her "good advice," and veiled orders.

There are moments in every analysis when dammed-up demands, fears, criticism, or envy break through for the first time. With amazing regularity these impulses appear in a guise that the patient has never expected or that he might even have rejected and feared all his life. (Cf. pp. 18–19.) Before he can develop his own form of criticism he first adopts his father's hated vocabulary or nagging manner. And the long repressed anxiety will surface in— of all things!—his mother's irritating hypochondriacal fears. It is as if the "badness" in the parents that had caused a person the most suffering in his childhood and that he had always wanted to shun, has to be discovered within himself, so that reconciliation will become possible. Perhaps this also is part of the never-ending work of mourning that this personal stamp must be accepted as part of one's own fate before one can become at least partially free.

When the patient has truly emotionally worked through

the history of his childhood and thus regained his sense of being alive—then the goal of the analysis has been reached. Afterward, it is up to the patient whether he will take a regular job or not; whether he wants to live alone or with a partner; whether he wants to join a political party, and if so, which one—all that is his own decision. His life story, his experiences, and what he has learned from them will all play a role in how he will live. It is not the task of the analyst to "socialize" him, or "to bring him up" (not even politically, for every form of bringing up denies his autonomy), nor to make "friendships possible for him"— all that is his own affair.

When the patient, in the course of his analysis, has consciously repeatedly experienced (and not only learned from the analyst's interpretations) how the whole process of his bringing-up did manipulate him in his childhood, and what desires for revenge this has left him with, then he will see through manipulation quicker than before and will himself have less need to manipulate others. Such a patient will be able to join groups without again becoming helplessly dependent or bound, for he has gone through the helplessness and dependency of his childhood in the transference. He will be in less danger of idealizing people or systems if he has realized clearly enough how as a child he had taken every word uttered by mother or father for the deepest wisdom. He may experience, however, while listening to a lecture or reading a book, the same old childish fascination and admiration—but he will recognize at the same time the underlying emptiness or human tragedy that lurks behind these words and shudder at it. Such a person cannot be tricked with fascinating, incomprehensible words, since he has matured through his own experience. Finally, a person who has consciously worked through the whole tragedy of his own fate will recognize another's suffering more clearly and quickly, though the other may still have to try to hide it. He will not be scornful of others' feelings, whatever their nature, because he can take his own feelings seriously. He surely will not help to keep the vicious circle of contempt turning.

All these things are not demands I make on my patients because of my own wishes or ideology; they are simply the result of the experience that I have gained through my work with my analysands, and that can be attributed to the effects of their regained sense of being truly alive.

Works Cited

Abraham, K. 1960 (orig. 1912). Notes on psychoanalytic investigations and treatment of manic-depressive insanity and allied conditions in *Selected papers on psychoanalysis*. New York: Basic Books, pp. 137–156.

Chasseguet-Smirgel, J. 1973. *L'ideal du moi* XIII⁰ Congrès des Psychanalystes de Langues romanes, R.P.F. 5 June, 1973.

Eicke-Spengler, M. 1977. Zur Entwicklung der Theorie der Depression. *Psyche* 31:1077–1125.

Fischer, R. (1976). Die psychoanalytische Theorie der Depression. *Psyche* 30:924–946.

Freud, S. (orig. 1914). Recollection, repetition, and working through. Standard Edition 12. London: Hogarth Press.

———. 1957 (orig. 1917). Mourning and melancholia. Standard Edition 14. London: Hogarth Press.

Ganz, H. 1966. *Pestalozzi*. Zurich: Origo.

Habermas, J. 1973. Der universalitätsanspruch der Hermeneutik. In *Kultur und kritik*. Frankfurt: M. Suhrkamp.

Hesse, H. 1965. *Demian*. New York: Harper & Row.

———. 1970. *Gesammelte Werke*. Frankfurt: M. Suhrkamp.

———. 1966. Kindheit und Jugend vor neunzehnhundert. *Herman Hesse in Briefen und Lebenszeugnissen 1877–1895*. Frankfurt: M. Suhrkamp.

———. 1971. A child's heart. In *Klingsor's last summer*. New York: Harper & Row.

Jacobson, E. 1971. *Depression*. New York: International Universities Press.

Joffe, W. and Sandler J. 1965a. Notes on a childhood depression. *International Journal of Psychoanalysis* 46:88–96.

———. 1965b. Notes on pain, depression, and individuation. *Psychoanalytic Study of the Child* 20:394–424.

Kernberg, O. F. 1970. Factors in the psychoanalytic treatment of narcissistic personalities. *Journal of the American Psychoanalytic Association* 18:51–85.

———. 1974. Further contributions to the narcissistic personalities. *International Journal of Psychoanalysis* 55:215, 240.

Khan, M. M. R. 1974. *The privacy of the self*. London: Hogarth Press.

Kohut, H. 1971. *The analysis of self*. New York: International Universities Press.

———. 1973. Überlegungen zum Narzissmus und zur narzisstischen Wut. *Psyche* 27:513–554.

Lavater-Sloman, M. 1977. *Pestalozzi*. Zurich and Munich: Artemis.

Levin, S. 1965. Some suggestions for treating the depressed patient. *Psychoanalytic Quarterly* 34:37–65.

Mahler, M. 1968. *On human symbiosis and the vicissitudes of individuation*. New York: International Universities Press.

Miller, A. 1971. Zur Behandlungstechnik bei sogenannten narzisstischen Neurosen. *Psyche* 25:641–668.

————. 1979. Depression and grandiosity as related forms of narcissistic disturbances. *International Review of Psychoanalysis* 6:61, 76.

————. 1979. The drama of the gifted child and the psychoanalysts narcissistic disturbance. *International Journal of Psychoanalysis* 60:47, 58.

————. 1980. *Am Aufang war Erziehung*. Frankfurt: Suhrkamp.

Müller-Braunschweig, H. 1974. Psychopathologie und Kreativität. *Psyche* 28:600–654.

Nagara, H. 1967. *Vincent van Gogh*. London: Allen and Unwin.

Robertson, J. 1975. Neue Beobachtungen zum Trennungsverhalten kleiner Kinder. *Psyche* 29:626–664.

Schafer, R. 1972. Die psychoanalytische Anschauung der Realität. *Psyche* 26:882–898 and 952–971.

Spitz, R. 1967. Vom Säugling zum Kleinkind. Stuttgart: Klett.

Stern, M. M. 1972. Trauma, Todesangst und Furcht von dem Tod. *Psyche* 26:901–926.

Winnicott, D. W. 1956. Primary maternal preoccupation. In *Collected papers*. New York: Basic Books, pp. 303–305.

————. 1960. The theory of parent-infant relationship. *International Journal of Psychoanalysis* 41:585–595.

————. 1965. *Maturational processes and the facilitating environment: Studies in the theory of emotional development*. New York: International Universities Press.

————. 1964. *The child, the family, and the outside world*. New York: Penguin.

————. 1969. The use of an object. *International Journal of Psychoanalysis* 50:700, 716.

————. 1971. *Playing and reality*. New York: Basic Books.

————. 1971. *Therapeutic consultations in child psychiatry*. New York: Basic Books.

Index

Praise for Conquistador

"In *Conquistador*, Buddy Levy offers a fascinating account of the first and most decisive of those encounters: the one between the impetuous Spanish adventurer Cortés and Montezuma. . . . Mr. Levy has an eye for vivid detail and manages to build a compelling narrative out of this almost unbelievable story of missionary zeal, greed, cruelty and courage." — *The Wall Street Journal*

"A sweeping and majestic history of a clash of civilizations that reshaped the New World. With its larger-than-life cast, bloody no-surrender battles, and empire-shifting finale, *Conquistador* is a pulse-quickening narrative. It is a mark of Levy's skill that I felt sorrow at the Aztecs' defeat as well as respect for Cortés's triumph." — NEAL BASCOMB, author of *Red Mutiny: Eleven Fateful Days on the Battleship* Potemkin

"To read *Conquistador* is to see, hear, and feel two cultures in a struggle to the death with nothing less than the fate of the Western Hemisphere at stake. Prodigiously researched and stirringly told, *Conquistador* is a rarity: an invaluable history lesson that also happens to be a page-turning read." — JEREMY SCHAAP, bestselling author of *Cinderella Man: James J. Braddock, Max Baer, and the Greatest Upset in Boxing History* and *Triumph: The Untold Story of Jesse Owens and Hitler's Olympics*

"Levy carefully picks his way through . . . [and] conveys with ghastly power the relentlessness of Cortés, the tragedy of Montezuma, the brutality of battle, and the utter bewilderment of one culture in the face of the other." — *Kirkus Reviews*

"Drawing heavily on both Spanish and Aztec sources, as well as major secondary works, Levy gives a straightforward telling of the entire story, stressing the military strategy, diplomatic initiatives, and personal relationship between Cortés and Aztec emperor Montezuma. . . . This well-written book is a good starting point for those seeking to understand the conquest of Mexico." — *Library Journal* (highly recommended)

"Levy provides realistic portraits of the two major figures and their initial meeting . . . in a factual, enthralling, enlightening — if at times disturbing — lush narrative that reads like good fiction." — MICHAEL I. SHOOP, *Historical Novels Review*

BANTAM BOOKS TRADE PAPERBACKS

CONQUISTADOR

HERNÁN CORTÉS, KING MONTEZUMA,

AND THE

LAST STAND OF THE AZTECS

BUDDY LEVY

2009 Bantam Books Trade Paperback Edition

Published in the United States by Bantam Books, an imprint of The Random House Publishing Group, a division of Random House, Inc., New York.

BANTAM BOOKS and the rooster colophon are registered trademarks of Random House, Inc.

Originally published in hardcover in the United States by Bantam Books, an imprint of The Random House Publishing Group, a division of Random House, Inc., in 2008.

Title page art: Ms Laur, Med. Palat. 220 f.406: The Spanish fleet disembarks in Mexico, from a history of the Aztecs and the conquest of Mexico (pen and ink), Spanish (sixteenth century)./ Biblioteca Medicea-Laurenziana, Florence, Italy/ The Bridgeman Art Gallery International

Library of Congress Cataloging-in-Publication Data
Conquistador : Hernán Cortés, King Montezuma, and the last stand of the Aztecs /
Buddy Levy.
p.   cm.
ISBN: 978-0-553-38471-0 (trade pbk.)
1. Mexico—History—Conquest, 1519–1540. 2. Cortés, Hernán, 1485–1547. I. Title.

F1230 .L45 2008   2007052178
972/.02 22
Printed in the United States of America

Maps by David Lindroth
www.bantamdell.com

19 18 17 16 15

Text design by Glen M. Edelstein

For Camie, Logan, and Hunter

CONTENTS

Men of God and men of war have strange affinities.

—CORMAC MCCARTHY, *BLOOD MERIDIAN*

CONQUISTADOR

INTRODUCTION

IN 1519 AN AMBITIOUS AND CALCULATING CONQUISTADOR named Hernán Cortés sailed from Cuba and arrived on the shores of Mexico with empire expansion in his veins. He intended to appropriate the new-found lands in the name of the crown of Spain, to convert the inhabitants to Catholicism, and to plunder the rich lands of their precious metals, namely gold. Cortés made land at Pontonchan, a considerable native fishing settlement, with a roguish, roughshod crew containing thirty crossbowmen, twelve men with muzzle-loaded handguns called harquebuses, fourteen pieces of small artillery, and a few cannons. Carefully, methodically, Cortés and his crew used ropes and pulleys to unload sixteen Spanish horses, highly trained and skilled warhorses of which the indigenous Americans had no concept or understanding, never having seen any. He also unloaded savage and well-trained war dogs: mastiffs and wolfhounds. In addition to his band of Spanish pirates and mercenaries, Cortés brought along a few hundred West African and Cuban slaves for use as porters. It was March 1519.

Cortés marched his small force over massive mountains and active volcanoes towering eighteen thousand feet high, straight into the Valley of Mexico and the very heart of the Aztec civilization.* What Cortés encountered when he arrived

---

*The term *Aztec* was originally coined (erroneously) by the nineteenth-century German naturalist-explorer Alexander von Humboldt. *Aztec* was actually an eponymous derivation of the legendary Aztlan, the mythical "Place of the White Heron," the ancestral homeland of the people who eventually came to the Valley of Mexico and settled there after long years of migration and founded the city of Tenochtitlán

at Tenochtitlán, the famed "City of Dreams," were not the barbarians that his conquistador predecessors had envisioned but
a powerful and highly evolved civilization at its zenith. The
Aztecs possessed elaborate and accurate calendars, efficient irrigation systems for their myriad year-round crops, zoos and
botanical gardens unrivaled in Europe, immaculate city streets
with waste-management methods, astounding arts and jewelry,
state-run education, sport in the form of a life-or-death ballgame, a devoted and organized military apparatus, and a vast
trade and tribute network stretching the entirety of their immense empire, as far south as Guatemala. Cortés and his
Christian brethren would soon discover that the Aztecs also
possessed a highly evolved and ritualized religion much more
complex than their own, a religion that its people followed
with equal, if not greater, faith and conviction. Instead of one
god, they zealously worshipped a pantheon of deities in elaborate and sophisticated ceremonies.

At Tenochtitlán—at the time among the most populated
and vital cities on earth, much larger than Paris or Peking—
Cortés finally confronted Montezuma, the charismatic and
enigmatic Aztec ruler. Their first meeting could be considered
the birth of modern history. The conflict that followed was a
religious one ultimately, pitting the monotheistic Catholicism
of the Spaniards against the polytheistic mysticism of the
Aztecs, and though in many respects the two empires were
vastly different, they were actually parallel in a number of striking ways. Both were barbaric in their unique traditions. The
Spaniards, fired and forged by the Crusades, would pillage and
rape and kill in the name of God and country, subsuming in-

---

in 1325. In only two centuries these agricultural and warrior people had developed a
remarkable culture. The term *Aztec* has been widely replaced—primarily by scholars
and historians—with the term *Mexica*, a designation that more accurately describes
the people of the Triple Alliance of Tenochtitlán, Texcoco, and Tacuba. Numerous
modern institutions such as the Metropolitan Museum, the Guggenheim Museum,
the Smithsonian Museum, and even the National Museum of Anthropology in Mexico
City still employ the term *Aztec*. *Conquistador* will retain the popular term *Aztec* and
use it interchangeably with *Mexica*.

digenous cultures with little respect for their centuries of existence; the Aztecs used military force and violence to subjugate independent neighboring tribes and performed rites of human sacrifice and cannibalism. Neither could comprehend the other, and neither was willing to acquiesce. Both were uncompromisingly devoted to expanding their already considerable empires, and each was under the guidance and tutelage of a great leader.

The most significant of all the conquistadors, Hernán Cortés was a late bloomer, arriving in the New World in 1504. He lived in relative anonymity for over a decade before asserting himself in the political scene of the West Indies colonies, by which time he was in his early thirties. Born in 1485 in Medellín, Spain, site of castles and strongholds used in the last efforts of the Reconquista (the expulsion of the Moors after seven hundred years of occupation), Hernán was the son of Martín Cortés, a low-level hidalgo not overly distinguished or well bred, and Doña Catalina Pizarro Altimirano. A frail and sickly child, Cortés began university at age fourteen in Salamanca but returned home, bored and distracted, after only two years. His mind must have been quick and perceptive, however, because his erudition in diplomacy and politics would surface later, serving him well. He studied government, law, and Latin and would later be described by his secretary Francisco López de Gómara as "restless, haughty, mischievous, and given to quarrelling."[1]

Wanderlust filled his heart early on, and in 1503 he was set to join an expedition to the West Indies with Don Nicolás de Ovando. On the eve of his departure, the young rake Cortés was injured leaping to his escape when caught in the house of a married woman; his injury cost him a chance on that ship, and he spent the next year carousing in Spain's rough southern port villages. In 1504 the impetuous young man had earned entry onto one of five merchant ships setting sail for Santo Domingo, the bustling capital of Hispaniola and first settlement of the New World. Cortés had for a few years now heard rumors of untold wealth to be garnered in unknown lands, where gold flowed like water from the mysterious mountains. Just nineteen and with an adventurer's spirit, having learned to ride as a youth while herding swine and gleaned the rudiments of cavalry tactics in school and from his father, as well as from the widely popular romances, Hernán Cortés was entirely anonymous and average as he booked passage to the West Indies. He had no way of knowing that in less than two decades he would command a Spanish force in one of the greatest assaults in military history and become among the most revered and reviled of men in all the world.[2]

CORTÉS'S rival had led the Aztec people for nearly two decades. The ruler of the Aztec empire, Montezuma* was born in 1480, just five years before Hernán Cortés. Sometimes also referred to as Montezuma II, he was trained as a priest and rose to become the military, spiritual, and civic leader of the Aztecs in 1503, just as Cortés was on the verge of arriving in the West Indies. At that time the Aztecs controlled most of what is now Mexico and Central America, their capital being the great city of Tenochtitlán (present-day Mexico City). Montezuma was enthroned as the *tlatoani* (great speaker) at the great temple built by his own brothers, and his coronation involved an elaborate ritual of bloodletting, self-piercing with bone slivers, the decapitation of two quails, and the spraying of their blood on an altar flame.

Moody, petulant, even tyrannical, Montezuma was zealously driven by his spiritual beliefs. He was the semidivine ruler of a devout people whose supreme being was the sun and whose highly stylized and symbolic religion was driven by seasonal festivals, feasts, and celebrations observed by all members of society. The Aztec religion was an amalgamation of

---

*Many modern scholars use the term *Motecuhzoma* (actually pronounced something akin to "Mock-tey-coo-schoma"), which presumably more accurately mimics the correct pronunciation, but the more popular and widely used *Montezuma* causes less confusion, so I opt for the popular usage.

ancient Mesoamerican rites and traditions centered on paying tribute and making offerings to the many gods who orchestrated human destiny. The Aztecs believed these offerings—incense, birds, flowers, and in the highest of all forms, human hearts and blood—appeased the gods and ensured rain for their crops, healthy harvests, victory in battle, and even the daily rising of the sun.[3]

Montezuma lived in an immense palace surrounded by his two wives, countless concubines, and more than five hundred attendants, noblemen, and emissaries. The palace complex was vast, the architecture and grounds were as sophisticated as any in medieval Europe, and the temples where the Aztec people worshipped were as impressive as the Egyptian pyramids. Montezuma's personal rooms, scented with floral perfumes, were on the upper floors overlooking his sprawling domain. He loved games and music, especially drumming, gongs, and the melodies of hand-honed flutes, sometimes accompanied by poems and singing. Majestic in carriage, with deep, piercing eyes, Montezuma wore gilded sandals and traveled by procession elevated in a litter. Ordinary Aztec citizens dared not gaze directly upon him, under punishment of death. His pride, a hubris of Greek-tragedy proportions, was such that he demanded to be treated as a god.[4]

By the time Cortés met the great ruler, Montezuma was the head of an immensely powerful triumvirate called the Triple Alliance, a confederation of the city-states Tenochtitlán, Texcoco, and Tacuba.[5] These three great populaces carved a wide and powerful swath across Mexico, and as in Europe, all subjugated peoples, no matter how far flung, were forced to pay tithes or taxes to their ruler, a circumstance that created tension and resentment among distant tribes seeking independence. At the height of Montezuma's rule, he was the supreme warlord of the most powerful military machine in the Americas, with effective dominion over some fifteen million people.

At the time of Cortés's arrival, the Aztecs and other peoples on the North American continent had been evolving, completely isolated from the rest of the world. The discovery of the Aztecs, whom the Spaniards had previously not known to exist, has been called "the most astonishing encounter in our history."[6] The Aztecs must have had a similar response at their discovery of these alien visitors.

The clash of empires that followed culminated in the bloody siege of Tenochtitlán, to this day considered the longest and costliest continuous single battle in history, with estimated casualties of 200,000 human lives.[7] Cortés's odyssey from the West Indies into the interior of the Aztec nation remains among the most astounding military campaigns ever waged, rivaled only by the epic expeditions of Alexander the Great. In just over two years, using horses and cavalry techniques developed over thousands of years on the Iberian Peninsula, employing nautical warfare and remarkable military engineering, and driven by political genius and an immeasurable will to succeed, Cortés vanquished the Aztecs and their ruler, which at fifteen million people was the largest empire in Mesoamerican history.[8] For the Aztecs, the onslaught was so sudden as to be incomprehensible. No other great ancient civilization suffered such complete devastation and ruin in so short a time.

The clash of these two empires is a tragic tale of conquest and defeat, of colonization and resistance, and of the remarkable and violent confluence of two empires previously unknown to each other. This confluence of cultures in 1519 is the unbelievable story of one of the greatest conquerors that history has ever known, the complex leader of the magnificent civilization he would destroy, and the cataclysmic battle that would be the end of one world and the making of a new one.

CHAPTER ONE

Setting Out for New Spain and the Serendipitous Gift of Language

HERNÁN CORTÉS STRODE TO THE BOW of his flagship *Santa María de la Concepción,* a one-hundred-ton vessel and the largest of his armada, and scanned the horizon for land. He had much to ponder. His navigator and chief pilot, Antonio de Alaminos, an experienced veteran who had been pilot for Columbus on his final voyage, had been in these waters before—on the Ponce de León expedition in search of the fabled Fountain of Youth—and he suggested that if they encountered foul weather, the entire fleet should make land and convene on the island of Cozumel, just east of the Yucatán Peninsula's northernmost tip. Since their hurried departure from Cuba, the fleet had been buffeted by foul weather, scattering the boats. Cortés brought up the rear, simultaneously scouring for land and for brigantines and caravels blown astray. A few, perhaps as many as five, had been lost during the night, an inauspicious beginning to such an ambitious voyage.

Cortés had staked everything he owned on this venture—in fact more than that, for he had incurred significant debt building the ships and stocking them with provisions. His hope to get off to a good start had been slightly compromised when his patron, the fat hidalgo Diego Velázquez, now governor of Cuba, attempted to thwart his departure, even after he had signed a contract officially confirming Cortés as captain-general. Velázquez's behavior was no surprise, given the contentious nature of their relationship. On his arrival in Hispaniola (the modern-day Dominican Republic) in 1504, Cortés had sought out the established countryman and worked under him, initially on a raid to suppress an Indian uprising on the island's interior, and later on an expedition captained by Pánfilo de Narváez to conquer Cuba, which they accomplished easily enough. After this successful venture Velázquez, feeling magnanimous, gifted Cortés a large plot of land with many Indians and a number of viable, working mines on it, effectively making Cortés rich. But the two men were both obstinate, and their relationship was soon fraught with tensions that would ultimately threaten prison, and even death, for Cortés.

Both men shared a passion for women, and a disagreement over one Catalina Suárez resulted in the governor's having Cortés arrested and placed in the stocks. Cortés escaped by bribing the jailor, and Velázquez had him arrested again, even bringing a suit upon him and threatening to hang him for his refusal to marry Suárez, a snubbing that had sullied her reputation. Eventually Velázquez calmed, and the two men smoothed over their differences, but their relationship remained volatile. At present, in mid-February 1519, Velázquez held the political upper hand, for Cortés sailed under his aegis, as his emissary on a mission to trade, to find gold, and to obtain more Indians to work the mines of Cuba. But the wily Cortés had other intentions as he spotted land and had his pilot make anchor at Cozumel.

Cortés's ship was the last to arrive, and on setting foot on the island he found that the local inhabitants had fled at the arrival of the first ships, dispersing into the hills and jungle. Cortés noted their fear, filing it away as useful information. Then he was met with vexing news, and a reason for the local Indians' behavior: one of his most trusted captains, Pedro de Alvarado, had arrived early, immediately raided the first village he encountered—brusquely entering temples and thieving some small gold ornaments left there as prayer offerings—and then seized a flock of about forty turkeys that were milling around the Indians' thatch-roofed houses, even taking a few of the frightened Indians, two men and a woman, prisoner. Cortés, incensed, contemplated how to handle the situation. He needed to trust Alvarado, and he respected the fiery red-headed countryman who also hailed from his homeland, Estremadura. Alvarado, already battle-hardened and having commanded the previous Grijalva expedition to the Yucatán, was cocksure and felt justified in making his own independent decisions. Cortés needed him and required a symbiotic relationship with his captains, but he also insisted that they obey his command, and he would tolerate no insubordination.[1] Such behavior, he impressed upon his men, "was no way to pacify a country."[2]

Cortés rebuked Alvarado by commanding his men to turn over the pilfered offerings and return them to their Indian owners. He also had Alvarado's pilot Camacho, who had failed to obey orders to wait for Cortés at sea, chained in irons. The turkeys had been slaughtered, and some of them already eaten, so Cortés ordered that the fowl be paid for with green glass beads and small bells, which he gave to the prisoners as he released them, along with a Spanish shirt for each. Then Cortés asked for a man named Melchior, a Mayan who had been taken prisoner during an earlier expedition and converted into something of an interpreter, having been taught some Spanish by his captors. Through Melchior, Cortés spoke to the Indians as he released them and sent them back to their families, instructing them that the Spaniards came in peace and wished to do them no harm, and that Cortés as their leader would like to meet personally with their chiefs or *caciques*.*

The initial diplomacy worked. The next day men, women, children, and eventually the chiefs of the villages poured forth

---

Cacique is a Caribbean Arawak word for "chief" that the Spaniards brought with them from the islands. Many of the chroniclers, including Bernal Díaz and to a lesser extent Cortés, use the term. The word would have been unknown to mainland Mexicans.

from their hiding places in the lowland scrub and repopulated their village, which soon was bustling again. Conquistador Bernal Díaz, a soldier under Alvarado's command who had been on both the Córdoba and Grijalva expeditions, remarked that "men, women, and children went about with us as if they had been friends with us all their lives." Cortés sternly reiterated that the natives must not be harmed in any way. Díaz was impressed by Cortés's leadership and style, noting that "here in this island our Captain began to command most energetically, and Our Lord so favored him that whatever he touched succeeded."[3]

The islanders brought food to the Spaniards, including loads of fresh fish, bundles of colorful and sweet tropical fruits, and hives of island honey, a delicacy that the island people nurtured and managed. The Spaniards traded beads, cutlery, bells, and other trinkets for food and low-grade gold ornaments. Relations seemed convivial, and Cortés decided to hold a muster on the beach to assess the force he had amassed in Cuba.

The ships included his one-hundred-ton flagship plus three smaller vessels displacing seventy or eighty tons. The remaining boats had open or partially covered decks with makeshift canvas roofs to provide shade from the scorching sun or shelter from the rain squalls. The bigger ships transported smaller vessels that could be lowered at ports or some distance offshore, then rowed or sailed to a landing.[4] The ships were packed belowdecks with ample supplies of island fare: maize, yucca, chiles, and robust quantities of salt pork which had a long shelf life, plus fodder for the stock.

The crew of mercenaries comprised chivalrous men bred on war and adventure. Over five hundred strong, these travel-hardened pikemen and swordsmen and lancers had either paid their way onto the voyage or come spurred by the promise of fortune. Cortés strode the beach and surveyed the sharpshooters, thirty accurate crossbowmen and twelve well-trained harquebusiers bearing handheld matchlocks fired from the shoulder or chest. Ten small cannons would be fired by experienced artillerymen, who also carried light, transportable brass cannons called falconets. The detail-oriented, highly prepared Cortés had the foresight to bring along a few blacksmiths who could repair damaged weaponry and, most important, keep the prized Spanish horses well shod. Extensive stocks of ammunition and gunpowder were packaged carefully in dry containers and guarded at all times. For land transport, Cortés brought two hundred islanders from Cuba, mostly men for heavy portaging, but also a handful of women to prepare food and repair and fabricate the wool, flax, and linen doublets, jerkins, and brigandines the men wore.

Cortés ordered the horses lowered from the ship's decks by means of strong leather harnesses, ropes, and pulleys, then had them led ashore to exercise and graze on the island's dense foliage. Curious islanders came forward. They had been observing the general muster, and now they were absolutely entranced by the horses—some islanders running away in fear at the sight of them—the first such creatures they had ever witnessed. Intrigued by the horses' impression on the locals, Cortés had his best cavalrymen mount the glistening and snorting animals and gallop them along the beach. Artillerymen tested cannons, firing them into the hillsides; the explosions were thunderous, flame and smoke belching from the muzzles. Archers shouldered crossbows and sent arrows whistling through the air at makeshift targets.[5]

When the smoke from the military display had cleared and the horses were put away, islanders approached the Spaniards more closely, and tugged at their beards and stroked the white skin of their forearms. A few of the chiefs became animated and gesticulated aggressively using sign language and pointing beyond the easternmost tip of the island. Cortés had Melchior brought forward, and after some discussion he reported some extraordinary news: the older chiefs claimed that years earlier other bearded white men had come and that two of them were still alive, held as slaves by Indians on mainland Yucatán, just a short distance, about a day's paddle, across the channel waters.

Cortés mused, deeply intrigued by the prospect of Spanish-speaking countrymen who had been living among mainland

Indians. This was an unexpected and potentially profitable windfall. He appealed to one of the main caciques, asking him for a few of his able men whom he could send over as scouts to see what they might learn of these Spaniards and to bring them back if they could. The chief conferred with others, but they balked, explaining that they feared sending any of their own people as guides because they would quite likely be killed and sacrificed or even eaten by the mainlanders. Alarming as this fear seemed, Cortés pressed, offering more of the green glass beads that the islanders appeared to covet, and the chiefs acquiesced. Cortés dispatched several men, along with his captain and friend Juan de Escalante, in a brigantine. Hidden beneath the braided hair of one of the messengers was a letter stating that Cortés had arrived on Cozumel with more than five hundred Spanish soldiers on a mission to "explore and colonize these lands." Flanking them in support were two ships and fifty armed soldiers.[6]

While he awaited news from this reconnaissance, Cortés scouted his hosts' island. He noted well-built houses, orderly and neat, and other evidence of a complex civilization, including their "books," elaborate series of drawings on stretched bark. What interested him most was a large pyramidal structure, a temple constructed of limestone masonry, with an open plaza or sanctuary at its top, overlooking the sea. Cortés climbed the pyramid steps and, upon reaching the temple, saw that the pavilion was spattered with the blood of decapitated quail and domesticated dogs, small foxlike canines that the people also ate. Bones were piled as offerings. Cortés and his men found these idols monstrous, even frightening. One was especially curious: it was hollow, made of baked clay and set against a limestone wall with a secret entrance at its rear, where a priest could enter and respond to worshippers' prayers, like an oracle. Around the idol, braziers burned resins, like incense. The caciques told Cortés that here they prayed for rain, and frequently their prayers were answered. Sometimes human beings were offered as sacrifice.[7]

Inflamed by the specter of human sacrifice, Cortés called for Melchior and through him pitched his first sermon and attempt at religious conversion. Speaking to the assembled Indians, Cortés railed that there was only one God, one creator — the one true God that the Spaniards worshipped. Bernal Díaz listened carefully, reporting that Cortés said "that if they wished to be our brothers they must throw their idols out of this temple, for they were evil and would lead them astray."[8] These evil abominations would send their souls to hell, Cortés said, but if they exchanged their idols for his cross, their souls would be saved and their harvests would prosper.

Melchior's Spanish was hardly sufficient to convincingly or accurately convey Cortés's message verbatim, especially the complex notion of the Christian soul (for which, at any rate, no Mayan terminology existed). But that did not stop Cortés from using an even more aggressive, highly symbolic tactic. The chiefs had responded that they disagreed — their own idols and gods were good, and their ancestors had worshipped them since time began. Cortés then brazenly ordered his men to smash the idols and roll them down the pyramid steps, where they crumbled at the feet of the mystified and terrified onlookers. The islanders, even the chiefs, remained too frightened by the previous military and cavalry demonstrations to do anything other than shake their heads in terror and confusion. Cortés then supervised a cleansing, a whitewashing of the blood from the prayer pavilion. The men scrubbed away the blood smears and animal entrails with lime, and carpenters erected a wooden cross, as well as a figure of the Virgin Mary. These were the new idols the people of Cozumel were to worship.

Cortés then ordered the priest Juan Díaz to hold mass. On leaving the newly altered shrine, Cortés sternly instructed the caciques of the village that they must keep the altar clean and decorate it frequently with fresh flowers. As a parting gift, Cortés had his men teach the islanders how to make candles from their beeswax, so that they could keep candles always burning before the figure of the Virgin.[9] In exchange, the islanders presented Cortés with gifts of "four fowls and two jars of honey."[10]

A week later Escalante and Ordaz returned from their foray to the Yucatán. They had delivered Cortés's letter to a village chieftain, they claimed, but nothing had come of it. Cortés was disappointed, but it was time to press on, so he summoned his captains, loaded the ships, packed some Cozumel honey and wax for his king, and, as the weather looked promising, sailed away from the island paradise that they had already renamed Santa Cruz. They set their bearings for the small island called Isla Mujeres, which Francisco de Córdoba had discovered and named on his unsuccessful voyage two years earlier, in 1517. Almost immediately distress shouts came from Juan de Escalante's brigantine; the vessel hove to and then ignited its cannon, signaling that it was imperiled. It was leaking badly, and the pilot feared it would not make the crossing. Escalante's ship carried the bulk of the expedition's important stores of cassava bread, which had been packed in Cuba, so Cortés decided to turn around and sail back to Cozumel, where they might repair the ship in friendly environs.

For several days, with the help of the islanders, Cortés's carpenters caulked the leaks. Meticulous, Cortés had his "gunners" clean and maintain all the weaponry, then pack and repack all the ammunition and powder. His "bowmen" ascertained that all the crossbows were in order and had "two or three spare nuts and cords and forecords."[11] Cortés took the opportunity to see if the Virgin Mary and cross were still affixed at the temple, which to his pleasure they were. The repairs complete, the stores of provisions dried and reloaded, the weaponry properly maintained, the fleet prepared to set sail once more.

It was March 12, a Sunday. Cortés requested that mass be held before they depart. That done, the expeditionary force readied to board—but just then they spotted the outline of a canoe heading toward them from the mainland, paddling furiously. The boat made land down the beach. Cortés dispatched his trusted captain Andrés de Tapia to investigate; Tapia and a few officers strode down the beach, swords brandished. There they met the arrivals, a half-dozen men "naked except that their private parts were covered. Their hair was tied as women's hair is tied, and they carried bows and arrows."[12] Seeing the Spaniards carrying drawn swords, the oarsmen in the canoe set to push off again and flee, but a tall man standing in the prow spoke to them quietly, telling them to wait. Then he stepped forward and called out to Tapia in broken Spanish, "Brothers, are you Christians?"

Tapia nodded and sent immediately for Cortés, then embraced the man as he knelt and wept. He was a priest named Jerónimo de Aguilar, and his story was miraculous.

Back in 1511 the ship Aguilar was on had struck low shoals off the coast of Jamaica, and he and about twenty other survivors had escaped in a rowboat with what little they could gather. Bereft of food and water, and trading shifts on their only set of oars, they caught a westerly current and washed up on the shores of the Yucatán, half their number dead and the rest nearly so.

Mayan tribesmen welcomed them by taking them prisoner, immediately sacrificing their leader, the conquistador Valdivia, and four other men, then eating these Spaniards during a festival feast. Aguilar and his remaining friends, including a man named Gonzalo Guerrero, were crammed into cages and could only watch in horror at the sacrificial ceremonies, as drums rumbled into the lowland jungle and celebrants blew mournful songs on conch shells. The Spaniards were being fattened for sacrifice. Realizing their potential fate, they worked together and broke the cage slats, sneaking away into the night.

Aguilar and Guerrero, along with a few others, found refuge in another village and were quickly enslaved. Aguilar became known as "the white slave." Through hard work, acquiescence, luck, and his faith, he had survived eight years among his Mayan captors and had earned his freedom.[13] He had received Cortés's letter from the messengers, and then visited his countryman Guerrero, who was now living in a nearby

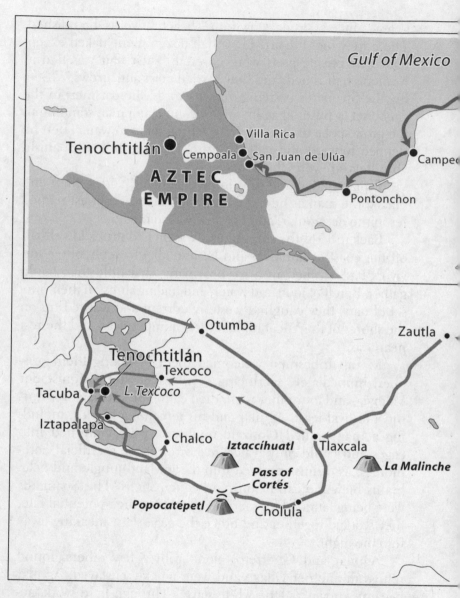

village. Guerrero had won his own freedom through impressive feats of manual labor and was now an accepted member of his tribe, a warrior and a military leader. He had taken a wife, a chief's daughter, and she had borne him a daughter

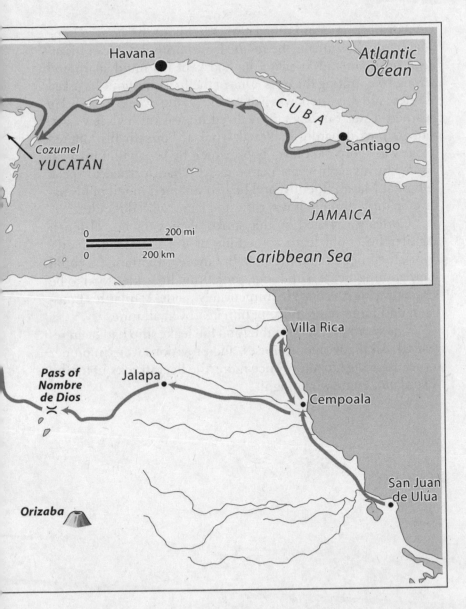

and two sons. His heavily muscled body was covered with tat-
toos, his ears were pierced, and he wore a hunk of jade in his
lower lip. He had gone native and told Aguilar he had no desire to return.

For his part, Aguilar had always held out the remote hope that he might someday be rescued, and from the day of his arrival on mainland Yucatán, he had kept his mind sharp and strong by counting the days. One of the first questions he asked Cortés and his men was what day of the week it was. He learned it was Sunday and realized he was off by a few days, but by now it hardly mattered. Tucked beneath his tattered cloak was a torn old prayer book, which he kept with him at all times. In his eight years marooned, he had learned to speak Chontal Mayan fluently, and he had retained much of his native Spanish, though it was rusty and came with difficulty.

Cortés was elated by this stroke of providence. Through Aguilar he could learn something of the mainlanders' customs, their beliefs and lifeways. But more important, he could now communicate with them, something he understood to be crucial to his success. He immediately made Aguilar his translator and interpreter and kept him nearby at all times.[14]

The weather was favorable, and the leaky ship had been repaired. All the weapons, horses, and provisions were in proper order. Leaving Cozumel once more, the fleet struck out for the mainland, come what might.

CHAPTER TWO

The Battle with the Tabascans and the Acquisition of La Malinche

AS THE FLEET CUT ACROSS THE OCEAN, Cortés plied Aguilar for information about the Mayan people, trying to determine whether they would be hostile. The mainland Mayans had successfully repelled Captain Francisco de Córdoba in 1517 at Champoton, killing twenty of his force and leaving over half of his expedition—including its leader—mortally wounded. Córdoba had made it back to Cuba, only to die shortly after. But he had managed to bring back gold, inflaming continued interest in the region. As Cortés paused on Isla de Mujeres to take on water and secure stores of salt, he mused on what his own reception might be like.

Fair winds pushed the fleet some four hundred miles around the nose of the Yucatán and into the southern reaches of the Gulf of Mexico, passing by the site of the Córdoba disaster. Cortés, patriot that he was and certainly game for revenge, brashly considered landing there and paying the inhabitants a visit, but his pilot Alaminos, noting unfavorable winds and also remembering the shallow reefs and shoals in the area, advised against it. They pressed on. Cortés sent Captain Alonso de Escobar, whose ship was "very fast and of shallow draught,"[1] ahead to do some scouting and reconnaissance. After being temporarily blown off course, Escobar made it safely to a harbor called Puerto Deseado, where to his amazement a greyhound, abandoned two years earlier during the Grijalva expedition, came yelping and barking from the woods, her tail wagging. The dog was sleek and fattened from the abundant game in the area. When they took her hunting, she led Escobar and his men to ample supplies of rabbits and deer.[2]

Reunited, the armada moved together under full sail before favorable winds and by March 22 anchored near a sandbar at the wide and tranquil mouth of the Tabasco River (renamed by the Spaniards the Rio de Grijalva), near the native settlement of Pontonchan. Because the water was too shallow for the bigger ships, Cortés assembled a force of two hundred soldiers and headed into the mouth of the river in brigantines and smaller vessels, the oar boats towed by the caravels. The boats slipped slowly upriver and into dank and briny mangrove swamps; the thick canopy overhead screamed and keened with shrill bird cries. The men found the place putrid-smelling. Cortés raised his hand to his pilot when he spied dugout canoes paddling furiously toward them from upriver. Along the banks of the river, interspersed among the trees, stood hordes of Tabascan warriors armed with bows and spears, their bodies painted ochre and red, plumed in feathers.

Cortés directed the bulk of his boats to a headland a safe distance away and had cannons and falconets unloaded while crossbowmen and harquebusiers stood ready. He hoped not to have to fight, but he would be ready nonetheless, and he entreated his men to remain at attention at all times.

With Aguilar at his side, Cortés moved upriver and neared Pontonchan, a thriving commercial center, and met the first of the Tabascan warriors in their dugouts. Through Aguilar, he called out that he came in peace and wished only to trade goods for food and obtain water. (That was a bit disingenuous, as he had plenty of both—he was in fact nosing around for gold.) The Tabascans responded violently, shouting back at Cortés that the Spaniards should not attempt to land. The Tabascans warned that all would be killed if they advanced beyond a line of palm trees the Spaniards named Punta de los Palmares (Point of Palm Trees).[3]

Cortés pondered his next move as he scanned the scene, estimating the town to possess some twenty-five thousand inhabitants. The Spaniards were dramatically outnumbered. Cortés continued to negotiate, reiterating his desire for food and underscoring that he was perfectly happy to pay a fair price for whatever they might provide. As darkness fell, both sides stood at an impasse, though the Tabascans said that they would report to their chiefs in town and determine whether they wished to trade. They told the Spaniards to meet them in the town square in the morning.

That night, sleepless on the sandy beach and anticipating battle, Cortés sent a force of one hundred men to the outskirts of the village with orders to support him in a surprise attack from the flanks if a skirmish ensued. While the rest of the Spaniards lay swatting bugs and sweating in their heavy armor, the Tabascans evacuated the town of all women and children and hid them deep in the river delta forests. To thwart the Spaniards' approach, Tabascan builders erected barricades and obstructions from tree trunks and branches around the town and along the river.

In the morning, the Tabascan representatives reiterated that they were unwilling to trade. Cortés and his men boarded their shallow-draft warships and proceeded upriver toward the town. A throng of war-painted Tabascans lined the river, chanting, shrieking, beating drums, and blowing weird siren-songs through conch shells. Standing at the prow of his boat with Aguilar interpreting and Diego de Godoy, the king's notary, as witness, Cortés addressed the Tabascan chiefs with Spain's legally required forewarning or *requerimiento*. This ironic, devious, and self-justifying speech called on the Indians to accept Christ in lieu of their own gods and the Spanish king as their sovereign. They must acquiesce to become vassals of Spain and agree to Christian preaching and education, for which they would receive untold rewards, including peace, prosperity, and everlasting life.[4]

The Tabascan response to this slick Spanish diplomacy was a rain of arrows, spears, and stones, and the first battle of Cortés's conquest was joined. Though he was a leader of men, until this moment in his career Cortés had never commanded men in battle.

Cortés was forced to think quickly. The Tabascans followed their onslaught with a full charge into the river, rushing to attack the boats and pouring forth in their own dugout canoes. Some Spanish soldiers disembarked and they fought hand to hand with the Tabascans in waist-deep water, war clubs and spears meeting for the first time the fire-hardened Toledo steel of Spanish swords. With great difficulty and severely outnumbered, Cortés and his men managed to slash their way to land, but the riverbanks were so mucky that Cortés lost a boot as he clambered ashore, one foot bare. The boot was retrieved. He then commanded from the densely foliaged bank. All the while men fought, and the Tabascan warriors cried out in their language to immediately "kill or capture the Captain."[5]

Surrounded, the Spaniards fell into tight ranks and fought as they had been trained, in well-organized and highly regimented squads, while their enemies came at them en masse in a series of surging and retreating waves. Their organization paid off, and soon the Spaniards were tearing down and breaking through the newly constructed timber barricades and pushing the Tabascans back, the harquebusiers firing deadly balls at close range. Just then, having heard the battle joined, Alonso de Ávila and his men, whom Cortés had ordered hidden the night before, made it through the palm woods and marshes in time to support, and now the Tabascans felt two-front pressure, as well as the deafening and utterly foreign explosions of cannons and falconets. They fled, retreating beyond the town to dense mangrove swamps and jungle, even still firing arrows and hand-thrown darts. The Spaniards' surprise tactic had worked perfectly, and as the last of the Tabascan warriors disappeared into the shadows, Cortés and his men convened in the village square, swords still brandished.[6]

With his royal notary Godoy at his side, Cortés strode to a great ceiba tree that stood in the central square. Raising his sword, he slashed the massive trunk symbolically three times, exclaiming before his men that he now conquered and took possession of this land "in His Majesty's name!" (This act would have had a profound effect on the native population, for the ceiba tree was sacred, believed to be the pillar holding up the heavens themselves.) Bernal Díaz, nursing an arrow wound in his thigh, recalled that he and a group of soldiers deeply loyal to Cortés replied with vigorous shouts of "Hear, hear," supporting Cortés's taking possession in the name of "His Majesty the King." Díaz added that he would "aid against any challengers."[7] But a small group of soldiers, followers of Diego Velázquez who were still loyal to him, grumbled that Cortés had conveniently forgotten to mention Velázquez, under whose sponsorship they were supposedly operating. In a brazen move that did not go unnoticed by the Velázquez camp, Cortés disregarded them, for the first time publicly ignoring his patron. His actions had placed him directly under the auspices of the king, and no one else. It was his first formal move to distance himself from Velázquez.[8]

Cortés ordered his men to rest and made an assay of his forces, determining that though a few were wounded, no Spaniard had been lost. They slept that night in the temple square, numerous sentinels posted on the perimeter, and awoke the next morning to some ominous news: during yesterday's battle old Melchior had fled, stripping himself naked during the melee and joining the Tabascans. He left as a parting gift his Spanish clothes hanging in a tree. Cortés feared that Melchior might inform the Tabascans of the Spaniards' numbers and details of their weaponry, but he could do nothing but scowl in disgust at the interpreter's treason.[9]

Cortés wished to maintain his ships' food stores but knew that his men needed provisions, so he sent two captains, Pedro de Alvarado and Francisco de Lugo, each with about a hundred men (including specialists—musketeers and crossbowmen), to scout the nearby countryside. They advanced in different directions into the interior. After only three miles Lugo discovered a promising sign: many well-tended fields of maize, apparently irrigated and drained by means of ditches. Lugo had little time to marvel at the Tabascans' agricultural ingenuity, however, for just then, according to Bernal Díaz, "they met great companies of archers, and others with lances and shields, drums and standards, who immediately attacked them, surrounding them on all sides."[10] The attack was so quick that all Lugo and his men could do was hold their shields above them to fend off a hailstorm of fire-hardened darts, stone-tipped spears, and thrown stones. The situation grim, Lugo dispatched a brave Cuban runner, who had been brought along for just such a purpose, to appeal to Cortés for reinforcement. In the meantime Lugo organized his small force in tight ranks and had his crossbowmen, falconets, and harquebusiers fire volleys at the swarming Tabascans.

Fortunately for Lugo and his men, Alvarado's drive inland had been thwarted by an impassable river crossing, and his division had arrived near the plain of Cintla. Hearing Lugo's musket fire, and the enemy's war-whoops and the beating of drums, Alvarado and his company sped to the battlefield. Alvarado arrived just in time to support Lugo, and together the two divisions defended themselves and repelled the onslaught as they backed into camp. They detained three prisoners, from whom Cortés was able to extract, through rough force, some shocking news: all the able-bodied Tabascan warriors from the vicinity would converge at the town of Cintla the next morning to make war on the intruding Spaniards. Most disconcerting of all (if the prisoner was to be believed), he claimed that these warriors numbered over 25,000, about fifty times Cortés's fighting force. They intended to surround the Spaniards and kill every last one of them.[11]

Cortés proceeded as if the main prisoner, who seemed important—a leader of some kind—was telling the truth. Then, in a move that would become one of his diplomatic trademarks, Cortés offered the prisoners gifts of green beads and released them, telling them to return to their chiefs with the message that he wished only to trade and that he came in peace. Once they were gone, he immediately prepared for war.

Cortés ordered his most seriously wounded men back to the ships to recuperate; the best of his special forces—the crossbowmen, harquebusiers, lancers, swordsmen, and light gunners—prepared for action. He called for more artillery, dry powder, and six of the heavy cannons to be removed from the ships and transported ashore. Then, sensing that the time was right, Cortés called upon his secret weapon: the entire cavalry of sixteen Spanish horses. The animals, stiff and sore from their long journey, were lowered by pulleys and led ashore. They were the first horses to set their hooves on the Mexican mainland since before the Ice Age, when the native animals became extinct in the northern hemisphere.[12]

As the sun went down, the horses were exercised and fed. The cavalrymen prepared for battle, donning heavy steel body armor—breast- and back plates—plus metal *tassets* for their thighs and *rerebraces* and *vambraces* for their arms. These they would sleep in, sweating through the humid night. The horses were fitted with breastplates of their own, and small bells that jingled as they went, serving to further frighten the enemy and to alert the Spaniards to the cavalry's location.

At daybreak Cortés heard Fray Bartolomé de Olmedo, the expedition's chaplain, say mass, then slung himself into the saddle of his dark chestnut stallion. He led his force of five hundred men out of the village and onto the plain of Cintla. From the woods beyond some ten thousand Tabascan warriors poured into the open maize fields; an equal number were strung behind in support. The well-organized warriors came in their traditional military garb and formation, some decorated in ornate feather crests, pounding drums and blowing trumpets to instill fear as they ran. Their screaming faces were streaked with white and black paints signifying rank, and they carried long bows and arrows, shields and spears, and even two-handed swords like the Spaniards'. The conquistadors noted that they wore quilted armor, made of heavy cotton, on their chests.[13] The Spanish infantry—foot soldiers and musketeers and crossbowmen—took the initial onslaught, and many were wounded in close hand-to-hand combat. An arrow pierced one soldier through the head, and nearly seventy others were badly wounded.

Cortés and the cavalry had been separated from the infantry by swamps and marshes and deep irrigation ditches that the horses could not cross, and so they were slow to arrive in support of the infantry. Meanwhile the infantry battled wave after wave of brave warriors, using skillful sword work to repel continuous and numerically superior assaults. They fired their matchlocks, falconets, and cannons, and the whistling balls and percussive explosions drove great numbers of Tabascans out onto the open plain, where they bent to the ground and threw up dirt and grasses to conceal themselves from the Spaniards. As the smoke and dust cleared, Cortés arrived from the rear with his cavalry to find thousands of the warriors regrouping on the open plain.

Cortés and his cavalry charged the field, the riders wielding spears in the first mounted combat in the New World. Horse and rider galloped into the fray at great speed, charging the crowd and impaling the warriors from elevated positions. Cortés and his men speared at will, then rode and wheeled and came again, skewering and trampling the confused Tabascans. Then they would retreat to the periphery, while cannon and gunfire boomed through the valley. The Indian warriors, having never before witnessed either horses or firearms, looked on in dismay as their compatriots were easily run down. They fought bravely but were no match for the killing efficiency of firearms or horses and expert riders. They fled in terror. Within a few hours smoke hung low in the Cintla Valley, and more than eight hundred Tabascans lay dead in the fields. Cortés's first major military engagement on mainland Mexico had been a rout.[14]

As the last of the Tabascans scattered into the hills, Cortés and his cavalrymen dismounted, unsaddled, and tethered their horses, treating some that were wounded. He ordered rest and medical attention for his wounded men, who amounted to nearly a fifth of his fighting force, though many of the wounds were minor. One soldier reported that "we bandaged our wounded with cloths, for this was all we had, and sealed the wounds of our horses with fat from the corpse of an Indian that we had cut up for this purpose."[15] That night more than a hundred additional Spaniards fell ill with fevers, cramps, and general malaise, likely from foul water drunk from the streams, coupled with the oppressive heat and humidity. Miraculously, only two of Cortés's men died on the plains of Cintla, one slashed through the throat, the other succumbing to an arrow in his ear. It was March 25, 1519, and the conquest of the Americas had begun in earnest.

Cortés and his men slept armed lest further hostilities erupt, but the night was calm and quiet. The next morning some thirty Tabascan emissaries walked into camp dressed in finery—ornately feathered cloaks and tunics elegantly embroidered. They carried with them offerings of maize cakes, fowl, fruit, and fish. Through Aguilar, they asked to see the Spanish chief, and when Cortés came forward, they requested that they be allowed to enter the savanna unharmed to burn and bury their fallen, to prevent their stench and avoid their being eaten by jaguars and pumas. Cortés consented, with the provision that the main cacique of the village of Pontonchan come personally to discuss a treaty.

Later, a lord did arrive with attendants in tow, bringing more food and offerings, including various turquoise objects and, more important, intricate masks, sculptures, and diadems fashioned in gold. Cortés noticed that the chief and his attendants seemed terrified of the horses, and the shrewd captain devised a plan to cement his dominance and get what he wanted: acquiescence and information. Realizing that these men understood neither the horses nor the fire-bursting cannons and guns, he ordered that a cannon be fired at dangerously close range. The thunderous report reverberated, and the hiss of the ball whistled past the Indians' heads and exploded foliage a great distance away. Then Cortés brought out a mare in season, followed by his meanest, most high-strung stallion. The stallion caught the scent of the mare and reared, kicked and neighed, then pawed and stomped the ground right at the feet of the Tabascan chief. It was a devious ploy, and it worked. The chief cowered, fearing that the cannons and stallion would attack him and his people. But Cortés calmed the horse, whispering to it and soothing it. He assured the chief that, if he cooperated, no further harm would come to them from these powerful weapons.[16]

Shaken and confused, a number of chiefs held counsel, returning at length with more gifts, more gold, small figurines of dogs, ducks, and lizards, and at last twenty young slave women, who they said could be used for various tasks, including cooking and preparing food like maize cakes. Pleased, Cortés inquired about the gold. Did they have more, and if not, where might he find more? Where were the mines? The Tabascans assured Cortés that they had no more gold, but they pointed to the northwest and said, "Culua, Mexico, Mexico."[17]

Cortés accepted the gifts and distributed the women among his captains, which boosted morale for the moment. One of the slave girls, whom Cortés presented to Alonso Hernández Puertocarrero, was a calm, confident, and precocious young woman originally from the north, in the province of Coatzacualco. The girl had been sold to the Tabascans, who now gave her to Cortés. Her native tongue was the Mayan language, but she spoke a number of other dialects as well. Her dark eyes sparkled with intelligence. Her name was Malinche.[18]

It was Palm Sunday 1519. Cortés had his carpenters erect in the center of the Tabascan town a large cross and a sturdy pedestal to support the figures of Mary and Jesus. He thanked the Tabascan chiefs, loaded the gifts of food, gold, and the slave girls, and readied to set sail for the north. They would search for and find this place called "Mexico."

CHAPTER THREE

Montezuma's Message

UNDER FAIR WINDS, NAVIGATOR ALAMINOS set a course to the
northwest along the coast, laying tight to shore, heading toward
what is now the port city of Veracruz. Cortés anchored off the
port that Juan de Grijalva, on his previous expedition,* had
named San Juan de Ulúa (first called the Isle of Sacrifices),
and from his flagship's bow he surveyed the land from a safe
distance offshore. The entire fleet arrived, and all anchored
close by, protected from strong northerly gales. Cortés ordered
Spanish pennants and royal flags raised on the *Santa María de
la Concepción*, while he continued to scan the shoreline and
the interior for a suitable landing site and for any activity.

He did not have to wait long.

Before an hour had passed, Cortés spotted two large
dugout pirogues paddling directly toward them. The boats
contained well-decorated priests and chieftains. They halted

---

*Grijalva, Velásquez's nephew, led an expedition to the Yucatán in 1518. He witnessed
evidence of thriving civilization, including pyramid towers and great buildings that
reminded him of the city of Seville. Grijalva and his crew also discovered evidence of
human sacrifice near what is today Veracruz, and they named the place the Island of
Sacrifices. Grijalva was unable to trade or settle and was eventually driven from Mexico
by the native inhabitants and lost over thirty men.

below Cortés's ship and motioned that they wished to come aboard. Intrigued, Cortés invited them up.

The conversation, however, was strained and awkward. Aguilar could not communicate with them in coastal Mayan, and Cortés grew frustrated, for he was deeply aware of the importance of communication as a tool for conquest and empire. Perturbed at the impasse, he was pondering what to do when he noticed one of the newly acquired slave girls speaking directly to the chiefs, their easy, fluid dialogue suggesting that she understood them perfectly. Cortés walked with Aguilar over to investigate and was delighted to learn that the girl spoke fluent Nahuatl, the highland Aztec tongue. She could speak to the highlanders, then translate the discourse into Mayan for Aguilar, who could relay the conversation in Spanish for Cortés. The communication proved cumbersome, but it worked, and Cortés was patient. He listened attentively, finding out what he could about these priests and chieftains. His ears perked when he discovered that they came from a place they called "Mexico."

Pleased, Cortés immediately elevated Malinche to interpreter and instructed her to stay always near him and Aguilar. A formal exchange of gifts ensued between the Spaniards and their visitors. The Indians offered featherwork, local cotton attire, and small trinkets in gold; the Spaniards reciprocated with food, cask wine, metal tools, and blue glass beads. It was a convivial exchange. The chiefs asked if they might have the wine to bring to their governor, a man they called Tendile, who resided some twenty miles away in a place called Cuetlaxtlán. Cortés consented, assuring the men that he came with peaceful intentions, wishing only to trade, but added that he intended to land and hoped that he might meet their leader personally, if this could be arranged. The men disembarked with the wine and their other gifts, responding that soon other leaders would come to speak with him.[1]

Cortés woke at dawn the next morning, rested and invigorated. It was Good Friday 1519. He orchestrated a landing, sending some two hundred soldiers (nearly half his force), the horses and war hounds, loads of artillery, and a handful of Cuban porters ashore in the brigantines and rowboats. As nothing better was available in the near vicinity, he and his troops camped on a sloped, inhospitable sand dune amid sparse tropical palms, erecting temporary shacks for shelter and shade. The place was oppressively humid, sultry, and swarming with mosquitoes. They positioned some cannons and other artillery on the higher dunes. As was becoming his custom (and in respect for Good Friday), Cortés ordered an altar installed and mass observed. Then, sweating profusely in their armor and swatting at the insect swarms, he and his men rested and kept watch.

The next morning emissaries began to arrive at the Spaniards' makeshift camp. The first group claimed to have been sent by their leader Cuitlalpitoc (incidentally, the same man who had been sent to parlay with Grijalva), and through Aguilar and Malinche Cortés first heard utterance of the name *Montezuma.*[2] This man Montezuma was said to be the magnificent and powerful ruler of the Mexica, a feared Triple Alliance of the city-states Tenochtitlán, Texcoco, and Tacuba, peoples who inhabited the Valley of Mexico (and who have since come to be known as the Aztecs). Cortés listened carefully, receiving Cuitlalpitoc with kindness and hospitality, and assured him that he came with peaceful intentions.

More ambassadors of Montezuma descended on the dune, bringing elaborate gifts, including a meticulously crafted feather garment decorated with golden rings, a war shield inlaid with opalescent mother-of-pearl, a large obsidian mirror, and large quantities of food.[3] They said that Cortés should expect a visit soon from a very important governor of Montezuma, then left.

On Easter Sunday 1519 the ambassador Tendile* arrived as promised with a few thousand attendants in tow, all dressed in feathered finery and elaborately embroidered cloaks, nobles carrying gifts and provisions. Perhaps for effect and as a show of

---

*Sometimes referred to also as Tentlil or Teudile.

religious conviction, Cortés instructed Fray Bartolomé de
Olmedo to say mass, which Tendile and his nobles listened to
with great curiosity and interest. When the Spanish priest had
finished, Tendile followed with a ritual of his own, as he and
some other noblemen performed a "dirt eating" ceremony, in
which they dampened their fingers, touched them to the earth,
then placed the dirt-smudged fingers to their lips in a show of
respect. They handed Cortés sticks of burning incense and
reeds dipped in their blood.[4] Tendile then brought forth bearers
carrying great chests, from which he proffered gifts from the
great Montezuma, his emperor from high above and far away
in the mountains, a deeply feared and sovereign leader who
ruled from the capital city, a place called Tenochtitlán.

Tendile presented Cortés with chests full of highly wrought
featherwork and gleaming gold objects and jewelry. Cortés
formally thanked Tendile and by extension his ruler, this
Montezuma. He reciprocated by giving Tendile a red Spanish
cap, embroidered in gold, depicting a mounted horseman
(Saint George) slaying a dragon; as a direct gift to Montezuma,
he offered an intricately fashioned, inlaid, and carved Spanish
armchair upon which, Cortés said, the ruler might sit when
Cortés arrived for his personal visit.[5] This highly presumptu-
ous and even brash suggestion was not lost on Tendile, who
responded quickly: "You have only now just arrived, and already you ask to speak with our prince."[6] His pride apparently
insulted, he instructed Cortés to accept the gifts first, and then
they would in good time discuss each other's wishes.

A bit affronted himself at being addressed in this way, the
clever Hernán Cortés took the opportunity to explain his situation, shrewdly fabricating some of the details and context. He
told Tendile that he too served a most powerful king, one who
lived across the vast seas to the east, and that his own king knew
well of the great Montezuma; in fact, Cortés said (and here he
laid it on thick), his monarch had dispatched him with instructions to meet personally with Montezuma and would expect
nothing less. As he waited for his words to filter through Aguilar
and Malinche, Cortés would have noticed the concerned

expression on Tendile's face when he learned of this ruler from the east, for there existed a myth proclaiming that very thing. For the moment, though, Tendile simply nodded and spoke to one of his attendants, who was sketching furiously on a large canvas made from the dried and stretched flesh of the maguey plant. Cortés inquired about it, and Tendile informed him that this was "picture writing," and that his painters were recording all the proceedings, so that they could report accurately to Montezuma what they had observed and learned. Bernal Díaz remembered the moment precisely, noting that Tendile gave his painters instructions "to make realistic full-length portraits of Cortés and all his captains and soldiers, also to draw the ships, sails, and horses, Doña Marina [Malinche] and Aguilar, and even two greyhounds."[7]

Cortés decided to offer a display of power to the artists and, by extension, to this ruler named Montezuma, so he ordered the cavalry to mount and ride through rigorous military exercises in full armor, their steel swords flashing in the sun. Artillerymen discharged firearms and cannons at close range. Tendile, the nobles, and the thousands of attendants shuddered in amazement and fear, marveling at the violent explosions. The disciplined artists drew their renditions of these phenomena, including smoke clouds billowing from the shot blasts that completely obliterated a nearby tree. They then turned their accurate picture-writing skills on the massive ships at anchor, vessels of a magnitude they had never before encountered, which they called "waterhouses." Astounded by the horses and the dogs, the artists depicted these animals racing about the beach, the "panting dogs rushing back and forth, their tongues dangling from their great mouths and their fiery eyes casting off sparks."[8] The impressive, awesome display quite literally put the fear of god in Tendile and his men, for indeed the weapons and the animals possessed such power and novelty that Tendile wondered if Cortés and these creatures might be *teules*—gods.*[9]

---

*The Spaniards, including Bernal Díaz, interpreted the term *teule* to mean "god" or "divine being," whether that was correct or not.

Tendile then inquired about a particular helmet worn by one of the Spanish soldiers who had been performing military exercises on the beach. He asked to see it. Fabricated of metal, with a peak sloping gracefully from front to back, Tendile noted that this helmet possessed a remarkable resemblance to those worn by their war gods, including Huitzilopochtli and Quetzalcoatl. Montezuma, Tendile said, would be very interested in seeing this helmet, and he asked Cortés if he might borrow it to show his ruler. Once again thinking on his feet, Cortés responded mischievously that Tendile could certainly take the helmet, under the condition that it be returned filled with grains of Aztec gold, which he might compare with that of his homeland in Spain and give as a gift to his own great monarch across the eastern oceans. Of his desire and interest in Aztec gold, Cortés added that "I and my companions suffer from a disease of the heart which can be cured only with gold."[10]

Finally, the artists having completed detailed portraits of Cortés and some of his captains, Tendile departed, assuring the captain that his people would supply the visiting Spaniards with food on the beach and that he would soon return with a response from his ruler in Tenochtitlán.

As a generous parting gift (likely on orders from Montezuma himself), Tendile had left Cortés with some two thousand servants, workers instructed to construct hundreds more huts and shelters for the Spaniards. They also offered women to make maize cakes and cook fowl and fish, which they provided daily. Cortés was impressed with their hard work and the apparent munificence, but he was also circumspect, figuring that among these men were likely spies and informants whose charge was to report back on the nature of these visitors, their habits and weaponry and numbers. So as he waited on the muggy promontory for Tendile's return, Cortés kept a watchful eye on the servants.

Never idle, Hernán Cortés also took the opportunity to get to know the beautiful Malinche, with whom he was developing something more than just good rapport. Technically he had given her to his friend Puertocarrero, but she had been at Cortés's side since the moment he discovered her linguistic prowess, and she would remain there for the duration of the expedition. Her talent for language acquisition was uncanny, and through Aguilar she began to learn Spanish with remarkable speed. Eventually, in her own words, she was able to tell Cortés her incredible, and in many ways sad, story. How, though she was of high birth, her chieftain father had died when she was very young, and she had been sold into slavery by her own mother. How she had been shuttled back and forth between slave traders, eventually landing in Tabasco, where the Tabascan chiefs had finally gifted her to Cortés. A deep intelligence burned in her dark eyes, and Cortés saw in her an ancient beauty. Before long, charmed, Cortés had her baptized and made her his primary confidante and then his mistress. Malinche would be present, and indeed instrumental, in all subsequent diplomatic proceedings, many of which would determine the history of the New World.*[11]

ABOUT ten days later Tendile returned from the interior leading a retinue of over one hundred bearers, strung in a long line behind him. Arriving before Cortés, Tendile and another important Mexican chief kissed the earth and perfumed the Spaniard and the soldiers around him with smoke from incense burning in earthen braziers. Then Tendile's attendants laid out numerous woven presentation mats called *petates*, onto which they spread before Cortés generous gifts from Montezuma himself: plates and ornaments and sandals, all of pure gold, and a strung bow and a dozen arrows of solid gold. They set out two enormous plates of gold and silver, which were, according to Bernal Díaz, "as large as carriage wheels."[12]

---

*Her name had been something approximating Malinali, which the Spaniards mispronounced, and it became Malinche—the name by which she is now commonly known. She was baptized and referred to as Doña Marina by the Spaniards.

One of these impressive disks represented the sun, the heavy gold carved elaborately with depictions of plants and animals; the silver plate, slightly larger, symbolized the moon. Cortés and his men marveled at the intricately woven and resplendently dyed cotton garments, cloaks of featherwork of inestimable beauty and value, created by highly skilled craftsmen. The jewelry—gold collars and necklaces and bracelets—was inlaid with shimmering precious stones and threaded with gleaming pearls. Also on the mats were laid golden deer and ducks and dogs, jaguars and monkeys and fish, golden rods and staffs. The Mexicans presented the helmet Tendile had taken, filled as requested with gold flakes and nuggets directly from the mines. Cortés stood amazed before the generous and wondrous artifacts, conscious for the first time that he was dealing with people of a highly civilized and established culture who could mine and then intricately fabricate precious metals. This was fine art of a kind to rival, and even surpass, anything being created in Europe or perhaps anywhere in the world.[13]

Tendile, seeing that Cortés was pleased, paused to let his pleasure sink in. Then he intimated Montezuma's wishes and his message: with great pleasure he offered these gifts to Spain's king, and he was happy to have this direct communication. The Spaniards were welcome to remain along the coast for a time if they so desired. But Montezuma would not come personally to see them, and under no circumstances could they venture through the mountains to visit him. Montezuma's instructions were polite but specific: the Spaniards were to take his gifts as gestures of good faith and evidence of his wealth and power— and leave. They must leave.

Montezuma's gifts had been sent to assert his unchallengeable and undeniable wealth and power, but they had an opposite and unintended effect. Their grandiosity piqued the greed and desire of the Spaniards. Seeing this imperial haul, Hernán Cortés had no intention of leaving. He had already come too far and risked too much, and though disappointed by Montezuma's refusal, he remained calm in his dealings with Tendile and the other chief. He decided to push Tendile, saying that his own king would be unhappy with him if he did not make direct personal contact with Montezuma, and in fact Cortés should feel it "impossible to present himself again before his own sovereign, without having accomplished this great object of his voyage," especially after having sailed over "two thousand leagues of ocean" to see Montezuma.[14] He thanked Tendile profusely for the gifts but wished him to return once more to Montezuma and express his deep desire for a meeting. He presented for Montezuma several tokens of his great respect, which included a number of Dutch shirts woven of fine linen, a Florentine glass goblet engraved with scenes of hunting, and handfuls of glass beads. Cortés must certainly have felt a little self-conscious with this scant reciprocity, as his gifts were paltry and few when compared to the literal treasure that Montezuma had presented to him, but Cortés gave what he could and sent Tendile away, still hoping for a personal audience.

Once Tendile left, Cortés assessed their situation on the dunes. It was untenable. Despite the numerous shacks and shelters they had built, the sands grew scorching hot during the day, and the area was surrounded by stagnant marshes that produced thick clouds of flies, gnats, and mosquitoes. Many of his men were racked with stomach cramps and bowel disorders, some even succumbing to tropical "bilious fever"—mosquito-borne malaria. So far some thirty of his men had perished from battle wounds and inexplicable disease. What food they had was spoiling in the hot sun or in the ships' holds.

Perhaps even worse, there were grumblings of discord among his men; some of the more influential members loyal to Velázquez suggested that they should take the gifts and return immediately to Cuba. Cortés attempted to allay their concerns by dispatching two expeditions—one over land and one by sea—to discover a more suitable location for settlement. He sent two brigantines, one piloted by Alaminos and captained by his own loyal friend Rodrigo Álvarez, the other under the captaincy of a Velázquez supporter named Francisco de Montejo, manned by some fifty soldiers, nearly all devoted to the governor of Cuba. Álvarez and Montejo were to seek a better, more sheltered harbor for the ships and a landing site that was not plagued by lowland marshes, swamps, and the attendant swarms. Cortés assigned Juan Velázquez de León, a relative of Velázquez, to foray into the interior for three days, also in search of more favorable surroundings for settlement and fortification. As it turned out, Cortés's choice to send away the bulk of the Velázquez sympathizers appears not to have been accidental.[15]

HIGH above, in the Valley of Mexico, Montezuma had difficult decisions to make. Deeply spiritual, having been a high priest before becoming emperor, he pondered the counsel of his priests, who suggested that the invading Spaniards be immediately driven back to where they came from or, better yet, killed. He learned from his spies and emissaries that along his route Cortés and his men had been destroying temples and replacing native idols with their own, a fact that perplexed and intrigued Montezuma. Moreover these Spaniards, these *teules*, were strangely served by beasts—they could conjoin themselves to the backs of great hornless stags to become one being—and they carried fire and thunder in their hands. One of the messengers' reports stated of the foreigners, "Their trappings and arms are all made of iron. They dress in iron and wear iron casques on their heads. Their swords are iron; their bows are iron; their shields are iron; their spears are iron; their deer carry them on their backs wherever they wish to go. These deer, our lord, are as tall as the roof of a house."[16] The emperor's priests reported omens and grim prophecies, including one that said, "The future has already been determined and decreed in heaven, and Montezuma will behold and suffer great mystery which must come to pass in this land. It comes swiftly."[17] The most disconcerting omen, already a general belief among Montezuma's priests, was that a long-standing prophecy was finally being realized, that Cortés, this strange and powerful bearded invader, might in fact be the plumed serpent god Quetzalcoatl, returned. He had, after all, arrived on the Mexican mainland on 1-Reed, which occurred only every fifty-two years and which was the exact date on the Aztec calendar on which Quetzalcoatl was prophesied to return.*[18]

As Montezuma listened to the counsel of his priests and messengers, he surveyed the grand lake cities of his domain. He knew that he must at all costs protect Tenochtitlán, the geographical, political, and spiritual epicenter of his vast empire, but he feared also that the arrival of this Cortés was predestined. Tradition held, and Montezuma fully believed, that the Aztec capital was the sacred center of the universe. The myth of Quetzalcoatl told that the bearded royal ancestor would one day arrive to "shake the foundation of heaven" and conquer Tenochtitlán. Montezuma listened to his priests and mused. He decided to be careful and judicious in his decisions, and he must discover whether this Cortés really was Quetzalcoatl: for if he was, then he was also a descendant of Montezuma's own ruling family, and the two were related by blood.[19]

Montezuma chose two of his trusted nephews and four of his priests (Tendile among them) and sent them again to the coast. They were to deploy spies to monitor all subsequent movements of the Spaniards and report back by means of their best "runners," relays of men who ran with astonishing speed and stealth through the thin mountain air, able to travel and dispatch messages across distances up to two hundred miles per day. Supported by a string of bearers, Montezuma's nephews and priests would once again carry the fine featherwork, cotton garments, and pieces of the gold with which the invaders

---

*The Aztecs used at least two calendars, one agricultural or solar, called the *xiuhpohualli*, the other sacred or ritualistic, called the *tonalpohualli*. The *tonalpohualli* was a calendrical system employing fifty-two-year cycles and the concept of "bundles of years." The sacred *tonalpohualli* used a pair of interconnected cycles: a cycle of thirteen numbers and a cycle of twenty day names.

seemed particularly enamored. Montezuma's envoys were to reiterate his ultimatum: take these gifts and leave.

WHILE Cortés waited for the return of his scouting expeditions, Tendile arrived again, once more trailing porters and gifts. Once more, with formal fanfare, he perfumed Cortés and his men with sweet, burning incense and laid out "ten loads of fine rich feather cloth"[20] and more gold pieces. He then brought out four large green gemstones (jadestones) that looked to the Spaniards like rough emeralds. These precious stones, Tendile explained, were direct gifts to the Spanish monarch from Montezuma, and they were much more highly prized and valued than gold, for they assisted the dead in the afterlife. Then Tendile became serious, and through Malinche he firmly reiterated the previous message from Montezuma, which now sounded like an ultimatum: as they now had everything they needed, the Spaniards should load up their ships and return to their own country at once. Their business here was concluded. Take these offerings with honor and dignity, and go. *Now.*

With that, Tendile, his officials, and his train of bearers turned and struck back toward the interior, headed for Mexico to report the successful delivery of his message to their emperor Montezuma.

The next morning Cortés awoke to find that all the huts previously inhabited by the two thousand workers Tendile had left for him were abandoned. The local inhabitants had also retreated into the woodlands, under direct orders of Montezuma, ceasing all trade and communication with the Spaniards. The locals no longer brought food for Cortés and his army. They had been cut off. They were now on their own.

FOR the duration of his expedition, timing was everything, and now the time appeared ripe for definitive action. From the moment of his rejection, Cortés became fixated on meeting in person this great and powerful (and wealthy) emperor they called Montezuma. But he would need to proceed carefully, and first he had internal divisions to contend with. With the bulk of the Velázquez faction away on reconnaissance with Montejo, Cortés drew on his legal training and orchestrated some deft political maneuvering. First, he held a meeting with his troops and remaining captains, explaining that he understood that there were factions among them, that they were essentially of two minds. He understood that the men were famished and miserable and that some of them even wished to return to Cuba—to take their spoils and sail.

But, Cortés argued, they had much to gain if they stayed the course. Simply look at the riches they had already received. True, most of it would have to be sent back to their king in Spain, but consider how much more there must be. Cleverly, Cortés opened the floor for discussion and heard arguments from both sides, but as most of Velázquez's men were absent, the discussion was relatively one-sided. That night, under veil of darkness in what was essentially a cunning coup d'état, Cortés gathered in his tent all his most powerful allies, and the majority agreed that rather than return to Cuba, they should stay and settle. To that end Cortés suggested that he would hereby resign his commission under Diego de Velázquez, in the presence of his notary, and together they would create and found their own legal settlement, a town and colony called Villa Rica de la Vera Cruz (the Rich Town of the True Cross, in reference to their arrival there on Good Friday). Quickly but precisely and with legal correctness, Cortés prepared formal documents that created a colonial government consisting of his own handpicked supporters and loyalists, complete with a chief magistrate (Alonso de Puertocarrero), town councilors (Alonso de Grado and Pedro Alvarado), a constable (Gonzalo de Sandoval), and a notary (Diego de Godoy). As a token and conciliatory political gesture intended to assuage unrest, Cortés nominated Velázquez's man Montejo as joint chief magistrate.[21]

Then Cortés left the tent so that his own supporters, his

newly assigned town councilors and governors, could "elect" him both chief justice and captain-general of the town that he had only moments before conjured into existence.

His actions reflected a brilliant legal mind and a profound knack for spontaneous diplomacy, for in resigning his previous command under Velázquez and founding a town, he was now under no further legal obligation to Velázquez. Cortés and his men were now answerable and accountable *only* to Charles V, King of Spain. With a few clandestine strokes of a quill pen, Diego Velázquez, Governor of Cuba, became the former patron of Hernán Cortés, legally excised of all authority, and within only a few days Cortés would begin a vigorous correspondence, a series of letters explaining, recounting, and in certain respects justifying his expedition and actions directly to his king.

THE maritime scouting expeditions returned with word that, though not ideal, there was another landing some forty miles up the coast, so Cortés wasted no time. They would depart, at last, the sultry sand dunes of San Juan de Ulúa. The bulk of his force he sent by sea to the new landing, while he and a smaller expeditionary army would march overland to meet them, giving him a chance to reconnoiter the lay of the land and its inhabitants.

Under fine skies and fair winds, the ships arrived shortly at a rocky promontory, an outcrop with a tranquil bay—though slightly too shallow for the navigator Alaminos's liking. Still, they were able to tie off on the rocks and anchor there. They began unloading artillery, provisions, horses, and dogs. They would make a stand here, near a village they learned was called Quiahuiztlán. This was to be the location of their newly formed town Villa Rica de la Vera Cruz.

Meanwhile Montejo and Velázquez de León, having returned from their scouting foray, had learned of the surreptitious proceedings during their absence. Fuming, they flatly stated that they would take no further commands from Cortés, who had clearly overstepped his authority. They held meetings of their own and attempted to sway the remainder of the Velázquez men to return to Cuba and report the schism. Unwilling to accept insubordination of any kind (and no doubt also because he knew that Velázquez, upon hearing the news, would certainly send ships after him to have him arrested or, more likely, hanged), Cortés had these men chained aboard the ships and kept under guard until they cooled down and he decided what to do with them. Soon, through his significant powers of persuasion, Cortés managed to convince most of the soldiers of the rightness of their mission and their duty to the crown, and within a few days even the most obstinate were released. But Cortés had sent a clear message to all his men: do not cross me.[22]

Cortés mounted up and led his small party inland and toward the north. Almost immediately he spotted a group of Indians regarding them from a safe distance on a hillside. They appeared different from Tendile and the interior Mexican highlanders and from any coastal Indians the Spaniards had yet encountered. He sent a few cavalry to bring them to him—and was both riveted and revolted when they came forward: they had pierced ears and noses, with holes large enough to run their fingers through; their lower lips were intentionally severed through ritual self-mutilation, revealing blackened teeth and gums; they wore in these grotesque stretched piercings great hunks of colored stone. They spoke a language that even Malinche did not understand, but some of them could manage a little Nahuatl. Malinche relayed a message from them to Cortés. They were called Totonacs, and they had been watching the Spaniards along the coast for some time now. They had been sent by their chief to see if the leader of the Spaniards would come talk to him—they lived only a few miles away, in a town called Cempoala.*[23]

---

*Cempoala was the principal city of the Totonac federation, who were reluctant tributaries of the Aztecs. The term *Totonac* refers to a member of the federation, while *Cempoalan* refers to a Totonac from the primary city of Cempoala.

Cortés suspected a trap, so he assembled a unit of cavalry, heavy artillery, harquebusiers, and crossbowmen and rode inland in formation to meet the Totonac chief. He also dispatched a few mounted spies and scouts to ride ahead and gather reconnaissance. One returned, breathless and wide-eyed, saying that he had seen their gleaming temples from afar, and they were burnished with silver; indeed, he believed their worship temples to be made of pure silver! (This scout was later humiliated, and Cortés disappointed, when they discovered that the silver was merely a mirage or optical illusion. The gleam was the bright midday sun reflected off the freshly whitewashed stones.)

Cortés and his men passed through dense foliage, rich and green as jadestone, the tropical trees filled with colorful parrots cawing overhead. They crossed muddy and roiling tributaries of the wide Río de la Antigua, the horses swimming, the foot soldiers on rafts fashioned from branches and tree trunks. They were mercifully shaded from the boiling sun by the crowded canopy of palms.[24] Cortés was encouraged as they flushed a variety of game, both large and small, from the thickets: deer, as well as turkeys and pheasants and quail.

As they arrived on the outskirts of the town, Cortés and his men noted the impressive stone dwellings, the roofs tidy and thatched, the walls cleanly scrubbed with lime. Many of the houses were of polished stucco and were brightly painted in yellow, blue, red, and green.[25] As they approached, the Spaniards were met by envoys of the Cempoalan chief, who led Cortés to a central square that lay below an impressive pyramid topped by a temple. Flanked by swaying palms, a series of pyramids had been erected with order and design across a magnificent flat plain. Amid them Cortés discovered a central ring of stones, which he later learned was used for religious "gladiator" battles, the victor winning his own life. Cortés dispatched scouts to inspect the main temple, where they found a scene that shocked them: freshly sacrificed young boys, blood still pooling from their viscera. The walls of the altar were bespattered with blood, and the victims' hearts were set out on plates. The scouts saw large, square sacrificial stones and sharp obsidian blades glistening with blood. They saw dismembered torsos, the arms and legs severed from them cleanly. All this they reported to Cortés, who immediately demanded to see the leader of these people.[26]

While they waited, Indian families poured from their houses and crowded about, pulling at the Spaniards' beards, staring transfixed at the mounted cavalry armed and ready, and at the horses, which they believed to be centaurs. Then the Totonac chief arrived, carried in a litter by many attendants. He was enormous, his distended belly supported by two men holding a solid pole between them as his corpulent flesh spilled over it.[27] The fat chief, named Tlacochcalcatl, spoke in his native Totonac, and some of his men used Nahuatl to relay his message through Malinche and Aguilar. As the chief bellowed, he kept gesturing toward the interior, toward the high mountains beyond, his voice becoming louder, his words faster and more animated. He had heard of the great power of the Spaniards and how with only a small force they had defeated the Tabascans. He was very impressed. Then he told Cortés that he had a slight problem of his own, and perhaps the Spaniards could help him. The proud and independent tribe of the Totonacs, whose central city of Cempoala boasted more than twenty thousand inhabitants, had recently been conquered by the neighboring Aztecs, the Mexica. Now, against their will, they were subjects of the emperor Montezuma. Worse, they were forced to pay exorbitant tributes to their new ruler, who demanded large numbers of victims for his ongoing human sacrifices. Montezuma had been taking their finest young men and women at will, and now he was even demanding their wives. It was too much. They no longer wished to comply, and Tlacochcalcatl wondered whether Cortés and the Spaniards could somehow use their great power to reduce the tributes the Totonacs were forced to pay.[28]

Cortés realized immediately how this discontent might

benefit him. Through Malinche he said that yes, likely they could strike a deal of mutual benefit. He scanned the well-organized city and decided that a good number—possibly thousands—of the inhabitants would make ready warriors and porters. He inquired offhandedly about the size of the Totonac confederation and asked the great hulking chief, who could barely walk without support from his entourage, how many warriors he might be able to lend Cortés in his effort. The chief responded that the Totonac confederacy comprised over thirty towns, all unified in dissension against the Aztecs. And other tribes were unhappy as well. One fierce tribe, the Tlax-calans, was in active revolt and had never surrendered to Mon-tezuma. The chief assured Cortés that if he would guide an offensive against the Aztecs, he could provide a massive army of warriors in support, a force numbering in the hundreds of thousands.

Cortés made a pact with the fat chief. Yes indeed, under those circumstances, he could most certainly assist them.[29]

CHAPTER FOUR

The Gambler Stakes All: "Either Win the Land, or Die in the Attempt"

OPTIMISTIC THAT HIS NEW VERBAL "allegiance" would solidify, Cortés mustered his troops for an inland trek to the village of Quiahuiztlán, just a few miles north and a bit inland from Cempoala. There, or somewhere close by, Cortés hoped to finally settle, build a fort, and formally secure Villa Rica de la Vera Cruz, which until now had been a mobile city, existing only in name and in documents. As a show of good faith, the chief of Cempoala, Tlacochcalcatl, offered Cortés more than four hundred porters, strong young men who could carry great weight for many miles. This gesture the Spaniard greatly appreciated, as it unburdened many of his finest soldiers and made their going easier and faster.

Cortés led his troops and their new porters to the outskirts, then into the town, which sat high on a steep hill overlooking the great gulf waters. The town appeared deserted except for a handful of priests who tended the temples there, sweeping and whitewashing. The priests explained that the inhabitants, fearing the four-legged beasts, had hidden. Just then breathless and agitated Totonac runners approached, informing the priests and the Spaniards that a delegation of Aztec tribute collectors was approaching the town—they had come for more men and women and boys.

Cortés viewed the tribute collectors carefully as they arrived: dignified and even haughty, their black hair slicked back tight on their heads and tied behind in a knot. They walked upright, in an orderly and unhurried fashion, each carrying a crooked walking stick and holding a rose to his nose (a sign of upper class). Servants walked next to them swishing the air with fly whisks. Their resplendent robes and loincloths were handsomely embroidered. They walked directly past Cortés and his men without making eye contact or even acknowledging their existence.[1]

Soon Totonac nobles arrived, scurrying about, rushing before the Aztec delegation to secure suitable accommodation for them, and plying them with copious amounts of food and drink. Affronted by their imperial air and apparent disregard of him, Cortés sent Malinche to see what she could discover about these visitors. She arrived to find the Aztec tribute collectors finished with their meal (which had included turkeys and chocolate) and vehemently berating the Totonac chiefs for peacefully receiving the Spaniards and then hosting them, without the Aztecs' (and by extension Montezuma's) permission. As punishment for such impudence, they demanded immediately twenty young men and women for ritual sacrifice. And this human fee was levied in addition to the other tributes they had come for.

When Cortés learned of this demand through Malinche, he quickly devised a ploy. He secretly met with one of the Totonac lords of Quiahuiztlán and instructed him to send some of his warriors to seize the Aztecs, collar them and tether them to long poles, and then imprison them in the quarters directly adjacent to those of Cortés, under strong guard. Fearing the repercussions from Montezuma, the Totonac chief hemmed and stammered, but Cortés convinced him that it would be all right. If the Totonacs wanted assistance from Cortés, they had to trust him and believe in his methods. They were to cease paying tribute of any kind to the Aztecs from that moment. Thereupon the Totonacs bound and collared the

Aztec tribute collectors. All their Aztec attendants fled, disappearing into the scrub, running off to report the news of their nobles' apprehension.

That night Cortés instructed his guards to surreptitiously release two of the Aztec prisoners and bring them before him. They were to make certain that the Totonacs did not see this take place. They did so, and then, in an elaborate and clever ruse, he called for Aguilar and Malinche to interview the prisoners. They made believe they were earnestly trying to discover who these men were (Cortés, of course, already knew) and listened to the appeals and explanations of the Aztecs carefully. The Aztecs explained their role as tribute collectors for their magnificent emperor, adding that they were quite shocked to have been treated so roughly. This was hardly customary, and they were indignant. Cortés listened carefully, nodding and agreeing. Then, through Malinche and Aguilar, Cortés assured the Aztecs that their arrest had been against his wishes, an independent act of the Totonacs, and that he personally hated to see agents of the great Montezuma, with whom he had already developed kindly communication and peaceful exchange, handled in this hostile manner. He gave them food and wine and treated them with kindness.[2]

Then Cortés had the two Aztec nobles released, promising that he would help them escape if they would report to their master Montezuma that Cortés had performed this act of generosity and compassion and wished only for friendship and peace. As the guards led the men away to freedom, Cortés assured them that by tomorrow he would have their three companions released as well and that he would personally ascertain that no harm came to them. To ensure that his stratagem worked, Cortés ordered six trusted seamen to smuggle the prisoners through the darkness to the coast, then load the two men on boats and row them some twelve miles north, beyond Cempoalan borders. The Aztecs thanked the Spaniards for their kindness and walked off into the night, headed home to Tenochtitlán to report the events to Montezuma.

In the morning the Totonac chiefs awoke, livid to discover that two of the prisoners had "escaped" during the night. They were so enraged that they threatened to sacrifice the remaining three Aztecs on the spot, but Cortés intervened. Feigning anger at the escape, he said he would take matters into his own hands and ordered the three tribute collectors to be chained and loaded aboard one of his ships. That way, he told the Totonacs, he could look after them himself to avoid another such escape. Once on board, and out of sight of the Totonacs, Cortés unchained the three Aztecs and repeated his routine, assuring them that he was a friend to them and to Montezuma and ordering their eventual release as well. The ploy worked; when the runners returned to Tenochtitlán and reported the imprisonment of his tribute collectors, Montezuma raged and threatened retribution. But shortly thereafter the first of the released prisoners arrived, explaining that Cortés had treated them with dignity and mercifully set them free, or they surely would have been slain by the Totonacs.

Cortés's machinations were succeeding—he had played both sides perfectly. The Totonacs were astonished and impressed by the courage of the Spanish captain-general. They could hardly believe his brash treatment of these Aztecs, and they marveled that he showed no fear whatsoever of the potential consequences. As well, they were quite pleased to be free from Aztec taxation. At the same time Cortés had, at least momentarily, appeased Montezuma, who decided that rather than punish the Spaniards, he would send a small delegation with more gifts.[3] When these men arrived, they explained that Montezuma still could not meet with him, but this time their position seemed to have softened. Cortés happily accepted the gifts and handed the last three tribute collectors over to these nobles, nephews of Montezuma, who seemed content when they left. Cortés's subterfuge and closed-door diplomacy were paying dividends.

Now Cortés set about establishing the fort and the town in earnest. On a wide plain about a mile and a half inland from Quiahuiztlán, he chose exact sites for the fortress itself, situating towers for defense. There would be a marketplace, a church and temple, a granary, and a host of other public edifices that a proper city would require. The bay here, discovered by Montejo and chosen for its tranquil and protected waters, was suitable for landings and the shipping commerce that Cortés hoped would be vigorous. The waters lay immune to the gulf's periodic gale-force northerlies. Excited by the prospects, Cortés worked long and hard and fast, reportedly the first among his men to "start carrying earth and stones and to dig the foundations."[4] His captains and soldiers quickly followed his example. The Cuban porters assisted too, as did many of the four hundred bearers that the chief of Cempoala had given over to Cortés. The work went quickly. Within only a few weeks some of the first buildings were completed; the rest were continuously worked on by any men stationed there. By June 28, 1519, Cortés had successfully founded the first colony in New Spain.[5]

While Cortés was engaged in these labors, the Cempoalan chief arrived, borne in his litter. He requested an audience with Cortés, who summoned Malinche and Aguilar to hear what Tlacochcalcatl of Cempoala had to say. The chief revealed that already he needed the help which Cortés had promised him. In a hill town called Cingapacinga, some twenty-five miles to the southwest, Aztec warriors were rampaging Totonac villages, destroying their crops and making war on the villagers. According to the Cempoalan chief, this was in retaliation for the Totonacs' alignment with the Spaniards and for the Totonac federation's refusal to pay tributes to the Aztecs. The chief wished to know if Cortés would honor his agreement and go there to stop the marauding Aztecs.

Though he hated to leave the construction of Villa Rica de la Vera Cruz, which was going so well, Cortés understood the importance of maintaining smooth relations with this new ally, so he agreed to help. He kept a small contingent of men to continue the work and to guard their stores and munitions. Then he mustered the bulk of his able conquistadors, including all the cavalry (which was now just fifteen horses, his own having died), and mounted his new horse, El Arriero (the Muleteer or Muledriver).[6] Ahead of a group of musketeers and crossbowmen, and leading more than two thousand Cempoalans, Cortés rode forward toward Cingapacinga.

Late in the day Cortés and his troops reached some villages to find other Totonacs already there, but rather than battling Aztec warriors, they appeared to be looting and pillaging defenseless villages, robbing stores of their food, dragging women and children away, and even killing innocent and unarmed people. Through Malinche Cortés discovered that this was an ancient intertribal skirmish over boundaries and land ownership between the Totonacs and the Cingapacingans, and there were no Aztecs anywhere to be found. Enraged, Cortés sent the Cempoalan soldiers away, adding that he would deal with them, and with their chief, when he returned. He rode in and physically subdued the Totonac pillagers, berating them for their behavior and for lying about Aztec involvement. He then told the relieved Cingapacingans that this looting was now at an end. They were safe, and their stolen food and kidnapped people were returned. Again, Cortés's definitive diplomacy worked: the Cingapacingans agreed right then to become Spanish allies.

Cortés rode back toward Cempoala to deal with the fat chief who had deceived him. During the return, Cortés witnessed one of his own men, a solder named Morla, coming out of a native house, a freshly caught chicken in each hand. This was the very kind of pillaging he had forbidden, and the kind they had just put a stop to. Wanting to set a firm example that such behavior would not be tolerated (and clearly having lost his composure), Cortés ordered two of his men to sling a noose around the thief's neck and string him up from a nearby tree. Stealing chickens was now, apparently, a hanging offense. Morla swung, suspended in the air and clutching at the noose, struggling for his last breaths. Just then Pedro Alvarado arrived at a gallop and, skidding to a halt, slashed the rope in two, sending Morla to the ground with a thud, alive. Alvarado took private counsel with Cortés, explaining that they needed all the soldiers they had and that this man had certainly learned his lesson, as had any witnesses. Cortés, reasonable, conceded, and they remounted and rode back toward Villa Rica and Cempoala.[7]

The next morning Cortés called together the chiefs of all the neighboring towns (including the chief of Cempoala and the cacique of Cingapacinga) and held a meeting. Before witnesses, Cortés told them that he could assist them, and help keep peace in the region, only under certain conditions, which they must agree to and live by. First, they must stop warring among themselves. The long-standing feuds must be forgotten and a new alliance formed. In principle (and apparently in practice, because according to chroniclers, this pact remained intact, never broken by either party), the Cempoalans and the Cingapacingans were to be friends. Cortés is said to have actually had the leaders shake hands on it, an uncustomary gesture that would have seemed at least strange, and probably awkward and meaningless, to the Indians.

Then, seeing that local border tensions were pacified, Cortés determined that the time was right for full-fledged conversion. Through Malinche, he delivered his "customary exposition of our holy faith, and his injunctions to give up human sacrifice and robbery and the foul practice of sodomy,* and to cease worshipping their accursed idols."[8] Cortés explained that only if they agreed to all of this would he assist them. If they did not, he would leave them as they were before, helplessly subjugated, vassals under the rule of the Aztecs. If they would cast aside their own beliefs and follow the belief of the one true God, they would become vassals of Spain (and receive other benefits as well, like everlasting life). Then, as he always favored action over words alone, Cortés had the chiefs bring all their soldiers and civilians together and assemble in

---

*According to Bernal Díaz and other sources, the practice of sodomy was frequent and also used as a form of prostitution. Díaz reports that the Cempoalans "had boys dressed as women who practiced the accursed vice for profit."

the central square of Cempoala. Curious villagers had also arrived from the outlying townships, and many filled the pyramid compound, where all religious ritual took place.

Hoping to make amends, a bit sheepish and contrite, the Cempoalan chief presented Cortés with eight native maidens, the daughters of chiefs, explaining that the Cempoalans wished to have the Spaniards as brothers and that he hoped these young women would bear them children. (One of these women Cortés would give to Alonso Hernández Puertocarrero, which was only fitting, seeing that Cortés had given him but then taken back Malinche.) With skillful improvisation, Cortés used the gift as leverage. He said that he much appreciated the gesture, but that the Spaniards could accept these women only if they became baptized as Christians. Moreover, he reiterated his condition that all the Indians of the region entirely give up the practice of human sacrifice. Every day Cortés and his men had witnessed this act, this barbarity, and it simply must cease, or he could not in good conscience be their ally and protect them from their "false beliefs."*

On the issue of removing their idols from the temples, the Cempoalan chiefs and priests argued vigorously, saying that these gods were responsible for bringing them good health, plentiful harvests, suitable weather, and indeed, life itself. It would be wrong to remove them. Cortés explained that, if they would not do it themselves, he was going to have some of his men ascend the pyramids and perform the service for them. The Totonac people, fearing that their world would come to an end if their idols were destroyed, began to shriek and howl and wail, and Tlacochcalcatl sent armed warriors to stand at the foot of the temple and defend it.

Cortés would not be bullied; nor would he compromise.

---

*Díaz also witnessed his share: "Every day they sacrificed before our eyes three, four, or five Indians, whose hearts were offered to those idols and whose blood was plastered on the walls. The feet, arms, and legs of their victims were cut off and eaten, just as we eat beef from the butcher in our country. I even believe they sold it in the *tianguez* or markets."

He marched fifty of his soldiers forward, armed and ready, swords drawn. As they neared the steps, the Totonacs strung their bows and aimed. Then Cortés turned on Tlacochcalcatl himself and held him at swordpoint. Through Malinche he explained in no uncertain terms that his men must be allowed to pass or Tlacochcalcatl and his priests would be killed on the spot. The air went tense and silent, all at an impasse, but the fat chief finally raised his hand. He called to his warriors to lay down their bows and spears and move aside. As the fifty Spaniards ran up the stone steps, all of the Totonac religious leaders and thousands of terrified onlookers waited below for their world to come crashing down.

The Spanish soldiers reached the top and paused before the giant stone idols, which they viewed as horrific and macabre. Among them were a "hideously ugly"[9] half-man, half-dog figure and a large, ferocious-looking dragon. Working together in teams, the Spaniards heaved the great carved-stone figures to the edge of the temple platform and then sent them rumbling down the steep steps and shattering into pieces. Horrified, the chiefs and priests threw their hands before their eyes and turned away, and the general wailing intensified. The assembled prayed to their gods to forgive this brazen act of the Spaniards, for it was not their fault. The Totonacs apologized to their gods for their inability to protect these symbols from harm.

When the dust from the crumbling idols cleared, they realized, with some confusion and clear relief, that their world had not come to a cataclysmic end, at least not instantaneously. But this act of conversion, Cortés-style, was the beginning of the end of their religion and their culture, and a mood of somber resignation fell about Cempoala as Cortés ordered the remains of the fragmented sculptures taken away and burned. Adding deep insult to this injury, Cortés forced the eight priests (*papas*) who were entrusted with the care of the shrine and the idols to perform the task of removing and burning them. These men walked with their heads down, moaning in lamentation. They wore long black cloaks, and their hair, which they never cut, was matted and congealed with sacrificial blood, and their ears were sliced from sacrificial self-mutilation.[10]

Cortés then directed the transformation of the pyramid temple into a Christian place of worship, calling on all the town's stoneworkers to assist him. They ascended the steps with wooden and earthen containers of lime and whitewashed the entire temple area, scrubbing the encrusted dried blood from the floors and the walls and from the surface of the sacrificial stone. They burned incense to eradicate the smell of blood. Then Cortés had an altar erected, laid over with fine linens and sweet-smelling roses. He called on four of the priests to guard and care for the new shrine, and as part of their conversion, their long hair, which fell all the way to the ground on some of them, was cut off, and they were given white robes to wear instead of their black ones. These new keepers were instructed in the art of candle-making and told to keep some always aflame on the altar, illuminating both the wooden cross that had been raised there and the figure of Mary. Remarkably, given Cortés's usual thoroughness in such matters, these Totonac priests were not baptized.[11]

To finalize the transfer of religions, Cortés asked Father Olmedo to say mass before all the Totonac chiefs, while the throngs of onlookers assembled below gazed up and listened intently to the Spanish language, translated by Malinche. Finally Cortés insisted, as a condition of his accepting them, that the eight virgin maidens recently given to him by the fat chief be briefed in the teachings of Christianity and baptized. That done, Cortés distributed the girls among his men, descended the steps of his new pyramid-church, and headed back to Villa Rica. As he and his cavalry rode away, the flames from the burning idols still smoldered, black smoke smearing the skyline of the coastal plain.[12]

BACK at Villa Rica, Cortés was intrigued to learn that a ship from Cuba had just arrived. It had been commissioned as part

of his original fleet, but at the time of their hasty departure was
not yet seaworthy, so it sailed later, and with good weather and
good fortune it had spotted Cortés's main fleet anchored in the
placid bay. Captained by Francisco de Saucedo, the caravel
carried much-needed provisions and food stores, sixty able soldiers, and—most encouraging and useful—twelve more horses
(including a few mares). Cortés's delight in these reinforcements was tempered by the news that arrived with the ship: a
letter from the king in Spain had recently arrived in Cuba, ex-
pressly authorizing Diego Velázquez to found settlements and
trade in these new-found lands, which included Cozumel and
the Yucatán. This message complicated matters.

Hernán Cortés always considered his difficult choices
carefully, then acted quickly, and in this instance too his move
was decisive and immediate. He gathered his captains and loyalists and explained that they must immediately dispatch one
of their ships directly to Spain. Cortés chose captains Puertocarrero and Montejo for the journey. They were to guard with
their lives and personally deliver to the king copies of the
documents that founded Villa Rica and dissolved the trading
venture with Velázquez. These two captains were carefully
chosen. Cortés trusted Puertocarrero as a friend, and by sending Montejo, he dispensed with an influential Velázquez agita-
tor, while providing the appearance of equality in his choice.
They were sent not simply as captains and envoys but as official *procuradores*, civic representatives of the newly founded
Villa Rica de la Vera Cruz. This designation gave the appearance of legitimacy, even if it was legally questionable.[13] With
the expert and experienced captain Alaminos at the helm,
their orders were to sail as fast as possible to Spain, avoiding
any unnecessary stops or delays.

Cortés explained to his men, who must certainly have bris-
tled, that they must load the ship with every ounce of treasure
they had procured along the way: all of Montezuma's wondrous gifts, the great disks and the resplendent featherwork,
including a magnificent headdress adorned with over five hundred quetzal feathers; all the gold they had been given from

Cozumel to Tabasco (except, mysteriously, what they had received at San Juan de Ulúa),[14] and every single item of precious jewelry, of stonework, down to the last golden trinket. When some of the men balked, protesting that they were required to send only the Royal Fifth, and would be giving away their hard-won spoils, Cortés argued that he understood, but in order to impress the emperor and win good graces for their continued mission, they must send a treasure literally fit for a king. Anything less would potentially undermine their credibility. It was a calculated maneuver, a roll of the dice. He had placed on his finest remaining ship some of the greatest riches ever assembled on a single vessel. In effect, it was an elaborate bribe.[15]

Cortés retired to his quarters to begin the first of five detailed and elaborate letters to the king describing their itinerary, recounting their actions in the new-found lands, and, most important, providing a political justification for his decisions at every step of the way.* The first letter contained an itemized list, down to the last golden bird and tiny bell, of the treasure he had sent, with the implication that there was plenty more where this came from, and the tacit assurance that Cortés and his men were going after it, right into the heart of the Aztec empire. Cortés well knew that, even under perfect sailing conditions (which were rarely guaranteed, and this ship would be leaving for Spain on July 26, nearly two months past the ideal departure weather), the treasure ship would take a few months to reach Spain, and that no response would reach him until spring of the following year, at the earliest. Cortés must have calculated that if all went well, by the time he heard back

---

*These five missives have come to be known collectively as *Letters from Mexico*. Written over a seven-year span directly to Charles I of Spain, they comprise one of the most impressive and detailed first-hand accounts of the conquest of the Americas. Though they must be read with severe circumspection, understood in broad context as highly political documents, and considered vis-à-vis all the other accounts, both Spanish and indigenous, they provide tremendous insight into the mind and character of Hernán Cortés. In these letters, Cortés repeatedly and vehemently underscores his loyalty to the king and to the church.

from his king, he would already have procured for him a prize much larger than this treasure: the Aztec kingdom itself.

Uneasiness simmered among some of the colony as they watched the pilot Alaminos sail away. Some diehard Velázquez loyalists grumbled, longing to board ships to return to Cuba, to their wives and farms and the creature comforts of home. This desire was reinforced when Cortés's intentions to march inland became obvious to them. They had been on the intemperate Veracruz coast for two months and, to their way of thinking, had achieved their initial goals. They were hungry and tired, and some were still run down with tropical malaises. They wanted to go home. Initially Cortés feigned sympathy, saying that any who wished to leave should be allowed to, but he soon reversed that decision, explaining that for the venture upon which they were about to embark, he would need every last man to combat the unknown dangers ahead.

But mutiny hung in the air. A small contingent of Velázquez supporters (championed by Pedro Escudero, Velázquez de León, Diego de Ordaz, and an able pilot named Gonzalo de Umbria) met secretly and plotted to board one of the most seaworthy brigantines, kill the captain, seize the ship, and sail after the treasure ship—which they would overtake and return to Velázquez. During the night they commenced preparations, loading flitches of salt pork, rations of cassava bread, water, oil, and some local fish, and planned a silent midnight departure. One of the original conspirators apparently lost his nerve and, fearing the wrath of Cortés if they were caught, decided to reveal the plot to his captain-general. He was right to have feared Cortés.

Cortés had all the known plotters arrested and, to send a message to his troops, imposed immediate, harsh sentences. Chief instigator Escudero would be hanged; the pilot Gonzalo de Umbria was to have his feet cut off; one of the lesser sailors was to be given two hundred lashes, in full view of the troops; and one of the expedition's priests, Juan Díaz, was imprisoned for a time and threatened with hanging. (Ostensibly Cortés wished him to be "scared to death.") Perhaps for dramatic effect, and to illustrate his compassion, Cortés would say of his decision, "It would be better not to know how to write. Then one would not have to sign death sentences."[16] With that, Escudero swung from the gallows. But not all sentences were carried out as originally conceived. Part of Umbria's feet, most likely his toes, were cut off, but he continued on the journey, and the rest of the men were held behind bars but eventually released, having learned their lesson.

Still, the mutiny unsettled Cortés. He could risk no further insubordination and knew that he must eradicate all entice-ments to future discord. In an act of incredible, calculated dar-ing, he confided in his trusted shipmasters and had them bore holes in the bottoms of the boats so that they began to list and groan and founder in the water. Then Cortés gathered his troops. The hulls of some ships were worm-eaten, he ex-plained, and others were weakened by the heavy gales and pounding surf of their long journeys. He ordered the boats stripped of sails and cables, cordage and nails, tackle and rig-ging, cables and pulleys, oars and all navigational equipment, and stowed all the usable hardware in the fort on the promon-tory above the beach.[17]

Then Cortés gave the order to have all the ships run aground or sunk. He scuttled his fleet.

As the last of the great ships fell below the level of the hori-zon and disappeared into the bottom of the dark gulf waters, Cortés stood with his men. He had staked everything, his very life and all of theirs, on the future. He later reflected that they now had "nothing to rely on save their own hands—and the certainty that they must either win the land or die in the at-tempt."[18] There would be no turning back.

CHAPTER FIVE

Into the Mountains

CORTÉS NOW SET ABOUT MAKING PREPARATIONS for an inland march, assaying his available troops and weaponry. He would need to leave some soldiers in Villa Rica to guard the fortress and continue working on the buildings. The weak, wounded, and sick would remain to recuperate, given the likely difficulty of the mountains, which he could see in the distance. As many as 150 would stay behind, under the command of Juan de Escalante, who was entrusted to keep his men fit and ready, to maintain convivial relations with the coastal Indians, and to survey the gulf waters for any maritime activity, friendly or hostile.

The journey up and over the mountains promised to be arduous, and Cortés requested assistance from the Cempoalan leaders. They agreed to provide him with fifty experienced warriors and, more important, a few hundred porters to help carry gear and weaponry, including the heavy falconets, which fired three-pound balls or even smooth, round stones if munitions fell short. Most of the larger cannons, the lombards, were too heavy to portage even with the addition of native porters and the remaining one hundred or so Cuban servants, so the bulk of them were left behind to shore up the fortress at Vera Cruz. There they could be wall-mounted and aimed from fixed positions. To assist the porters and speed travel, Cortés commissioned one of his carpenters to construct a few wheeled wooden carts that could be heavily loaded and pulled. These tools of war were the first wheeled vehicles ever used in Meso-america.[*1]

Cortés rode at the head of a fifteen-horse cavalry, all properly armed for battle, and between three and four hundred Spanish troops, including about forty to fifty excellent crossbowmen and twenty to thirty harquebusiers. All the soldiers were instructed to carry their own halberds, shields, lances, and swords and to wear the best armor they had at all times, even to sleep in it so that they would be prepared for combat at any time, day or night. The steel body armor and helmets they had brought from their homeland and the Caribbean were unmercifully heavy and cumbersome, poorly suited for the sultry tropics. Full armor radiated extreme heat approaching two hundred degrees, and quite soon Cortés and his men adopted some of the lighter, more breathable quilted cotton armor worn by the native warriors.[2] Cortés and some of his men also brought along a number of war dogs, well-trained mastiffs and greyhounds that would fight viciously alongside their Spanish masters.[3]

On August 16, 1519, Cortés assembled his troops in rank and file and spoke to them above the huff and snort of the horses and snarling hounds. They were a "holy company" of men about to engage in their own crusade, he said. They must "conquer the land or die," but belief in their savior would carry them to victory, as there was no option to turn back. "This assurance must be our stay," he hollered, "for every other refuge is now cut off, but that afforded by the Providence of God, and your own stout hearts!"[4] The men cheered, buoyed by the

---

*Though the Mesoamericans did invent wheels to use for children's toys, they never considered building larger ones for use as traction devices or transportation, in part because they lacked proper draft animals for such purposes but also because much of the terrain was unsuitable, especially during the rainy seasons. See Charles C. Mann, *1491* (New York, 2005), 19, 222–23.

rousing speech, and the train of warriors and bearers and beasts lurched forward into the unknown.

They marched westward, in the direction of Jalapa. Fit and knowledgeable Totonac scouts ran ahead on reconnaissance forays, returning periodically to report to Cortés the lay of the land and any hostile movements among the native populations. The conquistadors and their allies trekked through thick forests populated by ocelots and jaguars, into surreal and pungent stands of dense cacao and luscious vanilla, and across cultivated fields of maize and maguey plants and nopal cactus.[5] From high above them in the crowded jungle canopy came the shrill, cacophonous caw of parrots and macaws and the eerie buzz of iridescent insects unlike anything they had ever encountered. The route rose gradually into the Cordilleras, climbing up and up to the great Mexican tableland plateau, then up unmercifully steep trails. The air thinned and cooled as they rose to four thousand feet. To the southwest Cortés and his men stared in wonder at the gigantic, snowcapped dome of Orizaba, soaring nearly nineteen thousand feet above sea level, over twice as high as any mountain in their native Spain. Called "Star-Mountain" by the Mexicans, perhaps because of its fiery eruptions, it is the highest peak in Mexico, visible from a hundred miles off, and as such it engenders awe and reverence.[6] Temperatures plummeted as the conquistadors ascended. The poorly clad Cempoalan bearers shivered against the bitter cold, borrowing extra clothes and blankets from the Spaniards. Some fell gravely ill. After two days of forced marching on trails choked with thorny vines and *grandillas*, or passion flowers, they reached the town of Jalapa, at the far reaches of the Totonac boundaries.[7] There they rested for the night, being well treated, then kept on.

The route climbed again, up and over six thousand feet, passing through Coatepec, then on to Xicochilmaco, a walled fortress village and Aztec settlement. The Spaniards passed through unmolested and continued the long, cold slog, day and night, ascending to a steep and mountainous pass that Cortés named Puerto del Nombre de Dios (now called Bishop's

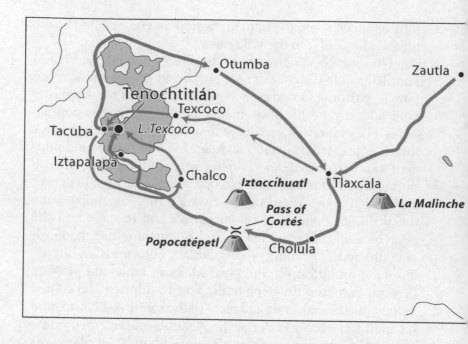

Pass). Harsh winds hurtled down the narrow canyon, followed by a severe mountain storm that pounded Cortés and his men with rain and sleet and biting pellets of hail, soaking them to the skin. Three of the Cuban porters perished from exposure in the high mountains of the Cofre de Perote.

The train of conquistadors and bearers pushed on, descending now from the rugged highlands onto a vast and desolate plain, a dry and barren sun-pocked pan. They swung north in the direction of the Río Apulco, skirting a massive salt lake, and marched for three days across the seemingly interminable plain, depleting all their stores of food and, worse, all their fresh water. Men, parched to delirium, knelt and sucked the water from brackish lagoons, but the salinity was so high it only made them thirstier, and some grew sick and vomited as they staggered along. Finally, after nearly a week of constant marching, they climbed again, as the austere maguey desert yielded to rough, flinty ridges. The narrow trails led Cortés and his ragged men to the town of Xocotlán (now called Zautla).[8]

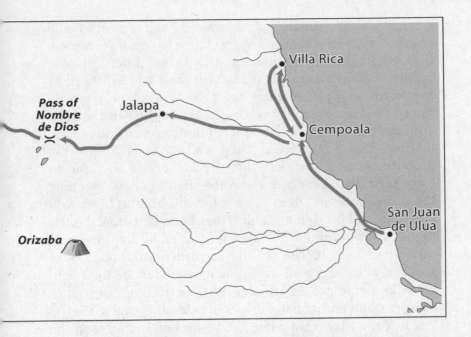

Exhausted, scorched, and ravenous with thirst, the Spaniards were now dangerously vulnerable, but by good fortune Olintetl, the chief of Xocotlán (and reportedly even fatter than the Cempoalan ruler), received them kindly, providing shelter, warmth, and food for Cortés and his men. Once rested and fed, Cortés made an inspection of the town, which was by far the largest they had passed through since leaving the coast and Cempoala, with a population of perhaps twenty thousand. In the town square Cortés discovered a giant skull rack (or *tzompantli*) displaying thousands of human skulls arranged in neat rows, beside which were great piles of thighbones and arm bones bleached white and luminous in the sun. Most shocking and repugnant to Cortés were the fifty or so recently sacrificed corpses, disemboweled and bathed in blood, and a large statue of the war god Huitzilopochi bespattered and still dripping with the lifeblood of these sacrificial offerings.

Cortés could not have understood that these skulls and corpses were the aftermath and remnants of complex and elaborate seasonal religious rituals that the native inhabitants considered essential, even vital to every aspect of their survival. Such sacrifices, they believed, ensured the daily rising of the sun. War captives were ceremonially led to high altars and sacrificed by five priests who placed each victim on his back on a special stone that depicted the sun. One priest held down the right arm, another the left, and two more priests splayed and pressed down the legs. A final priest clamped a large collar around the prisoner's neck while the village chief hoisted an obsidian blade high, then plunged it into the victim's chest. Opening the cavity, he would then remove the still-beating heart with his hands and lift it in a highly stylized and ceremonial offering. The steam from the heart was believed to carry a special message to the sun. The skull racks, made from thousands of sacrifice victims, served as constant reminders of their religion's immense power. Human ritual sacrifice also served to bring rain and ensure harvest, as well as fertility, enacted in the Feasts of the Flaying of Men, the Festival of Toxcatl, and the New Fire Ceremony.[9]

Cortés brought Malinche forward and through her asked Olintetl if he was a vassal of Montezuma. Olintetl waited a long time before answering, appearing both amused and amazed at the question. "Who is there that is *not* a vassal to Montezuma?"[10] was his curt and quizzical reply. Cortés assured Olintetl that he most certainly was not, and that he and his men served an emperor of their own in a far-off land to the east who had vassals and kingdoms to equal or surpass those of Montezuma. Not to be outdone, Olintetl launched into a cataloguing of Montezuma's empire, which he claimed spanned some thirty kingdoms of more than 100,000 warriors each. Cortés and his captains listened intently, sensing hyperbole in the claims but circumspect enough to be impressed and a little intimidated. What if the claims were true? Most interesting were Olintetl's detailed descriptions of the capital city Tenochtitlán, which he said was an impenetrable fortress on a great lake, accessible only by three major causeways containing removable bridges. When these were removed, no one could enter or leave the city except by canoe. The city's beauty was indescribable, Olintetl said, adding that the reach and power of Montezuma's empire was so great that over the years he had amassed riches of gold and silver beyond imagining, much of it won in his conquests over neighboring city-states.[11]

This last bit of information certainly piqued Cortés's interest, and he inquired whether Olintetl himself possessed any gold, as he wished to obtain samples to bring back to his emperor in their native land of Spain. Olintetl nodded that yes, he had some gold, but was unauthorized to give any to the Spaniards without the direct permission of Montezuma. Cortés, miffed by the rebuke, replied that soon enough he would be getting gold directly from Montezuma, whom he was on his way to visit. Still disgusted by the evidence of very recent human sacrifice, Cortés launched into his patented catechism on the virtues of Christianity and the evils of false worship, going so far as to suggest erecting a cross at the main prayer house, but Father Olmedo counseled the captain-general otherwise, suggesting that the act might provoke hostilities. Cortés took his advice and refrained.

Cortés remained in Xocotlán for four days; his troops were given meager supplies of food but enough to subsist on. The Spaniards were impressed by the town's organization, noting the carefully planted and tended agriculture: rows of giant cactus, and great plantations of maguey, their wide green leaves striped with yellow and their bright yellow flowers blooming on lengthy stems. The paddles of the nopal cactus, they learned, were stripped of their spines and eaten, and the juice from within the maguey plant was fermented into an alcoholic drink called *octli* (now called *pulque* and still consumed in Mexico today). The Spaniards learned, too, that the towns had laws against public drunkenness.[12] While they rested, the Spaniards were visited by fascinated townspeople curious to see their horses, dogs, and strange metal weaponry. Some onlookers stared warily from a distance, then ran away. The Spaniards bragged that their horses could run men down from great distances; their weapons could level entire armies from leagues away.

Many of these highlanders assumed the conquistadors and their horses to be gods, and the Spaniards said nothing to contradict the belief. They even encouraged the local belief that their dogs were vicious killers and that they could unleash either lions or tigers at will.[13]

Before departing, Cortés sent four Cempoalan chiefs ahead toward Tlaxcala. They carried letters (and were to convey the message verbally as well, since the Spanish-language letters were a formality and, at any rate, would not have been understood) stating that the Spaniards were coming soon, in peace, hoping to forge an alliance. The four chiefs also took some gifts: Spanish hats, a crossbow, and a sword—these last symbols of power. Cortés then asked Olintetl which route he ought to take to reach the Aztec capital. The chief recommended going through the town of Cholula, a city and shrine sacred to its former inhabitant, Quetzalcoatl. Some of the Cempoalans traveling with Cortés counseled against this choice, arguing that not only was the route longer, but Cholula was a heavily fortified Aztec outpost, and additionally the Cholulans were not to be trusted. By contrast Tlaxcala, on an alternate route, had never been conquered by Montezuma, and it was the Tlaxcalans' allegiance that Cortés sought. Plus, the route through Tlaxcala was shorter. Cortés pondered the advice as he readied to leave.

Olintetl came personally to see off Cortés and his troops, who were lined in tight formation. He offered a few gifts to Cortés—some cloth, a few lizards and small pendants of gold, some necklaces, and, most useful, four women to grind the local maize for bread—and bade the strangers farewell.[14]

The rested army, with Cortés at the head, moved out, snaking through the long valley of the Río Apulco, through a large town called Iztaquimaxtitlán. There they were also treated with guarded friendliness, apparently at the behest of Montezuma, whose spies and messengers roamed far and wide and reported the Spaniards' precise movements and locations. Here Cortés waited briefly for any response from his Cempoalan messengers, but there was no sign of them, so he pressed forward.

Unknown to Cortés, his native messengers had successfully reached the capital of Tlaxcala and had presented the gifts, letters, and message to the nobles there; but they had been immediately imprisoned, their release pending an inquiry by a high council. Through their own messengers and spies, the Tlaxcalans had discovered that already, along his route, Cortés had conducted several meetings with Aztec officials, and these dealings between the Spaniards and their arch-enemies made them nervous. They were especially dubious of any claims of peace and friendship, suspecting that the Spaniards might well have formed an allegiance with the Aztecs and were going to attack them. The Tlaxcalan nobles agreed that rather than be passive, they should be proactive. They would allow the Spaniards to enter their borders, then ambush them when the time was right. Some of the guards are reported to have taunted and threatened the imprisoned Cempoalans, saying, "Now we are going to kill those whom you call *teules* and eat their flesh. Then we shall see whether they are as brave as you proclaim. And we shall eat your flesh, too, since you come here with treasons and lies from that traitor Montezuma."[15]

Leaving the Zautla Valley, Cortés determined to take the shorter route toward Tlaxcala. After about ten miles he and his force approached a massive stone wall nearly ten feet high and twenty feet thick, which stretched a remarkable five miles across the valley. They halted and warily considered its elaborate construction, complete with defensive positions for archers and spear-throwers. They had reached the formal border of Tlaxcala, the great battlement constructed to ward off Aztec attacks. Cortés's men debated the virtues of entering the potentially hostile Tlaxcalan territory, especially since the messengers had failed to return. The fiercely independent Tlaxcalans might view their entrance as aggressive. But the tremendous fortification's single opening appeared unmanned, and deciding on action over discussion, Cortés urged his men through, the Spanish flag flapping from the staff of the standard-bearer.[16] Frozen winds howled down the valley flanks as the men rode and soldiers marched at the ready.

Cortés rode at the head of the vanguard, flanked by cavalry. As they reached the foothills of some mountains, he spotted a small group of fifteen Indians, armed for battle with two-handed obsidian swords, shields, and feather headdresses; seeing horses for the first time in their lives,* the Indians fled, scattering for the low hills. These were Otomi scouts, allies of the Tlaxcalans charged with monitoring the Tlaxcalan borderlands. Cortés pursued them at a canter, making hand signals in an attempt to convey that they came with peaceful intentions, but the presence of the large, loud, snorting animals only increased the Otomis' retreat.

Cortés sent horsemen to capture them, but the Otomis shrieked and wailed, and when the speedy Spanish horses overtook them, they turned and fought viciously, showing utter disregard for the charging animals, slashing at their necks and throats with their two-handed swords. One organized group of warriors unseated two riders and impaled their horses with spears, then beat them to the ground with stone-studded clubs. Chanting, they dragged the horses off, decapitated and dismembered them, and eventually (Cortés would later discover) distributed the remains of the horses among their villages in defiant triumph, offering the iron horseshoes up to their gods.[17]

Cortés dispatched infantry divisions, who quickly overwhelmed the remaining tenacious fighters, killing fifteen. Ten Spaniards had been seriously injured, and one of the cavalrymen died later from his wounds. Then, Cortés and his men saw, emerging from behind a rise, a moving throng of Tlaxcalan warriors numbering in the thousands, their faces painted brightly to signify their martial honors and accomplishments and ranks. Those who had previously taken captives wore red

---

*Cortés, it will be remembered, was the first to reintroduce horses to Mexico since their extinction from the northern hemisphere during the Ice Age.

and yellow. Warriors acknowledged for their courage and valor wore long black stripes on their faces; still others—"shorn ones"—wore shaved heads painted half blue and half red.[18] They came forward in organized ranks, which Cortés had not seen in Indians before. They were clearly a battle-honed fighting force, their shields and swords and helmets and crests bearing colorful insignia depicting ancient rulers, war gods, and even glorious battles of the past. Their insignia indicated rank and were taken so seriously that wearing insignia to which one was not entitled was punishable by death.[19] As the Tlaxcalans neared, they fired arrows and spears and piercing darts, hurled from special throwers called *atlatls*, and these missiles rained down on the Spaniards, who held their shields above them in defense. Under siege, Cortés called forth artillery and musketeers and crossbowmen, and his men assembled in offensive positions. The Tlaxcalans sent a group of warriors charging forward, and seeing the great numbers advancing and the waves coming behind in support, many of the Spanish soldiers feared for their lives. But by now the rest of the cavalry had also arrived, and after a brief but intense battle, the Tlaxcalans retreated, hauling their dozens of dead with them.[20]

Cortés wearily encamped his troops by a river and placed cannons on the perimeter, leaving the remaining horses saddled in case of a night attack. As they had no oil of their own, the Spanish soldiers who served as field physicians dressed their wounded with the melted fat obtained from dead Indians. They killed and cooked a number of small domesticated dogs that they found in deserted nearby villages, picked wild figs called *tuna*, and rested. That night his soldiers slept fitfully, trembling next to the cold streamside, their weapons clutched to their chests, their hands freezing. Cortés was uneasy, too, for he understood now that one of his tactical advantages had been undermined: the Tlaxcalans had discovered that the horse and rider were not one, and that each was as mortal as they were.[21]

At dawn the next morning Cortés roused his men, briefly discussed tactics with his captains, and then set off into the

rising sun toward the capital city of Tlaxcala. When they reached
a small village, they encountered two of the Cempoalan messengers, who huddled along the roadside, wailing in tears and
shaking in fear. They had been caged and were being prepared
for sacrifice, they explained, but had managed to escape when
news that the Spaniards had crossed the border wall sent the
city into commotion. They reported to Cortés that he and his
men were heading into an ambush. The Tlaxcalans and their
Otomi allies fully intended to attack, sacrifice, and even eat
them.[22]

Cortés had very little time to contemplate the implications
of this warning, for as soon as they advanced out onto a flat
plain, they saw on the horizon a horde of armed Otomi warriors, perhaps a thousand strong, who signified an imminent
frontal attack by chanting and stomping, blowing conch-shell
trumpets and pounding on drums, and shaking spears and
bows at the oncoming Spaniards. The instruments, employed
at the front, were used for tactical communication and to direct troop movements. The unit leaders bore tall feathered
standards called *cuachpantli*, which could be seen from great
distances, and armies followed these standards.[23]

Hoping to avoid a conflict, Cortés, along with Malinche,
Aguilar, and a few others, went forward. They brought notary
Diego Godoy to legally record the proceedings, and they presented the warriors with a handful of prisoners taken in the
previous day's skirmish. This gesture of peace, however, served
only to antagonize the Otomis, who shrieked and whistled and
leaped up and down shouting out the name of their town in
defiance, as was their warfare practice. Then they began throwing darts and spears.[24]

With conflict imminent, Cortés spoke encouragingly to
his men, instructing his infantrymen to thrust the points of
their swords through the enemy's bodies. The cavalry he urged
to lope at half-speed, leveling their lances at the Indians' heads,
and to avoid having the lances grabbed and the riders pulled
from the horses. He ordered them not to break ranks under any
circumstances, no matter how dire. The crossbowmen and

harquebusiers would support the flanks, and he urged them to fire constantly once the battle commenced. With a few final words of inspiration, Cortés and his force rushed forward.

The initial attack went well for the Spaniards. In the first few hours they killed and wounded a great number of the Otomis, who began to retreat into stands of woods and the mouth of a narrow canyon. Encouraged by the relative ease of their assault, Cortés pushed his men forward, but an astounding sight on either side of the ravine, extending to the open plains, gave him pause, and he reined his horse hard. The scene was truly daunting: an assemblage of warriors the likes of which he had never before witnessed, a massive army of perhaps forty thousand Tlaxcalan warriors, stood in great lines above and around them, stretching across an enormous plain. The naked common soldiers were brightly painted, and among them many chiefs and leaders continuously stomped and chanted and shrieked, their bodies draped in ornate feather costumes, their war helmets, embedded with gold insignia and precious stones, glinting in the morning light.[*25]

Bernal Díaz later wrote of the encounter, "They put so much fear into us that many of the Spaniards asked for confession."[26]

Though the numerical odds certainly did not favor him, Cortés understood that order, discipline, and superior weaponry were his only hope of survival. He moved his army cautiously forward in a tight quadrangle, stumbling with difficulty over undulating, broken ground that slowed even the horses. Soon an advance force of Otomis, whose excellent archers and throwers hurled missiles at them, stormed forward; the Indians threw darts and even stones as they came into hand-to-hand combat. Cortés's well-trained forces remained orderly despite the onslaught. His harquebusiers and crossbowmen fired

---

*The exact number of Tlaxcalan warriors is impossible to determine. Cortés, prone to exaggeration, estimated the army at over 100,000, while Bernal Díaz offered the more modest 40,000. Other sources confirm that Chief Xicotenga could quickly assemble, for battling the enemy Aztecs, an army of 40,000.

volley after volley at the charging enemies, and his infantry-men inflicted great damage with their tempered steel blades, which shattered their opponent's brittle obsidian swords on contact and impaled the mostly naked Indians. As a result of an embargo initiated by Montezuma, they possessed not even cotton armor.

Throughout the day Cortés pressed his army forward and repelled the Tlaxcalans, who poured forth again and again in unceasing droves, many mowed down in their tracks by can-non fire. Once or twice the sheer number of Indians was so overwhelming that the Spaniards did break ranks, but Cortés and his generals managed to reorganize them, and they some-how maintained their marching, four-sided fighting force of just over three hundred. During the repetitive attacks, cavalry-man Pedro de Moron was yanked from his mare and slashed repeatedly with obsidian swords, and though three cavalrymen came in support and pulled him to safety, his mare was killed and decapitated, and Moron himself died a few days later. But the Spaniards had inflicted a great deal of damage with their crossbows and guns and cannons, and miraculously, at day's end, the Otomi front guard and supporting Tlaxcalans re-treated.

The Spaniards nursed their wounds, which were consider-able, in a small abandoned hilltop village called Tzompach, which provided overlooks for guards. Cortés must have been somewhat encouraged that—other than Moron, who was fa-tally wounded—not a single Spaniard had died in the battle. But the rest of the troops he inspected were in dismal condi-tion. Many were cut and bleeding, badly wounded. These un-fortunates were cauterized and dressed with more searing fat obtained from slain Indians. Most of the horses were injured—slashed and bludgeoned even through their protective armor—and some limped, or stood lamely. Cortés himself began to convulse from bouts of malarial fever. Using an abandoned pyramid as a fort, he had some of his blacksmiths and carpen-ters fix broken crossbows and fashion more arrows. It was a tense and windy night on the deserted hilltop village. The

Spaniards knew they had narrowly escaped with their lives, but they did not know that part of the reason they had been "spared" lay in battle tactics. The goal of the Tlaxcalans (as later with the Aztecs), and indeed the design of their weapons, was to wound or injure in order to be able to take live prisoners for sacrifice, not necessarily to kill enemies on the battlefield. Great honor was bestowed on warriors who brought in leaders or chiefs alive. Cortés and his men lay in fear of what tomorrow might bring.

That night, his men hungry and exposed to the elements, Cortés brought Malinche and Aguilar to interrogate a few prisoners. One of the men was especially defiant, boastful, and arrogant. According to Malinche, he was related to Xicotenga the Elder, chief of the capital city of Tlaxcala. He warned Cortés that Xicotenga the Elder and his son, also named Xicotenga, were assembling more than 100,000 troops and that the Spaniards should surrender or else be defeated, captured, and then die at their captors' hands. Undaunted, Cortés gave him and a few other prisoners beads and sent them away with a stern message: we come in peace and wish only to pass through your lands on our way to see and speak with Montezuma. We come as your allies and brothers, but if we are further impeded, we will annihilate everything in our path. When these released prisoners made it to the camp of Xicotenga the Younger and conveyed to him Cortés's message, he simply scoffed. According to Bernal Díaz, the brash young warrior "replied that we could go to the town where his father was, and they would make peace with us by filling themselves with our flesh and honoring their gods with our hearts and blood."[27]

The next day the Tlaxcalans did not attack. Instead, they sent a delegation bearing a significant amount of food, including more than three hundred turkeys and hundreds of baskets of fresh maize cakes. Though Cortés and his men needed and relished the food, he quickly surmised that these gifts were merely a ruse to allow spies to assess the condition of his men, animals, and weaponry. He immediately had these men arrested and confined, and he decided that next morning, fueled by the fowl and cakes, he would march and meet the Tlaxcalans head-on if they had not by that time agreed to a truce.

Sunrise over the headland afforded Cortés and his men a daunting vista. Through the clear, cold air they could see the great army of the Tlaxcalans amassed on the cinderland below them, their mixed troops (including Otomis) finely bedecked for battle and arranged in tightly bunched squadrons. The thump of drums and mournful moans of conch shells resonated across the sprawling expanse. The Spaniards said their prayers, mustered and mounted, and marched and rode into what Bernal Díaz described as "a dangerous and perilous battle."[28]

Led by Xicotenga the Younger, a massive army swarmed the valley, the red-dyed warriors shrieking as they surged forward. But Cortés and his well-schooled divisions had planned for a mass attack, and his disciplined ranks held tight, despite a horrendous initial attack in which "stones sped like hail from their slings, and their barbed and fire-hardened darts fell like corn on the threshing floor, each one capable of piercing any armor or penetrating the unprotected vitals."[29] The Tlaxcalans hurled stone-tipped spears and charged, protecting themselves with leather-covered wooden shields.

But their numbers were so great as to prove a disadvantage. When they charged en masse, tightly bunched, they became easy targets for sustained crossbow volleys; the Spanish arrows mowed down dozens of warriors at a time. Artillerymen fired cannons into the mass—each heavy metal ball dropped many men and caused havoc and confusion among the Tlaxcalan squadrons, some of which dispersed. Seeing this disorder, Cortés sent cavalry in teams of four, which would gallop out, their riders slung low, slashing the steel swords with devastating impact, cutting down scores of warriors, then wheeling the horses back to their lines to rest and regroup, while another team went out. The Iberian horses and their riders, working in unison, became a killing machine, and the effect was terrifying for Xicotenga the Younger and his troops, who had never witnessed such efficient and frightening foes. To complicate matters, Xicotenga the Younger and one of his main captains were embroiled in a bitter dispute over tactics, so that even when directly ordered, young Xicotenga's captain proved insubordinate, refusing to support his leader or dispatch troops to his aid. Try as he might, despite sending wave after wave of his own men to their deaths, Xicotenga the Younger could not extricate the Spaniards from their position. As the Tlaxcalans retreated, they dragged their dead and wounded from the field, attempting to conceal their losses by scooping handfuls of dirt and parched grass from the ground and tossing it into the air, creating a low-lying dust cloud. By nightfall, both sides had returned to their own camps.[30]

Spanish losses were again astonishingly minimal. Though fifty or sixty men had been wounded, and now all of the horses were cut and at least slightly injured, only one Spanish soldier is reported to have died that day, and Cortés made sure he could not be discovered by the enemy. He ordered this man (and a few others who died later, from their wounds or the elements) to be buried deep beneath a house to avoid detection; he thereby hoped to maintain the perception that he and his men were immortal. The Spaniards remained in the hilltop village, utterly exposed on the ground. The night temperatures dropped dangerously low, and biting wind howled down from the surrounding snow-covered mountains and volcanoes. With his men hungry and shivering, Cortés dispatched yet another messenger to Tlaxcala, reiterating his desire for peace and brotherhood.

In Tlaxcala, the high council met, perplexed by their force's failure in the battlefield and wishing to determine the reason for it. The council gathered their finest wizards and shamans and soothsayers to look toward the stars for answers. They carefully studied the alignment of the constellations, consulted prophecies, and sacrificed many slaves, and after much contemplation, they returned to the council with the determination that though the Spaniards were not necessarily gods, still they received their power (as their own gods did) from the sun.[31] Therefore they must be attacked at night, when their powers were diminished. The notion was debated vigorously, especially among the chief Tlaxcalan military advisers, who were less than confident in night warfare, which they rarely if ever employed. After much argument, they agreed upon a night attack. As quietly as they could, some ten thousand Tlaxcalan warriors moved into position on the plain below Cortés's encampment.

The night was clear, illuminated by the rising autumn moon, and as usual Cortés had sentries posted on all sides of his camp. The sentries noted mysterious movements below and reported them immediately to Cortés, who roused his men quietly and whispered commands to his captains. They were to descend the hill in small divisions, conceal themselves in ditches and low depressions in the ground and in the maize fields, and when ordered, they were to erupt from the ground in a counterambush. As the Tlaxcalans approached, Cortés took his cavalry and small, fast regiments of harquebusiers and cannons and caught the Tlaxcalans unprepared on the open ground. The vaporous shadows of the horses and their thundering charge, the lightning flashes and deafening explosions of cannon fire, sent Xicotenga's forces fleeing in terror. The horses easily overtook many, wounding great numbers and killing more than twenty. The rest fled to report the grim news of the defeat to their leaders and soothsayers. Word of these miraculous victories would soon spread across the land, borne by terrified messengers to the Valley of Mexico.[32]

The Tlaxcalan high council met again, now utterly stymied. Many, including the sage Xicotenga the Elder, concluded that the Spaniards had proved themselves invincible during both day and night, and he argued that they ought to make peace now. But his son, brash and warlike, argued that he had seen the slain beasts of these supposed *teules* and had personally seen numbers of the soldiers wounded. They bled and, he believed, died as men. Divided, the Tlaxcalans agreed to once more send messengers to the Spanish camp to discover what they might.

Cortés was pleased by his night victory, though the warring was taking a toll on the men, some of whom were now hypothermic (a condition they would not have understood), and many, including Cortés, were suffering from malarial fever and salt deprivation. The mood in the camp was mixed, with some renewed grumblings among the ragged men about going home, and Cortés was forced to assuage their morale with promises of wealth, adding that it was better "to die in good cause than to live dishonored."[33]

About this time Cortés noted with great interest a small entourage of six Aztec nobles entering his camp on the hill, where he had now been for over a week. During the entire campaign between the Tlaxcalans and the Spaniards, Aztec runners and spies had kept the emperor apprised daily of the battles and outcomes. Montezuma seemed dismayed by the fierce Tlaxcalans' (whom he himself had failed to pacify) inability to subdue their foes. Now he sent the Spaniards a small embassy and their servants bearing an array of gifts: cotton garments, some lovely feather pieces, and a good deal of gold. The Aztec nobles expressed Montezuma's congratulations on their successful battles and warned Cortés not to trust the Tlaxcalans. Then they proposed a deal. Montezuma offered these gifts to Cortés and would submit to becoming a vassal of Spain, paying to the king an agreed-upon annual sum in tribute in the form of gold, slaves, women, and jade, if Cortés and his men would agree to return home immediately, forgoing their intended trek to Tenochtitlán, which would be too difficult anyway.

Cortés thanked the Aztec nobles kindly and willingly took the gifts but declined to return to Spain just yet. He expressed once again that he had specific instructions from his own emperor to personally visit Montezuma, and he did not wish to disappoint his ruler. He really had no choice in the matter. He bade them to return to Montezuma, explain the situation to him, and request once more a formal meeting.

A few days after the night raid, an entourage of fifty Tlaxcalans arrived with food, which revived the Spanish troops both physically and mentally. The famished men were gorging on roasted fowls, warmed maize cakes, and local figs and cherries, when Malinche informed Cortés that a good number of these "messengers" were actually spies, for she had seen them inspecting the perimeter of the camp and making notes concerning the condition of the men and horses. Cortés, enraged, had the men arrested, then questioned under physical duress. He was able to induce confessions from most. They were indeed spies sent by Xicotenga to assess the camp and troops for signs of weakness. As brutal punishment and to send a definitive message, Cortés assembled seventeen of the Tlaxcalan spies and had some of their thumbs amputated, then sent them back to Xicotenga with a clear warning: Submit or we will destroy you.*[34]

At least some of the dismembered spies made it back to Tlaxcala to display their maimed hands, because shortly afterward a delegation returned bearing much food and a message that soon the great warrior himself, Xicotenga the Younger, would arrive to make peace. The next day he indeed came, surrounded by many other Tlaxcalan noblemen and chiefs from the four main towns. They brought some gifts, apologizing for their modest nature but explaining that they were poor and that effective trade for goods had been impeded by their Aztec enemies. The warrior told Cortés that he was impressed with the captain's artistry on the battlefield and that the Spanish soldiers had defeated his finest, most skilled warriors. He apologized for the attacks on the Spaniards but explained that he had truly believed them to be allied with Montezuma and the Aztecs, their arch-enemies. The Tlaxcalans regretted not having been able to defeat the Spaniards, for they were a proud and defiant people, but now they were impressed and honored the Spaniards' military superiority. They wanted a

---

*A number of the chroniclers, including Cortés himself, say that he had the spies' entire hands removed, but this rings as exaggerated and highly unlikely, as they most certainly would have bled to death before reaching the city of Tlaxcala. Díaz mentions that Cortés had "some of their thumbs cut off," which seems more plausible.

truce. Xicotenga the Elder would be willing to strike a deal—they would agree to become vassals of Cortés and his king, if he would allow them to accompany his army in an attack against Montezuma and Mexico. Xicotenga the Elder had extended a personal invitation for Cortés and his men to come to Tlaxcala to rest from their battles, where they would be hosted like royalty.

Hernán Cortés nodded. He now had an army he believed sufficient to confront this man Montezuma, whoever he was and however powerful he might be.[35]

CHAPTER SIX

The Massacre of Cholula

CORTÉS WAS ELATED TO FINALLY LEAVE the rough and exposed hill of Tzompach behind. On September 23, 1519, three weeks after the first battle with the Tlaxcalans, he mounted his stallion and led his company to Tlaxcala. He came as an invited guest of Xicotenga the Elder, and here his bedraggled men and horses would rest and recover from the labors of invasion until they were fit enough to continue on to Mexico. Cortés insisted on bringing along a few remaining Aztec emissaries, to whom (and subliminally to Montezuma) he wished to demonstrate his allegiance with Tlaxcala and the force he was amassing.

Thousands of curious onlookers lined the streets as the Spanish army approached Tlaxcala after a trek of nearly thirty miles. Cortés and his men rode in as celebrated victors, the streets lined with flowers in anticipation of their arrival, and even inhabitants of outlying villages came to witness these strangers. Cortés was moved by the organization and layout of the city, remarking in a letter to his king: "This town is so big and so beautiful that all one could say about it would be unbelievable. It is bigger than Granada and better fortified. Its houses, its buildings, and the people that inhabit it are more numerous than at Granada at the time we conquered it, and very much better supplied with the produce of the land, namely bread, fowl, game, and fresh-water fish."[1] Robed priests along the route burned incense, their black hair tangled and matted with dried blood; their ears, recently mutilated in ritual sacrifice, dripped fresh blood. After dismounting and formally meeting the blind elder Xicotenga, Cortés followed a procession of hosts to his quarters, where his men were put up in large flat-roofed stone houses and palaces, and all the horses, many lame and limping, were provided with comfortable quarters. The Totonacs, who had fought bravely beside the Spaniards, were also given food. For three weeks the Spanish expeditionary force remained in Tlaxcala, gorging on fish and fowl at feasts and enjoying the company of some of the three hundred native women given Cortés as a gift in lieu of gold,* which their hosts claimed not to possess. By day they visited the bustling central market, where thousands of people from the region came to trade. Still, though they were being treated as royalty, Cortés positioned sentries and guards and instructed his men to sleep armed and ready.

While in Tlaxcala Cortés spent a great deal of time, flanked by Malinche and Aguilar, in conversations with nobles, elders, and members of the high council, who were remarkably forthcoming. Once their allegiance was formally and ceremonially sealed and Cortés had received assurances of significant Tlaxcalan military support, Cortés inquired pointedly about many aspects of the neighboring Aztecs and their ruler Montezuma. Xicotenga the Elder and his council informed Cortés that the great city of Tenochtitlán was, and had been for as long as they could remember, highly fortified and impenetrable. Its grandness was of a scale beyond measuring. The Tlaxcalans had managed to avoid complete conquest but only at very high costs. Montezuma maintained strict embargoes

*Cortés had said that he would accept them only if the Tlaxcalans would destroy their own idols and agree to give up human sacrifice; he later agreed to take them only if they were allowed to be baptized. Once they were baptized, Cortés distributed them among his men.

and blockades that denied the Tlaxcalan people many important trade items, including cotton goods (needed for armor), coveted gemstones, precious metals like silver and gold, and salt. The Tlaxcalans went on to describe, using hand-drawn illustrations on stretched maguey fiber, the Aztec arts of warfare and weaponry and even crucial details about the city, such as the fact that all its fresh water came from a single aqueduct at Chapultepec.[2]

Most interesting was the discussion of the generations-long Flower Wars that were held between the warring sides. Quite commonly practiced in the region (but utterly new and perplexing to Cortés), these were mock or staged battles between the finest warriors from each side, as well as young warriors hoping to prove themselves. More like competitions or tournaments than actual battles, these Flower Wars served a number of functions, including keeping the warriors practiced and trained for battle without killing them on such a scale as to deplete their forces. Most important, the winning side in a particular battle gained prisoners for human sacrifice, which both sides required (especially the Aztecs) in large numbers. Dressed in full regalia and fully armed, the enemies confronted each other at predetermined battlefields and engaged violently but took precautions to injure and subdue rather than kill. The Tlaxcalans and Aztecs had engaged in such staged wars for decades. Montezuma later boasted that his armies could have legitimately conquered the Tlaxcalans with ease anytime he wished, but the protracted Flower War provided convenient training for his men and never-ending sacrificial victims.[3]

While his soldiers rested, Cortés remained busy with diplomacy and military planning. He drafted a letter and dispatched it via mounted messenger to Juan de Escalante, who continued to hold down and construct the fort at Villa Rica de la Vera Cruz. He reminded Escalante of the importance of maintaining collegial relations with the Totonacs, who had fought bravely at his side. He instructed him to unearth from his personal quarters there two vats of wine and a sealed container of sacrificial wafers needed for mass and to send the messenger back with them immediately.

Roaming the city, some of Cortés's men came upon the disturbing sight of prisoners bound and pinioned inside wooden latticework cages. The prisoners were fed daily rations of a special diet designed to quickly fatten them for sacrifice and consumption. Seeing these unfortunates and their condition, Cortés railed against such practices, hoping to impress upon the Tlaxcalans the teachings and truth of Christianity, about which he lectured long and often through Malinche and Aguilar. He even suggested to the elders and nobles the benefits of destroying their own idols and replacing them with his, showing them illustrations and pictures of the Blessed Virgin Mary and the infant Jesus. They should convert immediately, submitting to baptism to avoid burning in a fiery hell in the afterlife. The elders, including Xicotenga, balked. They had no intention of forsaking their own gods. As in Cempoala, Cortés favored a forced conversion, but once more the judicious Father Olmedo argued for prudence, pointing out that real and lasting conversion took time and religious understanding, and at any rate the Spaniards certainly had no need to create conflict and tensions with their brand-new allies. And once more Cortés had the good sense to take the advice of his trusted religious counselor. For their part, in a remarkable show of religious concession and tolerance, the Tlaxcalans provided one temple where the Spaniards could erect a cross and worship their idols. Here Cortés had his priests hold daily public mass; the ceremonies were attended not only by his men but by scores of the city's inhabitants and those of neighboring villages.[4]

(Although Cortés is sometimes interpreted as feigning devotion and piety as a justification for his actions and behavior, he appears to have been authentically, deeply religious. As a product of his time and place, he could have believed in the rightness of his mission and viewed the conversion of the Mexican population—either forced, as he preferred, or by slower degrees and education, as his priests advised—as actually bringing them salvation. Obviously Cortés believed that he had much to gain financially and in terms of power by his mission of conquest, but his religious zeal as he marched through the country was at all times evident and consistent. He was to that end, in effect, the first man to sow the seeds of Christianity on the soil of the Americas.*)[5]

The Spanish men and horses and dogs were regaining strength, and Cortés discussed with his aides and captains their imminent departure and the best route to take. The Tlaxcalans and the Aztec emissaries who were accompanying him gave him conflicting opinions. The Aztec ambassadors vehemently urged Cortés to take the route through Cholula; its leaders, they claimed, were complacent allies of Montezuma and would treat the Spaniards well, and there he could await final word on Montezuma's decision to meet Cortés in person. The Tlaxcalans disagreed, countering that as allies of the Aztecs, the Cholulans could not be trusted—they were wicked and duplicitous people, and it might well be a trap. They argued for a route through the town of Huexotzinco, whose people were confirmed friends.

After some meetings and contemplation, Cortés opted to take the Aztec ambassadors as guides and go through Cholula, a decision that turned out to have both political and tactical reasons. To appease the disgruntled Tlaxcalans, who were visibly unhappy about his decision, Cortés offered presents of cloth to Xicotenga the Elder and said that he would happily now accept his host's offer of warriors to take along with him on his quest. The diplomacy worked, and the Tlaxcalan ruler offered an army of 100,000 men. Cortés thanked him for his generous support of his cause, adding that he would require only some six thousand at the moment.

On the tenth of October[6] Cortés mustered for departure.

---

*Cortés would eventually found a college for theology students training for the priesthood, a hospital, and a monastery, as well as provide financial endowments for the building and maintaining of Catholic churches.

With a train of Tlaxcalan and Totonac warriors and bearers that trailed for miles behind, accompanied by Montezuma's own ambassadors, Captain-General Hernán Cortés set out for Cholula. He was headed toward the city of Quetzalcoatl, at the time the most important pilgrimage destination in all of the Americas, famed because legend held that Quetzalcoatl, in his flight from ancient Tula (in Hidalgo, about 40 miles north of modern-day Mexico City) toward the Gulf Coast, had made his ceremonial first stop here.[7]

They marched most of the first day and camped that night on an exposed savanna; Cortés and his captains slept in slightly protected and sheltered ditches, with guards at watch. The next morning delegates from Cholula arrived, bringing turkey and maize cakes; the priests waved burning braziers to fumigate Cortés and his captains, while the robed dignitaries beat on drums and blew reed flutes and conch shells.[8] After some ceremony they invited Cortés and his men to come to Cholula, but they did not want the Tlaxcalans, their enemies, to accompany them. He thought about it, then acquiesced, telling the Tlaxcalans that they would need to wait outside the boundaries of the city proper while he conducted his business there. He appealed to their sense of pride by telling them that they could not enter because the Cholulans feared them.

Leaving the bulk of the Tlaxcalan force outside the city limits, Cortés led his cavalry, the Totonacs, and bearers into Cholula. Having been continuously inhabited for more than one thousand years (first by Olmecs, later by the people of Tula), the place was remarkably well kept, and the Spaniards were impressed as they rode in and first caught sight of the massive temple high on the hill overlooking the entire city, the great pyramid to Quetzalcoatl. One hundred twenty steps led to the top of the stunning structure, the largest free-standing man-made edifice in the world, twice as long as the great Egyptian pyramid of Cheops.[9] Highly revered as the former home of the man-god Quetzalcoatl, hundreds of thousands of pilgrims came to this towering holy center annually.[10] Cortés would say that Cholula was "more beautiful than any city in Spain, for it is very well proportioned and has many towers."[11] Organized and, to the Spanish mind, civilized (they noted freshwater wells), Cholula was a thriving city of more than 100,000 inhabitants, renowned widely for its fine pottery and craftsmanship in textiles, including jewelry. The Spaniards observed that the people here dressed in immaculate robes and took great care in their polished appearance.

Cortés and his captains were well housed and cared for initially, the food supplies—always of vital concern—sufficient. According to conquistador Andrés de Tapia, a young Spaniard of twenty-four who became a trusted captain under Cortés and one of the few chroniclers to produce a written account of the Mexico campaign, here the priests explained in detail aspects of the Quetzalcoatl myth that they had not heard before. When he founded the city, for example, he had commanded the people to cease the sacrifice of human beings and instead to build great temples "to the creator of the sun and heavens, in which to offer him quail and other things of the hunt."[12] The second day in Cholula another group of Aztec ambassadors arrived and asked for a meeting with Cortés, during which they said that the Cholulans had not the food stores to continue feeding the Spanish army, lest they themselves starve. (Cortés doubted the claim, having seen the size of their central marketplace.) They argued, additionally, that the road to Tenochtitlán was dangerous, barely passable, and that in the great city Montezuma possessed a magnificent zoo (he did), where fearsome animals like lions and alligators could be unleashed and set upon unwelcome visitors. This last was a thinly veiled attempt, perhaps issued by Montezuma himself, to keep the Spaniards from continuing their inexorable march toward the capital of Mexico. Cortés remained unmoved. He would take his chances with any savage beasts that might be loosed upon him.[13]

But the food supplies did indeed dwindle, then stop altogether by the fourth day, when they were offered only water, and some wood, presumably to cook their own provisions. And visits by Cholulan lower representatives (important civic leaders, despite requests by Cortés, had yet to make an appearance) diminished as well. Some of his Totonac bearers reported to Cortés that they had seen many people, carrying goods and possessions on their backs, leaving the city, women and children among them. More ominous still, rumors reached Cortés that large, covered trap-holes had been discovered in the streets, their bottoms lined with sharp stakes, and that a number of the city's streets had been cordoned off, with warriors positioned on rooftops, sitting next to huge piles of stones. Cortés had to wonder whether the Tlaxcalans had been right to suspect a trap.

Montezuma himself may have played a role in the perceived plot to ambush the Spaniards. While Cortés was battling the Tlaxcalans, Montezuma had summoned his high priests and oracles, seeking divine guidance in dealing with Cortés and these strange but powerful foreigners. He wished to discover their true nature and to see whether it might be possible to alter the prophecy of the second coming of Quetzalcoatl. After he spent days in intense meditation, an oracle came to him claiming to have experienced a vision, one that presaged that the Spaniards were destined to die in the great and sacred city of Cholula. Believing this prophecy, Montezuma immediately sent a division of his handpicked and best-trained warriors to Cholula, along with men carrying long poles to which they would tether the Spanish prisoners and lead them back to Tenochtitlán.[14]

Amazingly, a chance encounter by Malinche would propel Cortés toward his most uncharacteristic and perplexing act of the entire campaign. During their first few days in Cholula, Malinche had struck up a friendship with one of the local women, a wife of a Cholulan nobleman. The woman entertained Malinche in her home, fed her, and after a time suggested that for her own safety, Malinche should leave the Spaniards and come live with her—she could even provide a suitable husband, her son, for Malinche. Her husband was a captain in the Cholulan army, she informed Malinche, and the Cholulans, under Montezuma's orders, were massing a large force to attack the Spaniards on the road from Cholula to

Tenochtitlán. For their assistance in the ambush, the Cholulans would be given twenty Spaniards to sacrifice themselves. If Malinche wished to escape imprisonment and probable death by sacrifice, she should seek refuge with her.[15] But Malinche, now completely loyal to Cortés, convinced the noblewoman that she needed to get some things first, and she hurried to report her discovery to him.*

Cortés listened intently. The mood in the city was tense and ominous, and the exodus of the townspeople continued. Acting quickly on Malinche's intelligence, he rounded up a pair of Cholulan priests and bribed them with jadestone gifts; when they remained tight-lipped, he tortured them into submission. The priests admitted that as far as they knew, Aztec forces were indeed stationed outside the city, along the route to Tenochtitlán. The Cholulans' role was to help lead the Spaniards into the trap as they left the city. In preparation for a successful ambush, a special sacrifice was currently under way that included a handful of small children, both boys and girls. Cortés quietly fumed at this last, then demanded at swordpoint that they go to the city's chiefs and tell them that he wished to speak with them. When these nobles did arrive, Cortés calmly thanked them for their hospitality and informed them that he and his troops would be leaving in the morning so as to no longer burden the kind people of Cholula. They agreed to provide him with some bearers for his departure.

Cortés promptly convened his captains to discuss the situation. They disagreed about the best course of action, some suggesting they return to Tlaxcala or at the very least, should they proceed toward Mexico, take an alternative route. But Cortés

---

*Cortés mentions this episode in his second letter to King Charles V, and Malinche's "discovery" is widely and similarly reported by most of the Spanish chroniclers. Because the subsequent massacre is unprecedented by Cortés and might well have been unprovoked, the "discovery" rings to the skeptical ear as a bit too *convenient,* like an after-the-fact justification. For an intriguing argument against the likelihood of Malinche's discovery of this supposed "plot," see Ross Hassig, *Mexico and the Spanish Conquest* (Norman, Okla., 2006), 97–98.

had another idea, a punitive preemptive strike that would send a message reverberating through the badland plains and all across the Valley of Mexico.

Feigning preparations for departure, Cortés requested that all the lords of Cholula convene at the large central courtyard of the Temple of Quetzalcoatl, where he could bid them farewell. He also requested that his escort of Cholulan bearers be brought forth. Then he asked to speak with the leaders of the city, the main nobility, in private in his quarters. They came forth. Once they were inside, Cortés barred the doors. He accused them of conspiring with the Aztecs, said he knew of their plans and that for such treason they must die. The lords at first denied duplicity, but when pressed, they blamed the scheme on Montezuma, saying that as his subservient tributaries they had had no choice. By now the courtyard of the Temple of Quetzalcoatl had filled with Cholulans, including most of the city's dignitaries, as well as the many bearers Cortés had requested. Cortés waved for a harquebus to be fired, his signal for the massacre to commence. Spanish soldiers rode in and sealed off all the courtyard exits. The infantry—both Spanish and the few Tlaxcalans who had been allowed into the town—rushed the crowded courtyard, wielding their swords and spears, crossbowmen and harquebusiers in support. They fell upon the mostly unarmed populace in wholesale slaughter. Arrows whirred in horrific volleys, scything down scores in minutes as musket balls plowed others. Women and children ran screaming, many trampled by horses or by their own fleeing people. Some priests managed to escape to the top of the high Temple of Quetzalcoatl, from which spot they feebly hurled stones to defend themselves or, despondent, took their own lives. Witnesses later reported, "They hurled themselves from the temple pyramid...and they also hurled the idol Quetzalcoatl headfirst from the pyramid, for this form of suicide had always been a custom among them, and it was their custom...to die headlong. In the end, the greater part of them died in despair, by killing themselves."[16] Cortés ordered the temple set ablaze, and it burned for two days straight.

Within two hours nearly everyone who assembled in the courtyard had been slain. Uncharacteristically, Cortés then allowed many of his allied Tlaxcalans inside the city to vent their rage on their long-standing rivals. For hours the Tlaxcalans pillaged and burned houses, looted and slaughtered everyone they could find, until Cortés determined to put a stop to them lest they go on indefinitely, so inflamed was their bloodlust. By the time Cortés halted the butchery, nearly five thousand people lay dead on the stone streets of Cholula.

A great deal of gold and other precious items was looted from the palaces and homes of the nobles, and Cortés confiscated everything he could—though he had difficulty getting some back from the Tlaxcalans. Eventually Cortés ordered his men to clean the corpse-strewn city, removing the dead and scrubbing the place. What priests and nobles remained alive were brought forth, blamed for the slaughter, and instructed to send for their escaped friends and relatives, hiding in the plains or outlying villages, to return—no more harm would be done to them. Though this must have been difficult for them to believe, in time people did reluctantly start to return. Prisoners were released, and after a few days a semblance of order was restored.

As he had in Tlaxcala, Cortés found caged victims, including children, being held and fed for sacrifice, and he angrily broke the wooden bars and freed them. As usual, he instructed the Cholulan priests to cast aside their false gods in favor of his (who was clearly the more powerful) and subject themselves to Spanish authority. They agreed in principle to become allies and vassals, but as to the question of gods, they hedged, and once more Father Olmedo counseled Cortés to give conversion time.

The Aztec ambassadors had remained safely in hiding during the massacre, and now Cortés used their fear to his advantage. He told them that though the Cholulans had blamed Montezuma for planning an attack, he did not believe them, for Montezuma was a friend to the Spaniards and would never have perpetrated such a devious ploy. Cortés intimated that he still planned to march on Tenochtitlán, and he hoped and trusted that Montezuma would receive him peacefully. The Aztec ambassadors asked to send messengers to the capital to discover Montezuma's wishes, and Cortés allowed it.

With the massacre, Cortés had ensured a safe route between Cholula and Vera Cruz, which he figured would be crucial for resupply of arms, powder, and even men and horses, should any arrive from the islands. The smoke from the burning temples died down after a few days, and to alleviate continued Cholulan fears, Cortés again stationed most of the Tlaxcalans outside the city, but only after the two sides had agreed, begrudgingly, to a truce. Cortés and his men remained there, fed and hosted, for nearly two weeks, but the massacre sent shock waves through the land long afterward.

WHEN the messengers arrived in Tenochtitlán with explicit and detailed descriptions of the bloodbath in Cholula, Montezuma was stricken and perplexed. This style of slaying defied all protocols of traditional Aztec warfare. Even more confounding, Cholula was the spiritual house of Quetzalcoatl—how could his own shrine have been desecrated? How could Quetzalcoatl have allowed it to occur? It was inconceivable. The massacre cast doubt that this Spaniard, this Cortés, was really Quetzalcoatl. But that left an ominous question: who, then, was he?

Montezuma gathered a dozen of his highest priests to contemplate the matter. Cortés could still be a god, but which one? He might be a god of war, a demon of darkness, a deity of justice or punishment. Montezuma wondered what else he could possibly do to prevent these beings from arriving, or perhaps their arrival was preordained and could not be stopped. Maybe it was indeed the will of the gods. Montezuma and his priests climbed to the heights of their temples for meditation, fasting, and prayer. Visions appeared to Montezuma—he must sacrifice many men, which clearly the priests of Cholula had failed to do. For a week Montezuma remained alone, aloft in the temple sanctuary, fasting and waiting for signs. In the thin air he was visited by Huitzilopochtli—the hummingbird, god of war and sacrifice—who communicated with the emperor. After listening carefully to his gods, Montezuma at last left his sanctuary and descended the pyramid steps. He had come to a decision.[17]

AFTER a few days Aztec runners arrived at the Cholula city gates, runners sent from beyond the high mountains. Behind them trailed emissaries who asked for Cortés. Before him they laid offerings of food, many garments of the finest cloth, and, most impressive, ten plates of solid gold. The gods, and Montezuma, had spoken. The emperor would be willing now to receive Cortés. He was formally invited to come to Tenochtitlán.[18]

CHAPTER SEVEN

The City of Dreams

HERNÁN CORTÉS SPURRED HIS HORSES and men westward. They rose, the Spaniards and their great train of allied warriors in tow, winding up the scrubby sierra separating the vast plateaus of Mexico. Looking up, they glimpsed the enormous volcano Popocatépetl, its conical dome smoldering, spewing cinder ash and steam straight into the sky. As they marched higher, the horses' hooves kicked up fine ash and dust, cocooning them in a moving cloud. The Indians shuddered in fear, worried that their presence had angered the mountains. The Totonacs, who had never been this far from their homes in Cempoala, begged permission from Cortés to return to their coastal villages. Some of them were sick, growing queasy with the altitude. The looming mountains ahead, and the foreboding mysteries of the great Tenochtitlán, were more than they could bear. Cortés, appreciative of their assistance, plied them with presents and praise and sent them on their way, ensuring that one load of embroidered cloth be delivered directly to their chief. Cortés and his soldiers would now rely on Tlaxcalan bearers and those Caribbean and West African porters still with him to pull the heavy artillery up and over the mountain passes, and to grind and prepare their food. It was the first of November, viciously cold at night, the temperatures plunging well below freezing.

They lurched slowly up through the timbered foothills and then into the higher mountains. Men, sickened by great heights such as they had never before encountered, bent at the waist, coughing and gasping for air. The horses stumbled up the rocky trails, heaving and wheezing. Cortés began to wonder if he could lead them through this spare and hostile place, or if they would perish here on the mountain's flank. They progressed slowly, only a few miles each day, passing through tiny scattered villages where they would rest a day or even two, then press upward as biting winds hurtled down the narrow gorges; the poorly clad lowland and island bearers shivered through the nights. The Spaniards in full armor fared better, but they teetered as they climbed, burdened by the weight.[1]

As they approached the furiously smoking Popocatépetl (The Hill That Smokes) and its sister volcano Iztaccíhuatl (White Woman) Cortés watched a jet-plume shooting arrow-straight into the sky and decided to investigate this remarkable natural phenomenon. He dispatched Diego de Ordaz (a noted Velázquez man and coconspirator back at Vera Cruz, so perhaps Cortés wished to test his loyalty now) and nine fit soldiers to scout the mountain and determine whatever they could and whether it was dangerous. He might also, from high on the mountain, gain some view of the Valley of Mexico and Tenochtitlán. Ordaz took a handful of Tlaxcalan porters and began his ascent while Cortés moved slowly toward the pass between the two stunning snow-covered domes, where they camped and rested at a ridged col,* a pass named "The Sleeping Place." At this exposed and lonely depression, legend held that during Quetzalcoatl's flight from Tenochtitlán to Cholula, his followers, dwarfs and hunchbacks, had fallen asleep and frozen to death.[2] Cortés and his followers must have wondered if they would succumb to a similar fate, so frozen and exposed was the pass.

---

*"Col" is a pass or depression.

Ordaz and his men tramped slowly up the steepening terrain, game trails giving way to sheer talus slopes as they rose, up and up toward the sky, the air growing dangerously thin with every halting step of the boot. Stopping to rest at over thirteen thousand feet, they could see the summit beyond, but it remained elusive, a smoldering mirage in the distance. Here the Tlaxcalan porters began to murmur and shake with fear, saying that they would progress no farther, for they believed that beyond, inside the mountain, lurked evil spirits and malevolent gods. Ordaz took a compatriot and trekked on, hopping over lava streams, the shale and scree turning to snow as they rose up the massive living mountain. Snow and sleet and volcanic ash swirled around them, the heat from the dome almost unbearable as they came near the summit at almost eighteen thousand feet above the sea. Ordaz reported that he was just below the summit, a mere "two lances distant," before flames and fiery ash and burning stones made it unbearable to continue and their clothes began to catch fire.[3]

When the tremor subsided and they descended, the smoke diminished, and they gazed out from the mountain to the valley beyond, catching glimpses of the enormous city on the lake, or what appeared to Ordaz as "another new world of great cities and towers and a sea."[4] After a harrowing and dangerous descent over ice and snow, the two climbers managed to stagger down to safety, coughing and stumbling, their feet and hands numb with frost. They brought samples of snow, icicles, and cinder to show Cortés, who was impressed with Ordaz's tenacity and courage.*[5] Ordaz had also seen the way to Tenochtitlán, a track between the two mountains, which they followed (now called the Pass of Cortés). At length the company arrived on the ridge separating the two volcanoes, a fork in the main path. One of the roads was open, the other having

---

*Diego de Ordaz was himself so impressed with the volcano Popocatépetl that in 1525 he requested of his king, and was granted, the right to install the image of a smoking volcano on his family's coat of arms.

been blocked with trees and boulders. Cortés inquired of the Aztec guides why this was so, and they explained that the blocked road was the more arduous of the two, with poor footing and steep, rocky, dangerous sections. Sending Tlaxcalans forward to clear the debris, Cortés chose this route.

During that first week of November an early winter storm descended, fog and mist encircling them and snow coming down, lightly at first, then in pelting, blinding flakes. Cortés ordered camp made, using some of the downed trees barring their passage as shelter. They struck fires as they could, though the place was wet and windy. The night was deathly cold; men convulsed in their armor, and the Indians hunkered together to warm each other. Some of the captains found abandoned shacks, perhaps used by Indian traders, and sought shelter there.

By morning snow covered the ground, but the storm had subsided and the skies cleared. Cortés mustered and marched, the Tlaxcalans scrambling ahead to remove stumps and felled trees, and soon the group arrived at the top of the descent into the other side, overlooking the Valley of Mexico. Mist lifted like steam from the valley floor and afforded them views that left them breathless: the connected lakes and waterways glinting in the sun like iridescent blue gemstones, and houses magically built on them, and white trails of wood smoke lofting up from the many whitewashed houses that stretched out for miles. Surrounding and outlying the cities on the lakes were manicured, cultivated jade-colored fields of beans and maize, and beyond them, Tenochtitlán itself—grander and higher and larger than the other cities—seemed to float upon Lake Texcoco. They took it all in, amazed and even reverent, for they had never seen anything of its kind before, and many were left to simply gape in awe and wonder as they descended the steep switchback trail down into the valley.[6]

The trail snaked and wound sharply, and they eventually came to a large and well-appointed villa that, though abandoned, appeared to have been prepared and provisioned for their arrival. They found great quantities of food and fresh water, rooms large enough for shelter and rest, and fodder for the animals. There was even cut firewood laid by and ready to light, and neat walkways lined with trimmed plants and shrubs, the rooms decorated with wall hangings and draperies. Knowing that the place had been recently inhabited (and responding to reports that there were spies about), Cortés sent guards and sentries ahead and behind; he made certain that the horses remained saddled and the men were alert, but even with these precautions the men slept much better than they had on the snowy mountainside.

They passed the night without incident and early the next morning descended into the valley, passing through beautiful woods and small villages and eventually arriving at a town called Amecameca, home to nearly five thousand people. As they went, Cortés noted with great interest that the chiefs were vocal and forthcoming, often complaining about the high taxes they must pay to Montezuma, and how even their women, as well as their children, were often taken from them, along with valuable goods. Cortés filed the information, interpreting the discord so close to Tenochtitlán as a positive sign of potential future alliances, should he require them.[7]

During their descent they were also visited by yet another embassy of Aztecs, this one special, for Montezuma had included a handful of his best magicians and sorcerers who he hoped might be able to thwart the relentless approach of the Spaniards. The Aztecs reported that "Montezuma sent the magicians to . . . see if they could work some charm against them, or do them some mischief. They might be able to direct a harmful wind against them, or cause them to break out in sores, or injure them in some way. Or they might be able to repeat some enchanted word, over and over, that would cause them to fall sick, or die, or return to their own land."[8] Montezuma, running out of options and apparently becoming desperate, also sent an impersonator, a nobleman named Tziuacpopocatzin. He was to dress in regal finery, assume a kingly countenance and behavior, and claim to be Montezuma, the idea being that they could hold their formal meeting and then, just maybe, the Spaniards would turn back. They came bearing gifts, too, lovely featherwork of the quetzal bird and a good deal of gold, which sent the captains into a sort of delirium, for they were apparently still giddy from their high-altitude trek. Their response to the gifts was recorded by chronicler Bernardino de Sahagún,* who said they clung to the gold "like monkeys...they thirsted mightily for the gold, they stuffed themselves with it, and starved and lusted for it like pigs. They...showed it to one another, all the while babbling. What they said was gibberish."[9] Initially the Spaniards believed that the nobleman Tziuacpopocatzin might be Montezuma, for he claimed to be, but after consulting a number of the Tlaxcalans, Cortés determined that the man was of the wrong age and build, and the ruse was discovered.

The magicians and wizards, too, failed in their attempts, and the embassy returned to Montezuma with disconcerting news: all their witchcraft, spells, and conjurings were ineffective on these *teules*, these gods. Cortés, his cavalry and horses, and many thousand Tlaxcalans were still coming to Tenochtitlán. Montezuma sought more counsel, both from his priests and from his gods.

Cortés remained in Amecameca for two full days, where he was well housed and fed and given more gold as well as forty slave girls. He developed good relations with the city's chiefs, assuring them that soon he could relieve their burden of tribute to the Aztecs. Rested, he resumed his march, arriving next at the banks of Lake Chalco, the southernmost body of water in the lacustrine chain. The city teemed with thousands of people, and here the Spaniards watched with interest the many canoes pouring into and out of the town on the calm waters. Soon a very formal and official contingent of Aztec nobles arrived, bearing with them Cacama, Montezuma's nephew and king of Texcoco. They came, as Bernal Díaz remembered it, with

---

*A dedicated Dominican friar, Sahagún spent nearly forty years preparing his *General History of the Things of New Spain* (the Florentine Codex), a thirteen-volume work translated from Nahuatl Indians who were present before, during, and after the conquest. The work records every conceivable aspect of Aztec life and culture. (See "A Note on the Text and the Sources" at the end of the book.)

greater pomp and splendor than we had ever beheld in any Mexican prince. He came borne in a litter, most richly worked in green feathers with much silver decoration and precious stones set in tree designs that were worked with the finest gold. His litter was carried by chieftains, each of whom...was a ruler of a town. When they came near the house where Cortés was lodged, they helped the prince out of his litter, swept the ground, and removed the stones and straws from his way.[10]

Cacama faced Cortés and explained, through Malinche, that he regretted that the great Montezuma, his emperor, was unable to come himself but he felt ill. Cacama came to represent him in his stead and wished to extend every courtesy to Cortés and his men, who would now most certainly be his invited guests and would have a personal audience with Montezuma very soon. Until then, Cacama and his nobles and lords would escort the Spaniards to the city of Iztapalapa, and then into the capital, and they would have everything they would need along the way. Hearing this message and overcome with emotion, Cortés embraced the prince in an awkward (but customarily Spanish) hug, then hung from him a necklace of cut glass. He gave colored beads to the other attendees standing by.

Once these formalities were taken care of, Cortés followed his new dignitary hosts along the lakeshore, noting that crowds of curious onlookers flocked alongside the marching train. Soon they encountered the first of the marvelous causeways, a long straight road structure made of stone that ran some five miles across the water from Chalco to the adjoining Lake Xochimilco. The causeway was narrow—Cortés would say, only "as wide as a horseman's lance"—and they marched in growing awe and wonder as they neared the town of Cuitláhuac, which Cortés described as small but definitely "the most beautiful we had seen, both in regard to the well-built houses and towers and in the skill of foundations, for it is raised on the water."[11] His amazement was only being piqued. So too was that of Bernal Díaz, who remembered the place with

astonished wonder: "When we saw all those cities and villages
built in the water . . . and that straight level causeway leading to
Mexico, we were astounded. These great towns and temples
had buildings rising from the water, all made of stone, and it
seemed like an enchanted vision from the tale of Amadis.
Indeed, some of our soldiers asked if this was not all a
dream."[12] Cortés himself would refer to Tenochtitlán as "the
City of Dreams," exclaiming that it was without question "the
most beautiful thing in the world."[13]

When they arrived at Iztapalapa, Cortés was utterly impressed. The city was constructed next to a vast salt lake, half
on land and the other half suspended on foundations and pylons seeming to hover over water. It was the domain of
Cuitláhuac himself, brother of Montezuma and Cacama's uncle. Cuitláhuac invited Cortés and his men to stay there for
the night. They were shown about the nobles' villas, many
newly constructed, multistoried, and complete with kitchens
and outdoor terraced gardens connected by gorgeous stone
corridors lined by trees and herbs and flowers. The courtyards
and corridors were covered with awnings made of woven cotton, for shade and shelter. Cortés remarked that the craftsmanship and design surpassed anything built in Spain:

> They have . . . cool gardens with many trees and sweet-
> smelling flowers; likewise there are pools of fresh water, very
> well made with steps leading down to the bottom . . . In the
> garden is a large reservoir of fresh water, well built with
> fine stonework, around which runs a well-tiled pavement . . .
> Beyond the pavement, toward the wall of the garden, there
> is latticework of canes, behind which are all manner of
> shrubs and scented herbs. Within the pool there are many
> fish and birds, wild ducks and widgeons, as well as other
> types of waterfowl; so many that the water is often almost
> covered with them.[14]

Early the next morning Cortés gathered his troops and fitted them out in their most impressive battle regalia, determined

to march into the city in impressive fashion, but also because, despite their recent royal treatment, they would be exposed and vulnerable along the five-mile causeway. Ready, they rode and marched in strict order, scanning the periphery for danger, noting the crowds lining the lance-wide causeway for miles. Bernal Díaz chronicled their entrance:

> It was so crowded with people that there was hardly room for them all...The towers and the temples were full, and they came in canoes from all parts of the lake. And no wonder, since they had never seen horses, or men like us, before. With such wonderful sight to gaze on we did not know what to say, or if this was real what we saw before our eyes. On the lakeside there were great cities, and on the lake many more. The lake was crowded with canoes.[15]

The Spaniards marveled at the maritime architecture, such as they had never seen before. Small boats and canoes glided up and down an elaborate system of canals, the boats loaded with freshly harvested foods or handmade textiles and crafts for market. As they rode and marched, their mouths agape, they saw miraculous *chinampas*—floating gardens—islands of flowers and edible vegetables bobbing like living rafts along the waterways.*[16] The place appeared enchanted, like fairy tales they had been told as children, or told to their own.

Chinampas—fields constructed in the lakes of the Valley of Mexico—were a brilliant Aztec agricultural innovation beginning around 1450. It involved staking the lakebeds and dumping lake-bottom soil into these "enclosures," which created islands of extremely fertile soil (augmented with fertilizer that included human feces, a form of waste management) that did not require irrigation since crop roots could tap the water table below. The design also left crops impervious to frost. The creation of *chinampas* dramatically helped Tenochtitlán supply its own food and reduce the need for outside sources and is in large part responsible for the great size of the city, which, at 200,000 inhabitants, far outnumbered any other Mesoamerican metropolis. At their height the *chinampas* fields of the southern lakes Chalco and Xochimilco comprised approximately 2.3 million acres.

Zumpango

Lake Zumpango

Lake Xaltocán

Xaltocán

Tepotzotlán

Battle of Otumba ✕

Teotihuacan ■

Tenayucan

Lake Texcoco

Texcoco

Tepeyac Causeway

Azcapotzalco

canal for brigantines

Tlatelolco

Tacuba

Dike of Netzahuacoyotl

TENOCHTITLÁN

Tacuba Causeway

Chapultepec

Iztapalapa Causeway

Coyoacán Causeway

Xoloc

Iztapalapa

Coyoacán

Culhuacán

Lake Xochimilco

Lake Chalco

Chalco

Xochimilco

```
0              50 mi
0              50 km
```

The Aztecs were equally enraptured by the arrival of these foreigners from another world, and their own firsthand accounts recall the awe with which they regarded them.

They assembled in their accustomed groups, a multitude, raising a great dust. The iron of their lances and their halberds glistened from afar. The shimmer of their swords was as of a sinuous water course. Their iron breast and back pieces, their helmets clanked. Some came completely encased in iron—as if turned to iron, gleaming...And ahead of them ran their dogs, panting, with foam continually dripping from their muzzles.[17]

They stood back in fear at the snarling spotted mastiffs and the sun-sweated horses. The procession of Spanish soldiers brandished their swords; the crossbowmen were stoic, shouldering their weapons. In the rear rode Cortés himself, defiant and alert, surrounded by armed guards and harquebusiers. Malinche was there, too, near Cortés, and the Aztecs were awed and confused by her, traveling as she was alongside the Spaniards' leader.

The ride in, a regal display of bravado and daring, brought Cortés at last to a fortress bordered by two great towers. After a series of ceremonies orchestrated by Montezuma's welcoming ambassadors, Cortés was led over a drawbridge to the main island and the gates at the heart of the city of Tenochtitlán. It was November 8, 1519. Nine months after sailing from Cuba and after three months of forced marching and fighting since leaving Villa Rica, Cortés had arrived at the gates of the Aztec empire. Malinche spoke to Cortés and Aguilar, then conferred with the hosts, who regarded her with suspect curiosity and reverence, because they could see that she spoke many languages, and they believed she must be a goddess. Malinche stepped away and leaned to whisper to Cortés.

They must wait there. The emperor Montezuma was on his way.

THE stage was set for a moment unprecedented in human history: a meeting between two civilizations, two completely autonomous worlds with no prior encounters or understanding of each other. The native Americans whom Cortés saw for the first time were a race of people who had evolved, isolated from the rest of the outside world, for more than fifty thousand years, and the complex, advanced civilization he was encountering had until only recently been thought not to exist. Yet here it was before him.[18]

Cortés shifted in his saddle and eyed the gates, the crenellated battlements, and the rooftops of the houses overflowing with onlookers; he realized that he was utterly exposed here, his military position less than tenuous. He could not believe, despite everything he had been told about Tenochtitlán, the size and scope and grandeur of the place. He and his company, against great odds and perhaps against good judgment, had ridden into the most powerful and most populated city in the Americas, perhaps even in the entire world,*[19] and they were now surrounded by water on all sides. All he had left to do now was wait for Montezuma and see what would transpire.

Cortés looked up to see two long processions of people approaching. They were elaborately dressed Aztec nobles bedecked in ornately feathered headdresses, their dyed cotton garments embroidered with gold. In the center four noble attendants bore a gold-plated litter, its awning adorned with brilliant quetzal feathers and lined with silver, gold, gemstones, and pearls. Cortés dismounted as the attendants came to a halt, and from the litter the great monarch Montezuma emerged and stepped down onto cloaks laid at his feet so that

---

*The population of Tenochtitlán at the time is estimated to have been between 200,000 and 300,000; the entire Valley of Mexico, Tenochtitlán's metropolitan area, contained between 1 million and 2.6 million people. By contrast, Europe's largest city then was Paris, with 100,000 to 150,000. London had between 50,000 and 60,000. Many scholars agree that at the time Tenochtitlán was the largest city in the world.

they would not have to touch the ground; other attendants, averting their gaze, swept the ground before him as he strode regally forward to meet this brash and irreverent foreigner Hernán Cortés.

Lords Cacama and Cuitláhuac walked next to Montezuma, followed by other lords of local tributaries. Though the others were barefoot, Montezuma wore gold-soled sandals, the jaguar-skinned thongs bejeweled with precious stones. As they came face to face for the first time, the two regarded each other. Cortés observed a man five years his senior, regal, perhaps softened from the indulgences of kingship, but lean and dark, his black hair cropped tight, his eyes piercing, deep, and meditative. He wore a brilliant green quetzal feather headdress and an embroidered cotton cloak studded with jewels. His lower lip was pierced with a blue stone hummingbird, his ears with turquoise, and his nose with deep green jadestone. He moved with dignity and grace. In Cortés, Montezuma beheld a bearded man hardened by recent toil and battle, his white face and limbs scarred, his eyes defiant. There was an awkward pause, during which Montezuma leaned forward to smell Cortés, at which point Cortés wondered what to do next. He would later say of the exchange, "I stepped forward to embrace him, but the two lords who were with him stopped me with their hands so that I should not touch him."[20]

Though Cortés had met numerous lords and caciques along his route, the reverence required in greeting Montezuma was clearly of another magnitude entirely, with a level of pomp and ceremony Cortés had not previously encountered. He presented the emperor with a necklace made of pearls and cut glass and scented with musk. Through Malinche, he inquired with a directness that must have surprised the emperor: "Are you Montezuma?" With measured calm came the reply, "Yes, I am he." Flanked by dignitaries, the two men strolled a short distance up the street, and then Montezuma waved for an attendant to bring him a bundle of cloth, which he handed to Cortés. Wrapped inside were two necklaces, which the Spaniard graciously accepted. They were "made from red snails' shells, which they hold in great esteem; and from each necklace hung eight shrimps of refined gold almost a span in length."[21] Montezuma had given him the highly revered "wind necklace," a design said to have been worn by Quetzalcoatl himself.[22] He also presented his visitor with garlands of aromatic flowers.

Montezuma then took his leave, climbing again into his litter to be borne back to his palace. To Cortés he said, "You are weary. The journey has tired you. But now you have arrived...Rest now." Then he instructed Cacama to lead Cortés and his company to their accommodations. The Spaniard thanked the emperor through Malinche, saying, "Tell Montezuma that we are his friends."[23] Cacama led him and his company, including the Tlaxcalans (who were regarded with suspicion and enmity by the general Aztec populace), to an expansive and immaculate compound. The low-lying buildings with a walled central courtyard had formerly been the royal domicile of Axayacatl, Montezuma's father. Captains and men of rank were given the best quarters, with woven reed floors and palm-leaf mat bedding; even the horses were pampered, sleeping on beds of flowers.[24] The Tlaxcalans, the remaining few Cempoalans, and all the slave porters received more basic dwellings in the courtyards, exposed to the air but sheltered by cloth awnings. Cortés lodged in the Palace of Axayacatl, which was just northwest of the main plaza and adjacent to the Tacuba causeway, the western exit from the island city. Across the way, to the east, Cortés could see the city's ball court, and beyond, the sacred precinct including the Great Temple (Templo Mayor).

Cortés must have felt slightly apprehensive to be housed so near the religious and civic lifeblood of this magnificent city. He must have felt vulnerable, for he immediately placed guards and sentries all about his periphery and ordered cannons and artillery stationed at key points of defense around the Palace of Axayacatl and the courtyard. Then, as a show of military force and to herald their arrival, Cortés directed his men through some formations in the central square and had them fire repeated volleys with the harquebuses and falconets. The discharges erupted with noise and flame and smoke, amazing and frightening the onlookers, who coughed and choked at the smell of the spent gunpowder. The Aztecs later recalled how "people scattered in every direction...they were all overcome by terror, as if their hearts had fainted. And when night fell the panic spread through the city and their fears would not let them sleep."[25]

Despite this rude and aggressive display, Montezuma determined to try to understand these foreigners, perhaps learn from them, and if he could, even comprehend something of their powers. Later in the afternoon, after Cortés and his men had supped on fowl and tortillas, Montezuma summoned his visitor, his chosen captains, and Malinche and Aguilar into the great hall of the palace. The emperor took his seat on a throne and seated his guest next to him on another throne. There Cortés received a lengthy procession of gifts, constituting an immense display of Montezuma's wealth and power. There were thousands of woven garments and textiles, dazzling and intricate featherwork, and more gold and silver than Cortés had ever seen or could even have imagined. Certainly the exhibit impressed him, but it also had the unintended effect of further inflaming his greed and determination to possess what he saw, and more.

Montezuma then straightened in his throne and called for silence. He addressed Cortés with great formality and measured, even poetic language, conveying the following through Malinche:

> Our lord, thou hast suffered fatigue, thou hast endured weariness. Thou hast come to arrive on earth. Thou hast come to govern the great city of Mexico. Thou hast come to descend upon thy mat, upon thy seat, which for a moment I have guarded for thee. For thy governors are departed—the rulers Itzcóatl, Montezuma the Elder...who yet a very short time ago had come to govern the city of Mexico. O, that one of them might witness, might marvel at what to me

now hath befallen, at what I see now. I do not merely dream
that I see thee, that I look into thy face. I have been afflicted
for some time. I have gazed upon the unknown place
whence though hast come—from among the clouds, from
among the mists. And so this. The rulers departed, maintaining that thou wouldst come to visit the city, that thou
wouldst come to descend upon thy mat, upon thy seat. And
now it has been fulfilled; thou hast come... Rest thyself.
Visit thy palace.*[26]

Cortés, duplicitous and manipulative, would later interpret the great lord's words literally rather than figuratively (as
they likely were meant) and assume that Montezuma believed
the prophecy, that Cortés had returned to assume the mantle
of his authority. For now Cortés's response, through Malinche,
was clipped and clever and patently disingenuous:

Let Montezuma put his heart at ease. Let him not be frightened. We love him much. Now our hearts are indeed satisfied, for we know him, we hear him. For a long time we
have wished to see him, to look upon his face. And this we
have seen. Already we have come to his home in Mexico. At
leisure he will hear our words.[27]

Allusions to the story of the returning god appear in both
the Aztec and the Spanish versions of this initial discourse.
Cortés, for his part, appeared quite happy to embody the
myth—it would serve him well. Montezuma, on the other
hand, remained intensely curious and hoped to learn as much

---

*Montezuma's speech to Cortés will remain among the most perplexing, intriguing,
and problematic in history, the subject of endless interpretation and discussion. How
his speech is interpreted underlies and informs the essence of this unprecedented
meeting. Cortés's version appears in a letter he wrote to the king of Spain ten months
later, and it is suspect because of its highly politicized nature. The Nahuatl version
(quoted above), gleaned from oral histories and here translated into English, is deeply
poignant, revealing Montezuma as aristocratic and dignified but also burdened by
confusion, self-doubt, and an unwavering belief in destiny.

as he could about these Spaniards while he decided what to do with them. He wished to discover the secrets of their power and perhaps, if he could, possess these magical things for himself and for his people. It might cost him only a little gold, by which these Spaniards seemed intoxicated, as if drunk on pulque (liquor made from the maguey plant).

Montezuma closed the encounter by inviting Cortés and his men to roam the city freely, with Aztec guides, and behold its magnificence. Then he retired to his own quarters for prayer. He certainly had much to contemplate. The events back in Cholula had raised some doubts about whether this Spaniard was actually Quetzalcoatl; but Cortés had miraculously arrived on the mainland in 1-Reed, the precise year Quetzalcoatl was predicted to return, and even more portentous, today was 1-Wind in the Aztec calendar, Quetzalcoatl's day of "the whirlwind," the very day when wizards and robbers do their black bidding, thieving treasure while their victims slumber.[28] That night, having witnessed the arrival of these strange creatures, Montezuma and his people slept fitfully, if at all, for the atmosphere in the city was rife with apprehension. The order of their world seemed to have shifted, "as if everyone had eaten stupefying mushrooms, as if they had seen something astonishing . . . as if the world were being disemboweled. People went to sleep in terror."[29]

CHAPTER EIGHT

City of Sacrifice

THE FOLLOWING MORNING, despite the populace's palpable disquietude, the sun did indeed rise again over Tenochtitlán. The arrival of these strangers had not been the end of the world. Not yet. The city awoke as usual; women knelt in the kitchens of their sun-dried brick homes, fanned the fires for cooking, kneaded and slapped maize flour with their hands to make cakes, then left the house to carry goods to market. Canoes coursed the waters along the canals and causeways on their way to do business, or to trade, or to work the *chinampas* to the south. Craftsmen went off to workshops to produce their wares. Sons of the nobility walked to monasteries and schools to study religion and science and receive military training, while the priests and their attendants ascended the temples to clean them, filled the braziers with burning coals so that they would never extinguish, and made certain that the shrines were in suitable working order.[1]

Montezuma rose from a night of prayer and sent attendants to make sure that Cortés and his people lacked nothing. He provided them with servants to prepare meals for them, fruit and fowl and of course maize cakes, and to care for their animals, supplying fresh grain to the horses and meat scraps and offal to the dogs. He then summoned Cortés and

Malinche to visit him at his royal palace later in the day. Cortés took along Jerónimo de Aguilar to assist Malinche, as well as Pedro de Alvarado, Juan Velázquez de León, Gonzalo de Sandoval, and Diego de Ordaz, plus five others, including Bernal Díaz. The outside walls of the newly built stone compound bore banners of Montezuma and his ancestors, and painted images, including the coat of arms—an eagle, its talons outstretched, attacking a jaguar. The emperor greeted them in the center of a large hall on the ground level, which was the political and governmental nerve center of the city and indeed of the Aztec nation. Montezuma led them on a tour of the halls and rooms, which were commodious and beautifully finished, with painted walls and ceilings, trimmed in regional timber. Copal incense burned in earthen braziers at the corners of the rooms, perfuming them with a rich, musky scent. The complex consisted of more than one hundred rooms spread over an enormous area; in addition to the administrative offices there were also workshops where the best craftsmen in the city—jewelers, potters, and feather-smiths—did their work.[2] It was all very clean, well organized, and impressive, evidence of a highly ordered and structured civilization at its zenith.

After the initial tour Montezuma seated Cortés beside him on a footless, matted chair while the emperor took his throne, surrounded by some of his chiefs and servants. Malinche remained close by, as did Aguilar, and the two leaders fell into a discussion, though the slow, awkward translation made it really more like one halting monologue followed by another. Cortés thanked the emperor for his kindness and hospitality and assured his host that he and his company were now quite well rested. He then abruptly launched into his routine discourse on Christianity (which he had memorized by now), pointing out that it was in part to instill these truths that they had come, on behalf of their own king.* They worshipped the one and

---

*Cortés, of course, was exaggerating this part, since his king had not yet sanctioned his endeavors.

only savior, Jesus Christ, he explained, who was the son of God, and all humankind were brothers and sisters, the off-spring of Adam and Eve. God had created the world and had included a heaven for those who worshipped and believed and lived good lives, and a hell where sinners and nonbelievers suf-fered a fiery eternity. Cortés had the audacity to add that the gods Montezuma worshipped were ugly, vile, and demonic, as was the Aztec people's practice of human sacrifice. He reiter-ated that he hoped they could convince Montezuma to cease such false worship and embrace the true faith.[3]

Montezuma processed these words and ideas slowly and thoughtfully, and though offended, he betrayed nothing of his emotions or indignation. He spoke with erudition, using a measured cadence. He had known of the Spaniards' beliefs since his own ambassadors had returned from the sand dunes near the sea and brought back the books, paintings, and de-scriptions of those meetings. Then he straightened and spoke directly to Cortés: "We have given you no answer, since we have worshipped our own gods here from the beginning and know them to be good. No doubt yours are good also, but do not trouble to tell us any more about them at present."[4] It was more a command than a request, and Cortés took the cue to leave the matter. It had been his first real opportunity, and he had done his duty. He could press the emperor later, when the time was right.

Montezuma mentioned that others like Cortés had arrived on the coast two years ago; were they also Spaniards? Cortés, knowing that he referred to the expeditions of his countrymen Córdoba and Grijalva, nodded affirmation, saying that they too served their great king, and had come to explore the seas and landings and find the route to this land, which they had done, making possible his own arrival. Now here he was.

Montezuma waved to one of his nephews, who came over with more gifts, including finely embroidered cloaks for the captain-general and two gold necklaces each for the captains. Cortés thanked him, then noticed the late hour (and the hun-dreds of attendants moving about the quarters, preparing the emperor's meal) and begged his leave. Montezuma encouraged Cortés to use the guides and servants provided, for he had permission to make a full tour of his city, which he hoped he would enjoy. Then he rose to leave, promising that they would meet again soon. Montezuma departed to dine and then to pray. For the next five nights he would ascend the steep steps of the Great Temple, the highest in Tenochtitlán, and pray vigorously to his god Huitzilopochtli, the hummingbird god of war and sacrifice, patron of the Aztecs. After his priests sacrificed a dozen children, believing that the survival of the universe depended on them, Montezuma would kneel before flickering firelight and pray for vision, for truth. He would desperately try to understand Cortés and these strangers, whose victories against the Tabascans and the Tlaxcalans, against terrific odds, were difficult to fathom. Kneeling before the stone idol — human hearts smoldering on a brazier, priests attempting to see the future in the fresh viscera of sacrificed doves and quail — Montezuma waited for a sign.[5]

OVER the next week the remarkable City of Dreams unveiled itself to the Spaniards as they traveled about the thriving megalopolis accompanied by Aztec nobles. They toured the remainder of Montezuma's grand palace, which Cortés noticed was heavily guarded by as many as three thousand armed warriors. Here were housed a few thousand women (150 of whom, presumably, Montezuma slept with); the emperor was attended to daily by more than one thousand servants. His personal rooms on the upper floors offered vistas of his sprawling realm. His meals were elaborate, for he ate only on the finest Cholulan ceramic ware, and he touched each plate or platter or bowl, it was said, only once. He selected daily from more than three hundred possible specially prepared dishes — "cooked fowl, turkeys, pheasants, quail, tame and wild duck, hares and rabbits" — then removed to a low table, where he dined alone in silence but for the occasional low whispers of his closest priests and chosen relatives. He finished his meal with a cup of cocoa frothed with chocolate and long drafts from his tobacco pipe, entertained by foot-jugglers, singers, poets, and even misshapen hunchbacks and dwarfs and albinos.[6]

Cortés and his men were stunned by the range and scope of the palace, including the menagerie areas, which housed savage mountain lions and jaguars (rumored to be fed with the blood and remains of human sacrifice victims) as well as lynxes and wolves. There were deadly venomous snakes, rattlers and boa constrictors, and lizards and crocodiles. One house was devoted to birds of prey, with eagles and falcons and hawks in their own cages, and great tropical birds of resplendent plumage, including the highly revered quetzal; its chest feathers were the color of blood, and the long tail feathers were the color of polished jade. They strolled through immense and manicured tree-lined botanical gardens, where learned experts grew aromatic and medicinal herbs and roses the colors of sunrise and sunset.[7]

The central marketplace of Tlatelolco was astounding, surpassing anything the Spaniards knew of in Europe. Here daily more than sixty thousand people came from far and wide to buy and barter and trade, making it the greatest commercial center in all of the Americas. Everything imaginable (and much, to the Spaniards, that was previously unimaginable) was traded here, from textiles to slaves to butchered human body parts. All the items were grouped by kind in well-organized stalls (for which the vendor paid a sum to the government). There were stalls for pottery, for building materials, for the skins of animals—deer and jaguars tanned or raw, some with fur or hair, some without; there were feathers, skinned birds, and whole birds, the work of skilled taxidermists. There were crucial trade goods like salt and cotton, and sheaves of tobacco and slabs of chocolate, both novel to the Spaniards, and the important fibers of magucy and palm, used for pictographs. Apothecaries sold seeds and roots and bark and herbs for healing, while craftspeople manufactured toys for children, including some that rolled on small wheels.[8]

The food booths amazed the visitors, for the Aztec palate seemed to know no boundaries. Cortés later recorded:

> They will eat virtually anything that lives: snakes without head or tail; little barkless dogs, castrated and fattened; moles, dormice, mice, worms, lice; and they even eat earth which they gather with fine nets, at certain times of the year, from the surface of the lake. It is a kind of scum, neither plant nor soil, but something resembling ooze, which solidifies... it is spread out on floors, like salt, and there it hardens. It is made into cakes resembling bricks, which are not only sold in the market [of Mexico], but are shipped to others far outside the city. It is eaten as we eat cheese; it has a somewhat salty taste, and, when taken with *chilmole*,* is delicious.[9]

Cortés was most impressed by the quarter of the market comprising jewelers and metalsmiths, whose skill was such that they had no rivals in Europe. They made fish with intricate scales in gold and silver; tiny kettles cast with miniature handles; replicas of tropical birds, macaws and parrots, with moving beaks, tongues, and wings; and most remarkable, lifelike cast-metal monkeys that could move their hands and feet and even appear to hold and eat fruit. These men sold not only precious metals but turquoise and jade and pearls, all finely wrought.[10]

The Spaniards roamed the city, awestruck by its wonders. For his part, Cortés was all the while thinking how to make it his. He had to be impressed by Montezuma's power, by the incredible reverence paid him, and by the order he commanded. Even the streets they walked were washed daily with water and scrubbed with brooms. But there were disconcerting, even disturbing sights as well. Some of Cortés's men reported being shown a morbid place, an ossuary of human skulls, constructed

---

*A dark and spicy *recado* or seasoning combination.

to resemble a viewing theater of slain sacrifice victims. Set in stacks of five, on tiered poles between large supporting towers, were some 136,000 skulls, all the heads facing outward, the open-mouthed faces bleached to a bone-white patina from the high-altitude sun. For the Spaniards, it was a macabre and chilling sight.[11] During his tour of the palaces and market-place, Cortés would also have heard about other equally grue-some ritual practices, including the slashing open of the throats of infants, the beheading of young women, and the dressing of teenagers in recently flayed human skins. The shock and disgust that he felt (notwithstanding his own recent personal acts of barbarity) must have fueled his sense of mission and righteousness.*[12]

The Spaniards saw evidence of sports and leisure activities, too. Near Montezuma's palace they came upon large, well-constructed ball courts, laid out in great rectangles with stone-stepped viewing areas for large groups of spectators. The court itself was shaped like a huge capital I, and at its center were suspended two large stone rings or hoops through which com-petitors had to pass a rubber ball (which fascinated the Spaniards, who had never seen rubber) using only their elbows or hips. Participants in the game, called *tlachtli*, wore special leather shoulder, knee, elbow, and even chin guards for the violent encounters, performed primarily by and for the nobility. The "game" was as much ritual as play for the sake of play, and victory was considered to be determined less by the partici-pants' athletic abilities than by the will of the gods. As such, like almost every aspect of Aztec life, it bore a religious ele-ment. The ball game was often used to determine questions of divinity, solve perplexing problems or decide omens or prophe-cies. During discussions with Montezuma's priests, Cortés

---

*The hypocrisy of Cortés's response to Aztec ritual practices cannot be overlooked or overstated, especially given Spain's recent history of barbarity and cruelty during the Inquisition and its treatment of the Moors and the Jews. Cortés had just weeks before sanctioned the throat-slitting of six thousand innocent civilians in Cholula. His reaction simply reinforces the historical truth that one people's passion is another's perversity.

might have discovered an interesting and foreboding anecdote. A few years before the Spaniards came, the sage Nezahualpilli, ruler of Texcoco, had interpreted a comet blazing through the sky to be a sign of the end of the Triple Alliance and a portent of the destruction of the Aztec empire. Montezuma disagreed vehemently, so the two had played a game of *tlachtli* to let the gods rule on the matter. Montezuma had lost the game.[13]

AFTER four days of passing by the temples that defined the ritual center of Tenochtitlán, Cortés wished to see them for himself. He sent to inquire of Montezuma whether he might visit the Great Temple and see the shrine to Huitzilopochtli. The request was quite forward, even bold, for it was Montezuma's special place of worship and was sacred. Montezuma hesitated, wondering whether to allow it. Finally, in the afternoon, he made the decision to escort Cortés personally. He arrived borne in his litter, and Cortés brought Malinche, a number of his captains, and some armed foot soldiers and followed in the shadow of Montezuma's imperial train.

At the foot of the great pyramid Montezuma halted and descended from his litter. Once again servants spread out mats and swept the ground before him. He instructed Cortés to wait and ascended the 114 steps, which were dangerously steep (designed so that sacrifice victims would plunge, unimpeded, from the stone at the top the entire 150 feet to the bottom). The Spaniards craned their necks as, assisted by attendants, Montezuma rose to the summit and disappeared. Not long afterward some priests descended, sent as a courtesy by Montezuma, to aid Cortés and his company on the difficult climb to the top. Cortés was standoffish, ordering the priests not to touch him or his men. Some of his men even drew their swords, knowing what happened in these Aztec places of worship. The priests had backed off, and Cortés led his troop upward, awkwardly hiking the uneven steps one at a time, until he came at last to the flat top where the shrines were located. The high elevation of Tenochtitlán (7,400 feet) and their armor made Cortés and his men huff for air; Montezuma smiled and remarked, "You must be tired from the climb." Cortés, attempting to quickly catch his breath, retorted arrogantly, "Spaniards are never tired."[14] Montezuma must have found this claim amusing, given the gasping of Cortés and his men.

The summit area was wide and paved perfectly smooth with flat, broad stones. Montezuma swept his open palm in all directions, indicating the miraculous panoramic view of the city stretching for miles in all directions, the water of the lakes finally giving way to croplands, and indeed the entire Valley of Mexico, which Cortés viewed with a keen military eye. He peered down, hawklike, noting carefully the directions of the causeways and the placement of the drawbridges. It was all marvelous, literally breathtaking, and at the same time quite unbelievable.

Cortés found the shrines themselves both beautiful and unsettling. The two shrines were to honor Huitzilopochtli, god of war, and Tezcatlipoca, the "smoking mirror" and omnipotent power. In front of each was a sacrificial stone stained dark by the blood of many victims. Black-robed priests stood nearby, their faces eerily pale from fasting and bloodletting, their ears cut and shredded, their black hair matted and knotted with blood.[15] Steeling his nerve, Cortés asked Montezuma if he might see the inner sanctum of the shrine to Huitzilopochtli, where the emperor prayed. After consulting his priests, Montezuma consented and led Cortés inside, where the Spaniard witnessed images and scenes that few mortals other than the highest priests and chieftains had ever seen. The idol of Huitzilopochtli loomed over the room, his gigantic form seated on a litter. His eyes were of bright stone, and he bore in one hand a gold bow, in the other gold arrows. His face was bespattered with blood, both fresh and dried, and near him stood smaller idols equally frightening, dragons and "other hideous figures," including a "fanged serpent." From his neck hung a chain of gold and silver hearts, symbols of the most important sacrifice. Before the idols burned braziers, in which freshly extracted human hearts spat and sizzled.[16]

Sickened, Cortés could only look away in horror, casting his eyes against the blood-drenched walls. The smell of the place overwhelmed him. He faced Montezuma and spoke to him as Malinche translated, "I cannot imagine how a prince as great and wise as your majesty can have failed to realize that these idols of yours are not gods but evil things...devils." Montezuma heard these words with a steely-eyed stare but for the moment said nothing. Cortés, deciding the time was right, with brazen audacity suggested that a cross be erected here, as a symbol of the one true God. "Let us divide off a part of this sanctuary...as a place where we can put Our Lady, and then you will see, by the fear that your idols have of her, how grievously they have deceived you."[17]

Cortés did not comprehend (nor did he attempt to) the ancient, deeply held importance of ritual sacrifice in the Aztec religion, nor the importance of these idols in their worldview, though it was right there in front of him. For Montezuma and his people, the hearts and blood of the victims were not just desired but absolutely necessary. This was neither sport nor entertainment—it was a requirement, needed to live, like air or water, needed for the continuation of the world. Ritual human sacrifice was the supreme offering in the Aztec belief system. And here stood Cortés, this mysterious interloper, denigrating that which was most sacred. It was too much. It was inconceivable. Deeply affronted, Montezuma held up his hand in defiance. "If I had known that you were going to utter these insults, I should not have shown you my gods," he said angrily. "We hold them to be very good...they give us health and rain and crops and weather, fertility, and all the victories we desire. So we are bound to worship them and sacrifice to them...Say nothing more against them."[18]

Cortés and his men were led away. As they reached the bottom of the steps, they heard the slow, rhythmic, diabolical beating of death drums and the eerie evening conch shells blown by the priests from the summit of the temple, signaling the setting of the sun and the commencement of ceremony.

Montezuma remained in the shrine, dismayed and perturbed. He needed to make sacrifices now, to appease his gods for his transgression in bringing Cortés here, for surely they would be angered. He must pray to them. A religious war—between his innumerable gods and this one the Spaniards worshipped—was at full pitch.

CHAPTER NINE

Seizure of Empire

CORTÉS FELT LIKE PRAYING, TOO, and desired a formal setting, a prescribed chapel where he and the men could hold daily mass, properly. For a few days he considered Montezuma's rebuke to his suggestion of Christian worship at the Great Temple and waited for the emperor's mood to improve. Then he sent to know whether he might build a chapel near or about his quarters, in the Palace of Axayacatl. To his surprise the emperor consented, even providing some of his masons and carpenters to assist in the project. In just two days a small Christian chapel was erected inside the palace, a seemingly small concession in a city dominated by Aztec temples, but symbolically, and certainly to Cortés, a powerful sign of progress. He and his men now had a legitimate Christian place of worship (overseen by fathers Bartolomé de Olmedo and Juan Díaz) in the epicenter of the Aztec spiritual world. It would hardly be the last.

While constructing the chapel, one of Cortés's own carpenters, Alonso Yanez, stumbled on an interesting discovery. He found a door in one of the walls that had quite recently been boarded and plastered over but was cracked at the edges and could still be opened. Because the entire building was newly constructed, Cortés did not think much of it at first, but curious, he decided to investigate and brought men to pry the sealed door open. They followed a short corridor into a large hall, where they found woven baskets and crates. They began to open them quietly. They could hardly believe what they saw: a secret treasure of tributes and taxes paid or collected over Axayacatl's thirteen-year reign, the blood-wrought spoils of imperial expansion. There were piles of gold and silver, fine jewelry and trinkets and large platters and goblets, as well as many objects crafted in stone, including a good deal of jade. Numerous containers were devoted solely to rich feather work, much of it quetzal. Bernal Díaz said of the wealth contained there, "I was a young man, and it seemed to me as if all the riches of the world were in that one room!"*[1]

The men pawed the treasure in a frenzy of greed, until at last Cortés ordered them to halt—they must leave the treasure alone for now. Some objected, but their leader assured them that in good time, when the city was theirs, they would right-fully divide the plunder. So the door was sealed shut, and he ordered his men to say nothing to anyone about what they had seen, an order that was likely disobeyed almost instantly by some of the greed-drunk, loose-tongued men still giddy at the sight of all the jewels and shining gold.**

THOUGH they were being hosted like royalty, Cortés felt un-easy. For one thing, his men, accustomed to movement and action, were growing restless. And something else gnawed at the captain-general. The incredible view he had taken in from

---

*Aztec chroniclers also recorded the Spaniards' discovery of the treasure: "They went to Montezuma's storehouse where his personal treasures were kept. The Spaniards grinned like little beasts and patted each other with delight. When they entered the hall of treasures, it was as if they had arrived in paradise. They searched everywhere and coveted everything: they were slaves to their own greed."[2]
**Sometime later Cortés actually told Montezuma that he had discovered the treasure, and Montezuma asked only that the Spaniards not disturb or take any of the gorgeous and revered featherwork, which rightfully belonged not to him but to his gods. The gold, he said, they could keep.

atop the Great Temple had graphically illustrated to him the relative precariousness of their situation here in the water-bound capital. Even including the Tlaxcalans, many of whom remained in their barracks, Cortés's force, he now felt palpably, could be overwhelmed by sheer numbers with one command of Montezuma. Then, as if confirming these suspicions, word came from the Tlaxcalans that the Aztecs in their vicinity were no longer treating them well. Vocal Tlaxcalans also pointed out, again, that when and if they wished to, the Aztecs could quickly raise all the drawbridges and trap them all on the island city. Cortés listened intently. He understood that the Tlaxcalans' long animosity toward the Aztecs made them prone to mistrust and exaggeration, but they were right about the drawbridges. From a purely military standpoint, he was exposed. What if this was what Montezuma had intended from the beginning? Cortés mulled it over. If Montezuma had intended to ensnare him in this way, why would he have told Cortés not to come here under any circumstances? It made no sense, and he was inclined, at least for the time being, to dismiss the Tlaxcalans' fears.

But some of Cortés's captains approached him with similar concerns. They held a meeting in the newly built chapel and discussed the situation. Cortés, Sandoval, Ordaz, Alvarado, and Velázquez de León discussed their current situation and options, both military and political. While these conversations were going on, Tlaxcalan emissaries arrived bearing grim news from Vera Cruz: Juan de Escalante, captain in charge at the coastal fortress, as well as six other Spanish soldiers and a number of allied Totonacs, had been killed.* Montezuma still operated a system of tribute collection in the coastal regions, and his agent in Nauhtla (also called Almeria), a man named Qualpopoca, had been pressing for the Totonacs to continue

---

*Cortés had actually learned of this skirmish while mopping up the massacre in Cholula, but he had chosen to withhold the news from his men so as not to alarm them or cause discord among them. He also wanted further confirmation of the events, which he now had.

their payments, which they might do since Cortés had left. But the Totonacs explained that because of their allegiance with Cortés and the Spaniards, they were no longer vassals of Tenochtitlán, and they refused to pay any form of taxes. Enraged by this impudence, Qualpopoca determined to exact either payment or punishment. In a ruse he sent messengers to Escalante requesting a meeting, saying that he wished to seal an alliance with the Spaniards as well.

Escalante bought into Qualpopoca's trap. He sent a group of four representatives to the appointed meeting, and the men were ambushed; two of them were slain, while the other two somehow managed to escape and return to Vera Cruz. Escalante then mounted a force for reprisal, taking a number of his own men and a few thousand Totonac allies, and they fought Qualpopoca and his warriors in a heated battle. Escalante was knocked from his horse (which was killed) and badly wounded, while six of his men were killed. One, named Juan de Arguëllo, was taken alive and sacrificed; his severed head was brought by runners to Montezuma as a war prize. Montezuma found the white-faced, black-bearded head frightening and ordered it sent away from Tenochtitlán. Escalante straggled back to Vera Cruz, defeated, but soon perished there from his wounds.[3]

Cortés, from the moment he crossed the causeway and set foot in Tenochtitlán, had been scheming and planning, "thinking of all the ways and means to capture [Montezuma] without causing a disturbance."[4] Now, with a letter in hand describing the recent events at Vera Cruz, he had a pretext. On November 14, less than a week after being welcomed to the Aztec capital and treated as an honored guest, Cortés sent word that he wished to meet with Montezuma. He brought Malinche and Aguilar, plus captains Sandoval, Ávila, Lugo, Alvarado, and Velázquez de León and some thirty well-armed soldiers, and headed to Montezuma's palace. The letter from Pedro de Ircio, who had temporarily assumed Escalante's post at Vera Cruz, was tucked into his pocket.

As usual, pleasantries were exchanged. Montezuma offered

gifts, including jewels as well as women—he even offered one of his own daughters to Cortés, who thanked him but declined, saying that he was already married. Cortés accepted her on behalf of Alvarado, who was pleased. Cortés then became stern, producing the letter from Pedro de Ircio and saying that he had evidence of a conspiracy, perpetrated under Montezuma's orders, that had resulted in the deaths of six of his fine soldiers and one of his prized horses. He had his interpreters read and translate the letter. Cortés stressed that the letter made clear that Qualpopoca had acted on direct orders from Montezuma, but for his part Cortés could hardly believe this. He thought that Qualpopoca must have acted independently, but he had to admit he could not be certain, especially given the thwarted attack at Cholula, in which the Aztecs were also implicated. This business at Vera Cruz was a very serious matter indeed and required further investigation.

Cortés continued, facing Montezuma: "I have no desire to start a war on this account, or to destroy this city. Everything will be forgiven, provided you now come quietly with us to our quarters, and make no protest. You will be as well served and attended there as in your own palace. But if you cry out, or raise any commotion, you will immediately be killed by these captains of mine, whom I have brought for this sole purpose."[5] Montezuma, according to Bernal Díaz, was utterly "dumbfounded" and rightfully so—his guest had just threatened to imprison or kill him. His first response was to deny any personal involvement in aggression against the Spaniards, either at Cholula or at Vera Cruz. He immediately suggested that he would send for Qualpopoca on the coast, get to the truth about what had happened there, and have any guilty parties punished. With that he removed a bracelet from his wrist, a small figure of Huitzilopochtli, and said it would be sent along to ensure an immediate response. Cortés agreed that that was fine and said he would like to have a few of his men accompany Montezuma's messengers, but Montezuma would still have to come along with Cortés to his quarters and remain there until the matter was resolved.

Montezuma adamantly refused: "My person is not such that can be made a prisoner of. Even if I should consent to it, my people would not suffer it."[6] As an alternative, Montezuma suggested they take as prisoners his son and two daughters, but Cortés held firm, saying that there really was no other way, that he would have to come personally. He would still be ruling his people, just from the Palace of Axayacatl rather than his own. They argued the matter for a long time, until some of Cortés's men grew weary and nervous with the delay, suspecting that Montezuma might at any time call his guards, and they would all be killed. Velázquez de León was the most vocal and impatient, exclaiming, "What is the use of all these words? Either we take him or knife him. If we do not look after ourselves now we shall be dead men."[7] León's gruff, aggressive tone alarmed Montezuma, who asked Malinche what he had said. She calmly replied that her advice to him was to accompany Cortés and his captains to their quarters without protest, and he would be treated with honor. Otherwise she was quite certain that they would kill him.

Montezuma finally stood and summoned what little dignity he still possessed. He consented to go, but only if it was granted (and given the appearance) that he was accompanying Cortés of his own free will, not as a prisoner. He would inform his family, his high priests, his council, advisers, and guards that he had decided, after prayer and contemplation, that he wished to live with the Spaniards for a few days, to better learn their ways and to discuss religion with the captain-general. He then called for his nobles and his royal litter and was conveyed under the close armed scrutiny of Cortés and his finest soldiers, from his own palace, across the main plaza, to the palace of his dead father. Watching the weird procession, the people of Tenochtitlán could only stare in wonder at what strange and unprecedented events were transpiring in their magical city.[8]

Hernán Cortés's brazen, bloodless coup was perhaps the most audacious and astonishing takeover in the annals of military history. Deviously and deceitfully, Cortés had played on Montezuma's trust, generosity, and hospitality, then struck with viperlike venom from within. Cortés was likely ecstatic, and perhaps surprised, that his plan had worked so seamlessly; but little did he know that the real fight for the Aztec empire had only just begun.

AT the outset, the coup d'état appeared to be nothing more than a mutually agreed-upon arrangement between Cortés and Montezuma. To publicly give the appearance that everything was normal, Montezuma convened his nephews, his brother, and his trusted regional chieftains at his new accommodations and assured them that though he would be staying with the Spaniards for a time, all remained under his control. He would simply govern from a specially prepared room there now. He added that it had been his choice, as he had received a sign from Huitzilopochtli recommending this action. He instructed his men to maintain order and keep the populace at ease. There was nothing to worry about. But despite these assurances, a mood of fear and disquiet coursed through the city, for nothing of this kind had ever happened before. And those closest to Montezuma could see that within the palace he was under guard and surveillance day and night, and the permission of Cortés was required for anyone wishing to speak with the emperor. Whatever Montezuma was choosing to call his living and ruling situation, the public could see that he had been taken against his will and was imprisoned. The nobles, especially Cacama, Montezuma's nephew, while initially bowing to Montezuma's wishes, sensed calamity.[9]

About three weeks after Montezuma's confinement, Qualpopoca, his son, and fifteen chiefs returned from the coast, bearing Montezuma's bracelet. Qualpopoca rode regally, borne in a litter, and was likely a little affronted when his emperor Montezuma immediately handed him and his son over to Cortés for questioning. He admitted that his actions had resulted in the deaths of the Spaniards (including Captain Escalante) and of the horse. He was indeed a vassal of Montezuma (who was not? he wondered) but had acted independently, without Montezuma's direction. Later, after a series of rather strong-armed Spanish interrogations, Qualpopoca amended his confession, saying that Montezuma had given him the order to fight and kill any *teules* interfering with their tribute collections.[10]

Cortés sentenced Qualpopoca, his son, and the fifteen chiefs to burn at the stake, after which they would suffer eternal damnation for killing the Spaniards. The penalty was harsh, though hardly novel or original, having precedents in the Spanish Inquisition. By meting the punishment out so publicly, in a nearly ritual spectacle, Cortés certainly intended to send a message to the Aztec nobility as well as to the populace: killing a Spaniard would be met with the highest penalty. Having admitted their guilt, the Aztecs were tethered to poles and led to the square directly in front of the Great Temple. As they stood in confused horror, Cortés's men arrived from Montezuma's personal storage arsenals with javelins, swords, bows, and arrows, which they used to make great pyres. In the meantime Cortés visited Montezuma. After verbally lambasting him for his part in the deaths of his men, he ordered the emperor to be chained in ankle irons, an utterly humiliating and unprecedented indignity. Cortés then took Montezuma to watch as his own countrymen were burned alive at the stake; their horrific screams were finally subsumed by the snapping and cracking of the flaming wooden weapons. A large crowd gathered at the square to witness the atrocity, stunned into utter silence and confused as to how their emperor could have ordered it, or if he had not, how he could have allowed it.[11]

Cortés returned Montezuma to his quarters and personally released him from his chains, apologizing for the indelicacy of his bondage and even offering to set him free now—he could return to his own palace if he wished. Together, Cortés promised, the two could rule this land and those beyond, expanding the empire to those not yet subjugated.[12] But being placed in irons, and witnessing the execution, had terrorized Montezuma, broken his spirit and will. He was so humiliated that he was reduced to tears and a state of shock. His reputation had been publicly sullied, and his leadership was in serious doubt. He quietly thanked Cortés for the offer of his freedom (which may or may not have been genuine) but added that he preferred to stay in the house of his father. For one thing, his freedom might result in an armed rebellion by his nephews and lords, who had more than once suggested attacking the Spaniards. Were he back at his house, in their midst, they might attempt to convince him to rise up against Cortés, or they might even replace him with another leader who would do their bidding. No, for the time being he wished to remain with the Spaniards and continue governing, as much as he could, from the palace of his father.[13]

CHAPTER TEN

Cortés and Montezuma

HERNÁN CORTÉS WOULD REMAIN ENSCONCED in Tenochtitlán for the next five months, during which he and his captive ruler Montezuma would develop one of the most peculiar relationships in recorded history. Driven partly by political arrangement and partly by military necessity, the two men coexisted for nearly half a year in a bizarre captor-captive, ruler-puppet scenario of colliding religious beliefs and a regional power struggle.

During the awkward weeks following the kidnapping of Montezuma and the public executions, life in Tenochtitlán returned to a semblance of normalcy. Montezuma continued to rule, to hold meetings, and to dine in his intricate fashion; he even maintained his nightly forays to the summit of the Great Temple for prayer and sacrifice, a practice that disgusted and displeased Cortés (especially when the emperor returned, bloody and ashen from self-sacrifice), but that he begrudgingly tolerated, fearing a massive civic rebellion should he try to put a stop to it. Women were ushered into and out of Montezuma's rooms daily, and he continued to host huge feasts. Festivals went on as usual. Though Montezuma had lost some of his pride and regal air, he remained a gracious host, taking small groups of Spaniards, including Cortés, on excursions into the countryside, where they hunted rabbits and deer. Montezuma taught the Spaniards to use the native blowpipes, while he learned the workings of their more sophisticated weapons.[1]

Montezuma accompanied Cortés to exhibitions of *tlachtli*, the widespread Mesoamerican ball game, where they watched the padded participants leap and run and bludgeon one another (some became so bruised by the contact that, after games, they required physicians to lance and drain their hematomas) and bet on the outcome.[2] Cortés and Montezuma spent hours together, with only the interpreters and a few invited guests, Montezuma teaching Cortés how to play the games of *totoloqui*, (or *totoloque*), in which they tossed small gold balls, and *patolli*, a popular dice game something like backgammon that the general populace played with beans and stones and that the nobility played with small gold balls and gemstones; it was also gambled on. Bernal Díaz recalled that Cortés would have Pedro de Alvarado keep score for him; Montezuma often caught Alvarado cheating, adding an extra point or two to Cortés's score. This amused Montezuma, and the two laughed a great deal about it. They played for jewels, and if Cortés won, he would give the jewels to Montezuma's nephews and favored counselors in attendance; if Montezuma won, he gave his winnings to the guards. These interactions were all strangely convivial.[3]

Despite these pleasant diversions, Cortés never stopped calculating and planning. For all the superficial appearances of normality, he understood there was nothing at all ordinary about either his continued presence in the city or Montezuma's odd accommodations under Spanish guard. To bolster his tenuous military position, he devised a plan. He would build boats. Boats might just prove his only way out of the city. After meeting with his senior captains and experienced sailors and discussing the matter, Cortés settled on a young man named Martín López to oversee the ambitious project. Brave, adventurous, and highly intelligent, López quickly agreed to the post and organized a squad of skilled carpenters, blacksmiths, and laborers for the tasks ahead. Likely having planned for

their eventual usage from the time he scuttled his ships, Cortés
sent to Vera Cruz for spare ship parts, compasses and oars and
cordage, anchor chains and sails, enough gear to rig four brigantines. López drew up plans, designing the boats so that they
could either be rowed with oars or sailed; they would be fitted
out for numerous heavy cannons and large enough to carry up
to seventy-five soldiers and a few horses. Along with chief carpenter Andrés Núñez, López then set about their construction. They enlisted servants from Montezuma to cut, limb,
and portage back to Tenochtitlán timber from Tacuba and
Texcoco; the timber was planed and bent using steam to shape
the ships' hulls.[4]

Not long after the four vessels were completed and deemed
lakeworthy (a few months), Cortés invited Montezuma out on
a "pleasure cruise," a clever euphemism for "military reconnaissance." Cortés insisted that the primary use of these boats
would be for diversion—sailing and hunting—but Montezuma
must surely have noticed that they bore heavy artillery, with
four cannons on each. Still, having first seen pictographs of
these "water-houses" brought back to him from the coast, he
was fascinated by their novelty, their size, and their nimble
movement in the water, for they were remarkably fast for their
size. He accompanied Cortés and Malinche on one hunting
trip, riding under the ornamented awning with a few of his nobles, where he felt the exhilaration of wind in his face, the stiff
lake breezes puffing the sails full. He watched in amazement as
the forty-foot boat, powered solely by the wind, easily outraced
his finest canoes and oarsmen, leaving them churning feebly
in the wake. This naval superiority stunned him and was certainly observed keenly by Cortés as well, who all the while
made careful notes on the layout and topography of the lake
regions, including their depths, moorages, and prevailing wind
directions.[5] As a powerful exclamation point, gunners discharged the big cannons; the booming explosions filled Montezuma simultaneously with awe and fear. Cortés would claim
that Montezuma returned from such excursions "very happy

and content,"[6] yet his enjoyment must have been tempered by Cortés's blunt reminders that, should the emperor attempt to escape or raise any suspicions among the chiefs of the lake cities they visited, he would immediately be killed.

From the moment when the four brigantines were finished, they remained on the water throughout the spring of 1520, ranging widely and running daily reconnaissance across the whole five-lake system, recording valuable intelligence that the Spanish might draw on later.[7] They saw beyond the banks, in the distance, lovely cultivated maize and bean fields, men planting and tending, and along the northeastern shores of Lake Xaltocán, men cutting troughs of earth to solidify into salt lumps.[8] Cortés was keenly aware, having seen the deficiencies the Tlaxcalans suffered, of the politics and power of the salt trade.

Cortés used the success of the lake jaunts to push Montezuma even further, requesting that the emperor reveal to him the source of the seemingly endless supply of gold. As he had demonstrated on his numerous occasions of gift-giving, Montezuma and his people were much less enamored of gold than of jade and quetzal feathers, so the concession seemed trifling at the time—he told Cortés that the gold came from places far away, but he would certainly be willing to provide guides if Cortés wished to visit them. Excited by the prospect—not only of obtaining more gold but of continued military scouting of the region—Cortés happily agreed, immediately organizing three separate expeditions.

First Cortés summoned Gonzalo de Umbria, the former Velázquez conspirator who had been punished with the removal of his toes for his part in the attempted mutiny at Vera Cruz. By now he must have won back enough of Cortés's favor to be entrusted with this mission (and his feet must have been sufficiently healed), for he subsequently led a group, accompanied by Montezuma's handpicked noble-guides, to Zacatula (in present-day Oaxaca) to see the Mixtec mines and delicate gold work created there, which was thought to be unrivaled in the Americas. Cortés then called on Diego de Ordaz, who had recently distinguished himself (and atoned for his part in the clandestine attempt to hijack a ship and retreat to Cuba) by his daring ascent to the summit of Popocatépetl, to take ten Spaniards and follow the guides to the region of Coatzacualco (south of Vera Cruz on the Gulf of Mexico) in search of gold. They would also seek a harbor superior to the one where they had settled, one deeper and more protected. Last, Cortés asked Andrés de Tapia and Diego Pizarro to reconnoiter the Panuco area, on the northeast coast, for gold and to inspect the mines.[9] These expeditions were expected to take more than a month, and, though they forayed into unknown and potentially hostile lands without the benefit of interpreters, they were expected to return with detailed maps and notes of their findings.

Somewhat surprisingly, even to the optimistic Cortés, all three expeditions succeeded in varying degrees. They passed through previously unknown (to the Spaniards, at least) jungles, mountains, and deserts, mapping their routes and findings and developing for Cortés a detailed picture of some of the lands beyond the Valley of Mexico. The Spaniards brought back many objects, gifts they received along their routes, even from tribes and chieftains hostile to the Aztecs. Umbria was the first to return to Tenochtitlán, bearing excellent news: the Mixtecs had plenty of viable gold mines, and the rivers themselves were filled with gold, which the Indians mined directly, panning for it in handheld troughs. Gold could be dug from the nearby mountainsides as well. Ordaz came back next, and though he failed to locate a harbor suitable for large, plunder-bearing Spanish ships, he brought both valuable booty and news. A certain chieftain from Coatzacualco, named Tochel, not only offered gifts but pledged immediate vassalage to Cortés and his king in Spain, for he had long held deep animosity toward the Aztecs, even naming a famous battleground "*Cuylonemiquis*, which in their language means 'Where-the-Mexican-Swine-Were-Killed.' "[10] Cortés found this news comforting, as he always sought to nurture allies. Last to return were Pizarro and Tapia, who also brought a good deal of gold and similar news of Aztec loathing in the Panuco region on a scale to rival that of the Totonacs and the Tlaxcalans.[11]

CACAMA, king of Texcoco, had been observing his uncle Montezuma's behavior since his incarceration, and he despised the transformation. From the beginning, the pugilistic and short-tempered Cacama had argued for strong resistance against the Spaniards; he had urged the chiefs to fight Cortés and to refuse his entry to Tenochtitlán, though he ultimately bowed to the wishes of his more powerful uncle and the will of the other nobles. More than once, in private meetings at the Palace of Axayacatl, he had urged his uncle to try to escape, but to no avail. Now he had seen enough. From his point of view (which was significant and considerable, Texcoco being the second most powerful city-state in the Aztec Triple Alliance), the emperor Montezuma appeared to be giving away the empire. He hated seeing his uncle gallivanting on lake cruises with a man he perceived as an enemy of the state, and rumors had filtered out that the Spaniards had discovered Axayacatl's treasures. That Montezuma had been bound in irons to witness the burning alive of his brethren, including his entrusted ambassador Qualpopoca, was unpardonable. In private Cacama began to plot with other regional lords who were also dismayed by Montezuma's acquiescence to the Spaniards' presence. They planned to overthrow the Spaniards and drive them from the city or, if necessary, kill them all.

The plot, however, was leaked. Evidently Cacama was overzealous in his enthusiasm, attempting to enlist too many supporters, and one of them revealed the plan to Montezuma who, rather than risk an uprising in his city, passed the intelligence on to Cortés. Montezuma then helped orchestrate countermeasures. He lured Cacama to a lakeshore villa under the pretense of a meeting, where he was arrested, chained, and conveyed back to Tenochtitlán. The lords of Coyoacán,

Iztapalapa, and Tacuba were likewise duped and taken prisoner. At Montezuma's urging, Cacama was stripped of his powers, and his brother Conacochtzin was installed as the new king of Texcoco, which proved beneficial to Cortés, for he obeyed all of Montezuma's wishes, which were day by day becoming the wishes of Cortés.[12]

Cortés could see that, although he had thwarted Cacama's rebellion, things were beginning to unravel around him. Cacama's attempted coup indicated discontent and division among the neighboring Aztec city-states, and it could happen again. People had seen the king of Texcoco, and other important lords, hauled off in chains. The city, indeed the entire region, was flooded with anxiety. Cortés decided that he must do something to formally and publicly solidify his stranglehold on the city and on the whole Aztec nation. He requested that Montezuma convene all the leaders of the Aztec empire at the Palace of Axayacatl. (A few were already incarcerated there, still bound in irons.) Though Montezuma had given his word that he would pay tribute to Cortés's king in Spain, Cortés now wanted to officially (and to his mind, legally) and ceremoniously subject the Aztec empire to Spanish vassalage. As always on such occasions, he made sure that one of his notaries was present, and he also brought Malinche, Aguilar, a young page boy named Orteguilla (whom Montezuma liked and trusted, for the boy was a quick learner, able to speak a few sentences to the emperor in his native Nahuatl), and a few of his captains.

The room fell quiet as Montezuma spoke. He reminded his lords of the prophecy, long passed down from their ancestors, "that men would come from the direction of the sunrise to rule these lands, and that the rule and domination of Mexico would then come to an end."[13] He paused as his voice quavered, then continued. He now believed in his heart, from consultations with the gods, that Cortés and these Spaniards were the prophesied men. "At present," he went on, "our gods permit me to be held prisoner here, and this would not have happened, as I have often told you, except at the command of the great Huitzilopochtli." Seeing the emotion overtaking the once-proud emperor, even the Spaniards assembled felt pity and sorrow at these words. Montezuma sighed deeply, choking back tears as he tried to finish his speech: "Remember that during the eighteen years that I have been your prince, you have always been most loyal to me, and I have enriched you, extending your lands, and given you power and wealth ... What I command and implore you now is to give some voluntary contribution as a sign of vassalage." With this last, he broke down and wept, as did many in the room.[14]

Once Montezuma composed himself, he reiterated, stammering, that he needed his lords' assurances in these matters, and one by one they all promised to "obey and comply with all that was demanded of them" in the name of King Charles V of Spain. Under Spanish oath (if not their own), King Montezuma of the Aztecs and all of his lords of the empire (admittedly, some of them pinioned in irons and subjugated by terror, both overt and covert) pledged their allegiance to Spain, effectively ceding control to Hernán Cortés as the king of Spain's representative.

Hernán Cortés now had the relinquishment of the Aztec nation in writing.

ALMOST immediately Cortés began to exact tribute from the Aztec empire, explaining to Montezuma that, in particular, the Spanish king required as much gold as could possibly be gathered, from nearby and from far and wide. Montezuma sent collectors to the provinces with Spanish captains to bring in tributes, which began to pour in daily. Montezuma was amazingly (and from a modern viewpoint, incomprehensibly) cooperative about treasures housed within the city. He told Cortés that he knew the captain-general had discovered the secret treasure of his father, spoils from his reign, and he pledged to Cortés all the gold therein, which, as the Spaniards had seen, came in a dazzling array: necklaces, disks, bracelets, fans, toys, beads, and raw stones. All was melted into bars so that it could be properly weighed and appraised.[15]

Montezuma directed the Spaniards to his coveted House of Birds, part of his magical and exotic menagerie. Inside a hidden room there Andrés de Tapia and a handful of other Spaniards were led to more gold in various shapes and forms, including bars, platters, goblets, and jewelry, plus nearly indescribable featherwork, which they more or less ignored. Taking stock of the riches, Cortés was awestruck, marveling that the people of this land could "produce images in gold, silver, stone, and feathers of everything which exists in this domain and which, in the case of the silver and gold objects, bear such a remarkable likeness to the original that no jeweler anywhere else in the world could do any better."[16]

Despite the grandeur of these golden specimens, they too were summarily melted into bars.

The haul was significant, but the division of spoils was not without controversy. Melted, stamped, and weighed, the gold and silver plunder appeared at first to be of inestimable value, enough to make the men rich. It appeared that they had, in a very real sense, discovered the fabled mountain of gold El Dorado. The captains and soldiers were finally going to get what they had marched and ridden and bled and even died for.

But Cortés, ever judicious, pointed out to the men, who stared in awe at the booty, that the predetermined, legally required division agenda had to be adhered to. The king must get his royal fifth, and Cortés garnered an equal fifth himself. Cortés pointed out that he required personal reimbursement for his initial investments in staking the venture, which sums were considerable—he had purchased most of the horses and the food and had invested, along with Velázquez, in the ships.

In addition, wages were owed to the professional sailors, navigators, captains, and priests, on down the line, including, they must not forget, the soldiers who had remained in Vera Cruz. What had first seemed an infinite treasure now amounted to a paltry-looking sum per soldier, perhaps as little as one hundred pesos each. Many scoffed, refusing to accept such slighting. The men took to gambling away their shares. Rumors circulated that Cortés had embezzled plunder from the palaces himself, and in the end Cortés was forced to appease the disgruntled troops with promises of more gold and even bribes, which some took in behind-the-back payoffs.*[17]

Hernán Cortés had taken control of Montezuma's empire politically, in his mind legally, and with relatively constant tributes coming in, economically. But the niggling problem of religious differences remained. Feeling that the reins of power were firmly within his grasp, Cortés resolved that the time was right for a spiritual overthrow of the empire as well.

Human sacrifices had continued unabated since Cortés's arrival. Now, once and for all, he would call for a cessation of the vile practice. Gathering his interpreters and a small raiding crew that included Andrés de Tapia, Cortés marched to the Great Temple, climbed the sheer steps, and ascended the broad platform. Cortés and his men brandished their swords and sliced through the drapery entrance to the sanctuary, where Cortés once again came face to face with the invidious blood-drenched demon idols. The priests charged with the idols' protection stood in unarmed defiance as Cortés explained what he was about to do—destroy their evil idols and replace them with statues of Jesus and the Virgin Mary. The priests simply laughed, incredulous. These gods ruled the empire, and the populace of Tenochtitlán would most certainly die for them, as some did daily through sacrifice. Desecration of these idols would cause chaos and bloodshed, the likes of which the Spaniards could not imagine. The priests pointed to some alarmed citizens below who, having heard the commotion at the Great Temple, were beginning to organize a defense.

---

*According to William Prescott, some of the soldiers decided to take their shares of gold, which they had melted and then, with the aid of Tenochtitlán's best jewelers, fashioned into gaudy chains that they wore around their necks as displays of wealth. See Prescott, *History of the Conquest of Mexico,* (New York, 2001), 487–88.

Quickly Cortés sent one of his men to shore up the guard around Montezuma and bring, as soon as possible, a support team of at least thirty more men. Meanwhile he took matters into his own hands. He scaled one of the idols and attempted to tear the golden eyes from it, and he began to strike at the monstrous stone figures.[18]

Montezuma had learned of the proceedings from informants, before his guard was tightened, and through a fleet-footed messenger convinced Cortés to cease the destruction until he could arrive on the scene. Cortés consented, and the two met once again atop the highest pyramid in Tenochtitlán. Montezuma, who believed in and prayed to more than two hundred gods, decided to make room for one more. He diplomatically suggested a compromise: Cortés could erect his cross and idols on one side of the great platform, and leave the Aztec idols alone. They could share the area. That would be all right. Cortés, whose inflamed passions seem to have calmed during his wait for Montezuma, pondered this conciliation, no doubt eyeing keenly the gathering swarm below. He agreed to the deal, even as he dismissed the Aztec idols as merely stone, of no real consequence. But he had Montezuma promise to allow the thorough cleansing and whitewashing of the shrines, and he demanded an immediate end to human sacrifices there. These strange concessions were made by both sides, in a foreshadowing of the religious and cultural blending that would eventually become a hallmark of a new Mexico.[19]

A church was constructed on top of the great pyramid, and when it was completed, Father Olmedo said mass before Cortés and a select group of his men.

Though a crisis had been averted and the populace was apparently assuaged, shortly afterward Cortés received disconcerting intelligence, first from his page Orteguilla, then from Malinche. Both had overheard (the quick-witted page now capable of some translation) Montezuma, in consultation with his military advisers, talk of insurgency. Montezuma himself came to Cortés and encouraged him to round up his troops and leave as soon as possible, lest they be overwhelmed.*[20]

Cortés tended to agree with the emperor, but he had a problem. He could leave, but once he got to the coast, he had no ships with which to sail back to the Indies or anywhere else. He needed time. Montezuma said if that was the case, he should hurry. Cortés sent his fleetest messengers on an emergency run to the coast, instructing carpenters there to help Martín López build three ships to sail as soon as possible back to Cuba. They would need more men to pull off this conquest.

When Cortés's messengers returned, they brought the worst possible news. Eighteen warships were anchored off the coast at Vera Cruz, their Spanish flags flapping in the gulf winds, but they weren't reinforcements. Cortés understood that it could mean only one thing—Diego Velázquez had sent an armada after him.[21]

---

*Montezuma's acquiescence to Cortés while in captivity has long been puzzled over and debated, some calling Montezuma weak, cowardly, pathetic, and at the very least enigmatic. But it would certainly make sense to apply some modern psychology to him, and the Stockholm syndrome, in which a captive becomes sympathetic to and ultimately identifies with his captor (initially out of fear), certainly applies here.

CHAPTER ELEVEN

Spaniard Versus Spaniard

HERNÁN CORTÉS COULD FEEL HIS PULSE QUICKEN. He thought
about his former patron Diego Velázquez, choleric and at times
irrational, their past disagreements, and how Velázquez had imprisoned him—and even threatened to hang him. True, Cortés
had been less than communicative with Velázquez, but the governor of Cuba was generally forgiving, so something else must
have set him off. But what? Cortés could not be sure, as he considered his next move.

What Cortés did not know was that in late July 1519, nine
months before, a direct order of his had been ignored—or at
least had been interpreted liberally. When Cortés had sent the
treasure ship to Spain, with its immense wealth and the legal
papers concerning the founding of Villa Rica de la Vera Cruz,
as well as letters to the king, he had explicitly instructed his pilot Alaminos to navigate directly to Spain, without making any
unnecessary stops. He had both practical and political reasons
for this order. Piracy on the high seas was a very real threat, so
the faster the journey the better. And being spotted in the
Indies was undesirable, as it might raise suspicions regarding
Cortés's actions and exploits on the Mexican mainland.

Once in Spain, the conquistadors Cortés had chosen—
Francisco de Montejo and Alonso Hernández Puertocarrero—

were supposed to act as Cortés's representatives or *procuradores*. But once they set out on the *Santa María de la Concepción*, Cortés's prized flagship, Montejo convinced Alaminos to alter their proposed course and stop for a short period in Cuba so that he could tidy up some business affairs at one of his properties in a place called Mariel. Montejo reasoned that the stop was on their way, and they could load up on supplies there. Puertocarrero, suffering lingering effects of coastal *vómito*, was easy to sway, for he could use a few days ashore before the long voyage. So they docked at Mariel. In port, one of Montejo's servants, a man named Francisco Pérez, while assisting with provisioning the ship with cassava, water, and swine, happened to spot some of the treasure in the ship's holds, and his eyes grew as large as the great gold disks upon which he gazed.

He was asked to keep this knowledge to himself, but as soon as Montejo and Puertocarrero boarded the flagship once more and sailed for Spain, Pérez spoke with Velázquez in Santiago. The ship carried so much gold, he said tantalizingly, that it required no other ballast! Pérez also intimated what he had heard about the new colony Cortés had founded on the coast. Velázquez now had confirmation that the new-found lands were loaded with precious metals and that his long-held suspicions about the rebellious Cortés had been well founded.

Velázquez launched two fast ships to overtake the *Santa María*, but pilot Alaminos had already made it to the powerful Gulf Stream and was gone. When Velázquez's chase ships returned empty-handed, he decided to send a military force to capture or kill Cortés—whichever was most convenient—and reestablish the area under his control. The man he chose for the duty was his friend and trusted lieutenant Pánfilo de Narváez, who had helped him conquer Cuba in the first place, with Cortés under him.

Narváez was a large, muscular, formidable man, ruddy and red-bearded, whose booming voice was "very deep and hoarse as if it came from a vault."[1] He had gained valuable military experience in his exploits on behalf of Velázquez in Cuba, and before that in Hispaniola, earning not only Velázquez's trust but also power and personal wealth in the form of lands and servants to work those lands. Confident, even haughty, he appeared a good choice to chase down the rogue conquistador Cortés.

But the Narváez expeditionary force would not be traveling without some oversight. Back on Hispaniola, the Royal Audience of Santo Domingo (*audiencia*), a commission that looked after concerns of the crown, caught wind of Velázquez's punitive mission and sent a delegate to ensure that Narváez followed strict protocol—and even to put a stop to his mission if necessary, should he act outside their purview. Above all, the Audience wanted to ensure that bloodshed between Spaniards was avoided. It sent Lucás Vázquez de Ayllón, a legal-minded and devoted Spaniard who had arrived in Hispaniola in 1502 and had served in judicial capacities since that time. The arrogant Narváez chafed at having an official looking over his shoulder, but for the moment he could do nothing about it. So with financial backing from Velázquez, Narváez assembled a powerful fleet containing nineteen ships,* more than eight hundred soldiers (twice the size of Cortés's original force), twenty cannons, eighty harquebusiers, 120 crossbowmen, and eighty cavalry (over four times as many horses as Cortés had brought). This force set out for Vera Cruz on March 5, 1520.[2]

BACK in the capital of Mexico, the curious captor-captive relationship between Cortés and Montezuma—sometimes convivial, sometimes contentious, always mysterious—was about to become irreparably strained. Four days after Cortés learned that Spanish ships had arrived on the coast, he and Montezuma were in one of their daily meetings when the emperor, whose

---

*One of these shipwrecked in rough weather en route, claiming all aboard, including the ship's captain, Cristóbal de Morante, a good friend of Velázquez. So the usual number referred to is eighteen.

Portrait of the *Gran Conquistador*, Hernán Cortés, in armor. Ambitious, calculating, politically brilliant and unwavering in his beliefs, Cortés arrived on the shores of Mexico in 1519 and soon told the indigenous Mexicans: "I and my companions suffer from a disease of the heart which can be cured only with gold."

Portrait of the Emperor Montezuma, with feather cloak and feather shield, as he would have appeared when Cortés met him. Deeply spiritual, superstitious, and enigmatic, Montezuma was so revered and feared that ordinary Aztec citizens dared not gaze directly upon him, under punishment of death.

Quetzalcoatl, the plumed serpent, god of the wind, learning and the priesthood, master of life, creator and civilizer, patron of every art and inventor of metallurgy.

A

Priests perform a ritual human sacrifice, which they believed insured the daily rising of the sun.

To quell potential mutiny and prevent his men from turning back, Cortés ordered his ships scuttled in the bay of Villa Rica.

During the important Festival of Toxcatl, Pedro de Alvarado ordered the entrapment and slaughter of thousands of the Aztec's finest warriors and priests.

Under Spanish custody, Montezuma was ordered to a rooftop and forced to plead with his people not to attack the Spaniards. His appeals were met with a rain of spears and stones. The great emperor no longer held power over his own people.

The interpreter Malinche was instrumental in the Spanish conquest of Mexico. Not long after receiving her as a gift, Cortés discovered her skills with language and from that moment on she rarely left his side.

Spanish Captain Pedro de Alvarado's actions while in command at Tenochtitlán left the Spanish forces besieged inside the city and very nearly cost them the conquest and all of their lives.

The siege and conquest of Tenochtitlán, summer of 1521. The Spaniards fought along the causeways and on the water, using an armada of specially-built cannon-mounted "brigantines," which ruled the waters of the lake district for nearly three months and proved too powerful and maneuverable for the Aztec canoes.

After the Spaniards barely escaped with their lives during La Noche Triste, they fought the important Battle of Otumba. The battle was perhaps the Aztecs' last best chance to annihilate the intruding Spaniards, but the Spanish cavalry and horses proved too formidable on the open plain. Note the standard-bearer borne on the litter.

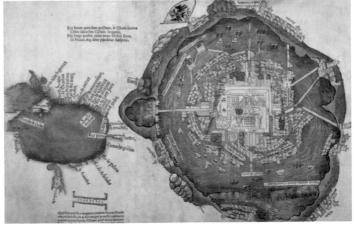

An early map of the
Aztec capital, which
was published with
Cortés's second letter
to Charles V.

After courageously defending Tenochtitlán for nearly three months of constant siege, Cuauhtémoc was finally captured on August 13, 1521, forcing an official Aztec surrender.

Portrait of an elderly Hernán Cortés, conqueror of Mexico.

mood seemed curiously exuberant given his circumstances, produced pictographs showing eighteen ships, drawn by spies and sent to him by his fastest runners. It turned out that Montezuma had known about these ships since the day of their arrival. Cortés felt slighted and a little suspicious. Why, he asked, had Montezuma chosen to withhold this vital information from him? Montezuma responded (rather coyly and disingenuously) that he had needed to ascertain through messengers (as he had done with the arrival of Cortés) the identity and intentions of the visitors. Montezuma was pleased, he said, because these ships could provide Cortés and his men with a way home. The pictures drawn suggested there were plenty of ships for the job. Montezuma conveniently failed to mention to Cortés that he had been exchanging political correspondence with Narváez.

Cortés confirmed, from his own messengers, that these ships were under the aegis of Velázquez and were captained by his old acquaintance Pánfilo de Narváez. Cortés knew what Montezuma did not: that he was swimming in dangerous political waters and would need to deal immediately with this threat to his effort to secure the empire. Angered with Montezuma for withholding the information, Cortés left to discuss matters with his captains-in-arms. The meeting was brief and heated. The Spaniards universally agreed that, though the mission was dangerous, Cortés should strike out for the coast and confront Narváez personally, to discover his intentions and, if necessary, fight for what they had already earned through their blood and sacrifice. Cortés sealed the meeting with a threat: "Death to him and anyone who argues about the matter."[3]

As Cortés always did when he met a crisis, he immediately launched into action. Though he hated to do it, he knew that he must divide his already dispersed troops. Pedro de Alvarado and 120 Spaniards would remain in Tenochtitlán to maintain guard over Montezuma and over the plunder they had garnered. Cortés feared it was too small a force, but with the support of the Tlaxcalans, he hoped for the best.

Cortés then organized a small but elite force of eighty soldiers to join 150 more Spaniards under Captain Velázquez de León (who remained out on military reconnaissance and gold-finding missions) at Cholula. He hoped to use diplomacy if possible, and to that end he dispatched Father Olmedo to the coast, accompanied by guides, to discover what he could about the nature and intentions of the armada. But Cortés had already determined that he would fight his own countrymen if forced to.

For his part, Narváez had disembarked on the coast and was learning as much as he could about the current situation in the region, both among the native population and with respect to Cortés. He soon stumbled on what appeared to be good fortune: three Spaniards, members of the recent Diego Pizarro scouting expedition who remained in the area. They were friendly to Narváez, homesick and disenchanted with their long and dangerous service under Cortés. Opening up to Narváez (especially when their tongues were loosened with copious Spanish wine and fresh food), they gave him much intelligence. They told him about the fort and township at Vera Cruz and about their alliance with Cempoala, and they regaled him with tales of Tenochtitlán. Narváez sensed their dissatisfaction and through promises was able to sway them to come over to his side. Having been for a time in the region, the three spoke crude but serviceable Nahuatl, enough to provide rudimentary translation between Narváez and the local population.[4]

Rather than attempt to overthrow Villa Rica de la Vera Cruz by force, Narváez sent three diplomats—a notary, a priest, and a soldier (named respectively Vergara, Guevara, and Amaya)—to speak to whoever was in command there and report the arrival of the Narváez expedition in the territory. Cortés, they were to explain, was a traitor with no legal claims to the settlement, and the garrison and soldiers were to join forces with Narváez, lest they be branded traitors to Spain and the crown as well. When the three men arrived, they were directed to Captain Gonzalo de Sandoval, whom Cortés had entrusted to run affairs there. Deeply loyal to his commander, Sandoval listened carefully to the claims and warrants of the three men, which they read from documents. But as soon as he heard Cortés called a traitor, he held up his hand and said that was enough. Sandoval motioned to his soldiers, who hurled strong woven nets over Narváez's ambassadors. Incensed, Sandoval ordered his men to enlist Totonac porters to physically haul the men over the mountains and deposit them at the feet of Hernán Cortés. They could read whatever warrants they might have to him personally and see how well they fared. He wrote a letter to Cortés apprising him of the tenuous situation on the coast and of Narváez's apparent intention to take over their town and fort. The Totonac porters, shouldering the writhing human bundles, hurried toward Tenochtitlán, led by Pedro de Solis.[5]

Cortés was still making preparations to depart and organizing his men and provisions when he learned of Solis's imminent arrival. He sent a small welcoming committee, including horses, to greet the party on the road. The prisoners were released from their nets and allowed to ride into the capital in style, for Cortés had shrewdly decided to placate them by treating them with the utmost dignity and politeness. Riding in, the men were as dazzled as Cortés had been by the City of Dreams. Cortés fed and housed them with great fanfare, wining and dining them and even personally giving them a tour of the magnificent city. He showed them the treasures he had appropriated and plied them with personal riches and enough extra to distribute among Narváez's more malleable soldiers upon their safe return to the coast, which he guaranteed in just a few days. Immediately, and rather easily, Cortés had bought their allegiance. He took care to include precious gifts for the judge Vázquez de Ayllón, about whom he had just learned.[6]

Cortés's manipulations had worked: the three Narváez men were now effectively his, and they faithfully followed their new commander's instructions. Cortés sent them away from Tenochtitlán well fed and flush with gold, which they carried on horseback, their return journey much more comfortable and dignified than had been their initial conveyance on the backs of bearers. With Narváez they were tight-lipped, telling him only that they had been imprisoned and waylaid when they had attempted to read the documents. Cortés, a decent Christian, had treated them very well, they said. They remained silent on the matter of the gold they had received, fearing its confiscation, but as instructed they delivered the gifts to Ayllón and began to clandestinely filter through the camp, telling Narváez's most impressionable soldiers about the immense wealth they had seen in Cortés's possession and how he had promised rich compensation for any soldiers willing to commit to his cause.

Ayllón remained dedicated to finding a peaceful resolution between Narváez and Cortés, but the "gift" certainly seemed to incline him in Cortés's favor. He approached Narváez, who was already irritable, and suggested that peace be sought between the rival factions. Narváez had resented Ayllón's imposed presence from the outset and was in no mood to hear his suggestions. He angrily had the upstart and meddling judge bound, placed on a ship, and sent back to Cuba, where he belonged. During the voyage Ayllón used his considerable powers of persuasion, telling the captain that, should he continue the course for Cuba, he would suffer death by hanging along with all his shipmates. The captain apparently preferred the potential future wrath of Narváez to swinging from a rope, so he altered his course, as directed by Ayllón, to Santo Domingo, Hispaniola, where Ayllón eventually argued in favor of Hernán Cortés before the Royal Audience, the report of which proceedings was later sent to Spain.[7]

Hernán Cortés was always thorough, especially concerning legal matters. Once the preparations among his elite corps of cavalry and foot soldiers were nearly complete, he thought it prudent to send a personal envoy to the coast, and for this important assignment he settled on Father Olmedo, hoping that a priest, an agent of God, might receive a fair audience. Cortés wrote a letter to Narváez expressing an interest in proceeding peaceably toward mutual goals and arguing for a collaboration that would quite probably benefit them both. He would gladly join forces with Narváez, he said, and share all the wealth that had so far been obtained, but one small detail, one minor sticking point, stood in the way: Narváez must produce legal documents from the crown in Spain denying or in some way overriding the foundation of Villa Rica de la Vera Cruz. If he could do so, Cortés (who was gambling that he could not) wrote slyly, and boldly, that he would be happy to submit to Narváez and, by extension, to Velázquez. But if Narváez did not possess such a writ, well then, the two were at something of an impasse; in fact, lacking such written authority, Narváez would have to depart, for he was trespassing. Cortés also entrusted Father Olmedo to deliver a personal letter to his old friend (and one of the original financiers of Cortés's expedition) Andrés de Duero, who was currently with Narváez. The letter to Duero came with a hefty portion of gold, and Olmedo was instructed to give yet more gold to certain of Narváez's captains as well.[8]

While Cortés readied to depart Tenochtitlán, Narváez was already busy moving into Cempoala. Sandoval's rebuke at Villa Rica had caused him to consider another approach to settling in the region, and the city of Cempoala seemed a feasible home, especially when Narváez learned that a certain obese chief in that city was friendly, in general, to the Spaniards. It was Tlacochcalcatl, the "fat chief," Cortés's original ally in the Totonac region. Through a show of military force, Narváez bullied Tlacochcalcatl into allowing him to move his forces into the city. He set up defenses right in the religious center, appropriating the main pyramid for his base of operations and establishing his own quarters on its summit. He put cannons at the steps around the perimeter, and evicted Cempoalans from their homes to accommodate his captains and soldiers.[9]

The fickle and easily duped "fat chief" bought into Narváez's claim that Cortés was defying the laws of his own king in Spain and that Narváez was the rightful leader to settle here. But he realized his mistake when Narváez ordered his men to pilfer the village, taking women and girls for his men and all the gold gifts that Cortés had sent with the Cempoalan bearers when they returned. Only after it was too late did Tlacochcalcatl realize that this new Spaniard whom he now harbored was a much greater threat to his people's security than Cortés.

Father Olmedo arrived and delivered Cortés's letter to Narváez, who interpreted Cortés's words as aggressive, even threatening. He was about to place Father Olmedo in irons on general principle, but the cooler head of Andrés de Duero prevailed, and Olmedo was allowed to move about freely. In hindsight, Narváez might have preferred to have acted on his passion, because Olmedo gained private audiences with some of Narváez's captains and swayed them toward the side of Cortés.

In the middle of May 1520, as the machinations between Cortés and Narváez were in full swing and the two had failed to reach any sort of agreement, Cortés rode out from the capital. Montezuma accompanied him and his small force as far as the causeway, where he descended from his litter and bade his captor farewell. Montezuma had offered him the services of many thousands of warriors and bearers, but Cortés rather arrogantly declined, saying he needed only the assistance of his God. The two even embraced, an odd display but one that suggested a mutual, if guarded, respect.[10] For half a year now the two had effectively cogoverned the Aztec empire. And now both men were barely hanging on to power. Montezuma's empire was on the precipice of civil rebellion, his people fearful, his lords and priests seriously questioning his leadership. Cortés, for his part, was being pursued by his own countrymen and he intended to confront, and perhaps kill, his own brethren—a notion both distasteful and unprecedented in the New World. As Cortés mounted his horse and spurred it toward the east, both he and the emperor Montezuma stared into a clouded and uncertain future.

CORTÉS marched down the southern causeway, out of the city, and back up through the mountains the way he had originally come, his small but select force supported by a number of Tlaxcalans. They passed between the two great volcanoes Popocatépetl and Iztaccíhuatl, once again amazed by their enormity and power. Fit and rested, they moved fast and arrived soon in Cholula, where they waited to rendezvous with more Spanish troops—some 250 soldiers under the command of Velázquez de León and Rodrigo Rangel. When they arrived, Cortés mustered his force of about 350 and struck out across the hard plateau for Tlaxcala. He also dispatched a messenger to Sandoval on the coast, saying that Cortés was en route and wished to meet up with him and the finest troops from the garrison at Tlaxcala.

Outside the city of Tlaxcala Cortés came upon Father Olmedo and his guides returning from Narváez's camp. Cortés gleaned as much intelligence as he could from the priest, who described Narváez's military positions and the number and deployment of his men. The general mood and attitude among the soldiers, Cortés was delighted to discover, was not entirely unified. Father Olmedo said that he had distributed bribe-gold to certain captains and that some seemed to have been won over. But then Father Olmedo turned to a most unsettling topic. Montezuma had conducted surreptitious communications with Narváez, Olmedo said, the import of which went beyond polite gift-giving. They had actually discussed Cortés in some detail, and Montezuma seemed even to have offered to aid Narváez and provide support for his army, in exchange for which Narváez was to free Montezuma and arrest or kill Cortés.[11] This news enraged the captain-general, who was now hell-bent on dispatching the interloper Narváez immediately. He would deal with Montezuma when the time came.

Cortés pressed on to Tlaxcala. There, as planned, he met Sandoval, who had brought sixty men from Villa Rica on a circuitous and arduous march through the thick woodlands and high mountains. Sandoval's men were in good spirits, eager to be involved in active duty again and pleased to hear tales from their compatriots who had been in Tenochtitlán for the last six months. Three hundred specially commissioned lances arrived, wrought by craftsmen in Chinantla in double-edged copper and of great length, to be used against Narváez's cavalry. Though Cortés hated to wound, let alone kill, any of the prized Spanish mounts, he would do what he had to.[12] After inspecting the weapons and the state of his troops—which now included some crossbowmen and a small number of horses but only a very few harquebusiers (most of them having been left with Alvarado in Tenochtitlán)—Cortés advanced toward Cempoala.

They crossed the parched tablelands, heading east until the trail finally spilled toward the sea. Humidity rose up from the smoldering plains of the *tierra caliente* below, and the men recalled the discomfort and stifling heat of the oppressive coast, but on they marched, until some forty-five miles before Cempoala they came upon a group of envoys from Narváez. Cortés was surprised to see among them his friend and business associate Andrés de Duero, who had been instrumental, back in Cuba, in planning and organizing Cortés's expedition. Cortés had certainly not forgotten their mutual allegiance. The secret meeting to install Cortés as the man for the expedition had been held at Duero's home, with support from the king's accountant Andrés de Lares. Duero had been the one to write the contract that made Cortés captain-general. But Duero also served as secretary to Governor Velázquez, so Cortés needed to establish where Duero's loyalties now lay.

Cortés greeted Duero warmly, wrapping him in a firm fraternal embrace. Duero would have noticed the beautiful and intelligent Indian woman always at the side of Cortés, whom the captain-general called Malinche. The two men talked privately. Cortés learned that shortly after the expedition had sailed for the new-found lands, Lares had died. Though the news saddened him, Cortés used this information to his advantage. He verbally reconfirmed their initial agreement, assuring Duero that he remained his business partner, and whispered to him tales of the vast wealth in Mexico. The two would share in all the spoils, he underlined, once the conquest was complete. But Narváez posed a serious, perhaps devastating impediment to those plans and must be dealt with.[13]

Duero suggested that Cortés seek a peaceful resolution with Narváez, primarily on the grounds that his force was superior and would trounce Cortés. Confident from the successes of his previous battles, Cortés scoffed, reiterating what he had told Narváez through messengers. "If Narváez bears a royal commission," he bellowed, "I will readily submit to him. But he has produced none . . . I am a servant of the king; I have conquered the country for him; and for him, I and my brave followers will defend it, be assured, to the last drop of my blood."[14] Duero could see that Cortés was a changed man, that his time on the mainland had steeled his will. He bore the scars of recent battles, and his face was creased by sun and wind. His piercing eyes darted about. He would not be swayed.

Still, Duero felt compelled to convey a proposal by Narváez that the two captains meet at a neutral location, each bringing only a handful of their men—ten at most—to discuss the situation. Cortés, after briefly conferring with his captains and Father Olmedo, concluded that it was a trap and summarily dismissed the idea. No, he would proceed to Cempoala with his complete complement of troops and give his answer on the battlefield. He treated Duero to handsome gifts of gold, reassuring him once again of their partnership and of the mutual benefit of turning Narváez away. Cortés then sent Duero and the other envoys, along with Father Olmedo, back to Narváez with a letter stating that Narváez and his men should submit to the captain-general as a representative of the crown, and if they did not, he would treat them as rebels and traitors. The letter was signed by Hernán Cortés, all of his officers, and a number of his best soldiers.[15]

Narváez was already in a foul mood when he received the letter. Tlacochcalcatl, annoyed by the Spaniards' rude behavior, had approached him, exclaiming, "I tell you that when you least expect it, he [Cortés] will be here and will kill you."[16] Narváez flew into a rage. He railed against Cortés and anyone under his command. Since Cortés appeared to be unyielding, he began shoring up his defenses around Cempoala. With his thunderous voice, he even made a loud public promise to pay two thousand pesos to the soldiers who killed Hernán Cortés and his captain Sandoval.[17] But Father Olmedo, and now Andrés de Duero, greased the palms of many more soldiers and crucial captains in Narváez's army, so that by the time Cortés and his men marched on Cempoala, perhaps as many as two hundred of the new arrivals (one-fifth of the force) were kindly disposed toward him. Tales of the City of Dreams, and the garish gold chains worn by Cortés's soldiers, clearly influenced these fortune-seekers.

CORTÉS made his move around May 28, driving his force forward in misty rain through vine-choked forests and dense stands of bamboo. At sunset they came to the Río de Canoas (River of Canoes), which was swollen to near flooding from the recent coastal rains, and while scouts sought fordable narrows, he mustered the rest of his men for a speech. To inspire them, he recounted the glories of their current campaign, the battles and spoils they had already won against great odds. They were outnumbered, he said, but this had been the case in most of their battles thus far, and they had always prevailed. And while they were experienced and hardened from battle and toil, he continued, Narváez's men were untested and soft, having just arrived from the comforts of their homes in the Indies. By now well practiced in the arts of rhetoric, Cortés ended his impassioned speech by saying: "So, gentlemen, our lives and honor depend, after God, on your courage and strong arms; I have no other favor to ask of you or to remind you of but that this is the touchstone of our honor and our glory for ever

and ever, and it is better to die worthily than to live dishonored."[18]

Rousing cheers went around the camp, and the men even
hoisted Cortés onto their shoulders until he ordered them to
put him down. There was much work to do.

As it grew dark, the rains increased. In the sputtering camp-
fire light Cortés gathered his now-inflamed men and told them
that they would make a surprise night attack. From their time
in Cempoala and the detailed intelligence he had received
from Father Olmedo and Sandoval, he knew the exact locations of Narváez's defenses, artillery placements, and troops.
He broke his army into companies, each with specific duties
and orders. Sixty would go to seize and subdue the artillery, as
well as provide cover for Sandoval. Sandoval was given the
most important responsibility: commanding eighty handpicked soldiers and a few of the best and brightest captains, he
was to personally seize Narváez and, if he resisted, "kill him on
the spot."[19] Diego de Ordaz led the largest company of nearly
one hundred men, and Cortés would lead the remaining
soldiers in a free-roving capacity, to be employed where most
required.[20]

While Cortés rallied his troops and organized his companies, Narváez, acting on messenger intelligence that Cortés
was in the vicinity, rode out with many of his cavalry and most
of his troops to an open plain, a likely spot for battle, about a
mile from Cempoala. There they stood, shifting and squelch-
ing in the dank muck, as the rain drenched them to the skin
even through their armor. Finally, after hours of waiting in the
deluge, night fell, and Narváez figured that the battle would
take place tomorrow. He left a couple of sentries to monitor
the area and sent out a cavalry force of about forty toward a
likely arrival spot. That done, he returned with the rest of his
men to Cempoala, where they could rest in more comfort for
the next day's battle.[21]

Cortés and his men moved through the night, the darkness concealing their progress and the pounding rains muting
the sounds of their movements. Undeterred by the pelting

rainstorm, and using their long spears for balance and purchase, they forded the roiling Río de Canoas, but with great
difficulty; some lost their footing on the slick bottom and were
forced to swim for their lives in the torrent.[22] Two men were
washed downriver. The rest made it across and pushed on,
forging through muck and mire until they came to the edge of
the woods, then the clearing. There they startled the two
Narváez sentries and in a brief skirmish subdued one of them;
the other avoided capture and slipped away into the darkness,
sprinting for his life toward Cempoala.

Cortés personally interrogated the captured sentry, and
though initially the man held his tongue, he eventually revealed (a noose tightened about his neck provided some incen-
tive) a little information. Even though the escaped sentry
might have made it back and alerted Narváez, Cortés made final preparations, stashing food and provisions and extraneous
equipment in a small ravine, to be guarded by the page Juan de
Ortega. Cortés took Malinche aside and requested that she remain safely with Ortega. Father Olmedo gave a quick mass.
Then Cortés ordered the stealthy nighttime assault, telling his
men to run swiftly and silently.

Sandoval sped toward the pyramid temple, bent on finding
Narváez, who was just now being awakened by the sentinel,
Hurtado. Out of breath from his sprint, Hurtado bounded up
the pyramid steps and shook Narváez vigorously, exclaiming
that Cortés was coming. Narváez roused slowly but did not
panic. Could Cortés really have made it here so quickly, in the
wet conditions and with the raging river to contend with? He
doubted it but pulled his clothes on (apparently not possessing
Cortés's discipline to sleep in full armor). As Sandoval's men
began ascending the pyramid, Narváez was still half-asleep in
bare feet. His call to arms came feebly and too late.

Sandoval and his eighty men flew up the steps and fought
the thirty guards along the platform in hand-to-hand battle.
The guards fought hard, but the speed of the attack and the
skill of Cortés's soldiers were overwhelming. Hearing the commotion outside his sleeping quarters, Narváez finally emerged,

brandishing a great two-handed broadsword, hacking away in the darkness. All around him the bizarre flickering of fireflies appeared like "the burning matches of arquebuses."[23] and only now that Cortés's crafty raiding forces were already swarming the square below, warning trumpets blew a mournful alarm.

Sandoval and his men, expertly wielding their pikes, swords, and the long, specially made copper-tipped Chinantla spears, surged forward, swinging viciously, and through the darkness they heard the bloodcurdling cry "Holy Mary protect me, they have killed me and destroyed my eye!"[24] The sharp tip of a pike had impaled Narváez's face, sinking deep into an eye socket. Blood spewed from the cavity, pouring down his face and over his bearded chin as he fell to his knees, gasping in agony.[25] Narváez must surrender, Sandoval barked, or the shrine would be set ablaze, consuming him and all his men. Narváez, thinking that he was dying, could only writhe in pitiful despair. When no order to surrender came, Martín López, the shipbuilder, set fire to the shrine's thatched roof, and flames enveloped the place. Shortly thereafter Narváez crawled from the burning wreckage, his bare feet scorched and blistered.[26] Ignoring his cries for help, Sandoval dragged him away and had him clapped in leg irons.[27]

Once the commander Narváez was seized and arrested, the remainder of the raid proved quick work for Cortés, whose clever and experienced warfare tactics hindered the little resistance Narváez's troops offered. On their way into Cempoala, Pizarro's men had slunk in and cut the girth straps of Narváez's cavalry's saddles; the riders now slammed ingloriously to the drenched ground as they tried to mount, and the horses bucked and galloped off into the night. The cannon-mouths of many of the artillery had been clogged with wax so that they either misfired or failed completely.[28]

By sunrise, the first pitched battle between Spanish forces in the Americas was over. Cortés had lost two men, while fifteen of Narváez's men had fallen during the invasion, which had lasted less than an hour. Among the dead was Diego Velázquez, the young nephew of Cuba's governor. Many men, mostly on the side of Narváez, lay wounded, and these Cortés had attended to by surgeons. Tlacochcalcatl, who had been in the wrong place at the wrong time, suffered a knife wound during the fighting, though it was not fatal.[29]

Pánfilo de Narváez, hauled in chains before his vanquisher, blood clotting in his spoiled eye socket, must have wished he had died rather than face the shame of this humiliating defeat. Diego Velázquez had entrusted him with an eighteen-ship armada, a cavalry of eighty horses, and an army nearly five times the size of Cortés's, and now he lay prostrate before Cortés, half-blind and half-dead. As the skies cleared and the sun rose over the Gulf Coast, he heard the growing chants of "Long live the king, long live the king, and in his royal name, *viva* Cortés, victory!"[30] He would have plenty of time to relive that ill-fated night, for Cortés would keep him imprisoned in sweltering, insect-bitten Vera Cruz for the next three years.*[31]

Quick to capitalize on his overwhelming victory, Cortés released all prisoners and converted them to his cause, dangling Mexico's wealth before them and distributing gold among those who had not already been bribed. His force of fighting Spaniards now swelled to thirteen hundred. He appropriated all the horses of Narváez's cavalry, giving him a total of ninety-six, which he desperately needed. Then he unloaded all the food stores, the wine, the provisions and equipment from Narváez's fleet, all of which he kept at Villa Rica, salted away for emergency and reserve support. As he had done the year before, he scuttled all but two ships, retaining again the sails, masts, hardware, rigging, and navigation equipment, anything he might use in the future. The two remaining ships he would send to the islands for domestic brood stock, including mares, goats, calves, sheep, and even chickens.[32]

But Hernán Cortés hardly had time to celebrate his victory.

---

*Narváez's star-crossed nightmare would not end there. In 1528, partly fueled by the stinging memory of his loss to Cortés, the one-eyed conquistador would lead an expedition to Florida, only to have all but four of his original crew perish during the journey. Narváez died at sea, without food or water and riddled with leprosy.

Soon a messenger arrived from the capital, bearing disturbing emergency news from Pedro de Alvarado. The hurried dispatch pleaded for the captain-general to return to Tenochtitlán immediately, with all the forces he could assemble. Alvarado was under siege, and the Aztecs were in full-scale rebellion.

CHAPTER TWELVE

The Festival of Toxcatl

WITH HIS FRESH NEW CONSCRIPTS trailing behind, Cortés rode hurriedly at the head of a formidable cavalry, back up into the mountains, bound for the scablands and the Valley of Mexico beyond. While he rode, back in Tenochtitlán, the lives of Pedro de Alvarado and his men hung in the balance.

AFTER Cortés left the capital, the situation had gone from uneasy to desperate within a matter of days. Rumors coursed through the streets that the chief *teule* Cortés had gone, never to return, and that another *teule* had arrived to take his place, perhaps even to free Montezuma. Others, including key members of the nobility, wondered why, with Cortés gone, their emperor remained in the custody of this small and insignificant group of Spaniards.

Alvarado and a remnant force of 120 noticed the changed and charged atmosphere, as they attempted to hold down the emperor and his city. Montezuma was seen whispering among his lords and priests, who came and went with frequency, and curiously, a number of his closest relatives had been sent away on errands from which they had yet to return. Montezuma himself, formerly convivial—even jovial—with Alvarado, no longer teased him playfully. He ceased playing games of *totoloqui* and *patolli* and appeared tense, distracted. His petulant mood and behavior worried Alvarado.

What worried him even more was that the Aztecs had ceased bringing food to the Spaniards. Ever since their arrival on mainland Mexico, the cessation of food by their hosts had been a bad sign, usually followed by armed conflict. A servant girl who washed and cooked for the Spaniards continued to bring food, but after a few days she was found dead, presumably killed for having aided the Spaniards, and from then on the soldiers had to purchase food from the market.[1] It was inconvenient, but they had to make do. Eventually even the market would be shut off to them.

Alvarado also received intelligence (though he suspected it was merely a rumor) that Montezuma and Narváez had been exchanging messages, even gifts. This fact, coupled with a lack of news from Cortés, heightened his tension. Had Narváez's larger force already overwhelmed Cortés, and was Narváez on his way to the capital? There was much Alvarado did not know with certainty.

The annual Festival of Toxcatl was now upon them. During three weeks in May, at the height of the dry season, prayer ceremonies were dedicated to Tezcatlipoca (the Smoking Mirror, Omnipotent Power) in supplication for the onset of rains that would fill the dry streambeds and parched crop fields with the life-giving liquid whose importance was second only to blood. Before Cortés departed for the coast, Montezuma had requested that this important festival proceed as usual, for failure to do so would incite confusion, perhaps even rioting, among the populace. Everyone, Montezuma had informed Cortés, from the lowliest servant to the emperor himself participated in the festival. Cortés had agreed that it should go on as usual.

Now Montezuma and a number of his high priests approached Alvarado to confirm that preparations for the festival were beginning. Alvarado consented, though he set the condition that there be no human sacrifices, a stipulation that was both naïve and unrealistic.

The very nature of the festival was predicated on human sacrifice, including that of four young girls who had fasted for twenty days, and culminating in the sacrifice of a special *ixiptla*, a handpicked virgin male youth, unblemished and embodying perfection. Selected a year in advance, he was an impersonator of, or manifestation of, Tezcatlipoca, and for an entire year he was instructed by the highest priests in music, flute playing, and singing. He was revered by all as a god incarnate, treated with veneration, and worshipped. After weeks of dancing and singing, the *ixiptla* would be paraded publicly through the streets, arriving finally at the Great Temple, whose high steep steps he would willingly ascend, breaking his conch flute in pieces as he climbed. At the top priests would meet him. He would turn and look down to acknowledge the power of the great lake, then acquiesce under the numbing euphoria of sacred mushrooms. Priests would hold down his arms and legs, as the obsidian blade impaled his thorax. His heart would be torn from him and offered, still pulsing, to the sun. Then he would be beheaded, his skull displayed on the skull rack for all to see. His sacrificial death signaled the birth of the next year's *ixiptla*, who was publicly named, and the cycle was renewed. The festival, its origins, and its enactment were integral to Aztec life.[2]

Toxcatl was considered the most splendid and important of all religious festivals, and the sacrifice of the *ixiptla* was its symbolic grand finale. So even had the priests and Montezuma told Alvarado that there would be no human sacrifices, they could hardly have upheld their promise. The very notion was absurd, akin to asking Cortés and his Christian followers to stop taking communion.

As the festival approached, Alvarado walked about the sacred precinct, inspecting the grounds and making mental notes. During these observations some of the head Tlaxcalans still in the city approached Alvarado in agitation, saying that they feared for their lives because each year at this festival many of their people, tribute prisoners or those won during Flower Wars, were ritually sacrificed. Trembling, they claimed to have heard that at the conclusion of the ceremony, when the city was teeming with hundreds of thousands of pilgrims, the Aztecs would assault the Spaniards.[3] Alvarado took their concerns under advisement and continued to scout the area of the main temple, where Montezuma had told him that most of the dancing, feasting, and celebrating would occur.

As he went, Alvarado came upon one strange and unnerving sight after another. At the central square he saw many large stakes fixed deep into the ground, which the Tlaxcalans warned were for tethering the Spaniards to before they were sacrificed. Alvarado noted that the main buildings of the temple area were draped in fine, resplendent canopies of rich cloth, which concerned him, for he had previously seen such cloth awnings shrouding sacrificial ceremonies.

Next he encountered a group of women who were busy working on a large statue of the war god Huitzilopochtli, whose image he recognized from the one in the shrine on the summit of the Great Temple. He stared at the weird figure, which was raised on poles and covered with the kneaded dough of ground amaranth seed, the dough laced with honey and thickened with the blood of fresh sacrifice victims. Above and below the ghastly eyes were painted crossbars, and the ears bore turquoise serpent earrings, gold hoops dangling from them. The nose was adorned with a ring in the form of a war arrow and was made of gold and gemstones. The women placed a headdress of hummingbird feathers on the statue's head.

The body of the statue was adorned with ornately decorated, flowing cloaks painted with images of skulls and human bones; the outer vest depicted "dismembered human parts: skulls, ears, hearts, intestines, torsos, breasts, hands, and feet."[4] The head of the god was matted with feathers and painted with brilliant blue stripes. The statue held a bamboo shield of eagle feathers aloft in one hand, with four arrows; the other hoisted a paper banner drenched in human blood.[5]

These images and rituals unsettled Alvarado, but the presence of what appeared to be sacrificial victims—men and women captives, drawn and diminished from fasting—particularly set him on edge. He learned, too, that for the Toxcatl festival the image of the Virgin Mary atop the temple pyramid would be removed and replaced with the elaborate, transformed statue of Huitzilopochtli. Alvarado's men reported seeing thick coils of ropes at the base of the pyramid, as well as pulleys and scaffolding that would be used to heave the statue up to the summit of the Great Temple.

Alvarado and his men encountered three finely dressed Indians with freshly shaved heads, each man tied to a separate Aztec idol and appearing very much like a potential sacrifice victim. Alvarado untied these men and brought them back to the palace for questioning, using an interpreter named Francisco. When they proved uncommunicative, Alvarado resorted to brutal torture, searing their stomachs with burning logs. Still these stoic unfortunates refused to speak, so after much torture Alvarado ordered one of the Indians heaved to his death from the palace roof, forcing the others to watch. (Apparently Alvarado deemed brutal physical torture and execution less repugnant than ritualized human sacrifice for religious purposes.) Seeing this, one of the others offered some information, saying he had heard that very soon after the festival the Aztecs were going to revolt and attack the Spaniards. Incensed, Alvarado called forth two of Montezuma's close relatives and tortured them until they confirmed an imminent rebellion among the Mexica; the Spaniards were to be taken prisoner and sacrificed.[6]

Alvarado called on Montezuma, telling the emperor what he had learned and demanding that he put a stop to any planned insurgence against the Spaniards. Montezuma replied only that, imprisoned as he was, he had no control over his people. Angry with this lack of cooperation, and made anxious by rumors that the Aztecs were chiseling holes in the palace's rear walls and setting up ladders to scale to the upper floors, Alvarado placed a large guard around Montezuma, putting him under constant surveillance. He ordered that Montezuma neither witness nor participate in the festival.

Alvarado attended the festival, nervously waiting for an attack. The first few days passed without incident. On its fourth day the impetuous and apprehensive captain struck in a way that shocked the Aztec world to its core. Leaving sixty men—half his soldiers—to guard Montezuma, Alvarado and the remaining sixty, plus a number of Tlaxcalan allies, moved in full battle armor into tactical positions. He posted musketeers atop the walls enclosing the Patio of Dances, where the elaborate Serpent Dance was to commence. And he positioned heavily armed horsemen and foot soldiers at the three main gates that accessed the sacred patio. These special gates had names and iconic connections: the Eagle Gate, the Gate of the Canestalk, and the Gate of the Obsidian Serpent.[7]

In anticipation of the Serpent Dance, the main patio began to fill with high and lesser nobles. The aristocracy were all dressed in their finest ceremonial costumes: they donned marvelous headdresses plumed with quetzal and macaw feathers. The dancers' cotton loincloths were intricately embroidered, over which were draped flowing woven cloaks made of feathers and fine animal skins of puma, jaguar, ocelot, and rabbit. The dancing nobles covered themselves in fine jewelry, with bracelets and armbands, some in gold, some in leather or hide and beaded with jade pieces. Dangling from their necks were shell or jade chains, and their pierced ears and noses displayed shining amber crystals. Their feet and legs, lifting and falling rhythmically to the beat of the drums, were covered in ocelot skin sandals, beautiful tan-yellow with black spots. Dangling gold bells jingled as they danced.[8]

By the time the drumming, flute playing, and dancing began, four to five hundred dancers and a few thousand Aztec observers—watching or participating in minor roles—filled the dance patio and courtyard. They swayed and gyrated in unison to the thumping of the drums, some upright, played by hand, others laid level and beaten with round, rubber-headed hammers. The dancers coursed and chanted, undulating in a roiling, rhythmical wave, to hollow horn sounds blown through bone fifes, shell conches, and flutes. On and on the dancers pulsated, consumed by spirits, enveloped and alive, the line of writhing Aztec nobles becoming the physical embodiment of a serpent. The music and drumming and chanting rose over the patio walls and poured into the streets of the city. Commoners stopped to listen in awe, aware of the sacredness of the spectacle.

Alvarado and his men observed the dancing in confused wonder, impressed by the elaborate ritual and the skill of the participants but unable to comprehend the euphoria or trance that infused the dancers, who seemed utterly consumed by the enactment. The Serpent Dance brought the participants into a unity of the senses, a whole-human awakening or *synesthesia*, combining the aural, visual, and tactile experiences of dance with the ritual spiritual experience of seeing their gods—both as icons and as human impersonators—all at once, so that the mood became frenzied.[9]

Pedro de Alvarado had seen enough.

The gates to all three entrances were slammed shut and blocked by his armed soldiers. Above the pounding drums and ecstatic chants, Alvarado bellowed the order "Let them die!"[10] and without warning set his men upon the unarmed, defenseless dancers. Musket shots from above pierced celebrants and spectators alike, scything them to the patio floor. The foot soldiers rushed headlong into the mass, swinging their sharpened Toledo swords. First they slayed the dance leader, a lone drummer. His arms were lopped from his body, and as he fell to the ground near his drum, he was beheaded with one stroke from a Spanish sword. The Aztecs, terrorized, ran for their lives.

But they were penned in. Trying to escape, they stampeded one another; some attempted to scale the courtyard walls, but few were successful, and the gates had been further blockaded by some one thousand armed Tlaxcalans.[11] Alvarado's swordsmen and pikemen hacked and slashed with impunity, cutting the hands from drummers who continued drumming, thrusting pikes and spears into the bodies of participants and spectators until runnels of their blood stained the patio stones. Aztec reports from a few nobles who managed to escape that day recalled the ruthless horror of the massacre: "They slashed others in the abdomen, and their entrails all spilled to the ground. Some attempted to run away, but their intestines dragged as they ran; they seemed to tangle their feet in their own entrails. No matter how they tried to save themselves, they could find no escape."[12]

Some of the Aztec nobles managed to find sticks and swing them; others fought bare-handed. Fighting for their lives, they killed a handful of the butchering Spaniards and wounded many, but in the end wood and flesh were no match for steel. Aztecs who survived later recalled the horror they had experienced: "The blood of the warriors flowed like water and gathered into pools. The pools widened, and the stench of blood and entrails filled the air. The Spaniards ran into the communal houses to kill those who were hiding. They ran everywhere and searched everywhere; they invaded every room, hunting and killing."[13]

In the grisly massacre, the music, drumming, and flute playing were supplanted by ghoulish screams and moans of the dying. In their frenetic bloodlust, the Spaniards killed until there was no one left to kill; then they knelt in the pooling blood to pilfer gold ornaments and stone jewelry from the slain and dying Aztecs.[14] By the time Alvarado ordered his men to return to the Palace of Axayacatl, many thousands of the finest Aztec soldiers and the highest nobility lay heaped in grotesque attitudes on the sacred patio floor.

The cessation of the music and the terrified cries of the celebrants told the general populace of Tenochtitlán that something had gone dreadfully wrong. After a time the frantic beating of war drums came from atop the Great Temple pyramid, a general call to arms. The fleetest messengers tore among the houses calling out, "Méxicanos, come running! Bring your

spears and shields! The strangers have murdered our warriors!"[15] Grief was subsumed by rage as many stormed the precinct with spears and swords and javelins, wailing and whooping.
The Spaniards engaged these furious Aztecs, fighting their way
back to the palace. During the retreat a stone struck Alvarado
in the head, gashing him deeply.

Once inside they bolted all the doors and entrances shut.
Alvarado soon learned that the second phase of his two-tiered attack plan had been perpetrated: those left to guard Montezuma
and the other highest lords had assassinated Cacama, the de-
posed lord of Texcoco, and a good number of others. They
spared only Cuitláhuac (ruler of Iztapalapa), Izquauhtzin (governor of Tlatelolco), and Montezuma himself. As the citizens of
Tenochtitlán stormed the palace, attempting to burrow beneath
the foundations and even lighting fires to burn the doors down,
they were beginning to understand the heinous scope of the
massacre—nearly the entire rank of elite nobles, the finest warriors, and the most skillful military leaders of the Aztec empire
had been slain. Their king, Montezuma, was shackled in leg
irons.[16] It was a devastating and deeply painful—and to the
Aztecs, inexplicable—act of barbarity, defying all protocols of
proper warfare.

As civilians and what warrior troops remained besieged
the Spaniards in the palace, mourners walked to the sacred patio to identify and recover their dead. Mothers, fathers, brothers, and sisters leaned over their loved ones, dumbfounded,
wailing and weeping. One by one the victims were carried
home for proper grieving. Many were later transported to sacred places, Eagle Urn and the House of Young Men, where
they were ritually burned; cremation smoke lifted blood-black
into the sky.[17] The mourning would continue for nearly three
months.

Alvarado ordered harquebusiers and crossbowmen on top
of the palace walls to contend with the gathering horde of
Aztecs; they bombarded them with cannon blasts as well.
Superior firepower allowed the Spaniards to hold their ground,

if barely, but the Aztec insurgency grew general and wide-spread. Alvarado then received terrible news: the Aztecs had set the four brigantines ablaze, sending Cortés's escape ships up in flames. When and if Cortés returned to the city, Alvarado would have much to answer for.

Fearing that all might soon be lost, Alvarado went to Montezuma, ordering him to calm the populace. Montezuma reiterated that as he was imprisoned, there was nothing he could do. Alvarado yanked a long knife from his belt and held the sharp steel tip at Montezuma's chest, saying that the emperor must speak to his people and calm them or be vented on the spot.[18] Both Montezuma and the lord Itzquauhtzin were then taken to the rooftop, where they reluctantly took turns appealing to the people to cease their attacks on the palace. With the sun dying in the sky, Itzquauhtzin was led to the edge and made this plea: "Méxicanos, your king, the lord Montezuma, has sent me to speak for him...We are not strong enough to defeat them...We are not their equals in battle. Put down your shields and arrows...Stop fighting, and return to your homes. Méxicanos, they have put your king in chains; his feet are bound with chains."[19]

The impassioned pleas did temporarily pacify the mob, many returning to their homes for a time. But the massacre had devastating and irreparable consequences, dismantling any semblance of political order in the region and turning the population resolutely against the Spaniards while publicly undermining Montezuma's ability as a ruler. The massacre had eradicated the Aztec military command and nearly all of the finest warriors, but for the Spaniards as well it came at a very high cost. They were out of food and fresh water and too fearful for their lives to leave the palace compound in search of more. Many of the bridges were being dismantled, they learned, reducing any chance for escape, and all Christian symbols—crosses and images of the Virgin—were being ransacked and removed from the Aztec temples and prayer houses.

At night, lying on pallets, their lips cracked and their tongues bloated with thirst, the Spaniards listened to the discordant, mournful beating of funeral drums and the lamentations of women and girls pleading for retribution from their gods. The harmony of Tenochtitlán and its people had been shattered.[20]

CHAPTER THIRTEEN

Montezuma's Ironic Fate

THE NEWS OF THE UPRISING IN THE CAPITAL spurred Cortés to action. At the conclusion of the battle with Narváez, he had sent out several colonizing and settlement expeditions, and now he recalled them, rerouting them for immediate rendezvous in Tlaxcala.[1] Each of these expeditions numbered about two hundred men, and Cortés knew he would need them all if he were to calm the siege and win back control of the empire. Once again only the weakest and least able were left at the outpost city of Villa Rica.

Cortés drove his force up and over the mountains and across the parchment-brittle badlands, the horses' hooves kicking up clouds of dust. In the rumbling electric skies to the north and west, spring rains, for which the unfortunate celebrants of the festival of Toxcatl had been praying, threatened but did not come. The ground Cortés and his men rode was rutted and wind-raked and furrowed with dry faults, offering only sunburned grass for the horses and scant water for the men. The original troops from the expedition were strife-hardened, grown accustomed to such trials, but the conscripts appropriated from Narváez suffered.[2]

At Tlaxcala Cortés met up with the other two expeditions, swelling his force to nearly twelve hundred, and he recruited a sizable number—perhaps as many as two thousand—of Tlaxcalan warriors.[3] Riding at the vanguard of his one-hundred-horse cavalry, Cortés heeled on toward Tenochtitlán, taking the northerly route through the city of Texcoco. From the shore of the great lake Cortés looked across to see smoke rising from the funeral pyres. The mood in Texcoco was dark. This time the Spaniards got no formal reception. "Not once on my journey," Cortés would recall, "did any of Montezuma's people come to welcome me as they had before."[4] In Texcoco only Ixtlilxochitl, Cacama's brother, came out to formally greet him.

Cortés pressed to learn all he could about the situation in Tenochtitlán. Though trapped within the palace complex, he discovered, Alvarado's main army remained alive. Six or seven had been killed in the fighting. A messenger arrived from the city by canoe, bearing communication from Montezuma. Cortés listened to the emperor's words, translated by Malinche, explaining that the revolt in the city was not his fault and that he hoped, he deeply wished, that the captain-general would not harbor anger against him. Montezuma assured Cortés that if he came once again to Tenochtitlán, order would be restored and Cortés would dictate.

Knowing of the clandestine dealings between Montezuma and Narváez, and the perilous current rebellion, Cortés had reason to suspect a ruse. He bedded his troops down for the night as he contemplated the best approach to the city.

In the morning Cortés rode ahead as his army arced around the lake to the north, heading for Tacuba and the shortest causeway. He took this route partly to scout that landscape, which he had seen mostly from the water, but also because he had learned that some of the other causeways had been blockaded or had their bridges removed.[5] The Spaniards encamped at Tacuba, where the local leaders were at least civil and at best conciliatory. Aware of the captain-general's recent victory on the coast, they could see the frightening evidence of an impressive cavalry. The civic leaders of Tacuba went so far as to suggest that Cortés remain out here on open ground, where he could better defend himself, rather than enter the dangerous city. If Cortés even considered taking the advice, he dismissed it, because the next morning, June 24, 1520, he rose, heard mass, then mounted and rode across the Tacuba causeway into Tenochtitlán.

No throngs of civilians lined the way to gape at the clomp of horse hooves or hear the clank and jangle of metal armor. Even the waters were spookily quiet, devoid of canoes.[6] Behind a mask of desert dust, Cortés scanned for trouble, but the caravan rode into the city unencumbered. The streets were entirely empty save for a few children playing and odd clusters of citizens hauling goods. The creosote smell of cook fires came from the low houses. Most residents stayed shut inside their homes, peering out warily from doorways or through timbered window slats. It should have been a time of great celebration and spectacle, but the slaughter of Toxcatl had imposed eighty days of mourning.[7] Even the famous market of Tlatelolco was shut down.

Cortés rode into a ghost city. His larger army required more quarters; Montezuma had provided them, sending the bulk of Narváez's men to lodgings nearby. Cortés and his men returned to the Palace of Axayacatl. On his arrival Alvarado rose, shaken and war-weary, his emaciated men gaunt from lack of food and shriveled by thirst; recently they had been forced to scratch holes in the earth of the courtyard, over which they knelt to slurp from brackish seeps. They looked upon the arrival of Cortés as a happy miracle. "The garrison in the fortress received us with such joy," Cortés recalled, "it seemed we had given back to them their lives which they deemed lost; and that day and night we passed in rejoicing."[8] But the festive mood of their reunion was short-lived. Cortés demanded an explanation for the massacre. Alvarado recounted the signs of rebellion, the rumors of impending attack and sacrifice, and the fear that Narváez had been on his way to free Montezuma. In the end, he explained, it had been a preemptive strike to avoid an Aztec attack at the conclusion of the festival, which, by all the information he possessed, had appeared certain.[9]

Cortés's face flushed with anger. "But they [the Aztecs] told me," barked Cortés, "that they asked your permission to hold their feast and dances." Alvarado could only nod sheepishly, agreeing, underscoring that to prevent the Aztecs from attacking, he chose to strike first. Cortés fumed, berating Alvarado, shaking his head that it was a poor decision, a madness, and saying that he "wished to God that Montezuma had escaped and he had never had to listen to this story."*[10] He stormed off, and they spoke of it no more. His only punishment of Alvarado was to informally demote him in rank, replacing him as second-in-command with the less volatile and more predictable Gonzalo de Sandoval.[11]

Anxious to mend a strained relationship, Montezuma waited expectantly in the courtyard to be received, but Cortés was in no mood for it. When two of Montezuma's attendants approached requesting a meeting, Cortés flew into a violent rage, cursing and swearing that they could go to hell: "Visit him? Why, the dog doesn't even keep the market open for us, or see that they send us food to eat."[12] When some of his captains heard Cortés's tirade, they hustled over to calm him. Had the emperor not ascended the wall and spoken reason to his people, they reminded him, the Spaniards would all have perished. This admonishment from his own men only enraged Cortés further, and his rant continued: "Why should I be civil to a dog who was holding secret negotiations with Narváez, and now, as you can see, does not even give us any food?"[13] The attendants must tell Montezuma to open the markets immediately, or there would be hell to pay. Cortés stomped away with Malinche hurrying behind, refusing for now either to

---

*Cortés's reaction to the massacre, and his calling it madness, ring a bit ironic, given the proceedings he orchestrated at the Massacre of Cholula. He may even have prearranged it in secret with Alvarado.

receive or to speak in person with Montezuma. (Later they did have one or two last fateful parlays, translated by Malinche and Aguilar.)

Despondent, Montezuma was led back to his domicile in the garrison, his leg chains dragging on the slate stone. Once revered as godlike, the highest mortal in all of Mexico—the nearest to a god—he now slunk imprisoned, withered and enchained and bereft of dignity. He had forsaken his people. When Malinche came to ask him to open the market so that the Spaniards could acquire food, he admitted sadly that he no longer had the power to do so. He did not believe anyone would listen. But after a time he suggested that one of the remaining lords, whose reputation remained unsullied, might have success. Cortés, through Malinche, agreed, saying that Montezuma should choose whomever he thought best for the job. Montezuma selected his brother, Cuitláhuac, who was unchained from his shackles and set free. Cortés did not know it at the time, but he had released a demon.[14]

Instead of procuring food for the Spaniards, whose presence he had argued against permitting from the moment of their arrival, Cuitláhuac met with the few remaining nobles who had survived the massacre, the last vestiges of the great council. Montezuma had fallen under a spell cast by the Spaniards, he reported, and charmed as he was, he no longer possessed the capacity to rule the Aztecs. It was a conclusion they had already come to themselves.[15] In a very short time, in a move unprecedented in the history of the Aztec peoples, the council annulled Montezuma's powers and bestowed the title of *tlatoani* on Cuitláhuac: he was now emperor of the Aztecs.[16]

When food failed to come, Cortés saw that his original scheme to win Tenochtitlán in a bloodless political overthrow would not come to fruition. The next morning at sunrise he sent a messenger toward the coast to keep the command at Vera Cruz apprised of the situation in the capital, but within a half hour the man returned, "beaten and wounded and crying out that all the Indians in the city were preparing for war and had raised all the bridges."[17] Within twenty-four hours, under the leadership of the new warlord Cuitláhuac, the Aztecs renewed their attacks, and the worst military fears of the conquistador Hernán Cortés and his company were stark realities. With the bridges up and the causeways blockaded, they were ensnared inside the City of Dreams.

Even as Cortés rushed his men to arms, the Spaniards could hear the cacophonic tremor of leather-thonged warriors marching and running toward the religious precinct. Peering out from the garrison watchtowers and cannon placements, the Spaniards saw a dark human tide pouring forth; the causeways, the streets, and even the flat rooftop terraces teemed with the violent surge of Aztec warriors. War canoes brimming with men churned from all shores of the lacustrine cities, racing toward the center, oars and paddles slashing through the saline wash.

Cortés's men were always armed for battle, ready and well organized, so they soon assumed their battle positions. But none could have liked their odds as the streets below and all around the precinct, even the plazas and courtyards, were filled to capacity with stomping, chanting, spear-wielding men. From the mass—numbering perhaps in the tens of thousands— rose a piercing, shrill war whistle that eclipsed even the beating of war drums and the alarum of the conchs. Cortés later remembered well the dreadful sights and sounds: "There came upon us from all sides such a multitude that neither the streets nor the roofs of the houses could be seen for them. They came with the most fearful cries imaginable, and so many were the stones there were hurled at us from their slings into the fortress that it seemed they were raining from the sky."[18]

Cortés sent Diego de Ordaz at the head of a few hundred men, hoping that the force of his weaponry and firepower might diffuse the onslaught, but the tactic proved ineffectual and costly. Despite their blazing guns and thrumming crossbows, a hailstorm of ancient ordnance from the terraces above—stones, javelins, and darts—battered their shields, helmets, and armor. A half dozen of Ordaz's men died in the initial barrage, and Ordaz was wounded badly, struck in three places.[19] Almost instantly Ordaz was on the defensive. Repelled by the sheer volume of warriors and the constant sleet of stone and wood from above, he ordered a retreat back to the palace. Once there the streets in front were so thick with Aztecs that the Spaniards were forced into close hand-to-hand combat, barely battling their way back inside to the temporary safety of the palace compound. There, slumped and bleeding, they found that Cortés had been injured—a war club had crushed his left hand—and so had as many as eighty other Spaniards.[20]

After regrouping, Cortés ordered a full-scale barrage of firepower from the rooftop. In unison, Spanish soldiers fired cannons, harquebuses, and falconets as fast as they could shoot and load; the crossbowmen sent searing volleys into the dense crowds. Hundreds of Aztecs slumped to the ground with each pelting, the metal balls ripping through dozens at a time, but for every man slain ten came behind in support. Conquistador Bernal Díaz and other soldiers were amazed by the Aztecs' courage and resolve: "Neither cannons nor muskets nor crossbows availed, nor hand-to-hand fighting, nor killing thirty or forty of them every time we charged, for they still fought on in as close ranks and with more energy than in the beginning."[21] The Aztecs surged forward with a torrent of their own, shooting flaming arrows into the wooden fixtures of the palace and igniting the Tlaxcalans' makeshift timber lodgings. Flames engulfed the compound. Cortés hurried to dismantle parts of walls, removing flammable sections and flinging mud and dirt until the fires were controlled.[22]

The fighting raged for nearly a week. At night some of Cortés's men nursed wounds and rested, while others worked to repair the great rifts in the walls protecting them. The Spaniards listened to chants and taunts hour after hour, the Aztecs calling them rogues and cowards and promising to sacrifice them and eat them, to consume their hearts and throw their viscera to the carnivorous zoo beasts. This taunting had a chilling effect on the morale of the soldiers. During the night the Aztecs sent sorcerers and wizards to vex the Spaniards, chanting and conjuring in full view at the palace entrance. In their delirium some of the Spaniards claimed to have had visitations, witnessing "heads without bodies bobbing up and down, cadavers rolling around as if they had somehow come back to life, and severed limbs walking about of their own accord."[23] The men—especially the newly arrived Narváez conscripts—trembled in sleep-deprived fits, uncertain whether these demonic apparitions were real or imagined.

By day Cortés launched courageous if ineffective sorties and assaults, all inevitably repelled. Constantly innovating and adapting his battle tactics as the situation dictated, he conceived an idea that he hoped would allow him to fight his way out of the palace with minimal damage to his men. Carpenters were to begin constructing wooden machines (Cortés called them "engines") called *mantas*, towerlike covered structures on rollers, to be carried or pulled with ropes by exposed Tlaxcalan bearers. The *mantas* would protect as many as two dozen soldiers, encased by the thick timber walls and ceiling. From inside, musketeers and crossbowmen could fire through narrow slats or loopholes, then duck to safety to reload. Cortés's invention, though similar to the medieval *mantelets*, was much more complicated and elaborate, having dual chambers, one above the other. The plan was for the men to use the *mantas* to shoot their way out, advancing through the mob and demolishing houses as they went. They could then use the debris and wreckage to rebuild the causeways and as fill so that the cavalry could more easily cross. The carpenters hurried, building three of the war machines in a matter of days.[24]

At this point Cortés was ready to try just about anything, for it was only a matter of time before they would be starved and thirsted out and overwhelmed by hundreds of thousands of Aztecs. So once they were completed and workable, he rolled out the first *mantas*, filling them with fine soldiers and enlisting strong and brave Tlaxcalans in waves to pull or push them into the enemy swarm. The initial shock worked well—the animate mechanisms lurched forward, spitting flame and smoke and lightning—and the Aztecs recoiled in fear and dismay, running from the monstrous contraptions. Soon, however, the Tlaxcalans had difficulty maneuvering the *mantas* over the uneven ground and through the thickening crowds. Canals also impeded their progress. Emboldened Aztec reinforcements heaved boulders from terraces that shattered the war towers into splinters. The shaken soldiers could only crawl out onto the ground and resume close combat, and though they tried to set a few houses on fire, they were forced to flee back to the palace, dragging the wreckage of the *mantas* with them.[25] Innumerable Tlaxcalans, exposed as they were, died during this attack.

From a purely military standpoint, Cortés was entirely on the defensive, his options—and his able-bodied soldiers—depleting with every passing hour. Even his vaunted cavalry, so devastatingly effective on the open field, proved inconsequential, held immobile in the tightly packed streets and struggling for footing on the slick cobble and flagstone. And the Aztecs were adapting and innovating as well, unseating charging horsemen with long lances, and erecting walls to slow or reroute the galloping animals. Cortés opted to make one last-ditch effort at diplomacy. Reason overriding his pride, he called upon Malinche and Aguilar and appealed to Montezuma to ascend the rooftop and speak to any below who might recognize him—some of his relatives had been spotted, even Cuitláhuac—warriors in regal battle garments, gleaming with gold.

Montezuma had no interest in trying to help Cortés and waved Malinche away. Despondent and humiliated, he said, "I wish only to die. Fate has brought me to such a pass because of him that I do not wish to live or hear his voice again."[26] The once-great ruler appeared slight and inconsequential in his robes, his voice tinged with melancholy and desolation. Cortés employed Father Olmedo, who had come to know the emperor well, to try to persuade him, but Montezuma shook his head, saying, "It is of no use. They will neither believe me, nor the false words and promises of [Cortés]."[27] He added, in words certainly intended to be translated verbatim to Cortés, "I believe I shall not obtain any results toward ending this war, for they have already raised up another Lord (Cuitláhuac) and have made up their minds not to let you leave this place alive; therefore I believe that all of you will have to die."[28]

Unable to convince the emperor to go voluntarily, Cortés ordered some men to strong-arm him to the roof. The Spaniards held him close as they led him to the edge, covering him with shields to protect him from the continuing barrage. At the edge, on a slight promontory, the soldiers removed their shields to display Montezuma prominently for all to see. They told him to start talking, to mollify the people below. If Montezuma spoke, his voice or words were unlikely to have been heard above the clamorous roar of battle. Seconds later stones drummed the rooftop and the terrace walls, arrows sizzled past, and spears fell in a clatter all around. Said Fray Aguilar, "It seemed as if the sky was raining stones, arrows, darts and sticks."[29] The emperor crumpled beneath the sting of stones, struck with at least three direct blows to the chest and head. Too late, the soldiers covered him with their shields and ran for cover.

Montezuma lived through the night but perished within a few days, on June 30, 1520, most likely from wounds caused by his own people. He had ruled the Aztec empire for seventeen years, leading it to the pinnacle of its magnificence. Its trade and tribute network stretched far beyond the horizons that he could see as he prayed atop the Great Temple, spanning to the oceans east and west and the lands as far south as Guatemala. It was a tragic end to an enigmatically tragic life.*[30]

---

*There are two distinct and opposing versions of Montezuma's death. The Spanish version claims that after being stoned, he lived for three days but had lost the will to survive and refused food, water, or any medical attempts to revive him. Aztec accounts are nearly unanimous that Montezuma recovered from his wounds but was stabbed to death by the Spanish or, some argue, "garroted" (an execution style using an iron collar to strangle or break the neck of a victim), then thrown from the palace roof to the ground and his people below. Scant evidence supports the garroting theory, since it was typically employed during formal, even public, executions, and virtually no other garroting incidents are recorded in the chronicles of the conquest. Alas, the exact nature of Montezuma's death must remain a mystery.

In many ways, he had been played by Cortés, duped or charmed into believing that his empire might actually be saved from ruin, if only he went along with the wishes of this strange and confusing visitor from another world. Perhaps Montezuma had allowed his deep religious conviction to cloud his political sense, for many of his family, his high counselors, and even his priests had cautioned him that the Spaniards were evil and not to be trusted. And certainly cultural and communicative differences plagued Montezuma, for the gifts he bestowed upon Cortés from the moment of his arrival—gifts that in the Aztec world were indications of wealth and power and meant to show dominance—only further fueled Cortés's greed and desire. Montezuma had allowed Cortés and the Spaniards into his wondrous city so that they might be awed by his immense wealth and power, realize it, succumb to it, and go away, but instead that wealth had only fortified Cortés's unyielding resolve.

Fray Diego Duran would say of Montezuma that he was "a king so powerful, so feared and served, so obeyed by the whole of this new world, who came nevertheless to an end calamitous and shabby so that even in his last rites there were none who spoke or bewailed him."[31]

Hernán Cortés certainly had no time to mourn. Back in Montezuma's chambers, after confirming that the emperor was dead, he ordered that all the remaining lords who were in custody, including Itzquauhtzin and as many as thirty others, be killed on the spot. This order released a great number of his soldiers from having to guard them, men he desperately needed. Below the balcony and out in the streets, flaming arrows sparked through the air, leaving trails in the sky like shooting stars or comets, and the hivelike Aztec imperial army continued assembling its immense force.

CHAPTER FOURTEEN

La Noche Triste

CORTÉS'S EFFORT AT DIPLOMACY had yielded only the death of Montezuma and an even more determined army, headed by the rabid warlord Cuitláhuac. Cortés must have berated himself for freeing him. Had it been Montezuma's plan all along? Perhaps Montezuma had agreed to let Cuitláhuac lead, then sacrificed himself so that Cuitláhuac might liberate his people. It made sense, really, a quiet and unceremonial parting gift from a once-proud king, the last effective military move of a ruler whose hands were literally tied. But if Cortés sought to understand the enigmatic lord Montezuma, he said nothing of it.

Weakened by hunger and thirst, the carpenters nonetheless toiled night and day to repair the battered *mantas*, and Cortés employed the war machines once more. Meanwhile the nearby temple of Yopico (where the Spaniards had previously erected a cross and a figure of the Virgin Mary inside the shrine of Xipe Totec, "the Skinned God") had been converted into a strategic Aztec command post.[1] From this aerie Cuitláhuac and his military advisers could monitor Cortés's movements (few and insignificant as they were) and direct the Aztec forces, sending squadron after squadron to replace those taking the heaviest artillery fire.

Cortés determined that, if he were to have any chance at all, he must eliminate the enemy's advantage of this elevated command post. He tethered a shield firmly to his left forearm, the injured hand palsied and useless, and directed a small detachment of perhaps forty soldiers. Using the ingenious *mantas*, they barrelled forward toward the base of the pyramid, the shored-up machines spewing balls and arrows from within. The *mantas* pitched and yawed toward the temple beneath a sustained onslaught from above, once more taking boulders rolled from rooftops and from the pyramid itself. By the time Cortés's engines reached the foot of the temple and men poured from inside, the *mantas* were for a second time splintered, but they had served their purpose.

At the steps, Spanish pikemen and swordsmen clashed with their Aztec counterparts, sun-swarthy warriors who according to Cortés wielded "long lances with flint heads wider than ours and no less sharp."[2] With great difficulty the Spaniards carved their way up the steps, battling not only armed warriors but armaments and stones and even tree limbs and trunks launched from the platform above. Hacking and slicing upward, fending off darts and missiles with their shields, Cortés and a small fist of soldiers fought to the pyramid summit, even as three or four Spaniards caromed to their deaths. The summit command fortress was heavily fortified, but by now more Spaniards and some Tlaxcalans had arrived in support, and a fierce hand-to-hand battle raged on the patio for over three hours. At one point Cortés was subdued and nearly tossed to his death by two Aztecs, but he managed to survive.[3] Most of the Spaniards were "streaming with blood and covered with wounds."[4]

Cortés and his men threw many priests to their deaths. Once inside the shrine to Xipe Totec, he saw that the Christian idols were gone, so he paid the Aztecs back in kind by heaving their statues down the steps. Then the Spaniards set the shrine ablaze and fought their way back to the palace, igniting what houses they could on their return.

Though Cortés would later bluster that this raid was a great "victory which God had given us" and further claim that "the loss of this tower so much damaged their confidence that they began to weaken on all sides,"[5] the sortie had been expensive, resulting in the destruction of the *mantas* (and their abandonment) and the deaths of dozens of soldiers. Cortés took priests as prisoners, but these men had virtually no bargaining or diplomatic value, so that the assault on the temple proved to be nothing more than a symbolic morale builder. Even if Cortés believed he had won the tower, he hadn't the manpower to keep it.

The excursion had afforded Cortés a demoralizing view of the city, which he could see was universally armed. Only the Tacuba causeway remained partially intact; the bridges on all the others were dismantled. He knew that the Tacuba causeway was the shortest of them all, and it now appeared his only remaining lifeline to the mainland. He had no way of knowing how long the causeway would remain usable and whether, even now, its bridges were being removed. Then one of the Spaniards, a soldier and astrologer named Botello who could read and write in Latin and had traveled to Rome, approached Cortés's advisers. For the last few days, he said, he had been casting lots and reading spirits and signs in the stars; the spirits had told him that if they did not leave the capital this very night, neither Cortés nor any of the Spaniards would survive.[6]

Cortés did not like the sound of this omen when it was whispered to him. He made up his mind, and his captains concurred. They must flee at midnight while the causeway could still be crossed; otherwise they were all doomed.

Cortés hated to let loose the gemstone that he had once held firmly in his hand. The prospect of explaining the loss to his king was unsavory, but the reality of the situation, coupled with the counsel of his trusted captains, confirmed that he had no choice. The sage Botello had foretold a stormy night shrouded in darkness, and the fact that the Aztecs were less proficient in nighttime warfare contributed to Cortés's decision. Once again when faced with a crisis, he made a well-considered decision and sprang into action.

But what would they do about Montezuma's immense treasure? The sheer bulk and volume of the booty presented a logistical problem. Carrying the munificence away in broad daylight under peaceful conditions would have been burdensome enough; but doing so stealthily, at night, and potentially while waging war hardly seemed possible. Cortés and his men pried open the sealed door to the palace treasure room and began to parcel out the treasure, separating the precious metals from the stones and the featherwork. Most of the gold was smelted and forged into hefty ingots, which could be accurately weighed for proper division. The haul was an astounding eight tons of gold, silver, and gemstones. They could not possibly cart it all on this run, so they divided it by importance. The royal fifth was laid aside and packaged—it must be protected at all costs by handpicked Spanish guards, portaged by eighty Tlaxcalans, one fit mare, and a few lame and wounded horses. Next was Cortés's personal fifth, as arranged through clever legal writing in the writ founding Villa Rica. The Tlaxcalans, uninterested in the gleaming metals, carried off armfuls of the iridescent quetzal feathers in bundles and bales.[7]

Cortés then gave permission for his men to fill their personal bags with what gold and treasure they could carry, though he cautioned them that weapons and food would serve them better in their present endeavor. "Better not to overload yourselves," he warned; "he travels safest in the dark night who travels lightest."[8] Narváez's men, seeing the fantastic spoils for the first time, went into a frenzy and ignored their new commander's advice; they loaded themselves heavily, stuffing their wallets, boxes, and bags to bursting. The seasoned Cortés men, including veterans like Bernal Díaz, were more sensible, taking mainly what they could carry directly on their person, aware of the travails to come: "I declare," remembered Díaz, "I had no other desire but the desire to save my life, but I did not fail to carry off... stones very highly prized among the Indians, and I quickly placed them in my bosom under my armor, and later on, the price of them served me well in healing my wounds and getting me food."[9]

The plunder secured, Cortés instructed his carpenters to destroy some palace walls and use this timber, as well as ceiling beams, to construct a portable bridge. It must be long and sturdy enough, he said, to span gaps in the causeway as well as bear the weight of the men, horses, and spoils as they crossed. The carpenters performed this ingenious feat of spontaneous engineering, but the bridge was awkward and unwieldy, requiring forty Tlaxcalans at a time to carry it; Cortés directed 150 Spanish soldiers to flank and cover some 200 bearers who would portage the bridge in shifts.[10]

Cortés placed 200 foot soldiers under his new second-in-command, Gonzalo de Sandoval. This vanguard would march directly behind the portable bridge and be supported by Diego de Ordaz, Francisco de Lugo, and two dozen skilled cavalrymen. Malinche would be heavily guarded up front, along with Cortés's priests, Father Olmedo and Father Díaz. Next, Cortés would lead the main militia, aided by a few captains. Behind them would come the bulk of the Tlaxcalan soldiers, who would also convey some key prisoners and dignitaries, including one of Montezuma's sons and two of his daughters.[11] The rearguard would be captained by Pedro de Alvarado and Velázquez de León, along with sixty more cavaliers.

Just after midnight in the black hours of July 1, 1520, Hernán Cortés and company heard a brief mass and then fled Tenochtitlán, marching and riding into a dense fog. Forcing open the heavy palace gates, the Spaniards moved out as quietly as they could under sustained summer showers. The rains that Montezuma and his people had prayed for during the Festival of Toxcatl had finally arrived, and many residents sought the comfort and shelter of their homes, so that the streets were quieter than they might otherwise have been.

The central plaza of the sacred precinct was eerily silent. The outlanders moved quickly, stealing along the empty streets past the Temple of the Sun, moving unhindered to the ball court, then striking west onto the Tacuba causeway. The expedition—men and horses and whimpering war dogs—trotted forward like some weird nocturnal millipede, making it across the first few intact bridges and to the first major breach in the causeway. They were readying to install the portable bridge when the cry of a woman's voice pierced the night. "Méxicanos!" she wailed. "Come running! They are crossing the canal! Our enemies are escaping!"[12] Soon guards sounded the alarm, and other sentries dashed to the top of the Great Temple. Within minutes drums pounded from the pyramid tops, accompanied by the howl of conch shells. Then the voice of a priest came echoing through the drizzle and mist: "Captains, warriors…follow them in your boats. Cut them off and destroy them!"[13]

As Captain Margarino, in charge of the portable bridge, yelled instructions to the Tlaxcalans, Aztec soldiers sprinted for their dugouts and shortly many canoes were pouring forth in pursuit, the oarsmen churning the lake to froth. Hurrying, Margarino got the bridge installed, and lines of soldiers sprinted across, pushing and shoving as they went two or three abreast. The bridge worked well, but the combined weight of the men and bearers loaded with weapons, and the tamping and compacting of the horses, wedged the bridge firmly into place; it was nearly cemented, and pull as they might, the strong Tlaxcalans could not budge it. The Spaniards and their allies were now strung out along the causeway, making it impossible to form organized ranks to fight. Then the first of the canoes arrived along the causeway banks, signaled by arrows and darts whooshing like birds of prey through the blackness. Still the bridge was stuck. The Spaniards had no choice but to abandon it and run for their lives.[14]

The Aztec canoes poured along either side of the Tacuba causeway as the Spanish vanguard reached gaps and bridgeless sections, creating panic and confusion. Bernal Díaz recalled the attack:

> The whole lake was so thick with canoes that we could not defend ourselves, since many of our men had already crossed the bridge…a great crowd of Mexicans charged down on us to remove the bridge and kill and wound our

men, who could not help one another...One disaster followed another. Because of the rain, two horses slipped and
fell in the lake. Just as we saw this, I and some others of
Cortés's detachment struggled to the other side of the
bridge, but we were borne down by so many warriors that,
hard though we fought, no further use could be made of it.
The channel or water gap was soon filled up with dead
horses, Indians...servants, bundles, and boxes.[15]

This place, the Toltec Canal, became a scene of chaos and
anguish for the Spaniards. Disorder and confusion became
general. In the dark, their numbers pressed together, the cavalry proved useless. Soon every man fought for himself, with
growing numbers of Aztecs arriving. In the melee, horses
reared and foundered, falling into the water, kicking and buck-
ing, some swimming aimlessly, riderless, only to drown. The
chants and war whoops of the blood-crazed Aztecs sent men
headlong into the water gap, and so many drowned there that
it was said a human bridge of the dead formed. Aztec accounts
recalled that "the canal was soon choked with the bodies of
men and horses, they filled the gap in the causeway with their
own drowned bodies. Those who followed crossed to the other
side by walking on the corpses."[16]

Cortés fought his way across, but he too plunged into the
water, where he was grabbed by warriors who tried to drag him
off. Two of his men hacked him free and hauled him ashore.
Cortés made the length of the causeway nearly to Tacuba but
there remounted and wheeled his horse back to help others
and learn the condition of the rearguard. It was disastrous.
Cortés found Alvarado stumbling along on foot, bleeding profusely, dragging his own sword in one hand and an enemy
spear in the other. His horse had been killed from underneath
him. Shaken, he reported that Juan Velázquez de León, his
cocaptain of the rearguard, lay dead on the road, riddled with
arrows.[17] The trailing detachments took a terrible beating,
swarmed from behind on land, and from either side of the causeway, bludgeoned with clubs, speared, many dragged away, pulled

into canoes, those not killed taken prisoner for sacrifice. Most of them were Narváez men, weighed down by the excessive gold they carried.

Alvarado gathered some men and offered to guard what little remained of the rear while Cortés and the rest struck for the safety of the mainland. The beleaguered Spaniards and remaining Tlaxcalans limped and staggered like ghouls to the outskirts of Tacuba, making the relative safety of the city at first light, weird broken bands of luminance angling through the fog. Cortés called for a makeshift muster to take quick stock. Dawn illuminated the brutal reality of the previous night, thereafter referred to by the Spaniards as La Noche Triste — The Night of Sorrows. Nearly six hundred Spaniards perished that night, including the bulk of the Narváez men, along with a great number of horses and as many as four thousand Tlaxcalans.[18] Also lost was most of the gunpowder, all the cannons, and perhaps most searing of all the smelted ingots, the gold and silver bars, the royal fifth and Cortés's fifth, all vanished in the cold dark waters. Somewhere buried in the brackish bottom of Lake Texcoco lay most of Montezuma's immense treasure. For a few minutes Cortés, utterly stricken with grief, mourned, standing in the rain beneath a giant *ahuehuete* tree (cypress), his hands and face bespattered with mud and blood.[19] But he did not allow himself more than a moment's regret. He took stock of the situation and regrouped.

He assembled the remains of his haggard company in the Tacuba plaza. The dead or missing included Chimalpopoca, Montezuma's son, and one of his daughters; Lares, one of Cortés's finest horsemen; and Botello the astrologer, along with his horse.[20] Cortés walked among his tattered, shivering ranks and was relieved to find his dear Malinche. He embraced her, thankful that she had survived the nightmare. His other chief interpreter, Jerónimo de Aguilar, also miraculously lived. Two dozen horses remained, but all of them were injured, none able to raise more than a trot. Captains Gonzalo de Sandoval, Diego de Ordaz, Alonso de Ávila, Cristóbal de Olid, and Pedro de Alvarado, all wounded and requiring treatment, lived.[21]

Cortés rarely dwelled on the past, and on that dismal July morning following La Noche Triste he once more, despite the tremendous losses, thought only of his present condition and what the future might hold. Looking around, he inquired about the fate of one man in particular—the master carpenter and shipbuilder Martín López. Where was he? Had he survived? Malinche went about the ghastly, ruined squadron and returned, calmly assuring Cortés that yes, Martín López was alive and with them, though he was wounded. This news reassured Cortés, who mounted his horse with renewed fire. Another ambitious idea was germinating in his mind. "Well, let's go," he said, "for we lack nothing."[22] Despite the disastrous night, the loss of more than half of his force, and near death for them all, Cortés already had a plan for reconquest. He led the remainder of his bloodied and limping force to the north, then into the rising sun to the east, heading for friendly Tlaxcala, more than fifty miles away.

At daybreak the Aztecs suspended their onslaught (a tactical mistake, for the Spaniards were devastatingly weak and vulnerable) to celebrate their victory. They had driven Cortés and most of his men from the city. A small contingent of eighty Spaniards had failed to make it across the Tacuba causeway and sneaked back inside the Palace of Axayacatl, but the inflamed Aztec warriors soon captured them and washed them in preparation for sacrifice. The Aztecs fished the dead and dying from the water, removing bodies from the canals and the lakeshore, separating Tlaxcalans from Spaniards. According to Aztec accounts, they then "loaded the bodies of the Tlaxcaltecas into canoes and took them out to where the rushes grow; they threw them among the rushes without burying them, without giving them another glance."[23] The slain Spaniards were stripped of their clothes and lay in bare piles looking to the Aztecs like "the white blossom[s] of the cane."[24]

Aztec warriors walked the causeway, picking spilled plunder from the muck: random gold and silver bars, necklaces and jewelry, and—most coveted—occasional sheaves of quetzal feathers. But they found very little. Most of Axayacatl's treasure sank during the night. Still some persisted, swimming and wading out into the water, feeling about with their hands and feet. Along the causeway they found many Spanish weapons— muskets and swords and crossbows—lying scattered, the tools of conquest thrown aside in the tumult and confusion. They unearthed lost and strewn coats of mail and breastplates, shields of metal, hide, and wood. The carnage had been heaved asunder, helmets squashed into the mud by the hooves of crazed horses.[25]

Any Spaniards who managed to survive the night were now dragged to the temple tops and held down screaming, their hearts cut still pulsing from their chests and brandished aloft in victory, spoils of war and bloodfood for the god Huitzilopochtli.[26] Later their bodies would be ingloriously dismembered, their heads skewered onto their own pikes and spears and swords and exhibited for all to see, thrust into the ground like monstrous fence-posts, alternating between blood-drenched, butchered horse heads.[27]

Although the Aztecs commonly ceased or suspended a battle in order to celebrate and consummate victory through ritual, in this case their time might have been better spent killing the rest of the Spaniards. The nighttime rout was already slightly uncharacteristic of traditional Aztec warfare, as they had killed at a greater pace and percentage than they had wounded, perhaps reflecting their anger at the death of Montezuma, at having their city held hostage for so long, and at the Spaniards' consortium with the Tlaxcalans. Whatever the case, while the Aztecs who had taken prisoners painted themselves in ochre and red, bathed in blood, and ceremonially cannibalized the slain,[28] and while the victors danced at the Great Temple steps to flaming brazier light, the Spaniards were getting away.

HERNÁN Cortés drove his train of ragged interlopers north over the top of Lake Texcoco, small bands of Aztec raiding parties attacking them constantly. He organized his vestigial force into rough squadrons: Tlaxcalan guides led the least injured and most capable to do battle up front, in the rear, and at the flanks, while the bulk of wounded men—Spaniard and Tlaxcalan alike—stayed in the center. The most seriously debilitated rode slumped on horseback; others limped behind or leaned on makeshift crutches or wooden walking sticks. Straggling and exhausted men, delirious from lack of sleep, clutched at horses' manes and tails to pull themselves along; others were so spent and hurt that they had to be carried by Tlaxcalan porters.[29]

For two days Cortés pushed his haggard and failing company, fighting on the periphery as they went. They skirted three shimmering lakes and banked toward shadowy mountains looming in the east, arriving at the town of Tepotzotlán. The ablest soldiers held their weapons ready, expecting a confrontation in the streets, but the town was deserted, the inhabitants having fled to nearby villages.[30] Here the troops rested in plazas and under awnings, sacking the place for water and whatever food they could rummage. They found maize, and boiled and roasted some, gnawing it down and larding stores away for the continued flight.

They rode next day into the rising sun, still harassed by bands of Aztec attackers, which kept them always on the defensive. The Spaniards followed their guides onto the plains, sleeping on the broken ground and leaving again at daybreak, passing just to the north of the famous ceremonial city Teotihuacán, with its mile-long Avenue of the Dead, its massive and stunning Pyramids of the Sun and Moon all vine-choked and shrub-covered, the once-great city having been abandoned years before the Aztecs arrived. Still, the place retained a powerful, even hypnotic religious importance, and as recently as the previous year Montezuma had made pilgrimages there with his highest priests every twenty days to offer sacrifices. The Templo Mayor of Tenochtitlán exhibited many architectural features borrowed from this magical and mythical ancient city.[31]

On Cortés rode. On the outskirts of a large city called Cacamulco, the Spaniards met fierce resistance. The attacks came from all sides, and the horses struggled to maneuver in the boulder-pocked terrain. Cortés reined up and called for a retreat. As he rode away, two hurled stones struck him squarely in the head, the injuries severe enough to require immediate bandaging.

The Spaniards were forced back out onto the flinty and esker-ridged chaparral. That night they camped in the open and tended their wounds and cooked and ate one of their slain horses. The animal sustained the famished men and provided their first meat since Tenochtitlán. "We ate it," remembered Cortés, "leaving neither the skin nor any other part of it. For we were very hungry and had eaten nothing since we left the great city save boiled and roasted maize—and there was not always enough of that—and herbs which we picked from the fields."[32]

Nearly a week of eastward wandering and fighting led Cortés and his bloodstained entourage to the Ápam plains, near Otumba, where they halted to rest. But the respite was short-lived, for soon a few of Cortés's scouts arrived with a frightening report. Ahead in the Valley of Otumba an enormous Aztec army had assembled. The new Aztec warlord Cuitláhuac, it seemed, was not content to let the Spaniards escape and was determined to finish them once and for all. Cortés realized that the nipping and heeling by small Aztec bands had actually been designed to herd them to this place, where a great force of Aztecs and their allies, including bands of Otomis, lay in wait. At the head of the army Cuitláhuac placed his brother Matlatzincatzin, who proudly took the role of *cihuacoatl*, equivalent to captain-general. He, along with his other chiefs and elite warriors, wore resplendent headdress, ornately jeweled. Matlatzincatzin bore on his shoulder the regal war standard—the Quetzaltonatiuh—"a Sun of Gold symbol encircled by quetzal feathers."[33]

Hernán Cortés certainly did not like what he saw as he crested a rise and looked down into the Valley of Otumba.

"There came to meet us," he said, "such a multitude of Indians that the fields all around were so full of them that nothing else could be seen."[34] Stretching to the far horizon all Cortés and his men could see were the bobbing shields and spears of warriors, the fluttering plumed helmets with black and white and green tail feathers. Given the dire condition of the men and their scant numbers, many of the Spaniards, including Cortés, believed that they faced their final hour. He addressed his troops, most of them hard men who had been on mainland Mexico since their arrival, tough and battle-steeled veterans. Once again he appealed to their sense of honor and duty, to their love of crown and cross, and gave last-minute military instructions. They were nearly out of powder, so the harquebuses would hardly play a role. The fighting would be up to footmen with pikes, swords, and lances and the few cavalry that remained operational. He hoped that the Spanish steeds could still run.

He commanded the horsemen to "charge and return at a hard gallop, and [they] were not to stop to spear the enemy but to keep their lances aimed at their faces until they broke up their squadrons."[35] Whatever happened, order and organization must be maintained. Then all knelt and prayed, crossing themselves and looking at the mountains beyond, the great volcano Popocatépetl to the south still spewing fumes and ash and steam.

The Aztecs closed for battle, charging with an array of screams and wails and high-pitched yips, and within moments the opposing ranks collided. "We could hardly distinguish between ourselves and them," said Cortés of the encounter, "so fiercely and closely did they fight us."[36] The Spaniards maintained a solid defensive rectangle, as commanded by Cortés, for the flatness of the plain allowed the rested Iberian stallions to do their work, charging at a gallop, their riders low-slung, crashing headlong into confused warrior ranks in a clatter of lance on shield, scattering the Aztecs. In the center of the combat the swordsmen swung and hacked and parried, side-stepping the slashing two-sided obsidian blades of their enemy.

From early morning until nearly noon the battle raged, and Cortés and his men hung on by lance-tip and sword-blade. As bravely as they fought, without the added firepower of cannons, falconets, and harquebuses, the Spaniards appeared doomed by their numerical inferiority. The Aztecs were squeezing them in a pincer.[37]

But Cortés noticed that the cavalry was causing havoc and disorder among the Aztec and Otomi ranks. The galloping charges, while not killing great numbers of the enemy, were disrupting their formations. Each well-timed cavalry charge plowed a huge gap in the enemy lines; Cortés was quick to move in afoot to exploit and maintain those gaps.[38] The prized horses, whose iron-shod hooves had skittered and slipped on the slick streets of Tenochtitlán, now found their natural footing and gait on the open plain, which more resembled their native Iberia. They seemed to gain strength and speed with each thundering pass. Some of the Otomis dispersed, fleeing under the devastating rush of the horses and the fury of the war hounds.

Then Cortés caught sight of the Aztec *cihuacoatl*, his garb gleaming in full glory. Wheeling his horse, he called for captains Sandoval, Olid, Alvarado, Salamanca, and Ávila to ride with him and attack the chieftains, all those wearing "golden plumes and rich armor and devices."[39] Riding with great purpose, Cortés galloped ahead, swung in, and bowled the commander to the ground, knocking his standard loose. Juan de Salamanca impaled the *cihuacoatl* with his sharp lance, swooping up his head-plume and the sun-standard as spoils.*[40]

Cortés and Salamanca had severed the head from the giant, and the body would soon wither. The loss of the principal military leader caused disruption among the Aztec warriors; perhaps worse, the all-important standard had fallen. The

---

*Juan de Salamanca attempted to give the plumed headdress to Cortés, saying that it was his by right for the initial gallant charge, but Cortés declined. Many years later, in 1535, Salamanca used the decorative plume as the model for his family's coat of arms, which was granted him by the king.

standard provided location and direction for troop movements and order, and without it the Aztec ranks grew hesitant and confused, many losing their morale, inciting a mass retreat.[41]

Cortés set more cavalry and hounds upon the withdrawing enemy, and the Aztecs and Otomis trampled one another as they fled. A short time later the Battle of Otumba was finished. Miraculously, the Spaniards had not only survived but prevailed. Despite apparently insurmountable odds, the swift and skilled warhorses and the strict defensive discipline of the Spaniards had won the day, which Spaniards remember as one of Hernán Cortés's greatest military achievements.

The Aztec command, including Cuitláhuac, had not reckoned on the power of the Iberian horses and could only look back on the day as a devastatingly squandered opportunity. Whether they realized it or not, they had been only minutes away from annihilating Cortés and his men and sending the Tlaxcalans running for home or hauling them away to the sacrificial stones.

Three days later, on July 11, 1520, Hernán Cortés led his men and small allied force into the outskirts of Tlaxcala, to a place called Hueyotlipan. There he slumped to the ground, requiring immediate medical attention. His skull was fractured in two places, two of his fingers had been crushed, and one knee throbbed, swollen violet and bulbous. As he lay semiconscious and writhing with the onset of fever, one of his surgeons operated on his left hand, staunching the blood flow by cauterizing the mangled stubs with searing oil, then picking shards of stone and bone fragments from his crevassed skull.[42] Cortés was carried to the home of a chief named Maxixcatzin and laid on a wattle bed. There was little more anyone could do but wait and pray that he recovered.

With Malinche and his concerned captains huddled anxiously about him, Hernán Cortés fell into a coma.

CHAPTER FIFTEEN

"Fortune Favors the Bold"

FOR SEVERAL DAYS HERNÁN CORTÉS lay dead still, sweat dampening his reed pallet as his body purged the fever and infection. Throughout his ordeal Malinche sat beside him, cooling him with dampened rags and coaxing droplets of water into the cracked corners of his mouth. She washed and cleaned his wounds, applied compresses to his bruises, and changed his blood-tainted dressings. After nearly a week he roused, his initial utterings like infantile babbling, incomprehensible and imbecilic, but in time he revived, sat up, and began to walk about hesitantly.[1] He awoke to find his troops in dire condition, a number having died, others nearly dead, their wounds septic and suppurating.

Cortés's host, Maxixcatzin, was pleased to see the captain-general ambulatory and improving, but he grew despondent about the flight from Tenochtitlán. He wept to learn that his daughter, whom he had gifted to Captain Juan Velázquez de León (the Spaniards had subsequently baptized her and christened her Doña Elvira), had perished on the causeway, as had Velázquez de León.[2]

Cortés and his men remained in Tlaxcala for twenty days; four men died during that time, while others recovered by slow degrees, aided by the dry, temperate climate. They were well fed and cared for, although their presence in the Tlaxcalan capital was not without controversy. Xicotenga the Younger still harbored ill will toward the Spaniards in general and hatred toward Cortés specifically. He had recently received Aztec emissaries, sent by Cuitláhuac, bearing salt and cotton and quetzal plumes, who urged the Tlaxcalans not to assist Cortés and his men. Seeing the Spaniards straggle back into his city, the young Xicotenga held council with his father, Xicotenga the Elder, and other regional chieftains, suggesting that the Tlaxcalans should kill all the Spaniards, which would be easy to do, given their condition.[3] The elder Xicotenga disagreed, as did the chief Maxixcatzin. They argued that their previously agreed-to allegiance should be honored and maintained. Heated debate broke out.

Eventually the elders reminded the young and impetuous warrior Xicotenga of the Tlaxcalans' long-standing animosity toward the Aztecs. Though they had to physically subdue him and remove him from the room, he finally accepted their counsel. Cuitláhuac's entreaties were ignored, and his emissaries sent away. Maxixcatzin, deeply mourning the loss of his daughter and fueled by a desire for revenge, through Malinche made verbal assurances to Cortés. "We have made common cause together," he offered ceremonially, "and we have common injuries to avenge; and... be assured we will prove true and loyal friends, and stand by you to the death."[4]

A great number of fine and brave Tlaxcalans had in fact already stood by Cortés to the death, so these were honored words. But perhaps because of the high death tolls, the Tlaxcalans wished to renegotiate their continued allegiance, which now came with specific provisions. Primarily they wanted everlasting exemption from paying tribute to the Aztecs, and should Cortés somehow manage to retake Tenochtitlán (this now appeared less likely than it once had), they demanded some share of the rewards. The Tlaxcalans also wanted control of Cholula and of Tepeaca, another region adjacent to their frontier. Both would have to pay them tributes. And last, they demanded that a Tlaxcalan fort be built in Tenochtitlán, which they would staff and guard.[5] Realizing the important role the Tlaxcalans had already played in his quest, and utterly cognizant of his continued dependence on them not only for their geographically crucial buffer zone but also for servants, porters, cooks, and warriors, Cortés immediately agreed.[6] He knew that without them his quest stood no chance.

The alliance with the Tlaxcalans reestablished and legal papers drawn up, Cortés moved on to other pressing diplomatic matters. Apprehensive about the state of Villa Rica, he wrote letters and sent Tlaxcalan runners bearing them to the coast. The missives underscored his urgent need for more soldiers, gunpowder, crossbows, and bow cords, and any ammunition they could spare. He sent specific instructions to Alonso Caballero, the sea captain in charge of the remaining two Narváez ships, to ensure that no one departed for Cuba under any circumstances. He was to scuttle the ships if he had to. Caballero was also to tighten security around Narváez, maintaining around-the-clock surveillance of the traitorous prisoner.[7] Seeing no need to create undue apprehension or loss in morale among those at the fort in Villa Rica, Cortés conveniently omitted the details of their near annihilation, including the fact that he had lost over half his troops and the majority of the Narváez contingent.

The garrison at Villa Rica responded quickly, though Cortés was less than impressed by the reinforcements that arrived. Seven soldiers made the arduous mountain trek up from the torpid coast, captained by a soldier named Pedro Lencero. They did bring some of the requested supplies and ammunition, but the soldiers themselves were a sickly, scurvy lot, covered with boils and pustules and complaining of liver ailments, their bellies grotesquely swollen and distended. If Cortés was not amused, some of his men, recovered enough to retain a sense of humor, were; they thereafter referred to any useless assistance as "Lencero's Help," and these pathetic reinforcements became the fodder of many jokes around the camp.[8]

As it turned out, the laughingstock of Lencero's Help was the least of Cortés's problems. He had other difficulties, political and practical, internal and external. He had recently made a demand on his men that, though necessary, proved to be universally disliked. Because of their recent losses (and especially the loss of Montezuma's treasure), their war coffers were depleted. Cortés ordered that, under penalty of death for disobedience, any and all gold now carried by soldiers must be handed over to him and Pedro de Alvarado, where it would be used communally as a continued war fund, part of Cortés's planned reconquest of the Valley of Mexico. Soldiers groused but grudgingly handed over their loot. Some, battle-maimed and even crippled for life, murmured that they should retreat to the coast and board ships for the islands and comforts of home. The remaining Narváez men, their allegiance to Cortés having only recently been procured, were most vocal. All of Cortés's promises of wealth and grandeur had thus far yielded them only lifelong scars and disfigurement.

There were other stinging financial losses. On his previous pass through Tlaxcala in June (after the battle with Narváez), Cortés had left boxes of gold and silver, presumably excesses from his stores of bribe booty, which he had ordered be transported to the fort at Villa Rica under the guard of Captain Juan de Alcantara. Cortés now learned that after Alcantara departed for the coast with five horses, about fifty foot soldiers, and two hundred Tlaxcalan porters, they were attacked by Aztecs (or Aztec subjects) at a place called Calpulalpan. All their party was slaughtered, and the attackers absconded with the chests of gold and silver.[9] Other Spaniards too, horsemen riding from Villa Rica toward Tlaxcala to provide support for Cortés, had been ambushed and killed along the way. The captain-general fumed at these losses, revenge boiling in his veins.

But his greatest immediate challenge came from an erstwhile friendly source—his business partner Andrés de Duero. A practical man possessing shrewd business acumen and a keen eye for fiscal matters, Duero surveyed the sorry state of Cortés's affairs and did not like the look of his investment.

Strictly from a business standpoint, things did not appear promising. Bolstered by the grumblings of the few remaining Narváez loyalists and other disenchanted Cortés men, Duero wrote an articulate appeal to the captain-general, laying out a litany of reasons that the expedition should now retreat, cut its losses, and strike out immediately for Villa Rica, where the party could regroup and reassess their circumstances. The letter pointed out (as was painfully obvious to Cortés, though he seemed to operate in a constant state of denial) that the troops were in dire condition: "Our heads are broken, our bodies rotting and covered with wounds and sores, bloodless, weak, and naked. We are in a strange land, poor, sick, surrounded by our enemies, and without hope of rising from the spot we fall."[10] They were without ammunition and weaponry and the flush coffers with which to fund a war.[11] Further, they did not trust the Tlaxcalans as Cortés did.

This formal remonstrance, signed by a good number of Cortés's company, was reasonable, even logical. But it also committed an error in tone, posited not as a request but as a demand, which surely rankled Cortés: "We therefore ask and beg your Excellency," the letter continued, "and, if necessary, *demand*, that you leave this city with all the army and set off for Vera Cruz."[12] The appeal concluded by formally *requiring* that Cortés personally pay for all subsequent damages and losses should he fail to comply with their demands.[13]

His head throbbing from his concussed and fractured skull, his body tattooed with lacerations and bruises, able to walk only for short periods, Cortés studied the document, holding the paper weakly in his one good hand, deeply pained by the words and distressed by the erosion of his command. Most hurtful of all, the letter stated that Cortés's pursuit of the present conquest was driven by "his insatiable thirst for glory and authority," and that "he thinks nothing of dying himself, and less of our death."[14] It was true that he was willing to die for this cause, for great enterprises required risk. He still believed the words he had spoken to his men on the shores of Cuba before their initial departure, that "great things are achieved only by great exertions."[15] Now, it was plain to see, these men were morally and spiritually exhausted. His only recourse was to lead them by example. He would not allow the expedition to crumble and fail. He must rally their sense of duty, pride, and above all honor.

Hernán Cortés found a quiet place and formulated his response, a written speech that was as rousing as it was definitive, its tenor in many ways similar to a pre-battle speech (which, in effect, it turned out to be). The glory that he and his men were in the process of winning was theirs as much as his, he said, adding that "the outcome of a war depends much upon fame, and how can you win greater fame than by remaining here in Tlaxcala in defiance of your enemies, declaring war against them?"[16] Yes, they had been routed and driven from Tenochtitlán, but he used the defeat as a rallying cry rather than a setback, his grandiose tone revealing something of his intentions: "What nation of those who have ruled the world, has not once been defeated? What famous captain, I say, ever went home because he had lost a battle or been driven out of some town? Not one, certainly, for if he had not persevered he would not have conquered or triumphed."[17] Yes, they were few in number, but even now, despite their losses, they had more men than they had when they originally landed. He punctuated this fact with an appeal to their pride and vainglory: "Victories are not won by the many but by the valiant."[18] It was an eloquent appeal to their dignity and honor, perfectly timed and paced, the stirring and patriotic oratory of a man born to lead men.

Hernán Cortés answered his men: under no circumstances would he quit this enterprise. They would not steal down the mountains to Vera Cruz and slink away defeated. "Never before in these Indies of the New World," he reminded Duero and the men, "have Spaniards been seen to turn back through fear."[19] Their course and duty remained constant, as clear to Cortés as the day he arrived on the mainland, their future bright and attainable and gleaming like Mexican gold. He closed with a flourish, reminding himself, his men, and his king that "fortune always favors the bold."[20] He then offered a slight concession. To assuage their concerns about the loyalty of the Tlaxcalans (concerns Cortés did not share), he developed a plan to test it once more. The Spaniards, with the Tlaxcalans in support as warriors and servants, would march on nearby Tepeaca, an Aztec stronghold and site of the recent killing of twelve Spaniards. "If the sortie turns out badly," offered Cortés, "I shall do as you request. If it turns out well, you will do what I beg of you."[21]

On the first of August 1520 Cortés and his reunited army of Spaniards and Tlaxcalans marched toward the province of Tepeaca.

THE Tepeaca campaign served a number of purposes; it was at once a reknitting of the fraying fabric of the men's morale as well as a punitive strike, an act of overt aggression meant to instill terror among Aztec satellites and tributaries. Geographically, Tepeaca was positioned along the best, most efficient route from Tenochtitlán to Vera Cruz, and Cortés needed the route open and secure. Cortés also well understood that the perception of power among the native population was often as important as actual power, and to that end he wanted to illustrate the fearlessness of the Spaniards, despite the debacle of La Noche Triste. He also hoped to send a stern message to Cuitláhuac, who he knew would be following his every move, that the proud Spaniards might bend but they would not break. Obsessed by his drive to recapture the great prize that was Mexico, he aimed to mow a wide swath around the region, carving the way for reentry into its capital, whenever that might be. "I resolved," he wrote to his king, "to fall on our enemies wherever I could and oppose them in every possible way."[22]

Unknown to Cortés, his military situation was being aided by a temporary political paralysis among the remaining Aztec nobility. Cuitláhuac's failure at the Battle of Otumba had been poorly received in the capital and throughout the dependant vassal states, and while he remained the de facto ruler of

Tenochtitlán (he would not be officially inaugurated as the tenth Aztec king until September 15, 1520), the loss cast some doubt on his ability to lead. The Aztecs' regional dominance and power was now dubious, and word of Cortés's renegotiated coalition with the mighty Tlaxcalans further heightened this uncertainty.[23] The Aztec empire's greatness relied in good part on the presence of an identifiable and highly visible ruler; for the last two decades Montezuma had been this man-god. Now, as Cuitláhuac tried to prove his worth as a war leader, the Aztec empire hung in a tenuous balance.

Cortés marched toward Tepeaca, which lay some forty miles southwest of Tlaxcala, with a force of about 450 Spaniards, seventeen horses, six crossbowmen, and nearly two thousand Tlaxcalans. He had mustered every able-bodied soldier, leaving behind only the most seriously debilitated, plus two captains to school the Tlaxcalan military in Spanish battle tactics. Tepeaca was at the time a well-fortified and flourishing city and religious center situated on an elevated rise in the tablelands that poured out from the rumbling Popocatépetl all the way to the foothills of giant Orizaba.[24]

Riding by day and camping at night, Cortés and his men reached the town of Acatzinco on the fourth day. There he stopped, sending an envoy of Tlaxcalans ahead to Tepeaca with an unyielding message: they must resubmit to Spanish rule (they had acquiesced on Cortés's first pass through, after his subjugation of the Tlaxcalans, but had reneged while he was entrapped in Tenochtitlán) or suffer severe punishment; they would be held in contempt as traitors to the throne and treated accordingly. The Tepeacans, perhaps confident of receiving Aztec military support, sent a haughty and defiant retort, saying that they were low on sacrifice victims and required more. The Spaniards would do just fine, they said, and if they came, they would sacrifice and eat them.

That was all Cortés needed to hear. As he later reported to his emperor, Charles V, "I will say only that after we had made our demands for peace on Your Majesty's behalf and they had not complied, we made war on them."[25] Cortés, to maintain an appearance of legal propriety, had his notary prepare written documents stating that all Aztecs and their allies were in breach of their previous submission to the crown, and that any whom the Spanish captured would be committed into "slavery."[*26] Two days later Cortés and his company marched in full battle armor to a plain of cultivated maize and maguey just outside the hilltop town, where they engaged the rebellious Tepeacans. The fully recovered horses proved devastating, chasing the overmatched Tepeacans from the maize fields and riding them down mercilessly on the flat and open plains, slaughtering nearly four hundred in the first day's skirmish without losing a single Spaniard. With morale burgeoning from that success, Cortés went forth and routed the enemy again the next day, and by afternoon the Tepeacans had capitulated, unable to resist the onslaught of the Spanish cavalry. They retreated to their city, or back to work in their maize and maguey fields, and the supporting Aztec divisions fled back to Tenochtitlán. "I have driven from these provinces," Cortés would confidently write, "many of the [Aztecs] who had come to help the natives of Tepeaca make war on us."[27] Leaving in his wake toppled idols, smoldering pyramids, and a terrified populace, Cortés marched into the city as the victor and established control.

Still seething from his bitter defeat in Tenochtitlán, and his narrow escape, he decided to take aggressive symbolic measures now. The measures he chose were public enslavement and terror. He would teach a lesson that burned across the region. He ordered his men to round up all prisoners of war from the two recent battles and conduct raids on all nearby towns where Spaniards were known to have been killed. They then herded these prisoners, including the women and children of

---

*Cortés had to be careful here, as he knew that the Spanish crown frowned on "slavery" in the strict sense of the word. In the West Indies (and subsequently, on the Mexican mainland) conquistadors had evaded this policy with the clever use of *encomienda*, which made captured or subsumed native inhabitants the propertied workforce of a land owner but not technically "slaves."

the slain and captive, into the central square of Tepeaca to await their fate. Cortés had one of his blacksmiths fashion a brand shaped in the letter *g* for the term *guerra* or "war." The brand was fired on hot coals and seared deeply into the faces of all the slaves taken, the skin of their cheeks blistering and bubbling as they were held down, bellowing out in anguish.[28]

For the next three weeks, fueled perhaps by a desire for vengeance for La Noche Triste, and certainly wishing to make a show of unyielding power, Cortés terrorized the region, ravaging villages and cities with brutal impunity. He turned his ferocious armored war-hounds loose on any Aztecs or their allies who refused to submit; the snarling, blood-crazed animals tore them to shreds.[29] Hacking and burning a wide and deadly course, Cortés took prisoner-slaves and exacted fealty from leaders until, as the thick smoke of sacked towns choked the horizon, he had subjugated the entire province of Tepeaca. Cortés would say of this bloody carnage, "Although...this province is very large, within twenty days we had subdued and pacified many towns and villages, and the lords and chieftains...offered themselves as your majesty's vassals."[30] Cortés would later justify his brutality and the taking of slaves by arguing that it was in response to widespread regional cannibalism, which both he and the crown despised, but this claim rang false, sounding like an excuse.[31]

The campaign reached, even for Cortés, shocking levels of atrocity and barbarity. In one city he is said to have lined up and killed two thousand civilian men, while four thousand women and children watched—and the latter were then branded and enslaved.[32] It was terribly effective, however, and on September 4, 1520, Cortés ensconced himself inextricably on the promontory of Tepeaca, where he founded a new town called Segura de la Frontera (Security of the Frontier). He appointed, as in Villa Rica, a city council, complete with magistrates, *alcaldes*, and all necessary officials of a functioning and "legal" Spanish city. Looking down from the hilltop fortress (on which he erected civic buildings and installed a garrison),

Cortés could survey his new domain with satisfaction, even optimism. He now controlled nearly half of Mexico, and, more important, he had won a strategic position that guaranteed secure and open passage from the high plains clear to the eastern shore, allowing unimpeded transfer of men, equipment, and goods. And by extension he had severed the Aztecs from this same crucial lifeline.

Brimming with confidence from his elevated base of operations, his physical health revived, Cortés held a secret meeting with his shipbuilder Martín López. The failed first attempts at taking Tenochtitlán had taught Cortés that the layout of the causeways made a straightforward ground assault impossible. But the innovative and engineering-minded Cortés had a new plan, one of unprecedented scope and magnitude, one that he may have conceived the moment he had arrived safely on the west bank of the Tacuba causeway on the fateful morning following La Noche Triste. Speaking in confidence, Cortés gave the shipbuilder strict and intriguing orders. Martín López was to take three skilled craftsmen as assistants, plus as many Tlaxcalan laborers as he needed, and head immediately for the western slopes of the mountain known as Matlalcueitl. (It would later be referred to as La Malinche, after Cortés's interpreter and mistress.) They were to strike into the dense forests of the foothills and cut great quantities of timber—pine and oak and evergreen oak—which could then be "fashioned into the pieces necessary to build thirteen brigantines."[33]

In a stroke of military brilliance, Hernán Cortés determined that if he could not take Tenochtitlán by land, then he would take the lake-bound Aztec stronghold by water.

CHAPTER SIXTEEN

"The Great Rash"

IF FORTUNE TRULY FAVORS THE BOLD, then in the next month, ironically, Hernán Cortés was the beneficiary of fortunes he could never have predicted or planned, arriving in forms both visible and invisible.

The first sign of good fortune turned up at the port of Vera Cruz in the shape of a small Spanish ship captained by Pedro Barba, an old "friend" of Cortés. Back in 1519, it was Pedro Barba whom Diego Velázquez had sent to attempt to thwart Cortés's departure from Cuba at the beginning of the expedition, but Cortés had won Barba over, who saw that he hadn't the power to arrest an armada and five hundred soldiers. Now here he was again, one of Velázquez's seemingly endless supply of henchmen. Velázquez had commissioned and dispatched the craft from Cuba to support the Pánfilo de Narváez expedition; the governor was currently aware of that expedition's ignominious fate and Narváez's imprisonment.[1]

As the ship anchored offshore, the clever captain Alonso Caballero, who was in charge at Villa Rica, lured some of the crew (including Barba) ashore in small boats, then held them at swordpoint and ordered them to surrender in the name of Captain-General Hernán Cortés. Barba's ship carried a light crew, just thirteen soldiers, a stallion, and a mare, but he did possess a great load of cassava bread and, most interesting, a letter from Velázquez to Narváez intimating that he believed New Spain was now his, telling Narváez that "if he had not already killed Cortés that he should at once send him as a prisoner to Cuba."[2] This goal would be difficult for Narváez to achieve from the tight confines of his own prison cell.

Alonso Caballero sent Barba, the soldiers, and the horses under guard to Segura de la Frontera. Cortés received his old crony with a friendly *abrazo*, slapping him on the back and welcoming him, clearly enjoying this fortuitous turn of events. Barba could see that Cortés was firmly in command of the situation (and of Narváez and his men), so he humbly accepted a new position as captain of Cortés's crossbowmen, and he was from that moment on loyal to Cortés.[3]

Then amazingly (for Cortés could certainly use reinforcement), a series of five more ships landed at or around Villa Rica. The first was another smallish ship sent by Velázquez, and Caballero similarly commandeered both its crew and contents; Caballero must have begun to enjoy the ruse of inveigling them ashore and then surprising them with the reality of the command situation. He conveyed under guard the captain of this ship, eight soldiers, and six crossbowmen over the mountains to Segura de la Frontera, along with numerous bales of much-needed cordage for fabricating crossbow strings, and yet another mare.[4] The newcomers consented without altercation or disagreement.

Shortly afterward another ship limped into port at Villa Rica, this one a caravel under the charge of Diego de Camargo, who was part of an expedition sponsored by Francisco de Garay, governor of Jamaica. Garay had intended to settle the area near the mouth of the Panuco River to the north of Villa Rica. (Cortés himself had sent reconnaissance voyages to that area and had, in his mind and on paper, claims to the region.) The Garay expedition fared poorly; it was overwhelmed by the local inhabitants the moment they landed, forced back to sea, and suffered a storm that took one ship, swallowing it and all its crew members. The remaining ships sailed south and finally listed into the port at Vera Cruz, arriving in grim shape. Cortés later claimed to have effectively saved the men's lives, since "they had arrived in great want of provisions, so much so indeed that had they not found help there they would have died of hunger and thirst."[5] At the garrison at Villa Rica Camargo and his sixty soldiers were well treated, fed, and doctored—and conscripted into the service of Cortés.[6]

Just as Cortés was counting these blessings, yet more miraculously fell into his hands. A few days later another Garay ship sought refuge at Vera Cruz. This ship contained fifty men and, to Cortés's growing enthusiasm, seven healthy horses. The captain of this wayward ship was none other than the experienced and intrepid conquistador Miguel Díaz de Aux of Aragón, whom Cortés had known well from his days in Hispaniola. Indeed, Díaz de Aux had been among the first colonists in Puerto Rico nearly a decade earlier; his sagacity and knowledge would prove beneficial to Cortés.[7]

There seemed no end to this divine providence. Another ship arrived in the next few weeks, still another of Garay's, containing forty crewmen, ten horses, and, most useful of all, numerous crossbows and string, muskets, and quilted cotton armor. The irony that all Garay's ships and provisions ended up in Cortés's lap was not lost on soldier and chronicler Bernal Díaz, who commented with an archery metaphor: "Thus, Francisco de Garay shot off one shaft after another to the assistance of his armada, and each one went to assist the good fortune of Cortés and all of us."[8] The last ship to arrive came all the way from Spain via the Canary Islands, dispatched at the behest of Cortés's father and some of Cortés's business associates who continued to support his endeavors in Mexico. The large ship was owned by a merchant named Juan de Burgos and captained by Francisco Medel; upon their arrival with tons of crucial combat merchandise (including kegs of gunpowder, more bowstrings, muskets, and three horses), Cortés paid with gold for the ship and contents and absorbed the crew of thirteen into his expedition.[9]

In a matter of a few weeks, Cortés's conquering force was increased by more than two hundred men (giving him now around thirteen hundred), plus supplies and tools of war necessary for reconquest. He had subdued the entire province of Tepeaca, and despite the poor condition of some of the new men, Cortés seemed confident in his military position and his plan to retake Tenochtitlán.

AT precisely the same time, an invisible and deadly enemy unveiled itself across Mexico, one that would prove devastating to the Aztecs and that would paradoxically assist Cortés in his pursuit of conquest. While he was training his new recruits, stacking and storing powder kegs and ammunition, and cleaning freshly arrived armaments, all across Mexico the native population began to suffer from an inexplicable illness. King and peasant alike were racked with fitful coughs and burning, blistering sores. Then after months of horrific suffering, those stricken would die. The pestilence was smallpox, a virulent killer that was foreign to and unprecedented in the New World.

The disease first reached Hispaniola in the last months of 1518, laying waste to more than one-third of the indigenous population; then it hopped from island to island, infecting both Cuba and Puerto Rico and, quickly, the Greater Antilles.[10] Then came perhaps the greatest and most destructive irony in the history of the Spanish conquest; certainly Hernán Cortés would not understand until much later how crucial it had been to his cause. On one of the Narváez ships (sent to either capture or kill Cortés) was an African porter named Francisco de Eguia, who was infected with smallpox and brought the first case to New Spain.[11] Unwittingly Eguia "infected the household in Cempoala where he was quartered; and it spread from one Indian to another, and they, being so numerous and eating and sleeping together, quickly infected the whole country."[12] By late October the pestilence had scoured its way to Tenochtitlán, so that just as the Aztecs were busy cleaning their

temples and ridding the pyramids of all memory of the
Spaniards' presence among them, the people began to fall sick
with mysterious and frightening symptoms.

The appearance of those afflicted was grotesque, for they
broke out in flaming pustules and weals that gouged their faces
and bodies; some welts and blisters were so prevalent on the victims' faces as to render them blind. The inexplicable epidemic
caused panic and paralysis across the lacustrine district. The
Aztecs long afterward remembered the pestilence and its symptoms: "Sores erupted on our faces, our breasts, our bellies; we
were covered with agonizing sores from head to foot. The illness
was so dreadful that no one could walk or move. The sick were
so utterly helpless that they could only lie on their beds like
corpses, unable to move their limbs or even their heads. They
could not lie face down or roll from one side to the other. If they
did move their bodies, they screamed with pain."[13]

Skin conditions were not entirely unknown to the Aztecs,
who understood their minor forms as punishments meted out
by the god Tezcatlipoca. But they had no experience with an
epidemic of this magnitude, which partly explains why the
Aztec soldiers were unable to pursue and finish off Cortés.
People died in such numbers that even cremation was halted.
Bodies were heaped into canals or taken by canoe to the middle
of the lake and dumped without ritual or ceremony.[14] Women
grew too sick to grind maize, so that a serious food shortage developed, and for seventy days—the period coinciding precisely
with Cortés's crucial convalescence in Tlaxcala and Tepeaca—
the general populace was too ill to function properly. The recently enthroned Cuitláhuac also contracted the disease.

The Aztecs attempted to deal with the pestilence as best
they could. Physicians treated the horrific sores with ancient
remedies, employing their considerable knowledge of the
medicinal properties of plants and animals. They sprinkled
finely ground obsidian powder into the wounds of the afflicted,
then wrapped them in plasters. They pressed special "blood-
stones," called *eztetls*, to the nostrils of the sick to stanch their
nosebleeds, and they tried plants like *sarsaparilla* and *jalap*,

and even crushed beetles, but none could remedy the scourge of the smallpox, against which the indigenous peoples of Mexico had no immunity.[15] Most of these attempted remedies merely failed, but one actually further spread the disease: communal bathing. Ritual and curative bathing was a widespread, established practice in everyday life, used for general cleanliness but also to purge maladies. Unfortunately, one of the most common medicinal techniques—that of the steam bath or *temazcalli*—perfectly suited the spread of smallpox.

A bather at a *temazcalli* entered through a low door into a low-slung stone dome fueled by woodstoves. He began tossing water onto the fire-heated walls, and he "was then enveloped in steam, and he switched himself violently with grasses. Often there would be another person there, particularly if the bather were an invalid, to massage him; and after the massage the bather would lie upon a mat to let the bath have its effect."[16] The touching of open sores, the sharing of infected water, and the breathing of the close communal air helped transmit the disease, and soon "the Great Rash" ravaged the mighty metropolis of Tenochtitlán and the rest of the Aztec empire.

Innumerable Aztec warriors died from the disease, and many of those who lived only barely survived, stricken woefully, "disabled and paralyzed"[17] by the pox, some permanently blinded. In less than three months body counts staggered the cities—in some cases smallpox claimed half of the population. The Aztecs lumbered about in a sickly daze, wondering yet again why their gods had forsaken them, why they were being punished. As the Aztec accounts sadly reported, "a great many died from this plague, and many others died of hunger. They could not get up to search for food, so they starved to death in their beds."*[18] Chronicler

---

*The exact number of deaths as a result of smallpox alone is impossible to determine, but the impact the disease had on the native population was catastrophic. In México some estimates suggest that more than half the population died from the disease, and according to recent projections, between its onset in 1518 and the early 1600s, as many as 100 million Indians perished from European-borne diseases, which was then the equivalent of one in five people on earth. See Charles C. Mann, *1491: New Revelations of the Americas Before Columbus* (New York, 2005), 94.

Francisco de Aguilar, who was there, noted the cosmic irony of the timing, observing that just "when the Christians were exhausted from war, God saw fit to send the Indians smallpox."[19]

While the pox decimated the Aztecs physically, it also worked against them psychologically. The Spaniards were immune to the plague's effects, most having been exposed as children. Their immunity made them appear ever more powerful, even superhuman; it most certainly rekindled the notion (which had been at least contemplated by the late Montezuma) that these men were not men at all but gods.[20]

THE catastrophic "Great Rash" smote friend and foe alike, and by late December 1520 it had taken not only the Aztec emperor Cuitláhuac but also Maxixcatzin, Cortés's chief ally in Tlaxcala, as well as the kings of Tacuba, Chalco, and Cholula and the leader of the Tarascans. The deaths of these key leaders, especially of those in the city-states of the central plain, put Cortés in an unexpected position of authority in the region. He was called upon to suggest successors for those whom the smallpox had taken. In this way he was allowed to handpick the new ruler of Izúcar (one of Montezuma's nephews) and the new king of Cholula.[21] Both of these new leaders were positively disposed to Cortés, or were at least malleable, and they greatly strengthened Cortés's growing political choke hold on the region.

WHILE the Aztecs lay dying, Cortés fortified his position at Segura de la Frontera and watched his soldiers grow stronger by the day. He used the opportunity, and the safety of the hilltop stronghold, to take care of some crucial legal and diplomatic business. He penned a number of legal documents to justify the actions and decisions he had made during his expedition and to underscore his continued efforts to procure gold for the crown. He informed Spain that Velázquez and Narváez had been serious impediments to his progress, costing him time, money, and lives, and he explained his rationale in seizing Narváez's ships, arms, and men.[22] He understood that he would eventually have to answer for his actions, and he laid the groundwork for his own defense with this correspondence. One document, confirming that the entire army believed in the enterprise and agreeing that Cortés should remain captain-general and chief justice of Villa Rica, was signed by more than five hundred of his men.[23]

He finished the second of his famous letters to the king (who Cortés had by now learned was also Holy Roman emperor Charles V as well as king of Germany), apprising him of the events since leaving Vera Cruz and of his present situation. He admitted to having temporarily lost Tenochtitlán, but he suggested, with his usual bravado, that this was only a minor setback: "I intend, as soon as such help arrives, to return to that country and its great city, and I believe, as I have already told Your Majesty, that it will shortly be restored to the state in which I held it before, and thus all our past losses shall be made good."[24] Cortés followed this confident claim with the rather bold suggestion (noting the tremendous similarities between Spain and Mexico) that the emperor formally call the newly discovered land "New Spain of the Ocean Sea,"[25] adding that he had already been doing so in the emperor's name and honor. Cortés closed by expressing the hope that a trustworthy legal emissary would be sent to "make an examination and inquiry"[26] of his dealings to ascertain their legitimacy. The letter was dated October 30, 1520, though it would not in fact be sent (either delayed by bad weather, as Cortés claimed, or for political reasons) until March of the following year.

Though his force had been greatly strengthened by the recent ship arrivals, Cortés decided to send four ships back to the islands for more arms, ammunition, horses, men, and political support. One captain was chosen to sail a ship to Jamaica to purchase mares for breeding, and another went to Santo Domingo to acquire horses and also to entreat the Royal Audience there to support the cause or at the very least not hinder it.[27] The animals, ammunitions, and equipment would be paid for with gold ingots, which Cortés had hoarded for just this purpose.

Some of the last of Narváez's men reiterated their desire to return to the islands, and Cortés now consented, cleverly divesting himself of a few potentially mutinous captains. Among them was his friend and business associate Andrés de Duero, who he hoped might in time smooth Velázquez's very ruffled feathers and serve as a kind of buffer between them. Cortés gave Duero a letter for his wife, Catalina Suárez Marcaida Cortés, and another for his brother-in-law, Juan Suárez, sending them both some gold bars and precious golden jewelry that he had personally retained from Montezuma's treasure.[28]

Cortés conferred with Sandoval and determined that the towns of Jalacingo and Zautla, which lay to the northeast on the route to Vera Cruz, had to be subdued in a similar fashion to Tepeaca. Sandoval left with two hundred soldiers, twenty cavalry, twelve crossbowman, and a considerable force of Tlaxcalans, riding out on a monthlong expedition. He returned having taken these towns without the loss of a single Spaniard (though eight were badly injured, and three horses had been killed). He brought back two Spanish saddles and a number of bridles that the natives had absconded with and offered at their temples as idols. Trailing behind Sandoval, tethered to poles, were a "great spoil of women and boys... branded as slaves."[29]

These people, like the slaves taken and branded at the conclusion of the brief but brutal Tepeaca campaign, were distributed among the Spanish soldiers. Some discontent arose among the men, who argued that the best-looking slave women were always stolen or hidden away for the captains and that they received only the old and ugly women; there was much grumbling and fighting.[30] Cortés's solution to the problem was to sell the women to his men at public auction; the men paid a higher price for the women they most desired, and a lower price for the older women and those deemed less attractive. Cortés figured that in this way his men could have no grievance with him.

His business in Segura de la Frontera was finally completed on December 13, 1520, and he prepared to set out for Tlaxcala, where he would spend Christmas. He wished to check on the progress of the brigantine project and shore up the final plans for his military reconquest. Before departing, Cortés placed artillery commander Francisco Orozco in charge of guarding the fortress at Segura de la Frontera, along with about sixty men, twenty of whom were still too wounded to march.[31] Orozco was also to monitor the passes and roads leading to and from the city, keeping the route clear of hostiles.

Cortés rode out on December 13, taking his position at the vanguard of twenty horsemen. He and the small cavalry would ride to Tlaxcala via Cholula, where he intended to gird their alliance, while his foot soldiers, under Diego de Ordaz, were to march straight to Tlaxcala without stopping. Cortés arrived in Cholula and was welcomed by the nobles, who well remembered his wrath and wished to appease him. Many of their highest lords had succumbed to smallpox, and Cortés was called upon to assist them in choosing new leaders, a role he happily fulfilled.[32] He spent three days there tidying up these appointments before continuing on to Tlaxcala.

Cortés's pleasure in arriving back at the seat of his central allies was tempered by the news he received there: his dear friend and crucial supporter, the Tlaxcalan overlord Maxixcatzin, had perished from "the Great Rash." He grieved deeply at his loss, entreating his captains and men to mourn by wearing black cloaks, and most of them did so. Remaining chiefs and elders, including Xicotenga the Elder and Chichimecatecle, asked him to help name a successor, and he suggested the eldest of Maxixcatzin's legitimate sons, a boy of just twelve. With all the nobles attending, Cortés then "knighted him with his own hand,"[33] likely the first such instance of formal knighting bestowed on an American Indian.[34] Through Malinche, Cortés urged the young boy to act in the manner of his noble and honored father, whom all had respected and loved. The boy was then baptized, as was Xicotenga the Elder, both becoming Christians with, according to Bernal Díaz, "the greatest ceremony that at that time it was possible to arrange in Tlaxcala."[35]

Cortés then met with shipbuilder Martín López to discuss his progress and was pleased to discover that things were going well. López and his carpenters had completed much of the planking and many of the crossbeams. They were basing the design of the ships on one of those that had been left at Vera Cruz; the ship had been dismantled and, in an excruciatingly difficult operation, carried in pieces by Tlaxcalan porters over the mountains. Now López used it as a template on which to pattern the thirteen brigantines. Cortés could see his grand plan coming together, and he launched once more into aggressive action. "I then sent to Vera Cruz," he wrote to Emperor Charles, "for all the iron and nails they had, and also for sails and rigging and other necessary things, and as we had no pitch I had certain Spaniards make it on a hill close by."[36] This gear was retained from one of the scuttled ships, confirming his foresight to use the materials again when needed. It required one thousand Tlaxcalan bearers to hike over the mountains and convey the needed gear back.

Since September Martín López, his carpenters, and a great many Tlaxcalan assistants had been laboring in the dense forests on the western flanks of Matlalcueitl. Here López and his skilled carpenters stalked the woods looking for perfect oak and evergreen trees, which they felled and sawed into beams and planks. The rough-hewn timbers were then transported by Tlaxcalans across the fifteen or twenty miles of rolling scrub back to the city, where they were stacked and ordered for further refining, trimming, and dressing. This was merely the beginning of the most ambitious undertaking of the entire campaign, and it is still among the largest landlocked naval operation ever conducted in the history of warfare.

Cortés had decided, since his narrow escape from Tenochtitlán, that the brigantines were the key to the whole conquest.

But the task was so bold as to be almost incomprehensible. Martín López, by now personally invested monetarily in the project, believed it could be achieved, and to that end "he toiled in everything connected with [the brigantines'] construction, all day long, and often after dark and before dawn by the aid of candles, working himself and directing and encouraging other workmen, with the zeal of a man who comprehended the urgency of the case."[37]

The grand scheme was to carry the rough-cut planks and beams from the mountains to Tlaxcala and to fashion and finish them there, beyond Aztec reach and knowledge, whetting and drying and shaping them. Then the boats would be assembled at a makeshift shipyard on the edge of the Río Zahuapan, which López would dam to ensure a deep enough flow. The boats, which would be between forty and fifty feet long, would be tested for seaworthiness, checked for leaks, and then disassembled. Once they were deemed worthy, at Cortés's order the boats were to be transported some fifty miles over the mountains and down into the Valley of Mexico, to Texcoco, where they would (assuming that everything went according to plan) be reassembled. Then, under the direction of López, an army of Tlaxcalan workers would dig a mile-long canal twelve feet deep and twelve feet wide, so that they could launch the reassembled armada of brigantines from a safe and defensible distance.

The plan was overly ambitious—some might even say that it was insane. Nonetheless, as Christmas fell cold and clear over the Mexican highlands, it was the master plan of Hernán Cortés. His vision for the reoccupation—and ultimate reconquest—of the Aztec empire hinged on skeletal staves of timber plucked from the hillside of a dormant volcano.

CHAPTER SEVENTEEN

Return to the Valley of Mexico

WHILE CORTÉS WAS FINALIZING HIS PLANS to return to the Valley of Mexico, the Aztecs foundered in confusion and despair. On December 4, 1520, the new king and warlord Cuitláhuac died after a brief battle with smallpox, leaving the Aztec rulership uncertain once again. The people who had just survived nearly three months of plague mourned for their short-lived ruler, praying and making sacrifices at his passing, but they had little time for proper tribute. They were still busy disposing of bodies fallen to the pox. They made one lengthy prayer to him, an incantation, as part of the deliberations used to contemplate and select his successor. "Who now shall order matters for the good of the people and the realm?" chanted the priests. "Who shall appoint the judges to minister justice to the people? Who shall bid the drum and the flute to sound, and gather together the veteran soldiers and the men mighty in battle?"[1] Those questions would haunt the empire for two months, during which time the Aztecs lived without a ruler.

The answer finally materialized in the form of Prince Cuauhtémoc,* nephew to both Montezuma and Cuitláhuac

---

*Cuauhtémoc would not be formally inaugurated as the eleventh (and last) Aztec king until February 1521.

and son of King Ahuitzotl, the eighth emperor of the Aztecs. The choice made sense given the dire conditions in the valley and the fractured imperial system. Cuauhtémoc had battle in his blood, and as a devout worshipper of Huitzilopochtli, he vehemently opposed any concessions to Christianity. His imperial parentage certainly played a role in his selection as well.

Initially Cuauhtémoc had been among the cool-minded leaders who were against confrontation with the Spaniards, but that time had long since passed, and he in fact had led the throng to the base of the Palace of Axayacatl and cried out at the weakened and, in his mind, pathetic Montezuma as the puppet emperor stood on the parapet and attempted to calm the horde. One native source claims that Cuauhtémoc had thrown the stone that fatally wounded Montezuma.[2] He was young and strong and pugnacious; Bernal Díaz described him as "not more than twenty-five years old, and elegant in his person . . . very valiant, and so terrible, that his followers trembled in his presence."[3] He had distinguished himself in the battles in the capital, and once installed as ruler, he rapidly took charge, sending spies and runners to report to him on the movements and condition of Cortés and his army.[4]

Cuauhtémoc possessed much military training, but he also understood, now more than ever, the importance of allies and of diplomacy. He assessed the city's defenses, noting that before his death Cuitláhuac had done a decent job of shoring up ramparts, but there was more to be done. Cuauhtémoc set about buttressing the high walls to divert cavalry, digging caves for hiding, and fabricating armaments, including retrofitting the confiscated long Spanish lances that were adapted to impale oncoming horses and dismount their riders.[5] Cuauhtémoc, employing what few remaining lords of power he had at his disposal, sent ambassadors to all the city-states around the lake and across the valley urging them to join him and their Aztec brothers in the fight against the Spaniards, who were surely coming back. These appeals came with generous gifts, and some city-states were lured by the promise of abated tribute-paying. Other lords agreed in principle, though their support remained tenuous, even flimsy. Some, having learned through runners and messengers about the annihilations and enslavements in Tepeaca, Zautla, and Jalacingo, deeply feared Cortés. Still others harbored long-held animosity toward the Aztecs, making alliances difficult for Cuauhtémoc.

OVER the mountains in Tlaxcala, on December 28, 1520, Hernán Cortés reviewed his troops and readied for the descent into the Valley of Mexico. The troops looked fine, though he worried about his scant powder supplies and hoped for reinforcements from the coast, and soon. He possessed nine efficient field guns. Of the 550 foot soldiers mustered, eighty were skilled harquebusiers and crossbowmen. Forty ready cavalrymen trotted and wheeled their mounts. Cortés assembled the ranks; the cavalry was split into four squadrons of ten, the foot soldiers into nine units of sixty each. Cortés's Spanish army, well convalesced, had remained active and trained over these last few months, and they appeared ready.[6]

Their allied support was now strong, and the recently baptized Xicotenga the Elder (now called by the Spaniards Don Lorenzo de Vargas) offered as many as eighty thousand Tlaxcalan warriors. Cortés knew that feeding such a massive army on the move would be nearly impossible, so he took about ten thousand, leaving the rest in Tlaxcala, to be called upon later if required.[7] Chichimecatecle would command the Tlaxcalan contingents.

Before departing, Cortés assembled the entire allied force—the Spaniards in clanking and shimmering armor, the Indian warriors in feathers—at the central square of Tlaxcala. By now more than proficient in rousing oratory, Cortés spoke to his men (translated to the Tlaxcalans through Malinche and a few pages who had learned Nahuatl) reminding them of (and cleverly providing legal precedent for) the task ahead. They embarked on a "just" cause, he said, simultaneously appealing to honor, faith, and greed. "The principal reason for us coming to these parts," he bellowed across the plaza, "is to glorify and preach the Faith of Jesus Christ, even though at the same time it brings us honor and profit, which infrequently come in the same package."[8]

Cortés went on, attempting to justify, both to the crown and in accordance with Spanish law, his proposed military actions by suggesting that the Aztecs were not a liberated nation but rather were vassals of Spain in rebellion, murderers of Spanish citizens who therefore required "a great whipping and punishment."*[9] While the argument was weak and rather dubious, it achieved the desired effect: the army rallied with whoops and cheers. Cortés closed this portion of his speech with a salient reminder of the Aztecs' vile practices of human sacrifice, cannibalism, and even sodomy (this last an appeal against a taboo, seemingly for punctuation). Then he called upon a crier to shout out a list of seventeen rules of engagement, recently scribed by his new war secretary. The irony of some of them is so egregious, given Spanish brutality and duplicitous behavior, that in reading them, one does not know whether to laugh or to cry.[10]

The highlights of this list, which Cortés called "ordinances for good government and other matters concerning war,"[11] include the following. The purpose of the war was to impart to the local inhabitants of Mexico a "knowledge of our holy faith" and to "subjugate them, under imperial and royal yoke and dominion of His Majesty, to whom, legally, the lordship of these parts now belongs."[12] The terms "subjugate," "dominion," and "belongs" betray Cortés's true intention: to bring this land to its knees and possess it.

Then followed a series of unintentionally amusing "No one mights" (resonating the biblical "Thou shalt nots"),

---

*By calling the Aztecs "vassals in rebellion," Cortés was directly referring to his initial (now famous) discussion with Montezuma, in which Cortés interpreted (rather too conveniently) Montezuma's speech as a concession, and donation, of his empire to Spain via Hernán Cortés. It was a devilishly shrewd bit of diplomacy on the part of Cortés; the "justifications" for war later were referred to in the *Siete Partidas*, the Spanish legal code.

rendered concisely by Cortés's secretary Francisco López de Gómara: "No one might blaspheme the Holy Name of God; no Spaniard might quarrel with another; no one might wager his arms or horse; no one might force a woman; no one might insult friendly Indian warriors, or use the *tamemes* [bearers] as gifts; no one might take the Indians' clothing, do violence to them, or sack their towns, without Cortés's permission and the consent of the council." The last provision, "without Cortés's permission," is the most darkly conspicuous order, suggesting as it does that Cortés could ultimately do whatever he wanted, as shown recently in Tepeaca. The "no gambling" rule also made a curious provision for cards, "under certain limitations,"[13] which included Cortés's own private quarters.

Many of the rules were targeted at maintaining strict military order and discipline, and disobedience—including desertion during battle, abandoning one's post, and sleeping while on guard—was punishable by death. Certainly Alvarado's assault at the Festival of Toxcatl partly inspired one that prohibited any captain from attacking the enemy without orders. Cortés had seen only too clearly the devastating result of such an action. The last ordinance, also punishable by hanging, "prohibits any man, officer or private, from securing to his own use any of the booty taken from the enemy, whether it be gold, silver, feather-work...slaves, or other commodity."[14] Clearly Cortés had his own, and the king's, fifths in mind when he wrote this provision.

When all had heard these proclamations, Cortés took Malinche aside and directed her to give special instructions to the Tlaxcalan leaders, warriors, and workers whom he would be leaving behind. He told them that he would depart the following day to confront the enemy, adding that "the city of [Tenochtitlán] could not be won without those brigantines which were being built." He asked that the Tlaxcalan people "give the carpenters and all the other Spaniards...all they might require,"[15] in order that these vessels be completed as soon as possible. When the time was right, many bearers would be called upon to carry the planking, crossbeams, and rigging over the mountains. These bearers had best be ready.

After a last consultation with Martín López to finalize the brigantine plan, Cortés led his Spaniards and his long line of ten thousand west, toward the pass at the origin of the River Atoyac (modern River Frio). At nightfall they reached Texmelucan, a safe pueblo under Tlaxcalan control. Cortés chose this pass (north of their original route, now called The Pass of Cortés, but south of the path they had used in their escape-retreat) because it was more remote and severe than the others and thus less likely to be contested. The next day they climbed the steepening ground toward the pass, the ridgeline of the mountains ahead looming ragged and shadowy, the air thinning. Miles to the north they could see the snow-domed summit of the volcano Iztaccíhuatl dominating the skyscape.

The boulder-strewn trail narrowed and swept sharply upward. Bearers heaved the heavy artillery along. The mountainside was scabrous with thornbrush and dwarf pine, wind-gnarled tree branches choking the trail. They encamped that night near the top of the pass at over twelve thousand feet, huddled together around fires. Sentries and scouts stomped their feet and swung their arms so as not to freeze. "Although it was very cold," Cortés remembered, "we managed to warm ourselves with the great quantity of firewood we found there."[16]

At dawn the troops heard mass amid freezing spindrift, then moved again, cresting the talus ridge of the sierra and nosing down into a desperately declining ravine. As it narrowed and plunged, Cortés sent four cavalry ahead to survey the trail, followed closely by harquebusiers and crossbowmen, armed and ready. They were now in Aztec territory. Cortés grew concerned at what they discovered: "They found the road blocked with trees and branches; very large and thick pine and cypress trees, which seemed to have been cut very recently, had been felled across it."[17] The conditions appeared perfect for an ambush. Cortés and his men continued forth cautiously, scouring the hillsides for signs of enemy movement, conjuring screaming warriors in their imaginations.

No attack came. With great difficulty men cleared away the tangles of timber, hacking passage for the horses, and for a few frightening hours the train streamed slowly and exposed down the mountainside beneath the shadows of hovering prey birds. At length the trail widened and spread onto an alluvial plain far below. Cortés halted his horsemen and sent word back to the rear for the train to hurry along. The great Valley of Mexico once more unfurled before him, the whitewashed cities rising up out of the water, the cultivated maize and maguey plantations rimming the lakes. But this pastoral vision was disrupted by something else: "the enemy, who had already observed us, now suddenly began to send up great smoke signals all over the land,"[18] and he warned his men that they should remain organized in tight formation on the trail. He entreated his men that they should "not turn back until they had taken Mexico or died in the attempt."[19]

The trail sloughed away below them and narrowed again at a rocky, vine-cluttered path, where a dilapidated timber footbridge spanned a deep ravine and a rumbling waterfall. Beyond, lying in wait, was a "large squadron of Mexican and Texcocan warriors."[20] Concerned but undaunted, Cortés dispatched fifteen horsemen, who galloped forward with their lances lowered, spearing and dispersing the warriors and scattering them to the hills. The way cleared, Cortés marched his units in formation down the mountain. Local inhabitants of the farms, many perched atop the ravine walls, shouted jeers and obscenities. Despite Cortés's recently drawn up "ordinances," a few enraged Tlaxcalans broke ranks to pillage farms, absconding with fowls and maize. When officers reprimanded them, they pointed out that the jeers and cries were hostile and justified a response.

They rode into the valley, camping that night at Coatepec, a tributary village of Texcoco, which they found abandoned. Worried about a nighttime attack, Cortés took ten horsemen and led the first watch, reminding all his men to sleep fully armored, their arms clutched to their chests. That night, instead of an attack, Cortés received a welcome visitation from Ixtlilxochitl, the brother of Cacama (whom Cortés had ordered slain) and of Coanacochtzin, current king of Texcoco. He secreted to Cortés a gold peace chain and a solemn promise to fight with the Spaniards against the Aztecs, even agreeing to march next to Cortés at the vanguard as a symbol of his allegiance. He would fight against his own brother, his rival, whose ascent to Texcoco's throne had been controversial. Cortés gladly accepted both his golden token and his support, delighted by the unexpected windfall, for it paved the way for his unencumbered entry into Texcoco, the city most crucial to his grand military plan.[21]

On the last day of 1520 they rose and marched in strict order for six miles. Cortés and his captains surveyed the landscape and discussed their approach to the city of Texcoco, which they prayed would be peaceful, though, given their recent reception, they fully expected hostilities. Soon some of Cortés's scout riders returned at a gallop, reporting that they had met peaceful chieftains ahead, men who wished to speak with the captain-general of the Spaniards. Though initially suspicious of subterfuge, Cortés was encouraged to see that he knew one of the chiefs, who approached with a half dozen others, one hoisting a heavy golden peace flag. The leader of the delegation apologized for the rude reception Cortés had received, and the skirmishes up in the gorges, but he assured the captain-general that those attacks had been ordered by Cuauhtémoc, who remained hostile. The flag-bearers came, they said, on behalf of their own leader Coanacochtzin, who desired only peace and friendship and was at this moment waiting to receive Cortés as an ally in Texcoco; he would provide quarters for them in the palace of the late king Nezahuapilli and whatever food he could spare.[22]

Cortés, through Malinche and Aguilar, responded that he accepted their peace offering but pointed out that not long ago, very near here, many of his men had been killed and most of his treasure, given to him by Montezuma, had been stolen.

He said that though the dead could not be returned to life, his treasure could be returned, and if they did so, he would spare their lives. The delegation murmured among one another, then responded that any confiscated treasure had been the work of the Aztecs of Tenochtitlán. They were themselves quite innocent, they said, but if Cortés would come to the quarters prepared for him, they would speak with the chief of Texcoco and do whatever they could to regain the missing treasure.

Cortés reached the center of Texcoco around noon on December 31, 1520. It was, at the time, the second most populated city in the Triple Alliance, sustaining 25,000 to 30,000 people, but during their march through the suburbs Cortés noted that the streets were uncharacteristically quiet: "We had not seen a tenth of the people who are normally to be found in the city, nor any women and or children, which was a rather alarming sign."[23] The men they did see appeared frightened, well bundled, and skittish, darting sheepishly behind doors at the Spaniards' coming. Cortés sent some of his captains and soldiers, including Pedro de Alvarado, Cristóbal de Olid, and Bernal Díaz, to the top of the city's great pyramid (which was actually slightly higher than that of the Great Temple in Tenochtitlán) to scan the area and report their findings.

What they saw from this impressive promontory explained the empty streets, for most of the populace was fleeing the city in canoes; some eight or ten thousand coursing furiously across Lake Texcoco, westward toward the capital. The streets and roads leaving the city to the north and west were clogged with people, including thousands of women and children, carrying their belongings on their backs, scattering toward the lake and woods and mountains. The mass departure was widespread.

Unable to arrest the exodus, Cortés called for the arrest of Coanacochtzin, but he was among the first to have fled, ahead of his people. He was clearly aligned with Cuauhtémoc. Cortés fumed, and to vent his rage he sanctioned some carnage, ordering the idols on temples shattered, random buildings set afire, and a roundup of the remaining citizens, including women and children. These people were branded, enslaved, and sold among his men as before.[24] Cortés soon learned that all the lords who had met him on the plain and given him the golden staff had now bolted for the capital, so while he had not been attacked, he had been deceived, and—worse—he had fallen for their ploy. A master of deception himself, he might have been at least a little impressed.

Cortés established himself in the commodious palace rooms that had been prepared for him and contemplated his situation, which presented both problems and opportunities. On the one hand, a vacated city was not ideal, for though he had entered unopposed and lost no men, he now had only the bare shell of a citizenry and infrastructure for food, provisioning, and daily living. Additionally, the departure of the city's lords meant that this new emperor, Cuauhtémoc, had at least some local support; Cortés would need to test the attitudes around the lake—south to Chalco and Iztapalapa, and west as far as Tacuba—to see how far the emperor's influence reached. On the positive side, the evacuations left him in control, essentially, of Texcoco, which had been his plan and desire all along. But these city-states functioned only with visible (whether actual or symbolic) rulers, and now the rule of Texcoco sat vacant, creating civic tension and doubt.

The industrious Cortés, having recent experience in such placements, figured he could remedy this problem in his favor. Ostensibly with the support of the few remaining Texcocan dignitaries, he suggested a puppet-ruler, a boy named Tecocol. Curiously, Tecocol would die after only two months (perhaps as a result of smallpox, though the epidemic seems to have subsided by this time), and the position was then filled by Ixtlilxochitl, Cortés's convenient new ally.[25]

For a few days Texcoco remained a ghost village. Cortés and his men pillaged the palace and nearby homes for food to feed themselves and the ten thousand Tlaxcalans, finding some but not enough. The people had taken much of their stores with them when they left. As they foraged about the city,

Cortés and his men encountered a magnificence that nearly rivaled that of neighboring Tenochtitlán, with remarkable botanical gardens, an outdoor theater for public performances, a music hall, a ball court, a zoo, and a great market (which was closed). The nobles' houses were immaculate timbered buildings built on high wooden pylons, with terraces overlooking the lake.[26] Though the city and environs impressed Cortés, after a few days he grew discouraged, for without the commerce and trade of a vital, working city, he could not hold out for long and would have to reconsider his plans.

On the third day, lords of three nearby Texcocan tribute towns—Tenango, Huexotla, and Coatlinchan—paid Cortés a visit. They admitted to having participated in the evacuation of Texcoco and their own villages. Weeping, they asked Cortés for forgiveness, saying that they had reconsidered and now wished to submit to Spanish authority. Cortés agreed to pardon them provided they returned to their cities and brought their children and women back to their homes.[27] These leaders complied, and within a few days people began returning to the surrounding cites. When word spread that Texcoco had a new ruler, other people started coming back as well, partly out of curiosity to see the new boy-king, but also because they preferred the comforts of their homes to life in the woods and on hillsides. Soon the city was functioning normally again.

This was a significant political coup for Cortés, who now had a military base in the imperial palaces of Texcoco, with vantage points from the terraces and temples overlooking the lake and the entire valley. Not only did he now possess the perfect staging area for his planned attack on Tenochtitlán, but his new allies strengthened his growing political stranglehold on the lake district, and his occupation of Texcoco's palace provided him with both a symbolic and an actual position of authority. He controlled an utterly unimpeded supply line from Vera Cruz, through Tlaxcala, all the way to the shore of Lake Texcoco. At the same time he was depriving Tenochtitlán of crucial coastal goods like saltwater fish and tropical fruits, essentially creating an embargo of this trade lifeline.

All that remained now was to subdue and incorporate any holdout Aztec allies, and to pray that his brigantine scheme would work. The enormous undertaking of conveying the dismantled boats over the mountains had yet to be done. There was no telling how long it might take, if it worked at all. Even now the Aztecs might be massing for an attack. The whole plot was a long shot, a toss of the Aztec *patolli* dice, but Cortés remembered beating Montezuma at that game, and now the gambler from Medellín was ready to wager everything once more.

CHAPTER EIGHTEEN

The Wooden Serpent

THE WINTER AND SPRING OF 1521 saw a series of moves and countermoves in the Valley of Mexico, as Cortés maneuvered to consolidate his allies while Cuauhtémoc sought to undermine them and bolster his own. Cuauhtémoc quickly learned that a number of the Texcocan tributaries had allied with Cortés, and he sent emissaries to try to subvert those recent agreements, but his plan backfired when his messengers were captured and brought before Cortés. The captain-general used these messengers as an opportunity to glean information about current conditions in Tenochtitlán and to establish a direct line of communication with the new emperor, with whom he hoped he might be able to negotiate, perhaps even convincing him bloodlessly to sue for peace. Cortés dismissed the prisoners, sending them back by canoe to the capital with an appeal for peace that included an implicit warning: agree to revert to Spanish vassalage, or your cities will be besieged and destroyed.

When no response came after a week, Cortés organized a reconnaissance mission targeting Iztapalapa, an important Aztec bastion some twenty miles to the south, an easy two days' march. He divided his army, leaving 3,000 or 4,000 Tlaxcalans and about 350 Spaniards in Texcoco under Sandoval. Cortés would personally lead a reconnaissance force of 200 Spaniards and as many as 7,000 Indian warriors and bearers, both Tlaxcalan and Texcocan allies.[1] Cortés took along captains Andrés de Tapia and Cristóbal de Olid, as well as twenty able chiefs of Texcoco, leaders suggested by Ixtlilxochitl, who had become a crucial and trusted ally. The captain-general rode out with a small cavalry of fifteen to twenty horses and modest but skilled firepower—ten harquebusiers and thirty crossbow-men—and headed south to the jutting isthmus of land that separated the great lakes Texcoco and Chalco into two distinct bodies, one salt water and the other fresh. It was here, in this large and beautiful waterborne city of Iztapalapa (nearly two-thirds of the houses were built on stilts over water) that Cortés and his men had spent their last night before their original historic entrance into Tenochtitlán via the long Iztapalapa causeway, the southernmost land route into the capital.[2]

As Cortés marched south, he noticed plumes of smoke rising in the distance; the inhabitants of the outlying villages signaled his movements. When he neared the outskirts of the city, he saw Aztec warriors congregating in the farm fields, and many war canoes lining the lakeshore. The Aztecs attacked in small bands of skirmishers, and Cortés fought minor combats for nearly five miles into the city proper. Most of the Aztecs then retreated, and as Cortés investigated the empty city, a startling thing occurred: the ground at his feet began to fill with water. In an ingenious ploy, the Aztecs had intentionally opened the dike of Nezhualcoyotl, sending salt water pouring into the low-lying ground. Their intention was to drown the Spaniards and their allies as the Aztecs retreated to higher ground. Apparently this was Emperor Cuauhtémoc's response to Cortés's recent communiqué.

The plan nearly worked. The Aztecs had hoped that Cortés would camp in the city, and be drowned that night. Instead, on the advice of the Texcocan chiefs who understood what was happening, Cortés moved quickly, fighting his way toward higher ground and killing rogue warriors as he went. "We drove them back into the water, some up to their chests and swimming," Cortés remembered.[3] The Tlaxcalans, inflamed with a lust for revenge, lingered in the city, killing citizens with impunity. Cortés ordered his men to set many of the houses ablaze, and in the smoldering dusk he realized that by now much of the city was under water, and he was forced to retreat. "When I reached the water," Cortés said, "it was so deep and it flowed with such force that we had to leap across it; some of our Indian allies were drowned, and we lost the spoil we had taken in the city."[4] Cortés and all but one of his Spanish force made it to the shoreline just in time; only an hour or two more, and they all would have drowned. Most of their gunpowder became wet and had to be abandoned. Many Tlaxcalans lost their lives.

Cortés and his men shivered the night away, soaked to the bone and weak with hunger. They awoke to find that hordes of Aztecs lined the lakeshore in their canoes, poised to attack. Shrieking, they leaped from their boats to fight, and Cortés ordered defensive maneuvers, fighting a retreat all the way back to Texcoco. Though the raid had not gone as planned, it could have been disastrous, and Cortés felt lucky to have escaped. The Aztecs considered themselves victorious, though a good portion of this vital city now lay swamped and burned, its inhabitants reeling in fear and confusion.

Word of Iztapalapa's destruction spread quickly around the valley and even beyond, as far as Otumba, and while Cortés remained in Texcoco planning north-lake forays, chiefs from all over began to arrive to negotiate allegiances. The chiefs from Otumba apologized for their involvement in that famous battle (in which Cortés had had his skull fractured), blaming the Aztecs for forcing them to participate. Cortés agreed to pardon them provided that from now on the Otomis would capture and imprison any Aztec messengers or soldiers in their land and bring them directly to him. The most important and intriguing correspondents came secretly from nearby Chalco, a reluctant Aztec stronghold on the far eastern shore of Lake Chalco. The messengers revealed that, though they wished to make peace with Cortés, their situation was precarious and compromising. Cuauhtémoc had established a military post within the city, essentially forcing their support. The messengers intimated that if Cortés could extricate the Aztecs from their city, they would oblige him with their support.[5]

Cortés called on Sandoval to lead a substantial force to Chalco at once to drive out the Aztecs. During the march Aztec warriors in small squadrons pestered the rearguard but caused little damage, and Sandoval arrived successfully at the outskirts of Chalco. A formidable force of Aztecs met the advance on a level expanse of cultivated maize and maguey. They had learned from previous experience and adapted some of their weapons—they used long lances fashioned with spear tips. But engaging the Spanish cavalry on the open, level plain proved a serious tactical blunder.[6] Sandoval and his horsemen galloped upon the Aztec foot soldiers, dispersing their ranks and riding them down, killing a great number with few Spanish casualties. Ixtlilxochitl of Texcoco commanded an organized allied thrust, helping Sandoval fight his way into the city, where he took control of the central plaza and drove the Aztecs from their garrisons.[7]

Leaving a force of Tlaxcalans to guard and maintain control of Chalco, Sandoval returned triumphant to Texcoco, bringing with him live war spoils in the form of the two sons of Chalco's recently deceased emperor, who had been claimed by smallpox. According to Bernal Díaz, the late emperor believed that "their lands would be ruled by bearded men who came from the direction of the sunrise, and his own eyes told him we were those men."[8] Cortés was delighted by the successes in Chalco and quite happy to perform the ceremonial inaugurations of the two sons, making one his puppet ruler of Chalco, the other of two nearby cities. The region, and Cortés's web of vassal alignment, was falling into place. In the last cold days of January, as winter gales whipped the lakes into white-capped chop, Cortés once more called upon Sandoval, this time to head back over the mountains to Tlaxcala to check on the progress of the brigantines.

Sandoval took a light and fast force via Zultepec, where he

was instructed to inflict punitive measures on any holdout Aztecs. The year before, forty-five Spaniards had been killed there, and Cortés saw Sandoval's expedition as an opportunity to exact revenge, since it was en route to Tlaxcala. Sandoval did his bidding, driving a few insurgent Aztec warriors from the town and securing it. Some of the local inhabitants then took Sandoval and his captains to a nearby village and led them to an abandoned temple. Here during the previous year the contingent of forty-five Narváez men, trekking to meet up with Cortés, had instead met a gruesome fate in an ambush as they led their horses through a narrow ravine. The blood of the Spaniards had been spattered across the walls, and one of the party's members had carved a message onto the wall with a knife: "Here was imprisoned the unfortunate Juan Yuste, and many others of his company."[9]

The eerie message hardly prepared Sandoval for what he next witnessed. Splayed out, stretched, and tanned before the idols were the full skins of five horses; the hair was preserved in perfect condition, while the hooves and shoes were displayed in offering. More grisly still, the weapons and clothing of the Narváez men hung lifelike, and the flayed faceskins of two Spaniards had been placed before the Aztec idols, the beards clotted with blood. Disgusted, Sandoval and his men could only imagine the morbid cries of his countrymen as they met their fate on the sacrifice stone.*[10]

Sandoval found these remains so repugnant that he took some of the villagers as slaves even though they blamed the Aztecs for the sacrifices. He pardoned the chiefs of Zultepec and the surrounding villages, on the condition that they bow to Spanish authority, to which they agreed. Then Sandoval mounted, quirted his horse, and rode toward Tlaxcala.

---

*The flaying and wearing of sacrifice victim skin was relatively common and part of particular ceremonies, including the Feast of the Flaying of Men. Immediately following ritual sacrifice, the face (and sometimes the arms and legs as well) would be flayed, removed, and donned by priests while the skins remained slick with blood and membrane. See David Carrasco, *City of Sacrifice* (Boston, 1999), 140–63; and Diego Duran, *History of the Indies of New Spain* (Norman, Okla., 1994), 169–74.

He had not gone far, just to the border of Texcoco and Tlaxcala, when he spied on the horizon Spanish banners waving at the head of a convoy shrouded in a thick cloud of dust. Sandoval's small group of thirty rode up and greeted Martín López and Tlaxcalan commander Chichimecatecle. Sandoval was amazed: behind López and Chichimecatecle strung a line of Tlaxcalan bearers so long that Sandoval could not see its end. He pulled up and conferred with López, who explained that the shipbuilding had been completed. As planned, he had dammed the Zahuapan River near Tlaxcala and carefully assembled each of the thirteen brigantines there and floated them, checking their seaworthiness (though at this point, he skipped the final process of caulking). As it passed muster, each ship was dismantled, organized, and stacked. Now here they were, the timbers borne by some ten thousand Tlaxcalans, with an equal number of warriors in support, protecting the precious cargo. It was an awesome spectacle.[11]

Sandoval escorted the immense train to Texcoco, leading an organized march of the caravan that was heavily guarded at the front, rear, and along all sides. Cortés had more than once impressed upon him the crucial importance of this weapon—he had said it was the key to the entire campaign. The vanguard included eight cavalry, one hundred Spanish foot soldiers, and ten thousand ready Tlaxcalan warriors. Next slogged those bearing the skeletal brigantines and their entrails: eight thousand *tamanes* trudged along beneath the excruciating weight of the long-ribbed hull timbers and planking, as well as iron anchors, tackle, cordage, chains, nails, sails, and everything else required by the vessels. Another two thousand *tamanes* carried and prepared food, as this miraculous convoy strung itself over the difficult passes of the mountains. Another one hundred Spanish foot soldiers, seven cavalry, and ten thousand more Tlaxcalan warriors guarded the rear and the flanks.[12]

Once the caravan was set in motion, it lurched and spiraled continuously for four days; Sandoval drove the remarkable serpentine train all through each day, resting only at night. From head to tail the "Wooden Serpent"[13] stretched over five miles long, and Cortés attested that it took a full six hours for the great column of perhaps fifty thousand to pass a single point. The sprawling caravan kicked up a dust plume visible for miles. Each day Sandoval feared an Aztec attack, but none came. Finally, on the fourth day of constant movement, the vanguard saw the outline of Texcoco's buildings and temples in the distance. The Tlaxcalans at the front donned their finest cloaks, and headdresses with feather plumes, announcing their arrival with an exultant thump of drums and the cry of horns and conch shells, whistling and singing out, "*Viva, viva* for the emperor our Lord!" and "Castile! Castile! Tlaxcala! Tlaxcala!"[14]

The populace of Texcoco (as well as many excited Spaniards) ran out to the edges of the suburbs to witness their grand entry; the unbroken procession took half the day to march into the city center. Watching the parade, Cortés must have understood that he had orchestrated a task of nearly inconceivable scope, for the thirteen ships and tackle had been carried overland for fifty miles. In the day's final light a long skein of dust-haze hung over the valley, and the boats were safely laid and stacked along the banks of the channel project at the shipyard. The overland portage that they had just completed ranks among the most astounding achievements in military history: ingenious, audacious, unprecedented, and unequaled.*

Though elated by the arrival of the brigantines, Cortés understood that one more herculean endeavor remained if the ships were to prove the difference in his battle plan. After heartily congratulating Martín López, Cortés set him to the

---

*The exact route of the transport of the brigantines is not known, though two primary possibilities seem most likely. The most level route, with the least amount of vertical gain, would have been the one north of the Telapon mountain. Another possibility is the Pass of Ápam, which Cortés took in his retreat during La Noche Triste and knew to be secure. See C. Harvey Gardiner, *Naval Power in the Conquest of Mexico* (Austin, Tex., 1956), 117–18 and 117n, for discussion. Also see Manuel Orozco y Berra, *Historia Antigua*, (Mexico City, 1880), 4:523–24.

task of reconstructing the boats and, even more important, bade him to oversee the massive engineering feat of trenching the canal through which the boats would be launched onto Lake Texcoco. It was now mid-February, and for the next months all available Tlaxcalan hands (unless employed with Cortés on lake reconnaissance) participated in digging the channel. The proud Texcocan warrior and chieftain Ixtlilxochitl commanded a work crew of forty thousand Texcocans. For nearly two months, toiling ceaselessly in shifts of eight thousand men at a time, they simultaneously dug and removed dirt from the canal and buttressed its banks with timbers to keep it from caving in. The launch channel would be over a mile long, twelve feet deep, and twelve feet wide, a staggering work project. The Aztecs in the vicinity could certainly see the daily commotion and progress, and desperate smoke signals rose over the valley all the late winter and early spring of 1521.[15]

With Texcoco a bustling hive of activity, Cortés decided to reconnoiter the north lake communities on a mission of subjugation, for a number of these cities remained loyal to the Aztecs and had thus far snubbed Cortés's overtures of peace. Cuauhtémoc seems to have had more success in maintaining alliances in the north, where the Aztecs knew that Cortés's entreaties for peace really were demands that they surrender to him. The first city Cortés set his sights on was Xaltocán, a small waterborne city about fifteen miles to the north that, like Tenochtitlán, was linked to the mainland by causeways. Though Xaltocán did not represent any major military threat (or its capture, any major coup), Cortés had tactical and operational reasons to engage his allied troops there. Because of its layout and design, and since it was surrounded by water, Xaltocán presented a microcosm of the battle that Cortés was planning to fight at Tenochtitlán, including channels filled with water that impeded his cavalry's progress. Cortés may well have wished to use it as a training mission, not only to see how his Spanish-trained Tlaxcalans fought but to test out causeway battle tactics once more—a kind of fighting of which he did not have fond memories.[16]

Riding at the head of his cavalry as usual, Cortés made good progress up one of the causeways but soon came to a point where Cuauhtémoc had ordered it breached, making it impassable for either horse or man afoot. The lake swarmed with canoes, and the "enemy yelled at us loudly and attacked us with darts and arrows."[17] Cortés and his men reined up and returned fire, scattering the canoes, which appeared to have been reinforced with light wooden bulwarks for protection against crossbow and musket fire: the Aztecs had adapted their warfare to try to defend against the superior Spanish fire-power.[18] At an impasse on the causeway, Cortés began a retreat, when two of the Indian allies he had brought along told him that the causeway had only been flooded over rather than actually breached, and that it was shallow enough for them to ford. Cortés asked the two allies to guide the foot soldiers across while he and the cavalry covered them from the rear, guarding against an Aztec foot assault. According to Bernal Díaz, "little by little and not altogether, sometimes skipping along and sometimes wading waist deep, all our soldiers crossed over, with many of our allies following."[19] The Aztecs resumed their water attack, but the Spanish firepower and allied numerical power prevailed. Cortés moved in and sacked Xaltocán, burning much of the city and absconding with some booty, including cloth and gold.

Seeing Cortés and his imposing force of Tlaxcalans coming, most of the inhabitants fled in canoes, as did the Aztec warriors, but Cortés felt uneasy and chose not to camp on the island city, certainly remembering the feeling of being trapped in Tenochtitlán. After plundering for most of the day, they moved out again to cross the causeway and camp on the mainland, in open ground that they could guard from all sides and where the horses could be most effective if called upon. Cortés marched around the northern headland of Lake Xaltocán for the next few days, finding abandoned cities as he progressed, the inhabitants having dispersed at his advance. Spent signal fires smoldered as the Spaniards rode through the deserted streets.

Most residents of these towns sought refuge in Tacuba (formerly called Tlacopan). Cortés was bent on taking Tacuba as well, perhaps drawn to it for revenge from La Noche Triste, perhaps because of its importance politically and logistically. As he had already discovered, the Tacuba causeway was the shortest of all the major causeways into Tenochtitlán. But more than that, as the third city in the Triple Alliance, Tacuba possessed important influence and reach, its territories stretching to the Tarascan borderlands (in present-day Mexico, northwest to the boundary of the states of Mexico and Michoacán). Tacuba was the third most powerful of the triumvirate, which made it potentially vulnerable.

Cortés would later claim that he came to Tacuba to initiate discussions with Cuauhtémoc, if he could, but he certainly also had designs on establishing a base of operations there, given its proximity to the capital. His greeting was less than convivial. When he and his men arrived on the west shore of the lake at Tacuba, they saw that the Tacubans and their Aztec brothers were waiting expectantly for them. "When we came close," said Cortés, "we found that there also the enemy had dug a great number of ditches and were well prepared for our arrival."[20] Aztec forces attacked immediately, the air filled with conch sirens, drums, screams, and war whoops. Cortés and his cavalry met the advancing Aztec lines at a gallop, supported by harquebusiers and crossbowmen (and many thousands of Tlaxcalans*), and after a considerable effort the horses managed to disband the Aztec ranks and break through their ragged lines. Cortés entered the city, the Aztecs and Tacubans seeking safe positions in the periphery and suburbs. Cortés took lodging in the abandoned city center.

Dawn broke to widespread looting and burning by the Tlaxcalans, whose numbers were so great, and whose ancient

---

*Cortés said they left Texcoco with 30,000 Indian allies, while Bernal Díaz halves that number to 15,000. In any event, the great numbers of warriors and bearers made the Spanish assaults on the lake cities possible.

enmity toward the Aztecs was so deeply rooted, that they could hardly be controlled. Cortés and his forces spent the next week in Tacuba fighting fierce engagements every day. He seemed content to let the Tlaxcalans do the bulk of the fighting, keeping his own men safe and enthralled by the traditional modes of warfare engaged in by these ancient enemies. "The captains of the [Tlaxcalans] many times challenged those of [Tenochtitlán]," Cortés recalled with wonder, "and fought most beautifully with them; they argued at length, shouting insults and threats to each other, all of which was truly a remarkable sight."[21] Verbal taunting was common and expected, and the Spaniards received their share of it. Luring Cortés out onto the causeway (which had been reconstructed), the Aztecs would part their defenses slightly, feigning a move to let him through, then tease him and his men with banter like " 'Come in, come in and enjoy yourselves.' "[22] They even referred to their fallen emperor, their tone suggesting disapproval of his methods and steadfast defiance of their new ruler: " 'Do you think there is now another [Montezuma] to do whatever you wish?' "[23]

Cortés was careful on the causeway, but one day he ventured too far. At a bridge near the center, the Aztecs attacked from everywhere, in canoes from all sides of the water, and afoot from the rear, pinching him in. Cortés charged his horsemen in a disorderly retreat, and a number of the animals were wounded and a few soldiers killed. A Spanish standard-bearer was knocked from the bridge into the enemy-filled water. Aztecs dragged him into a canoe, but he managed to fight his way ashore and escape with the banner.[24]

After hours of close hand-to-hand fighting, Cortés and his men made the Tacuba mainland, thankful to have come away with their lives. One of the men, exhibiting false bravado given their narrow escape but apparently drawn into the taunting game, called back to the Aztecs, saying that they would all die of hunger, for the Spaniards vowed to encircle them and not let them leave to gather food. The haughty response came quickly. The Aztecs assured the Spaniards that they had no shortage of food and as a parting gift tossed some maize loaves at them, adding indignantly, " 'Take these if you are hungry, for we are not.' "[25]

Cortés failed to arrange a meeting to speak with Cuauhtémoc, so after six days he beat a retreat back to Texcoco via the towns of Guautitlán and Acolman, fighting all the way. The attacks were not significant, for the Aztecs seemed reluctant to engage Cortés's troops away from the water and the causeways (they were learning and adapting). Cortés made it back to Texcoco harried but more educated for his efforts, having seen once more that he would need to modify his tactics to deal with battle on the causeways. The Aztecs retained the advantage there, the canoes able to hit both flanks simultaneously and the cavalry ineffective.

He had been gone nearly two weeks during this campaign, and his men at Texcoco were happy to see him return safely. They had much to report, including good news from the eastern coast. A number of native confederacies on the Gulf shore had pledged fealty to Spain, securing Cortés's influence to the north of Villa Rica. Even more encouraging, news arrived by messenger that in the last few days (late February 1521) yet another expedition had arrived from Hispaniola, three ships carrying two hundred men, sixty or seventy horses, and loads of gunpowder, swords, crossbows, and harquebuses. Already the Spanish soldiers were making their way over the mountains from Vera Cruz, led and supported by Totonac porters.

Cortés could certainly employ these reinforcements, but most intriguing was the arrival in Texcoco of a man named Julián de Alderete, a well-heeled Spaniard (and self-proclaimed expert crossbowman) sent by Hispaniola to oversee the royal fifth as treasurer. Cortés received Alderete kindly, taking him to the patio and offering him the grand view of Tenochtitlán across the water, as enticing as a mirage. Cortés garnered important intelligence from Alderete, learning that his efforts in New Spain were making a great deal of news in Hispaniola as well as Cuba, and that were it not for the destructive skullduggery of Velázquez, even more Spaniards would be flocking to Mexico to aid Cortés in his cause (and for mercenary reasons, to seek riches of their own).

Most interesting of all, Alderete brought news from Spain itself: Puertocarrero and Montejo had made it to Spain with the treasure ship, and after some difficulties (the treasure was initially impounded for a time while the *procuradores* awaited an audience with the emperor), they had ultimately been received by the king, to whom they explained the vast richness of Mexico and the importance of Cortés's endeavors there. This was most agreeable news indeed.*[26]

In response to the news from the mother country, Cortés dispatched a ship for Spain. It carried the important second letter to Emperor Charles V; whatever plunder (gold and other artifacts from the Palace of Axayacatl) Cortés had managed to squirrel away from La Noche Triste; and other regional curiosities, including enormous bones that came from what the Spaniards believed to be giants who either once lived in Mexico or perhaps still existed.[27] The legends of these "giants" fueled speculation and wonder, perpetrating the continued mystery and allure of these exotic new-found lands.**

Cortés checked on the progress of the brigantines and the canal (both were going well, perhaps only a few weeks from completion) and assessed and absorbed his new troops. About this time a soldier named Rojas asked for a private meeting,

---

*Puertocarrero and Montejo, sailing with pilot Alaminos, reached Spain at the end of October 1519. They were not received as heroic conquerors of the New World, as it turns out. Their ship, Cortés's flagship the *Santa María de la Concepción*, was impounded, and much of the treasure they carried was embargoed and some of it seized (including five Totonac Indians sent as evidence of their amazing discoveries). It would take *procuradores* Montejo and Puertocarrero many months to finally receive an audience with the crown, finally gaining it (and then only with the assistance of Cortés's father, Martín Cortés) in late April 1520.
**The bones, thought to be from giant humans, were actually those of the mammoth (*Bison antiquus*) and other prehistoric elephants. Based on the size of the femur bones, Spanish scientists hypothesized that the giant men would have been over twenty-five feet tall.

wherein he informed Cortés that there was a conspiracy in the works involving as many as three hundred soldiers still loyal to Narváez and Velázquez. The plot's leader was Antonio de Villafaña, a veteran of the Grijalva expedition who had arrived on one of Narváez's ships. The plan, according to Rojas, was to wait until Cortés was meeting with all of his captains (including Sandoval, Tapia, Alvarado, and Olid), then bring a forged letter to Cortés, claiming that it was from his father in Spain. Then while Cortés was raptly engaged in reading the letter, the followers of Narváez would fall on him and all his captains and stab them to death. Presumably, once Cortés was dead, Francisco Verdugo, brother-in-law of Velázquez, would replace the captain-general, and men would be dispatched to Villa Rica to release the imprisoned Narváez, who would escape by ship to Cuba.[28]

Cortés called for Sandoval and other captains and, heavily armed, stormed to the quarters of this Villafaña, from whom he extracted a confession. According to Bernal Díaz, Cortés pulled from Villafaña's shirt "the memorandum which he possessed with the signatures of all who were in the conspiracy."[29] Cortés then shrewdly pocketed the list, but so as not to alarm the other conspirators, he spread the report that Villafaña had swallowed the list before he could get it from him. In this way Cortés was able to keep close watch on those who remained hostile to him. From that moment he employed a good friend and trusted soldier named Alonso de Quiñones as a full-time bodyguard and reportedly ever after slept in a coat of mail.[30] After the formal confession was taken, Villafaña was immediately sentenced and hanged from the window of his own lodgings, in full view of the rest of the plotters and anyone else who cared to look.

This unsavory business concluded, Cortés went to the shipyard alongside the creek, which was now a full-fledged canal, to make another inspection of the brigantines and the waterway. The scope of the project, and its progress, amazed even Cortés. Each boat was being carefully assembled, and this time (as had not been done on the dammed Zahuapan

River in Tlaxcala) the gaps between the hull planks took on
heavy caulking, stuffed with hemp, cotton, and flax, and were
sealed with human fat rendered from the dead Aztec victims of
the recent campaigns. Though the Spanish soldiers were a little squeamish about the process, they had before used boiling
human fat to sear wounds and staunch blood flow, so they did
not object when the Tlaxcalans cut open the slain Aztecs and
sat streamside, extracting and heating the fat.[31]

Martín López oversaw even the smallest details for each
ship, including proper bow placement for the mounting of
cannons, exact measurements, cuttings, the fastening of sails
to spars, and the raising and securing of the tall masts. The decision by Cortés and López to assemble the brigantines away
from the shore of Lake Texcoco turned out to be a stroke of
brilliance, and probably made completion of the project possible, because on three separate occasions during the construction phase, Aztec foot forces attacked the shipyard and had to
be repelled.[32] One sunset the Aztecs sent a stealth force, hoping to burn the brigantines, but these fifteen were captured.
Had the shipyard been any closer to the lake or at its shore
(where a lesser tactician might have placed it), the Aztecs
could have sent thousands of canoes and seriously hindered,
and possibly even stopped, their shipbuilding. As it was, the
placement a mile off, though it required the elaborate and difficult canal construction, allowed the work to continue.

Martín López promised Cortés that in just a few weeks,
barring any unforeseen setbacks, the thirteen ships would be
completed and the canal would reach the waters of Lake
Texcoco. What had once sounded impossible was now almost
upon them—an attempt at the reconquest of Tenochtitlán. All
day long, across the valley, the Aztecs could hear foreign and
ominous sounds: the pounding of thousands of nails and trun-
nels into planks and beams, the metallic clang of blacksmiths
beating metal into shape, and the raspy sawing of boards to
line the great ditch. Those Aztecs who ventured forth in canoes could see the giant Wooden Serpent transform itself before their eyes into individual "water-houses," and some would

have remembered the boats that Cortés and Montezuma had sailed around Lake Texcoco, stunning floating wooden structures that belched fire and spat flames and metal balls from their mouths. As he prepared to defend his city, Cuauhtémoc would have been able to see the tall white sails flashing in the spring daylight, the canvas snapping and billowing in the valley winds, looming like mammoth war flags from some enormous Spanish battle standards poised in that chilling stillness just before the charge.

CHAPTER NINETEEN

Encirclement

AS SPRING CAME TO THE VALLEY OF MEXICO, the peoples on the southern reaches of Lake Texcoco remained unaligned. Cortés sent Sandoval toward Chalco and farther south to extricate Aztec elements in those provinces. Rumors abounded that a significant Aztec army was congregating there to prepare for an attack and to disrupt the important route to the coast that Cortés had worked so hard to establish and keep clear. Sandoval left Texcoco with two hundred Spaniards, twenty cavalry, a handful of harquebusiers, and twelve crossbowmen. In support he had about one thousand allies, primarily Tlaxcalan and Chalcan. The force rode and marched beyond the southern reaches of the Valley of Mexico, piercing a gap between the Serrania of Ajusco and the foothills of Popocatépetl, descending into the sprawling plains of Morelos and Cuernavaca.[1] The country far to the south, which the Spaniards were seeing for the first time, was magnificent; the plains were scoured by numerous streams running down from the mountains and by the burned-out remains of recent lava flows and extinct volcanic craters. High, jutting barrancas formed promontories that the enemy used as natural fortifications.

Sandoval and his army fought brief skirmishes along the

way; the cavalry prevailed easily on the level chaparral. The Aztecs fled to the hills and ravines. He arrived at Oaxtepec, and secured the town, his allies ransacking houses for clothing and any other booty they deemed valuable. Sandoval remained there for two days, then marched on nearby Yecapixtla, which proved more difficult because of its strong elevated position and rough, narrow topography which was unsuitable to cavalry attack. Sandoval sent messengers urging them to peacefully submit rather than die in battle, but all he received in reply was a hailstorm of stones and darts from the cliffs above, an onslaught that injured many of the allied Indian forces.

Sandoval, enraged by the enemy's affront, charged forward, up through the narrow gorges, determined now "to take the heights of the city or die in the attempt."[2] With great difficulty and suffering many injuries (the Aztecs rolled boulders and heaved large rock fragments down upon them), Sandoval drove up the steep escarpment and onto the plateau, dispersing Aztec warriors from the hilltop garrison. His head bled from a contusion, but he managed to stay atop his horse and unleash his allies on the fleeing enemy. Many Aztecs were hurled headlong from the cliffs into the river below, and others tried to escape by climbing down the rock faces but fell to their deaths. So many Aztec warriors perished in the river that day that Spanish lore later claimed the water ran red with their blood for over an hour, and the men grew thirsty waiting for the river to clear.[3]

Sandoval returned triumphant to Texcoco but was unable to bask in his glory for very long. When Cuauhtémoc learned of the defeat of his garrison at Yecapixtla (and of the allied involvement of Chalco), he sent some twenty thousand soldiers in two thousand canoes to inflict a punitive strike on Chalco. The leaders of Chalco sent frantic messages to Cortés asking for help, and Cortés, livid that Sandoval had returned without ensuring Chalco's safety, angrily ordered his immediate return to remedy what he should have ensured at the outset. Sandoval turned around and struck southward for Chalco. He arrived to discover that the chiefs of Chalco had enlisted assistance from nearby provinces, and without any help from the Spaniards, they had bravely defended their city, driving Cuauhtémoc's forces back to Tenochtitlán in disgrace. This was a painful loss for Cuauhtémoc to bear, and it signaled to Cortés that the Aztec forces might be weakening, losing their hold over their tributaries.

The victory by the people of Chalco also allowed Sandoval to save face, for he returned to Cortés in Texcoco with forty Aztec prisoners. They were branded and interrogated (though, according to Bernal Díaz, many "good-looking Indian women" were hidden away by soldiers and not branded, but were said to have escaped and then were clandestinely distributed among the captains).[4] From his strong-arm interviews with prisoners Cortés learned that Cuauhtémoc had no intention of surrendering or making peace but would fight to the death to defend his city. The prisoners told Cortés that appeals to peace would be futile, that he should save his words and prepare to fight.

Though he was quite liberal in making threats, Cortés did not take kindly to hearing them. He determined to secure for himself the regions recently visited by Sandoval. Cortés wanted firsthand knowledge—both topographical and political—of the entire Valley of Mexico (and beyond, south as far as Cuernavaca), which would help him as he made final preparations for his siege of Tenochtitlán. Cortés took newcomers Julián de Alderete and the priest Father Melgarejo along, hoping to dazzle them with the wonders of the valley and illustrate his military leadership. Under captains Pedro de Alvarado, Andrés de Tapia, and Cristóbal de Olid, Cortés organized an expeditionary force of three hundred soldiers, thirty cavalry, twenty crossbowmen, and fifteen harquebusiers. On April 5, 1521, they heard mass and rode out at the head of more than twenty thousand Texcocan-Tlaxcalan allies. Sandoval remained behind to guard Texcoco and make certain that Martín López had everything he needed to complete his shipbuilding projects.

Cortés hoped to circumnavigate the valley, including the lands to the south, eventually tracing a northward arc on the western side of the lakes, passing Tacuba once more and returning to Texcoco by means of a full circle. "For I believed that once I had finished this task, which was most important," Cortés remembered, "I would find the brigantines completed and ready for launching."[5] He passed through Chalco, stopping only to apprise the chiefs there (through Malinche and Aguilar) of his itinerary and intended route. He pushed south, passing Amecameca and arriving at Chimalhuacan (present-day San Vicente Chimalhuacan), where he appropriated many thousands more allies, perhaps as many as forty thousand.[6] Cuauhtémoc, seeing allied support of this magnitude, would have been deeply distressed, and for good reason. Given the devastation caused by the recent smallpox plague in his city, and the many tributaries now capitulating to Spanish authority, he would have difficulty matching the numbers that Cortés was amassing.

Cortés marched his ranks, swollen with the new recruits, toward Cuernavaca, traversing steep and precarious mountains. The plateau tops were covered with entire villages of civilians watching the Spaniards approach. Cortés surveyed the well-protected hilltop garrisons, noting that "the slopes were covered with warriors, who soon began to howl and make smoke signals, attacking us with stones, which they hurled down by hand or from slings and with spears and arrows, so that in approaching them we received much harm."[7] Below, exposed in the ravines, Cortés and his allies were vulnerable, and though he considered a retreat, he did not want the new allies to think the Spanish cowardly, so he halted to survey his options. The base of the mountain atop which the main fortress sat (the hilltop village of Tlaycapan) was huge, nearly three miles around, and well defended; Cortés later admitted that it was "madness to attempt to take it."[8] Cortés thought that it would take too long to go around, so he opted instead to scale directly up the face in three places that appeared climbable. He sent flag-bearer Cristóbal Corral and sixty foot soldiers up the steepest gorge, supported by crossbowmen and harquebusiers. He sent a handful of other captains and light troops up alternate trails leading to the plateau. He remained on the plain below with the main force, guarding against attack from the flanks and rear.

The assaults proved foolhardy and costly. As the captains and their charges scrambled up the steep rock faces, at times reduced to a literal crawl on their hands and knees, they arrived at points that left them exposed to the garrison above. Repeating the tactic used recently against Sandoval, the Aztecs hurled giant boulders that thundered down, shattering into pieces that ripped through the Spaniards at the front, killing a few and maiming many others. Bernal Díaz was in the vanguard alongside the standard-bearer Corral, and as stones from the overhead crag crashed and caromed past them, sparking against the rock walls, they sought shelter—Díaz beneath a protective overhang, Corral behind a knot of thick thornbushes, clinging for his life to the sharp branches. Corral's face streamed blood as he called out for Díaz and the others to go no farther—it was futile. Looking back, Díaz saw that the flag on the standard was torn to shreds. Through word of mouth the men hollered their predicament down the ravine to Cortés, who ordered a retreat, and the men descended as best they could, a great number badly wounded, the healthiest carrying the dead.[9]

Down below on the plain, the cavalry was able to disperse small bands of Aztec warriors and return. Cortés and his company spent a difficult night on the open chaparral, the men and horses brutally parched, as there was no water, and no one had drunk for an entire day. Bernal Díaz remembered the terrible night they spent huddled in a dusty mulberry grove, "half dead with thirst."[10] The men struggled to sleep, haunted all night long by the sounds of drums and trumpets and taunts of ridicule from the enemy above.

At sunrise, the first order of business was to water the horses in a spring that a scout had found nearly three miles away. Cortés took a few captains with him on foot to scout another approach to Tlaycapan—and noticed two options that appeared less steep. As Cortés and his captains moved forward, many of the Indian allies followed behind (though they had not been instructed to do so), and all the activity warned the Aztecs above that the attack would be coming from one of the more gradual approaches. The Aztecs who had been guarding the steep ravine therefore abandoned their posts. Cortés immediately capitalized by sending Francisco Verdugo and the king's treasurer Julián de Alderete with fifty men to fly up the gorge and capture the top if they could. After a difficult climb, the Spaniards reached the top and fired crossbows and harquebuses; the loud and violent discharges of the guns frightened the Indians, many of whom surrendered. Alderete distinguished himself, proving as good as his word with his crossbow. After some time Cortés could see the Castilian banner waving from the rocky pinnacle, and he followed up the narrow defile with reinforcements to secure the garrison.[11]

As it turned out, the Aztecs here sued for peace partly because, like Cortés and his men, they were out of water and thirsty. The Spaniards were pleased to see that the women of the village made the sign for peace, clapping their palms together to indicate that they would be happy to make maize cakes, and that the warriors laid down their weapons and ceased hurling stones and darts at them.

Cortés and his troops remained here for two days, during which time Aztec forces abandoned the fortresses and the local inhabitants sued for peace, agreeing to Spanish vassalage. Cortés sent his wounded back to the more comfortable lodgings of Texcoco for treatment before he continued south on his quest of reconnaissance, subjugation, and encirclement.

The departure south took them down the steep descent of the Cordilleras, which plunged nearly two thousand feet from the plateau over lava-blackened ground in less than a day's march. The men and horses breathed easier and gained strength as they lost altitude. Cortés observed the more temperate climate; the spring flowers were already in bloom, and vegetables and fruit grew along the trailside. At Oaxtepec, which Sandoval had recently marched through and subdued, Cortés was received warmly and "quartered in a chief's country house amid the most beautiful and refreshing gardens ever seen."[12]

The captain-general found himself amid what were arguably the finest botanical gardens in the world, begun by Montezuma I* during his reign and maintained immaculately ever since. Resplendent summer homes sprawled over miles of spring-fed countryside; small streams meandered through the tidy city punctuated by lovely ponds. Cortés was impressed, choosing to rest there for a day. "There are summer houses spaced out at distances of two crossbowshots," he recorded for his emperor, "and very bright flower beds, a great many trees with various fruits, and many herbs and sweet-smelling flowers. Certainly, the elegance and magnificence of this garden make a remarkable sight."[13]

The deep impression was well earned, for these were the most famous and revered botanical gardens in all of Mexico, a place of pleasure for the political elite. The gardens were also experimental and medicinal. Flowers and trees were brought from all over the country, including the sultry lowland of the *tierra caliente*, to see if they might prosper in Oaxtepec in the gardens of the nobility. The tremendous nurseries and orchards were all carefully nurtured by skilled botanical experts, under sanction of the Aztec government. Cortés and his men would have been able to sample flavorful (and to them, novel) pineapples, guavas, avocados, and yams.[14]

Rested and refreshed by the garden setting, Cortés moved on the next day, taking two days to pass through a series of small towns on his way to the more important Cuernavaca,**

---

*Montezuma I reigned from 1440 to 1469.
**Originally called Cuauhnahuac by the Mexicans, but Cortés and the Spaniards mispronounced the term enough so that they eventually renamed it Cuernavaca, the name it still bears. It is considered to be among the most beautiful and dramatic places in all of Mexico, with a lovely temperate year-round climate, situated at five thousand feet above sea level. Cortés would eventually establish a large sugar plantation there and maintain a stronghold palace fortress (now called the Palacio de Cortés) atop conquered Aztec buildings. Diego Rivera painted murals on the top floor of the palace between 1927 and 1930. Cuernavaca is today the capital of the state of Morelos.

an immensely wealthy city bounded by severe ravines and accessible only in two places by bridges spanning these deep ravines. Cortés was struck by how well defended the city was, noting that the bridges had been raised to thwart their entry, and that the defenders were "so safe that had we been ten times our number they could have held us with scorn."[15] He learned that there were a few places about a mile away where horses could cross the barrancas, and he rode for those while captains and soldiers looked for ways they might cross the removed bridges, all the while ducking a steady barrage of stones and spears and darts.

Bernal Díaz observed that there were two large trees growing toward each other from opposite banks of the ravine, their branches intertwining. Though it was dangerous, a brave Tlaxcalan warrior began to shinny across, clinging to branches and inching along the trunks. When he made it across, others were emboldened and followed suit, including Díaz, who remembered how frightening it was to look down: "When I was crossing and saw how bad and dangerous the crossing was, I turned quite giddy, but still I got across."[16] Others were less fortunate. Three soldiers lost their nerve and their grip and plunged into the water below, one of them breaking his leg. About thirty Spaniards made the arduous crossing, followed by a substantial number of Tlaxcalans.

While this acrobatic aerial crossing was under way, Cortés rode with his cavalry into the mountainous outskirts and discovered an alternate passage at a narrow gorge, and though under attack the Spaniards made it across. The Aztecs defending that side of the city rallied to fight the incoming cavalry, leaving Bernal Díaz and company free to push forward toward the city. At nearly the same time Cristóbal de Olid, Andrés de Tapia, and a few other horsemen partially repaired and crossed a dilapidated bridge, and they came alongside Bernal Díaz and his men, as did Cortés and the rest of his cavalry. All of them proceeded to surprise and frighten the Aztecs, who were shocked to see so many Tlaxcalans streaming across. Many of the Aztecs, terrified by the horses, fled and hid in ditches and behind bushes and shrubs, while others ran off to the mountains.[17]

Cortés and his men arrived at the center of the city to find it mostly vacated and much of it already mysteriously burned, perhaps as a punitive Aztec strike. He took control of one of the chiefs' houses in a gorgeous garden, and his men scoured the nearby aristocratic lodgings, appropriating a "great spoil of large bales of cloth as well as good-looking women."[18] A short time later some twenty chiefs of the town arrived, unarmed, holding their hands up in peace. They gave Cortés gold and jewels and asked his pardon, saying (truthfully) that the Aztecs had forced their warriors to try to defend their city. Cortés granted the pardon, and with the usual legalistic proclamations Cuernavaca and its people were made the property of Spain.[19]

This was as far south as Cortés would venture during the present expedition. The next day he struck northward, climbing from the lovely garden enclaves of Cuernavaca and Oaxtepec up through scrubby pine forests into high mountains, the trails devilishly steep and narrow and the streambeds dry. The Spaniards and their allies strung out in a long train that struggled slowly upward, climbing higher and higher into the Serranía de Ajusco, crossing a cold pass at over ten thousand feet. Without water for most of the day, the men grew tired and weak, and a few of the Indian allies fell along the bony trailside and perished from thirst. On the descent, Cortés discovered a series of farms with scant shelter, and Bernal Díaz found a small spring near one of the farms with a bit of water. He filled a pitcher and brought it to Cortés, worried as he hurried along that it would be stolen from him, for as he put it, "thirst has no laws."[20] Cortés and a few of his officers guzzled the water and camped that night in the bitter cold under wind-driven light rain, without food or more water.

At sunrise they were up and on the move again, and from their height they could see the familiar Valley of Mexico and the town of Xochimilco ("Field of Flowers"), a beautiful and powerful city built primarily over the water on the far southwest side of the lake district. Tenochtitlán counted on Xochimilco's annual tribute of vegetables and flowers, which grew in the rich organic *chinampas* along the southern lakeshores.[21] Like Tenochtitlán, Xochimilco was protected and accessed by causeways, being suspended over the water some half-mile from the southern shore, though its causeways were shorter.

Small bands of enemy skirmishers attacked Cortés and his men as they approached, using light volleys of darts and spears followed by quick retreats. The captain-general and the vanguard were content to withstand these brief assaults and continue forward, though cautiously, for he could not be certain what level of reinforcement the city might garner from the capital itself, beyond to the north. Dismounting and joining the foot soldiers, Cortés decided to try to take the main causeway; he found a great number of Aztecs there, sent by Cuauhtémoc to defend it. He ordered divisions of crossbowmen and harquebusiers ahead to fire on the defenders, and after constant bombardment the Aztecs weakened and dispersed, allowing the Spaniards in the vanguard across the causeway. Given his previous negative experiences with causeway battle, Cortés was less than comfortable with the situation, and in this case he was right to worry, for the retreat of the Aztecs had actually been a successful ploy to lure him across.

Though some of his men in the front made it into the city and the chiefs of Xochimilco were ostensibly surrendering and asking for peace, at that moment Aztecs were paddling ferociously in droves to come in support, appearing in large numbers on either side of the causeway in the early evening light. Cortés and many of his men had crossed the causeway and remounted, now using the horses to great effect, and the fighting grew fierce in the city streets. The Aztecs used special swords that they had adapted using found and confiscated Spanish steel points, and they caused dire injury.[22] Cortés rode at the head of the fighting on his dark chestnut stallion El Romo, ("The Flat-nosed"), and after continued battling for over an hour Cortés's horse "broke down, and the Mexican warriors who were around in great numbers laid hold of Cortés and dragged him from the horse," wounding him severely in the head.[23] Though he struggled mightily, Cortés was overwhelmed by the numbers of warriors who attempted to carry him away as a spoil of war, and ironically, their desire to take him prisoner probably saved his life. Just then a soldier named Cristóbal de Olea came along with a Tlaxcalan soldier, and they hacked their way through to Cortés and wrested him from the enemy's grasp. Slinging him back onto El Romo, they fought their way out of immediate danger. Olea suffered injury for his courage, sustaining three deep sword wounds.

Cortés had barely escaped with his life, but a few unfortunate Spaniards did not. A number were taken alive and later sacrificed and dismembered by Cuauhtémoc personally, their severed limbs paraded through the provinces to illustrate that the Aztecs were indeed defeating these vile *teules*, these Spaniards.[24] Soon afterward Andrés de Tapia and Cristóbal de Olid rode up, blood pouring down Olid's face, and his horse appeared painted with blood, as did a number of others. A large number of Spaniards and Tlaxcalans were badly wounded. They took shelter behind a barricade wall, searing their wounds with hot oil and spending a sleepless, anguished night being pummeled with javelins and slingstones. The crossbowmen, overseen by Pedro Barba, bided their time fixing copper arrow points and feathering the shafts. Cortés discovered that the causeway bridges had been removed to trap them inside the city, so he ordered thousands of Tlaxcalans out onto the causeway to fill in the gaps with stones and wood to allow escape at dawn.

At first light Cortés and a few of his captains ascended the pyramid of Xochimilco, which afforded them a panoramic view of the city below and the capital on the north lake. Cortés could hardly believe what he saw, and he would certainly have cursed at himself for falling into the trap. Coursing across the lake at great speed from the capital were some two thousand canoes, each brimming with warriors in full battle regalia, the captains in front, wielding captured Spanish swords. Cortés learned from messengers that another ten thousand Aztecs were on their way from Tenochtitlán over land. Cuauhtémoc planned to pinch Cortés from all sides and snare him within the water-bound city. From below on the water Cortés could hear the chant echoing across the valley, a cacophonic cry from the warriors paddling fearlessly toward them, calling out in unison "Mexico! Mexico! Tenochtitlán! Tenochtitlán!"[25]

Cortés and his captains ran down the pyramid steps and immediately ordered a retreat from the city. The Tlaxcalans had done their work well, filling in the removed bridge on the causeway, allowing passage by foot soldiers as well as cavalry. During the night able-bodied soldiers had looted the palaces, finding large bales of cotton cloth, as well as gold, but Cortés regretfully informed his men that most of it should be left behind so they would not be slowed in their exit from the city. Amid their grumbling Cortés hastily assembled his captains in divisions, himself taking twenty cavalry and five hundred Tlaxcalans in orderly defensive formation. They battled their way across the causeway to the mainland, harried continuously from all quarters.

With cavalry protecting the rear as well, Cortés and his troops made it back to the mainland, leaving the beautiful water-bound metropolis of Xochimilco a smoking ruin. "In the end," remembered Cortés with cold candor, "we left it burnt and ruined, and it was a notable sight, for there had been many houses and towers for their idols all built of stone and mortar."[26] After regrouping at the foot of a large hill about a mile from the lakeshore, Cortés spurred his horse and slung his company north, heading to the town of Coyoacán about seven miles away. They rode into the town on April 18, after three days of continuous fighting, relieved to find the city (a major tribute center for the Triple Alliance) almost completely deserted. Seeing the damage done at Xochimilco, civilians along the southwestern lakeshore were now fleeing before the Spaniards' advance.

Cortés continued his forced march north to Tacuba, pestered all the while by small divisions of Aztec foot warriors and men arriving in canoes from the lake. During the nights the Aztecs taunted the Spaniards, so that sleep proved impossible, and Cortés and his men plodded on, wounded and fatigued, toward the safety of Texcoco. At one stretch along the western shores Cortés was ambushed and in the fighting lost two young pages, Francisco Martín Vendabel and Pedro Gallego.[27] Though Cortés always suffered at the loss of his men, he grieved particularly hard for these pages on account of their youth and their commitment and courage during the campaign. The youngsters had been taken alive, and Cortés grew speechless and despondent at the thought of their fate at the hands of Cuauhtémoc.

Perhaps to ease his anguish and his conscience and perhaps to remind himself to stay focused on the prize, at Tacuba Cortés took Father Melgarejo and the treasurer Julián de Alderete to the top of the main temple, affording them a spectacular view of the lake and the capital. They watched the canoes coming and going, some loaded with goods for the market, some taking men out to catch fish in nets. They marveled at the sprawl of complex metropolises that truly appeared to be floating on the water. The two men assured Cortés that they would report these wonders directly to His Majesty their emperor.[28]

The weather turned and the rains came in sheets as Cortés rode for Texcoco, his reconnaissance encirclement complete. The fires spat and smoldered in the rubble of towns he had left behind him. He and his men squelched through deep muck and mire, arriving finally at the outskirts of Texcoco on April 22, 1521, after a campaign of nearly three weeks. Most of the Spaniards and horses were badly wounded, and untold numbers of Tlaxcalans and other allies had been hurt or killed, but Cortés had managed to tighten the noose around the neck of Cuauhtémoc and his stubborn Aztec empire. Gonzalo de Sandoval rode out to greet Cortés as he approached, covered in mud and blood. Sandoval bore good news: while Cortés had been away, more reinforcements—Spaniards, arms, and horses—had arrived, and, even more important, the brigantines were completed. The rains that should have dampened the captain-general's spirits were now filling the canal in which the thirteen freshly caulked warships floated, poised to be launched.

CHAPTER TWENTY

The Siege Begins

IT WAS TIME FOR FINAL PREPARATIONS on both the east and the west sides of Lake Texcoco. In Tenochtitlán, Cuauhtémoc and his highest military advisers assessed their situation and now took defensive measures. They ordered that thousands of canoes be retrofitted with wooden shields, converting them into the armored bulwark canoes called *chimalacalli*.[1] Although forays to destroy or at least hinder Cortés's shipbuilding efforts had failed, Cuauhtémoc garnered a good deal of intelligence from his messengers concerning the boats, and he understood that ships much like those he had seen sailing around on hunts and pleasure cruises with Montezuma would be employed against him. Cuauhtémoc held secret meetings with some of his most skilled military builders and ordered certain underwater traps constructed, to be sprung when the time was right.

Cuauhtémoc called for as many soldiers and weapons as possible to assemble within Tenochtitlán, though a number of factors hurt mobilization. The recent secession of Chalco particularly stung,[2] casting serious doubt about the Aztec power and slowing much-needed tribute payment (especially in the form of food) to a trickle. This presented a major crisis, since perhaps as much as fifty percent of the capital's population relied on a steady flow of food from outside the city proper for subsistence. There was also the problem of the season. It was planting season, a crucial time for the Aztec agricultural economy, and thousands of able-bodied men were preparing the maize and maguey fields as well as the southern *chinampas*.[3] These men doubled as soldiers, and planting time was not traditionally a time for battle, making it difficult for Cuauhtémoc to amass the size of force he would need to effectively contest Cortés and his growing allies. Still, Cuauhtémoc did all he could to prepare: he had men dig pits in the streets and line the beds with sharp stakes, then cover these openings with planks and dirt.[4]

Cuauhtémoc would certainly have been organizing his elite forces, his jaguar and eagle knights, proud and revered warriors among the highest military orders attainable in the Aztec army. They attained their high rank either through noble birth or by taking live prisoners in battle, and they served in battle as officers, in charge of divisions or smaller units. They were distinguished by their dress and helmets: a jaguar knight wore a jaguar pelt and an elaborate helmet, his face staring from inside the animal's growling mouth; an eagle knight wore a feathered helmet with a great cawing beak. With these elites Cuauhtémoc would have discussed tactics and strategy, planning as much as possible given what he already knew from watching Cortés's military work over the last months. But he could never have predicted how these strange and ominous water-houses would shape the course of battle on the lake.[5]

Lore records that as a last symbolic action, Cuauhtémoc gathered up the remnants of Montezuma's treasure and had it taken by canoe to a mysterious and fabled part of the lake, the whirlpool of Pantitlán, and tossed into a massive, roiling whirlpool where Cortés could never get to it. In retribution for his people's predicament, Cuauhtémoc perhaps also wished to dishonor the fallen ruler.[6]

Across the water in Texcoco, Cortés made preparations of his own. He was impressed by the work of Martín López and especially by the hardworking relay teams of Tlaxcalans who had been digging constantly in shifts. He wrote with pride,

"More than eight thousand natives...worked for fifty days on this task because the canal was more than twelve feet deep and as many wide. It was well lined with stakes, so that it would fill with water from the lake, and thus the brigantines might be transported without danger or effort; it was certainly a magnificent achievement and a notable sight."[7] The brigantines themselves looked impressive, fitted out with their sails and rigging and their newly fashioned oars. Cortés decided on a big official launch in about a week, complete with rousing fanfare and ceremony intended to inspire his troops and send a message to Cuauhtémoc.

In the meantime he sent out a call to all neighboring towns that he needed eight thousand copper arrowheads fashioned to a specific Spanish pattern, as well as an equal number of arrows, straight and of durable hard wood. He was delighted when, just a week later, the regional military craftsmen brought in more than fifty thousand arrowheads and as many arrows. They were divided among the crossbowmen, and overseen by Pedro Barba, the arrows were feathered, oiled, and polished with great care. The clang of metal on metal rang through the town as blacksmiths fashioned new shoes for the horses, and other metalworkers carefully honed the tips and blades of swords and lances. Dry gunpowder was packed and secured in containers, cannons and artillery cleaned and well oiled, the fittings and firing mechanisms gone over. Once the horses were newly shod, riders were instructed to take their mounts on daily training rides, running the warhorses at hard gallops, halting and wheeling them in simulated battle exercises.[8]

Cortés put out a call for more allied support, for he knew he would need strong bodies to take and retake the causeway bridges. He had witnessed the usefulness of auxiliaries in the recent near-disaster at Xochimilco, and he understood that a continuous ability to repair bridges destroyed by the enemy would be crucial if he was to successfully infiltrate and ultimately take the city. Cortés sent letters via messengers to the Tlaxcalan leaders Xicotenga the Elder and the always contentious Xicotenga the Younger alerting them to the time

frame of his attack and his need for men to work and to prepare food. Cortés expected to have this assistance within ten
days, if that would be possible. He specifically asked these
leaders for as many as twenty thousand men.

He organized a ceremonial launching of twelve of the brigantines on Sunday, April 28. Despite the recent rains the canal
had failed to fill sufficiently, but the clever naval engineer
Martín López had designed and overseen the construction
of twelve dams—running all the way from the lake to the
shipyard—and these ingenious devices allowed the ships to be
floated the length of the canal to the mouth of the open water
on the east bank of Lake Texcoco. Here Father Olmedo performed mass as thousands of citizens, warriors, and Spaniards
lined the banks of the canal to witness the send-off of these in-
geniously designed boats that, at nearly fifty feet, held twenty-
five to thirty men. Cortés's personal flagship brigantine, *La
Capitana*, was slightly larger and bore a heavy iron cannon.[9]

To the alarum of blaring trumpets and synchronized cannon fire, the sails on the warships were unfurled and Spanish
banners waved atop the high mastheads. Great cheers went up
along the banks as the flat-bottomed, low-draft ships, powered
by both sails and paddles, made their way through the canal
and onto the lake. As the vessels cruised out onto the open water for final test sailing and preparations, Hernán Cortés and
Martín López had much to be proud of. In just over seven
months they had conceived of and manufactured a full-scale
navy capable of amphibious assault on the two-hundred-year-
old city of Tenochtitlán. It was a stupendous spectacle and
something of a military miracle.[10]

Fitting out the crews for the armada, however, had been
no simple matter. Cortés originally called for volunteers,
assuming that men would fly to the posts, but that had been
optimistic—very few were forthcoming. He needed some
three hundred men. For each ship he required twenty-five
men: twelve would be needed to paddle (six on a side) if the
winds were light; otherwise these men could set the sail and
fight from their gunwale posts. Then each boat required

another dozen harquebusiers and crossbowmen to fire on
Aztec canoes or on foot warriors along the causeways. Each
ship also required a couple of skilled artillerymen to operate
the bronze bow-mounted cannons, a sentry or lookout, and of
course a competent captain.

Cortés was less than impressed with the response to his call
for volunteers. Apparently many thought paddling, and naval
orders at all for that matter, to be lowly duty, unbefitting their
rank and station. They may have also believed that infantry detail promised better access to the plunder. In the end, frustrated by his men's reluctance, Cortés personally staffed the
ships from muster rolls, ordering any men who had previously
sailed, or served on sailing ships, to come forward. Lacking
enough numbers, he ultimately drew on any Spaniards hailing
from port towns, figuring they must know something of naval
matters.

Cortés hand-selected the captains based on their previous
naval experience as well as his trust and confidence in them.
Notable brigantine skippers included newcomers such as
Miguel Díaz de Aux, who had only recently arrived with one
of the Garay expeditions, and veterans who had originally accompanied Cortés to Mexico, including Juan Jaramillo. Newer
arrival Pedro Barba, most recently associated with the crossbowmen, had apparently won Cortés's favor as a strong leader,
for he too earned the captaincy of a brigantine, where he would
again distinguish himself. For the next three weeks these sea
captains and the others would perform test missions and training shakedowns on the eastern waters, identifying and repair-
ing any leaks or mechanical problems while Cortés made final
preparations with his ground troops.

Continuing the pomp and ceremony of the brigantine
launching, Cortés held a formal parade and review of troops
in the plazas and streets of Texcoco. The recently arrived reinforcements certainly helped matters. Cortés now inspected
86 fine horsemen, 118 harquebusiers and crossbowmen, and
700 foot soldiers armed with swords and shields. His artillery

included three heavy iron guns, fifteen lighter field pieces, and ten hundredweight of gunpowder.[11]

He organized his Spanish force into four divisions—one aquatic, which he would personally command, and three land commands. The land divisions would be captained by experienced and trusted men: Alvarado, Olid, and Sandoval. Each one would have for troops approximately 150 infantrymen, about thirty cavalry, and fifteen crossbowmen and harquebusiers. They would also orchestrate large numbers of allied divisions, a combined total probably on the order of 200,000.* The major forces of allies—those from Texcoco and Tlaxcala—would operate under native commanders, Ixtlilxochitl and Chichimecatecle respectively, men who had already proved instrumental in the buildup to the siege.[12]

The allied divisions were so numerous that they had to assemble a short distance from the city of Texcoco where there would be room for them all. Bernal Díaz remembered the great pride and pageantry of the warriors as they arrived from the provinces prepared to fight:

> They approached in fine order, all very brilliant with great devices, each regiment by itself with its banners unfurled, and the white bird, like an eagle with its wings outstretched, which is their badge. The ensigns waved their banners and standards and all carried bows and arrows, two-handed swords, javelins and spear throwers; some carried mancanas and great lances and others small lances. Adorned with their feather head-dresses, and moving in good order and uttering

---

*None of the chroniclers, of course, had accurate means of counting the large allied forces. As a result, the numbers attributed to Cortés's allied reconquest force vary considerably, with 200,000 on the conservative but reasonable side, given modern military scholarship. Some writers place the number closer to half a million. Whatever the actual number, Cortés clearly employed large numbers of allied forces in various crucial capacities, including combat, the destruction and construction of bridges on the causeways, the demolition and incineration of houses, and the all-important transporting and preparing of food.

shouts, cries, and whistles, calling out: "Long live the Emperor our master!" and "Castile, Castile, Tlaxcala, Tlaxcala!"[13]

The train of troops was so long that it was said to stream into the city for three consecutive hours. The men were housed and fed at many lodgings within the city. They were well trained, well rested, and for the most part battle-tested. Now it was only a matter of time before the siege of and battle for Tenochtitlán began.

In the last weeks before the official commencement of operations, Cortés had yet one more political problem to contend with. As he had hoped, his call for men and arms had been well responded to, especially from Tlaxcala. Xicotenga the Younger had arrived, as requested, at the head of a few thousand of his best men. But on the eve of the initial assault Xicotenga the Younger abandoned his post during the night and left for his home in Tlaxcala. Cortés inquired about the matter, suspecting that, because Xicotenga the Elder was infirm with age and because most of the rival nobles of power were assisting in the Spanish conquest effort, Xicotenga the Younger— who had been hostile toward Cortés from the beginning— realized that the opportunity was ripe for him to take over the rulership of Tlaxcala. This same young and impetuous upstart had been restrained, then physically removed, during political meetings between the Spaniards and Tlaxcalans just months before.

Cortés now viewed young Xicotenga's actions as mutinous. He sent Tlaxcalan nobles with armed guards and two Spanish captains to pursue and overtake him, which they did. The delegation asked him to return, to captain a squadron, but he refused. Then, as ordered, the Tlaxcalan delegation brought their countryman, bound as a prisoner, before Cortés. Though Pedro de Alvarado intervened and attempted to persuade Cortés against taking the harshest actions, the haughty Cortés could not be swayed. Desertion, Cortés reasoned, was to the Spaniards a crime punishable by death. At this stage of their expedition, on the eve of battle, given all that had been risked and lost and

all they stood to gain, Cortés would not tolerate such insubordination, such treason. He ordered Xicotenga the Younger
hanged in the open, in broad daylight in the center of Texcoco
for all the allies to witness, to serve as an example.[14]

Flags flapped on the masts of the brigantines down on the
water. Late spring breezes were freshening. All was ready. The
military plan Cortés had conjured was as ingenious as it was
simple, but like most plans of warfare, enacting it successfully
would prove much more difficult than drafting it on paper.

THE battle plan was in every respect organized as an extended
siege, involving perfectly timed land assaults on the causeways
at crucial points, coupled with synchronized naval support
from the brigantines. Cortés also intended to cut off the city's
supply of fresh water and, if possible, cripple trade of any kind
with the outside world. Each ground division captain (Alvarado,
Olid, and Sandoval) had a strict mission to adhere to, and the
success of the overall siege plan required the success of each
independent but connected mission. Alvarado and Olid were
charged to march northward from Texcoco, over the top of the
lake, and swing down to Tacuba, where Alvarado was ordered
to secure the all-important causeway there. Olid would continue south to Coyoacán, whose short connector causeway was
linked to the long Iztapalapa causeway. Once Olid and Alvarado
were positioned, Sandoval would depart Texcoco and march
on the eastern lakeshore to Iztapalapa, where he would take
that causeway. Once all the ground divisions were in place
and had commenced their offensives, Cortés would direct the
brigantines to those positions and offer cannon, harquebus,
and crossbow support and flank protection. Clearly Cortés
understood that any entrance into the heart of the empire depended on gaining command over the causeways.

On May 22, after hearing mass in the main plaza of
Texcoco, Cortés addressed his troops once more. A crier bellowed out the rules of warfare, and Cortés spoke to his men of
the ideals of honor, of their duty to fight for God and country.

With that, Captains Olid and Alvarado marched north to begin their mission, and the siege of the Aztec empire was officially under way.

The beginning of the coordinated blockade, siege, and assault was marred by internal strife, and by the end of the first day Cortés must have wondered how his plan could possibly work if his own men could not get along. As the troops of Alvarado and Olid arrived that first evening at Acolman, a Texcocan subject city where they had been instructed to pause on their way to Tacuba, a dispute arose over which division (Alvarado's or Olid's) should take up the best lodgings in the town; Olid's men had ridden ahead and secured most of the good dwellings. Bitter arguing ensued between the factions, and swords were actually drawn on both sides. The tension was severe enough that someone dispatched a fleet horseman to gallop to Cortés and report the conflict to him.[15]

Certainly miffed by this petty disagreement but realizing its import, Cortés immediately sent the rider back to Acolman with Father Melgarejo to mediate the situation. He had begun to trust Father Melgarejo, which made sense for he, along with Alderete, was influential in Spain.* The priest arrived at Acolman bearing stern letters of reproach from Cortés, which he directed to the captains, suggesting they quiet their men and remain focused on the mission at hand. By the next day the matter had been smoothed over, but from that moment onward the relationship between Alvarado and Olid remained contentious.

The next day, their troops poorly rested, Alvarado and Olid marched on to Tacuba as instructed, noticing that nearly all the towns they passed through and stopped in had been

---

*Father Pedro de Melgarejo had arrived back in February carrying an impressive supply of "indulgences," in the form of papal bulls (*bulas de cruzada*), officially stamped sheets that, if purchased and signed by a priest, guaranteed absolution from any sins committed during their expeditions in México. Needless to say, Melgarejo turned a solid trade among the mercenary soldiers, and Cortés seemed to favor him from the moment of his arrival.

abandoned. Tacuba was deserted as well, and the Spaniards took lodgings in the royal palace where Cortés had stayed just a few weeks before. A quick reconnaissance of the entrance to the causeway revealed that it would not be taken without a fight, for already large numbers of Aztecs swarmed about in their canoes, and a force of foot soldiers stood ready to guard it. Minor skirmishing ensued, but it was near nightfall, and though the Aztecs taunted and provoked the Spaniards through dusk and all through the night, the Spaniards showed discipline and were not drawn into an attack but kept to Cortés's strict battle plan.

During his lengthy stay in Tenochtitlán, initially as a welcome guest and later as an unwelcome one, Cortés had come to know the design and layout of the great lake city extremely well. In fact, he had sent his own hand-drawn maps of the city back to Spain in his first letters. One feature that had caught his attention was the impressive Chapultepec aqueduct, a two-mile-long conduit engineered to carry fresh springwater from the hillside town of Chapultepec across the western waters of Lake Texcoco and into the center of Tenochtitlán. (The aqueduct met the city at the terminus of the Tacuba causeway.) It was a remarkably vulnerable lifeline, for though there were a few freshwater springs and wells within the major island city, they were certainly not enough to provide a population of a few hundred thousand with potable water. The aqueduct served that purpose, and Cortés knew it. He planned to sever this crucial conduit early in the siege.

The Aztecs, of course, understood the vulnerability too, having relied on this aqueduct since its construction during the reign of Itzcóatl (1426–40), fourth king of the Aztecs.* As a result, when Alvarado and Olid rode the few miles south from Tacuba to Chapultepec with orders to demolish the aqueduct, they arrived to find hordes of Aztec warriors already there,

---

*The aqueduct was improved upon and maintained by Itzcóatl's successor, his nephew Montezuma I.

waiting for them. The fighting was fierce: the Aztecs attacked with spears and javelins and hurled stones from slings, wounding a handful of Spaniards in the initial assault. Although the broken ground was not ideal for the horses, still the Spaniards managed to drive the frontal squadrons to flight and eventually took possession of the spring. "As soon as these squadrons had been put to flight," remembered Bernal Díaz, "we broke the conduits through which the water flowed to the city, and from that time onwards it never flowed into Mexico so long as the war lasted."[16] For the next seventy-five days, the residents of Tenochtitlán would defend themselves without this vital liquid lifeline, and Cortés would proudly describe the tactic as a "cunning stratagem."[17]

He had struck a major offensive blow in the earliest moments of the siege. Olid now continued five miles south as directed, where he found Coyoacán deserted and undefended; he was able to take up his position without a fight. Cortés took the cue to release Sandoval and his forces from Texcoco and deploy them at Iztapalapa, near the entrance to the main and longest causeway. On May 31 Sandoval marched the twenty-five miles without incident, but they were attacked once they finally arrived at the abandoned city. Sandoval's sheer numbers easily thwarted the small Aztec squadron. As Sandoval and his men appropriated the best houses there, smoke signals began to puff and rise from shrines around the lake, which the Spaniards assumed was a battle cry among the Aztec forces.

So far the Aztec ruler Cuauhtémoc had yet to act, choosing not to defend the positions the Spaniards were taking up with any real zeal, content for the moment to observe their movements. Clearly he was concerned about spreading his forces too thinly at various positions around the lake and was nervous about what that flotilla of water-houses would mean once they were brought into the action. He seemed to tacitly understand that he would need most of his canoe power to defend against these floating war machines, and he was right. As tradition and religion dictated, Cuauhtémoc appealed to his priests and his war god Huitzilopochtli for guidance in the forthcoming battles, and he made many sacrifices of special prisoners held in cages, including the two young Spanish pages captured from Cortés.[18]

Then on June 1, as smoke signals plumed the lake district, Cortés climbed aboard the flagship *La Capitana*, with Malinche at his side and Martín López as fleet pilot, and ordered the hoisting of the sails. The warships moved out of Texcoco using both sail and paddle, the winds too light to be of much assistance. They sailed south toward Iztapalapa, aimed at supporting Sandoval there. The brigantines lurched slowly along, and to the fascinated Aztecs watching from Tenochtitlán, they must have appeared cumbersome and plodding. Cuauhtémoc had organized thousands of his best and strongest canoe warriors, who filled the canals, waiting to be launched.

Cortés and his fleet kept on, reaching an inlet on the southern shore of the lake lying beneath the long shadowy outline of a lone peak, then called Tepepulco. He would have well remembered the inlet: it was here that he had gone with Montezuma, then disembarked to hunt on the emperor's royal island game preserve. Cortés later renamed it El Peñón del Marqués. Now the outcrop was covered with Aztec warriors who appeared to have expected the Spaniards and the brigantines to pass this way, so many were there. Cortés recalled the encounter: "When they saw the fleet approaching, they began to shout and make smoke signals, so that the other cities by the lakes should know and be prepared."[19] Although Cortés had planned to head for the portion of Iztapalapa built over the water and support Sandoval there, he decided to anchor first at Tepepulco and go ashore with 150 soldiers, hoping to extinguish the elevated communications post that was being used for smoke signaling.

Cortés led a squad of men up the steep and rocky terrain, encountering difficult hand-to-hand fighting along the way, and after a tough battle at the promontory, he managed to destroy the defense fortifications erected there and extinguish the signal fires. Though twenty-five Spaniards were wounded in the skirmish, Cortés relished it as "a most beautiful victory."[20] But the view from the knoll afforded him an image less appealing: a few thousand Aztec canoes were coursing across the lake from Tenochtitlán, headed straight toward them. Cortés and his men hurried back down the escarpment, embarked once more aboard the brigantines, and rowed out onto the open water to face the enemy.

Cortés and his naval captains watched the approaching Aztec canoe fleets with concern, even trepidation. He had his ships remain still, so that the canoe warriors would assume they had the upper hand and that the Spaniards were paralyzed by fear. The ruse worked—the bulwarked, reinforced canoes approached with great haste, pausing when they came within a distance of "two crossbowshots"[21] of the brigantines. For a moment of tense impasse the two sides faced each other, each waiting for a sign, or for the other to make a move.

Just then the flags on the brigantine masts began to flutter, and the sails billowed and filled as a strong breeze stirred on the lake. Cortés strode to the bow and tested the air, hoping for gusts, which soon arrived. Mountain winds whipped down the valley, winds that he deemed "very favorable to attacking [the Aztecs],"[22] so he ordered all oars in and sails full. The brigantines launched headlong into the lines of canoes, prow cannons blazing. Reaching their considerable speed, they rammed headlong into the canoe lines, shattering and splintering the smaller craft. They tacked and turned and slammed through again and again, sinking countless canoes and drowning droves of floundering warriors. Cannon fire from the bronze guns upended plenty more, and the harquebuses and crossbows fired and reloaded and fired again, until the water was strewn with wreckage and blood and the floating bodies of the dead and dismembered. A descendant of the warrior Ixtlilxochitl, who was there fighting with Cortés, reported that "so many were killed that all of the great lake was so stained with blood that it did not look like water."[23]

The canoe warriors eventually realized the futility of firing slingstones and spears and arrows at the hulls, which only pattered against the sides of the big boats and fell away into the water. Before long they were in retreat, paddling furiously for the safety of the canals, where the brigantines could not sail. Cortés and his warships chased the tattered canoe fleets for six miles, due north all the way to the capital. The initial deployment of his armada had brought a resounding and impressive victory, one that would clearly send waves of shock and dismay across the lake waters. Cortés had predicted that his brigantine launches would be "the key to the war," and their maiden voyage had made the Caudillo appear prophetic.

In Iztapalapa and Coyoacán, the Spaniards had observed the fight on the water and they were spurred on by what they saw. They later intimated to Cortés that they were overwhelmed and elated "to see all thirteen sails over the water with a fair wind, and us scattering the enemy canoes."[24] Inspired by the rout, the Spaniards under Olid pressed forward along the short causeway toward Xoloc. Olid took most of his cavalry and infantry and pushed the Aztec foot divisions back, finally managing to gain ground when Cortés and the brigantines arrived, having sailed through and crossed a number of channels where bridges had been removed in the causeway. Near evening Cortés positioned for a landing and amphibious assault at Xoloc, which was the confluence point of the causeways coming from Coyoacán and Iztapalapa and the site of an important Aztec fortress. Disembarking there with thirty men, Cortés would certainly have recalled the towers at Xoloc, the historic place of his first meeting with Montezuma. Now, assisted by Olid's forces, Cortés took possession of the two temple towers. Still, the causeway beyond swarmed with Aztec soldiers, and the water on all sides teemed with returning canoes.

Cortés ordered three heavy cannons landed from his flagship, and they were hoisted and conveyed to the captaingeneral. The largest of the three guns was loaded, aimed, and fired at the assembled Aztec foot soldiers, and the ordnance exploded into the enemy, causing a great deal of damage and panic. Then, ironically, a Spanish mistake actually aided their cause. The artilleryman in charge of the heavy cannon aimed another round into the Aztec lines and fired. But in his enthusiasm he carelessly ignited all the powder that had been landed and piled for the assault, and the powder kegs erupted in a massive explosion so powerful and concussive that it not only sent the enemy fleeing but knocked a number of nearby Spaniards into the water.[25] Cortés encamped that night at Xoloc, keeping the brigantines anchored just near the towers and close enough for immediate boarding. He sent one of the brigantines to Sandoval, indicating that he needed more gunpowder as soon as possible.

Night fell, and Cortés remained watchful and attentive. For the next few hours he could hear the sloshing of canoe paddles in the water all around, and the voices of Aztec soldiers echoing across the lake surface in the eerie darkness. The Aztecs issued forth from the city deep into the night, a fact that concerned Cortés gravely. "At midnight," he remembered clearly, "a great multitude of people arrived in canoes and poured along the causeway to attack our camp; this caused us great fear and consternation, especially as it was night, and never have they been known or seen to fight at such an hour unless they were certain of easy victory."[26] The Aztecs attacked with fury, charging forward from all quarters with battle cries piercing the night, screams and whoops calling out behind mournful conch whistles and the thumping of war drums. The surprised Spaniards had not expected such a concerted night attack.

The brigantines came into position flanking the causeway, firing repeatedly from their fieldpieces, the harquebuses and crossbows chiming in behind with sustained volleys. The brigantines thus repelled the first evening Aztec attack, and at dawn Cortés and his boats had won the day. But it was only the first day of their deployment. He had no way of knowing, as he watched the sunrise shimmer the color of roses over the *chi-nampas*, that he would need these boats every day for the next two and a half months. He would discover very soon that Cuauhtémoc and the proud people of Tenochtitlán had only just begun to fight.

CHAPTER TWENTY-ONE

Clash of Empires

CORTÉS, ALWAYS FLEXIBLE AND ADAPTABLE to his current situation, felt that his position at Xoloc was the best for his headquarters. It may have been merely circumstantial that the site he chose was the place of his historic first meeting with Montezuma, or it may have been intentional, for symbolic reasons. Less than two miles south of the capital, he could monitor the lake for incoming canoe activity and had access to ground support along the causeway from both Sandoval and Olid. Alvarado was to force his way inward from Tacuba, and thus Cortés planned to maintain his pressure around the throat of the city. But Cortés knew that the best-laid plans did not always come off smoothly, and though the first day's victory on the lake gave him cause for optimism, taking the causeways proved to be another matter entirely.

For the first weeks of early June, Cortés and his divisions engaged in a strange ebb and flow, a surge and withdrawal, that left the captain-general wondering whether he was really making any progress at all. By day the Spanish divisions fought toward the interior of the city, struggling mightily along the narrow causeways, contending with constant harassment from canoes on all sides, and slowed by stake-lined pits, strong wooden breastworks erected to block their progress, and Aztec

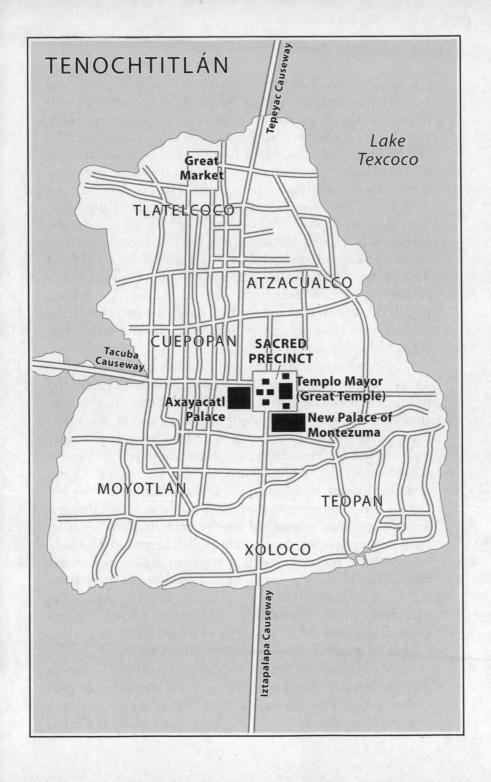

soldiers wielding Toledo-bladed spears and swords, adapted
from lost and abandoned Spanish weaponry. Not wanting to
risk being thinly scattered and vulnerable along the causeways,
Cortés and his captains drove inward all day, filling causeways
and hacking a path toward the capital, but by evening they returned to their three camps to rest, where they could post sentries and maintain brigantine support. The problem was, the
Aztecs used the cover of night (again, an adaptive departure
from their traditional practices) to rebreach the causeways,
erect new barricades, dig more pits and line them with sharp
wooden stakes, and unfill the causeway gaps of the rubble that
the Spaniards' Indian allies had worked so hard to fill. It was a
painstaking process for both besieger and besieged, and it exhausted all the combatants, but probably the Aztecs suffered
more, compelled to continue shifts both day and night, with
virtually no fresh water.

Cortés was quick to contrive innovations of his own. When
a group of Sandoval's men could not cross a large gap in the
Iztapalapa causeway, Cortés called for two of the smaller brigantines to sail into the gap and then anchor end to end, effectively creating a bridge over which Spanish soldiers and allies
and even horses were able to cross, then continue their forward
movement.[1] This was one of many in-field innovations. Cortés
also used hundreds of Indian workers to intentionally breach
the causeway, allowing four of his brigantines to sail through
so that they could assist Olid and his men, leaving the other
eight warships on the eastern side of the causeway.[2] The brigantines had to negotiate plenty of stakes in shallow waters, but
they managed to either evade or destroy many of these traps,
and the boat captains discovered a few deeper canals along
which they could sail or paddle right up into the suburbs and
outskirts of Tenochtitlán, where they set many of the houses on
fire before retreating back out into the open water.

The early stages of the fighting were as hard and vicious as
any the Spaniards had encountered. Cuauhtémoc continued
to send canoes from the capital in waves, which pestered the
causeways continually, the Aztec warriors, according to Cortés,

"shouting and screaming so that it seemed the world was coming to an end."[3] They were initially chased off by the cannon-firing brigantines, but the Aztecs adapted, learning that the cannons fired only in straight lines, and that if the canoe warriors bobbed and weaved as they paddled, they could successfully dodge the balls fired from the bronze guns. Cortés, noting this new evasive tactic, called for a fleet of several thousand canoes from Texcoco, which arrived eagerly to assist in driving the Aztec canoes from the proximity of the causeways.

During the first week of fighting, Cortés learned from Alvarado that the Aztecs were using the Tepeyac causeway—a short one at the north end of the city linking Tlatelolco to Tepeyac—aggressively as their primary access to the world outside the city, and that a constant stream of canoes was bringing in food and perhaps even water from the outside. Much of this activity was being conducted at night, under veil of darkness. Now Cortés had something of a dilemma. He had intentionally allowed that northernmost causeway to remain open as an enticement for Aztecs to flee the city, where they could easily be ridden down and slaughtered in the open by Spanish cavalry. Cuauhtémoc had not taken this bait, however, and the plan seemed to have backfired. Cortés could not allow the continued Aztec use of this thoroughfare, as it undermined his siege.

Although Gonzalo de Sandoval had been impaled through his foot by a javelin in recent fighting, Cortés trusted him to march north via Tacuba and secure the causeway. The movement of food into the city could not be tolerated, so Cortés from here on also ratcheted up brigantine patrols of the lake, targeting all canoes that looked to be conveying goods into the city. Once Sandoval reached and took the Tepeyac causeway (with the help of a couple of the brigantines, plus twenty-three cavalry, twenty crossbowmen, and about one hundred foot soldiers, as well as innumerable allies), Cortés had successfully inflicted a tight blockade on the city. He figured that as the Aztecs' supplies of food and water dwindled, so would their will to fight, and he reckoned that it was only a matter of time before Cuauhtémoc would realize that his cause was lost, and surrender. But Cortés had underestimated the last emperor of the Aztecs.

With his noose around the city, Cortés was determined to enter it and take it. Daily the brigantines made their way through the deeper channels and, at Cortés's direction, burned whatever flammable houses they could. "In this manner," he recalled, without betraying any emotion at the initial destruction of the city he had come to covet and admire, "six days were spent, and on each day we fought them; the brigantines burnt all the houses they could around the city, having discovered a canal whereby they might penetrate the outskirts and suburbs."[4] Perhaps a part of Cortés still believed it might be possible to take the city intact, and that setting buildings ablaze might just illustrate to Cuauhtémoc that his situation was hopeless, but in any event, a course of destruction was now under way. Only Cuauhtémoc and the military situation could dictate whether this course could be averted.

On June 10 Cortés determined that a concerted assault into the center of the city was worth a try. He took Olid and his two hundred infantry (plus many thousands of Chalcan and Texcocan allies) and marched due north from Xoloc, flanked by brigantines on either side of the causeway. He had sent messages ahead both to Sandoval at Tepeyac and to Alvarado at Tacuba to fight their way to the main temple, near the Palace of Axayacatl, which they would remember well.[5] It took much of the day, but by afternoon, having filled breaches and gaps where bridges had been removed, and destroyed barricades and battlements, Cortés and his soldiers arrived at the end of the main causeway. There they stood gazing up at the Gate of the Eagle, the doorway to the great city. It was a tall and impressive stone structure, with a large eagle in the center and a fierce jaguar standing on one side, a ferocious wolf on the other.[6] Here an extremely large bridge had been removed, but having learned from experience, Cortés positioned two of his boats and used them as a pontoon bridge, and in this way he and his men were able to cross into the city.[7]

As they pushed deeper inside the city, the Spaniards discovered that many of the bridges crossing canals had been left intact. Cuauhtémoc and his Aztec military advisers had not envisioned that Cortés and his forces would be able to infiltrate so far into the city so quickly. Seeing the Spanish divisions and allies moving forward all at once, the Aztecs took shelter behind stone pillars and columns and positioned themselves on the rooftops of the houses lining the streets. Cortés, following closely behind his vanguard, progressed to the edge of the plaza and set up a large cannon on the round gladiatorial sacrifice stone. Seeing great numbers of Aztec warriors overflowing the plaza, he began firing into the mass, causing much damage and a general panic and stampede as cannon smoke blackened the horizon.[8] Many Aztecs scattered to the temple precinct, and the drums atop the Great Temple boomed a warning call across the religious center. According to Aztec accounts, "the deep throbbing of the drums resounded over the city, calling the warriors to defend the shrine of their god. But two of the Spanish soldiers climbed the stairway to the temple platform, cut the priests down with their swords and pitched them headlong over the brink."[9]

The call to arms had nonetheless been heard, and Aztec warriors rallied to defend their city, many arriving in canoes. The Aztecs surged forth, swinging their obsidian-bladed swords viciously. Cortés tightened and ordered his divisions to attack, then called on his artillery and crossbowmen to fire at will. The plaza became riotous and confusing, a crisscross of arrows and darts and artillery fire, and in the melee, Cortés saw that the sheer numbers of Aztecs were too great. He ordered the Lombard cannon at the sacrificial stone abandoned, and the Spaniards commenced a defensive retreat back down the causeway, their progress aided by the gaps the allies had been filling in all day long. As the Spaniards departed the city, Aztec warriors seized the abandoned cannon, dragged it to the lakeshore, and heaved it into the water, where it sank at a place they called the Stone Toad.[10]

Inflamed by the Spanish retreat, the Aztecs pursued Cortés

from the main plaza all the way down the street and onto the causeway until it was nearly dark. Still, though attacked from the flanks and from the rooftops above, Cortés was planning his immediate return and taking necessary precautions. "We set fire to most of the better houses in that street," he said, "so that when we next entered they might not attack us from the rooftops."[11]

By nightfall Cortés and his troops were back at their camp at Xoloc, and through messengers he learned that both Sandoval and Alvarado had battled all day from their positions as well, but fierce resistance had kept them from reaching the center of the city. Bernal Díaz, who was with Alvarado attacking from Tacuba, reported that the causeway was much riddled with staked pits and that as the Spaniards approached the city, they were attacked from both land and water, peppered with darts and stones that were "more numerous than hailstones."[12] Compounding the problem, the Spaniards learned once again that the cavalry was ineffectual on the causeways. As cavalrymen came into contact with Aztec warriors and tried to ride them down, the Aztecs would leap into the lake and swim to safety, clinging to canoes or to the banks, their swimming skill and comfort with the water a serious advantage. The horses were too exposed on the causeways, and too valuable to risk, so the infantry did the bulk of the work, and many were wounded. Alvarado's and Sandoval's forces retreated to their camps at night as well, where they cauterized their wounds with searing oil and prayed to their god for the strength they would require during the next day's fighting, and the next.[13]

This initial incursion into the city had a few immediate and significant results. Cortés had had a firsthand look at how the entry, and subsequent fighting there, was likely to play out. He also clearly understood that the burning of buildings would be necessary to eradicate (or at least reduce) the elevated bombardment, and that this torching of the interior (coupled with the burning already being done by brigantine amphibious raids on the outskirts) had set the destruction of the city into motion. But the most important result of the foray all the way into the religious precinct was its effect on the vassal states that had, until now, been reluctant to send warriors in support of the Spanish cause. Word quickly spread beyond the lakeshores and across the valley, and within a day or two, Cortés received pledges of support from formerly hostile Otomis, as well as from the people of Chalco and Xochimilco, all groups with whom the Spaniards had previously skirmished.

The support from these peoples came in numerous forms, including manpower, war canoes, food, and shelter. The Spaniards had grown weary of the constant diet of maize cakes, and when sustenance arrived in the form of fish, fowl, and local cherries (and even prickly pear, which was coming into season), their morale strengthened.[14] The allied laborers would be sent ahead to fill in removed bridges and breaches in the canals and causeways, a full-time job, and they also began to build temporary shelters (houses or huts that the Spaniards called *ranchos*) along the causeways for the Spaniards, allowing them protection from night raids as well as summer squalls. When the Texcocans sent some fifty thousand reinforcements, Cortés decided on June 15 that he was ready for another offensive drive into the city's heart.[15]

The second sortie replicated the first. During the interim the Aztecs had been busy breaching the causeway once more and constructing more stalwart and impressive bulwarks. After hearing mass, Cortés left his encampment with twenty or so cavalry, three hundred Spanish soldiers, and all his Indian allies, whom he described as "an infinite number."[16] The allied divisions went first, filling in the gaps and destroying the ramparts, followed by the Spanish infantry, artillerymen, and cavalry when the causeway was partly cleared, flanked as always by brigantine support, which made the entire incursion possible. Crossbowmen and artillery slung their arms over the boat gunwales, picking off Aztec canoe warriors and forcing Aztec infantry to flee their positions, so that once again Cortés found himself beneath the Gate of the Eagle and ready to infiltrate the city. The fighting was again brutal and bloody, and the Aztecs defended their religious precinct with even greater vigor than they had on the first occasion.

Cortés decided that, rather than continue his advance, he would take some ten thousand of the allied laborers and concentrate on filling the breaches everywhere as permanently as possible, using stone and wood and rubble, and compacting the fill to make it difficult or even impossible to remove. In this way the cavalry could quickly cross and be of use in the wider plazas, where Cortés hoped to employ them. While inside the city, he dispatched messengers appealing to Cuauhtémoc to sue for peace, but the only reply was a constant volley of spears, stones, and darts from all quarters. By nightfall, Cortés was safely back on the southern portion of the causeway, having illustrated that he could come and go into the city as he pleased, if with some danger and difficulty.

During this second foray Cortés had something of a grim epiphany. All day long he had ridden with the cavalry and seen the bitter determination on the faces of the Aztec soldiers, men who would not yield but would fall to their deaths where they stood and fought. "When I saw how determined they were to die in their defense," Cortés remembered matter-of-factly, "I deduced two things: that we would regain little, or none, of the riches which they had taken from us, and that they gave us cause, and indeed obliged us, to destroy them utterly."*[17]

This last realization, according to Cortés, weighed heavily on his soul, for he certainly preferred, if possible, to take the city without destroying it entirely. But that appeared unlikely. As a last-ditch effort, thinking he would hurt the Aztec leadership to their very core, he sent amphibious raiding parties via brigantine to infiltrate the city and destroy and torch the "towers of their idols and their houses," including the Palace of Axayacatl as well as one of the former emperor Montezuma's

---

*Cortés is of course referring to the riches *he took* from Montezuma but lost when fleeing the city during La Noche Triste.

most prized buildings, his gorgeous and magnificent House of Birds.[18] And though the tactic caused the Aztecs extreme grief, it only spurred them to fight that much harder out of anger and hatred.

Cuauhtémoc was certainly unsettled by Cortés's progress into the city, and as a defensive strategy he began to move his base of operations and the bulk of his troops from the sacred precinct in the center to Tlatelolco, the island city at the far northwest tip of Tenochtitlán proper. Tlatelolco was home to the famous market, where what provisions the city still possessed remained, and more important from a military standpoint, Cuauhtémoc used the temple there (among the highest and most prominent in the city) to direct his defenses. From there he could see everything, including former Aztec vassals, now allies of Cortés, arriving from all directions in numbers too great to count. Standing atop the pyramid, Cuauhtémoc took in the grim situation—he would be fighting not only the Spaniards but fellow Indians, in effect his brothers. And perhaps worst of all, he could see the dismantling, burning, and razing of his city, could hear the crashing of stone walls as they toppled, could watch the smoke from the smoldering rubble. But he had vowed to his people, and to himself, to defend the city to the death, so he ordered smoke signals lit, a sign from the emperor that the Aztecs must rally and fight.[19]

For many days Cortés continued his approach in a repetitive way, each time supported by brigantines up the causeway, using allied labor to fill ditches, thrusting forth to the sacred precinct just a little bit farther each day, always nudging the Aztecs just a bit farther out of their city. Despite appeals from some of his less patient captains to set up camp within the city, Cortés always ordered the evening return to the relative safety of his causeway camp, reminding his men of the danger of being trapped inside the city. He had come this far and had planned methodically, and he had no intention of letting petulance and carelessness undermine his well-conceived battle and siege plan.

One of the impatient captains turned out to be Pedro de

Alvarado, which should have come as no great surprise to
Cortés. Alvarado had shown his impetuousness on multiple
occasions, most notoriously in the attack at the Festival of
Toxcatl. So far during the siege Alvarado had done as instructed, and each day he made good headway along the
Tacuba causeway, infiltrated the city, and then near sundown
returned to camp at Tacuba, perhaps not only for safety but to
share a bed with his indigenous spouse María Luisa.[20] But on
June 23, perhaps feeling overconfident by his daily ingress or
simply overanxious, Alvarado made the decision to encamp
half of his cavalry well forward on the causeway, almost within
the city itself, feeling that there was limited exposure there as a
result of all the houses they had destroyed.

It was a devastating mistake. Almost immediately three
squadrons of warriors attacked from three separate directions,
and the Spaniards engaged them at all points, including the
rear. The Aztec warriors at the vanguard retreated within the
city, with the Spaniards in pursuit, crashing through barricades
and then charging through the shallow water of a breach.
Tossing javelins and hurling darts, the Aztecs retreated up a
lesser causeway inside Tlatelolco, and Alvarado, inflamed,
sent men rushing ahead. Soon the Spaniards were among
houses, from which, and from the streets beyond, poured innumerable warriors, including those whose feigned retreat had
drawn the Spaniards in. Bernal Díaz reported that soon the
Aztecs "dealt us such treatment that we could not withstand
them,"[21] and the Spaniards turned to retreat, heading for the
shallow gap they had just crossed.

But the Aztecs had planned their ruse well, and the
Spaniards arrived to discover that the shallow breach they had
crossed was now filled with hundreds of Aztec war canoes,
forcing them in another direction, toward a deeper channel.
Pursued now at all points, some fifty Spaniards had no choice
but to wade and swim into the deeper ford. Many Spanish soldiers now plunged into stake-lined pits, some impaled on the
sharpened spears, others wedged and bogged down and unable
to flee as the Aztecs surged upon them. The Aztecs bludgeoned

the floundering Spaniards mercilessly, dragging a half dozen or so away for sacrifice, spearing and hacking many others to death. Bernal Díaz managed to swim to the safety of the other side, but as he crawled out of the death trap, he discovered that he bled profusely from one arm and could barely stand from the injuries and blood loss. It was fortunate, in fact, that more Spaniards were not lost, for the cavalry had been unable to assist, the pits keeping them on the other side. A lone horseman did attempt to aid the infantry, but both he and his horse were killed in a stake-lined pit.[22] Nearly all of them were seriously injured.

When Cortés learned of the rout, he was livid. He hated to lose men, and, worse, he knew that the Aztecs' success would encourage their spirit and bolster Cuauhtémoc's confidence. He immediately dispatched a letter to Alvarado, rebuking him for his overzealous maneuver and reminding him that under no circumstances should he ever leave a causeway breach unfilled, especially one behind his rearguard. Alvarado acquiesced, and his troops spent the next four days filling gaps that they should have filled in the first place, using the rubble— mostly stone and wood—from the houses they had torn down along the way. For assurance, all the horses were to remain saddled and bridled all night long, and their riders were to sleep at their sides.[23]

Cortés decided that a personal reprimand was in order, and he boarded a brigantine and visited Alvarado at his camp within the city. But once Cortés saw the distance Alvarado had infiltrated, he could muster only praise and congratulations for his countryman. Cortés admitted, "When I reached his camp...I was truly astonished to see how far into the city he had gone and the dangerous bridges and passes which he had won, and I no longer blamed him as much as he seemed to deserve."[24]

Instead, Cortés held a meeting with Alvarado, where they agreed that a concerted push to the Tlatelolco marketplace should be their central focus, as that appeared to be where the Aztecs were massing for a final showdown. That taken care of, Cortés returned to his own camp for the evening.

During this time the brigantines had continued to assert their dominance of the lake, maintaining unremitting day and night cruises to disrupt food and water importation by Aztec canoes. But the Aztecs were adapting to the new military techniques and quickly deduced that the brigantines were a significant problem that they must deal with if they were to save their city. To combat the ships, the Aztec command conceived a scheme that involved elaborate decoys, feigned retreats and aggressive counterattacks.

One morning Spanish brigantine captains sighted a flotilla of canoes moving along the open water in plain view; the canoes were camouflaged with brush and rushes as if hiding their contents—likely food, water, and other provisions desperately needed in the city. Two of the brigantines launched forth under sail and paddle, aggressively pursuing the supply canoes. Before the Spanish captains (among them Pedro Barba and Juan Portillo) realized they had been duped, the brigantines ran aground on stakes that had been buried underwater in a shallow channel, and the boats ground to a halt. While paddlers dug furiously, struggling to extricate the ships, lines of larger Aztec war canoes (as many as forty, all brimming with the finest warriors) emerged from a reed bank, where they had lain in hiding. It was a well-conceived trap, and the canoes attacked fiercely from all quarters. Soon the oarsmen had to abandon their posts and brandish swords in defense as the Aztec canoes surged forth, swarming over the brigantines.[25]

Numerous Spaniards were dragged from the ships, battered with clubs and taken away alive, while others, including Captain Juan Portillo, died in the struggle. More brigantines came in support and managed to wrest the two stranded vessels from the stakes and free them, but severe damage had been inflicted. Captain Pedro Barba died a few days later from the wounds he suffered. The Aztecs had shown ingenious and creative adaptability. Now the Spaniards would need to be ever wary on the water, always cautious of potential entrapment.[26]

Despite this setback, the three-pronged assault into the

interior of the city appeared to be yielding dividends for the Spaniards, as each invasion brought the three divisions closer to their desired confluence at Tlatelolco. But the length and difficulty of the siege was wearing on the captains as well as the soldiers. Seasonal rains kept the men drenched to their core, and they slept uncomfortably in their armor, dank and putrid within. Though the three divisions all had sufficient food supplies, Alvarado's division, now encamped within the city at the very battle front, was surviving almost solely on maize cakes, cherries, and herbs. In his own camp Cortés received pressure from certain captains (among them newcomer Alderete, the king's treasurer, who longed to get his hands on some of the gold he saw dangling from his compatriots' necks) to make an all-out assault on the marketplace. Other captains, including Olid and Tapia, also supported the idea of a concerted offensive, rather than the redundant daily surges and withdrawals that had come to characterize the siege.[27]

Contributing to this general edginess, the three Spanish divisions had a competitiveness, a point of Spanish pride, each wanting to be the first to take the marketplace. Cortés remarked, "For this reason, Pedro de Alvarado was much importuned, ... for they held it a point of honor to take it [the marketplace] first."[28] Cortés listened intently to the urgings (even demands) of his captains, but he hesitated to act, clearly understanding the disadvantages of such a rash undertaking. The houses in Tlatelolco remained intact, providing rooftops from which the Aztecs could position and fire stones, darts, and spears. Even worse, in Cortés's mind, deep inside the city the Spaniards would no longer have the benefit of brigantine support, which time and again had proved lifesaving. He held a meeting of the primary captains. Many were of the mind that if the Spaniards could take the marketplace, Cuauhtémoc would be so devastated that he would have no option but to surrender. They had grown exhausted, both physically and mentally, from filling every single channel and gap, only to see their day's labor undone by the Aztecs during the night. This frustrating seesaw had begun to seriously wear on the men. Also, there appeared to be allied support for an all-out attack, instigated by Ixtlilxochitl.[29]

After hearing all the different arguments for and against an assault, Cortés (probably against his own intuition and better judgment) agreed to a major offensive. He drafted letters to both Alvarado and Sandoval, apprising them of his operation plan and their responsibilities within it. From the north Sandoval was to leave a small part of his troops and cavalry at their encampment on the Tepeyac causeway; the bulk were to join up with Alvarado and his men. (The plan here was to make it appear that he was breaking camp and, when the Aztecs pursued him, to have the straggler division ambush from the rear.) Supported by a half dozen brigantines (for as long as the boats could navigate the lakeshore, narrow channels, and remain within firing cover range) and three thousand allied war canoes, Sandoval and Alvarado were instructed to take a large number of their Indian laborers and hurry to the dangerous breach where Alvarado's men had suffered such a defeat, take it if contested and fill it in with haste, then continue their advance toward the market area, where Cortés planned to meet them.[30]

Cortés intended to move up the southern causeway en masse, his customary approach. Then, once deep enough in the city, his force would splinter into three separate divisions and take the three primary roads leading into the marketplace, each of which required fording a significant watercourse that separated Tenochtitlán from Tlatelolco. The captain-general would lead one hundred infantry, eight cavalry, and a throng of allies up a very narrow road heading to the market. Andrés de Tapia would captain a separate division, comprising eighty Spaniards and perhaps ten thousand Indian allies, along a wide road heading toward the Tacuba causeway. The treasurer Alderete commanded his own column, by far the largest, having seventy Spaniards and an impressive twenty thousand allied warriors, bearers, and porters, guarded at the rear by eight able cavalry.[31]

At sunrise on Sunday, June 30, just after hearing mass, Cortés ordered the assault. The brigantines led out, followed by the allied canoes, and after taking two near bridges and a couple of heavily fortified ramparts, the defending Aztecs were driven back as usual. Cortés had been confident at the beginning, saying of the skirmishes with the Aztecs: "Our allies who attacked them on the roof tops and other places were so numerous it seemed that nothing could resist us."[32] This estimate turned out to be overly optimistic. Cortés's progress was soon hindered by the narrow, unfamiliar streets and the long distance he had to travel, coupled with concerted ambushes orchestrated by elite Aztec divisions who had been in hiding behind houses and public buildings.

Alderete's division moved quickly, and soon it was closing in on the marketplace, and the troops could even hear the cannon and musket fire near the market. Spurred on by the opportunity to converge with them, they hurried forward, coming to a water gap some eight feet deep and a dozen paces across. In his haste to get over to the other side, Alderete ordered an impromptu filling of the breach, and men hurriedly threw in reed grasses and wooden pieces until the makeshift bridge could support one soldier at a time, and in this way they dashed quickly over it. However, when most of Alderete's Spaniards reached the other side, a furious ambush awaited them.

The surprise attack was so quick and so concerted that it drove many of the Spaniards instantly back into the deep water; the Aztecs, quite comfortable with water, charged right in after them. Cortés, having heard there was a problem, rode hard to see for himself and arrived to find "the water full of Indians and Spaniards as though not a straw had been thrown into it. The enemy attacked so fiercely that in attempting to kill the Spaniards they leapt into the water after them. Then some canoes came up the canals and took some of the Spaniards away alive."[33] The place was in chaos, the cries of the Spaniards drowned out by the shouting, shrieking, and whistling of the Aztec squadrons enveloping them in waves. Cortés

leaped from his horse and fought his way down the embank-
ment, determined, as he put it, to "make a stand and die fighting."[34] The rout was so bad that Cortés was reduced to pulling
his dead, dying, and drowning countrymen from the bog and
hoisting them onto the shore, where they lay covered with
mud and blood. He could only watch helplessly as Aztec warriors dragged his soldiers away on the other side.

At that moment he felt a tug on his arms and realized he
had been surrounded. Despite his struggle he was overwhelmed, seized, and carried away. Under the circumstances
they could certainly have killed the captain-general, but the
Aztecs wanted him alive. Then, with remarkable similarity
to the scene that had taken place at Xochimilco back in
February, captain and personal bodyguard Cristóbal de Olea
swooped in, sword in hand, and slashed with all his might to
free Cortés from the enemy clutches. Olea is said to have
hacked the arms off of several Aztecs in order to free his commander; his efforts allowed other Spanish soldiers, including
Antonio de Quiñones, to aid in the rescue. Only through the
efforts of the brave Olea, who had now saved Cortés's life
twice, Quiñones managed to pull Cortés momentarily to
safety. But this time cost Olea his own life. Overwhelmed by
sheer numbers, he was slain on the spot—but not before taking four Aztecs down with him.[35]

Back up on the level causeway, Cortés and a dozen of his
men fought a difficult retreat. Holding their shields before
them, they swung swords and bucklers as hard as they could,
and soldiers tried desperately to get a horse to Cortés, for his
own had either been killed or galloped off in the frenzied fighting. Cortés turned and attempted to continue fighting at the
breach, but Captain Quiñones, who had now taken over the
responsibility of personal bodyguard, warned him against it.
"Let us go and at least save your own person," he hollered over
the din of battle, "for you know that if you are killed, we are all
lost."[36] Cortés knew this to be true and reluctantly agreed. One
of his attendants arrived with a horse, but that man was impaled through the throat before he ever reached his captain-

general. Another rider, a steward of Cortés's named Cristóbal de Gúzman, attempted to convey a horse but was captured and hauled away to Cuauhtémoc.

At last the remaining Spaniards did manage to get a horse close enough for Cortés to swing onto and ride, and deeply wounded in the leg, he clung for his life, as they galloped back toward their camp to assess the damage inflicted. The losses turned out to be monumental, not only in life, but in morale. Just a few dozen Spaniards (and a multitude of allies) had died in the fighting, but sixty-five to seventy Spaniards were taken alive and herded toward the pyramid, where already copal incense rose from the towers signaling an Aztec war victory.[37]

During Cortés's devastating defeat, Alvarado and Sandoval had been battling in Tlatelolco, near the market, in close proximity to each other. Alvarado's men had fared well, progressing close to the market center, when they were confronted with a macabre and disheartening sight. A large contingent of Aztec warriors came forward, bedecked in ornate headgear with sprawling quetzal plumes and carrying magnificent standards. Clearly driven by bloodlust, the Aztecs in the vanguard screamed and taunted the Spaniards, hurling the severed heads of five Spaniards at their feet, heads just taken from Cortés's troops. The heads had been tied together by their hair and beards. As Alvarado and Bernal Díaz looked to see if they recognized any of the men, the Aztecs yelled, "We will kill you, too, as we have Cortés and Sandoval, and all the men they brought with them. These are their heads, and by them you may know them well."[38] Thinking the worst but needing to confirm it for himself, Alvarado ordered a retreat. He and his men could hear the loud drumming from the temples as they rode to their camp.

Sandoval as well was forced back toward the Tepeyac causeway, berated similarly as he went, and more decapitated heads were hurled at him. Near the end of the day all three units were tending their considerable wounds back at their camps (Sandoval had been struck in the face with a large stone); the brigantines and their captains returned to offer what token security they could provide. All the Spaniards could see the ritual proceedings taking place at the great pyramid of Tlatelolco. Drums pounded all across Tenochtitlán, and warriors blew long on conch shells. Others played flutes and pipes, whistles and trumpetlike horns, some jangling instruments resembling tambourines. Bernal Díaz, who straggled back with Alvarado, described what they all witnessed as his comrades, stripped naked, were led up to the sacrifice stone:

> When they got to a small square in front of the oratory, where their accursed idols are kept, we saw them place plumes on the heads of many of them and with things like fans in their hands they forced them to dance before Huitzilopochtli, and after they had danced they immediately placed them on their backs... and with stone knives they sawed open their chests and drew out their palpitating hearts and offered them to the idols that were there, and they kicked the bodies down the steps, and the Indian butchers who were waiting below cut off the arms and feet and flayed the skin off the faces, and prepared it afterwards like glove leather with the beards on, and kept those for the festivals... and the flesh they ate in *chilmole*... and the bodies, that is their entrails and feet, they threw to the tigers and lions which they kept in the house of the carnivores.[*39]

All night long the Spaniards watched the temples, illuminated by eerie torchlight coupled with the burning ceremonial copal incense. They listened to the chants, to the drums, and to the horrific screams of their compatriots as they succumbed to the sharp obsidian blades. Cortés could only say with deep

---

*These sacrifices are recorded, if with less dramatization, by Nahuatl accounts, including the Florentine Codex (book 12, ch. 34), which states: "Then they pursued the Spaniards; they went knocking them down and taking them. And when they had gotten [the Spaniards] to where they were to die... they stripped them. They took away from them all their war gear and their cotton upper armor, and they made them drop everything that was on them to the ground. Then they performed their office and killed them; their companions watched from out on the water."

regret and resignation, "And although we greatly desired to put a stop to this we were unable to do so."[40]

Cuauhtémoc, flush with victorious pride, immediately dispatched messengers to the chiefs of his former vassals Cuernavaca, Xochimilco, and Chalco, bearing the news of a great conquest. More than half of the Spaniards, these despicable *teules*, had been slain. As evidence, the messengers carried with them the flayed heads of slain Spaniards, as well as some amputated feet and hands and a few flayed horse heads. As word of these trophies went around the lake, support for Cortés began to shift, and within only a couple of days nearly all of Cortés's Indian allies disappeared. Fickle, having seen that Cortés could be defeated, and superstitious of prophecies presaging their doom, they broke camp and vanished beyond the lakeshores.

With the situation now firmly in his favor, Cuauhtémoc issued a bold and definitive proclamation, one he ordered spread far and wide: he had consulted his gods, and they had spoken. Within eight days not a single Spaniard would be left alive.

CHAPTER TWENTY-TWO

The Last Stand of the Aztecs

FOR THE NEXT EIGHT DAYS THE SPANIARDS hung on, the wounded men (almost everyone) resting and recuperating as best they could, while the fittest continued the work of daily breach-filling. The nights were difficult to endure. Each evening the Aztecs continued their elaborate rituals, and the Spaniards watched the flickering lights of bonfires licking the horizon, heard the ominous and eerie horns and flutes and conch shells and the thumping of drums, then the screams of their comrades as the sacrifices continued night after night.[1] Cortés learned that Cuauhtémoc's messages to the provinces had been successful: the skinned heads and torsos of Spaniards and horses had encouraged the ancient tribes at Malinalco, near Cuernavaca, and in Otomi territory, at Matalcingo, to wage war on their neighbors who had aligned with the Spaniards, and to assist the Aztecs in Tenochtitlán, for the end was near.[2]

The uprising in the provinces was confirmed two days later when representatives from Cuernavaca (who had formally acknowledged allegiance with Spain) arrived at Cortés's camp to say that their city was being attacked vigorously, under orders of Cuauhtémoc, by highland barbarians from Malinalco and

Huitzuco. The delegation from Cuernavaca complained that these tribes were laying waste to their crops and fruit orchards and that Spanish support would be necessary to quell the raids. Cortés clearly had enough problems with the desertion of so many allies and his own troops devastated by injury. Spreading thin his already exhausted (and recently drubbed) force concerned him. "And although our defeat was so recent and we needed help more than we could give it," Cortés explained later, "I determined to go to their aid because they entreated me with such insistence: so, in the face of opposition from some who claimed that I would destroy us all by reducing our number in the camp, I sent back with those messengers eighty foot solders and ten horsemen under the command of captain Andrés de Tapia."[3] He gave Tapia ten days to quell the uprisings in the south.

Cortés then dispatched Sandoval, accompanied by eighteen horsemen and one hundred infantry, to deal with a similar situation near the Tlaxcalan boundary. False bravado or not, Cortés intended to send the message to the outlying provinces—and especially those now contemplating coming to Cuauhtémoc's assistance—that the Spaniards were far from finished and could mount expeditions at will.

Tapia rode south and joined the Cuernavacan warriors, and using the advantage of the cavalry on the open plain, he routed the highlanders and chased them all the way to their perched strongholds, where they fled to shelter. Tapia returned victorious in the allotted time, having squelched the opposition and reestablished strong ties (and manpower support) with Cuernavaca.[4]

Sandoval's expedition to the Otomi territory was similar in that his horsemen benefited greatly from level topography. After two days of riding he came upon the enemy crossing a river, and the Spaniards pursued and quickly gained ground. The hostile tribesmen, running for their lives before the charging Spanish horses, began discarding heavy bundles, spoils and plunder from an Otomi town they had recently sacked.

Sandoval and his men stopped to inspect the bundles of booty, which included bales of maize and stacks of fine clothing. Among the garments were also the remnants of roasted babies, the sight of which spurred the Spaniards to pursue the fleeing warriors for over five miles to an elevated and walled fortress, where the survivors (some two thousand were slain) sought refuge.[5] They wailed, beat drums, and blew horns into the night, then slunk away under cover of darkness. By sunrise there was no sign of them, and Sandoval was able to return to Tenochtitlán with more than seventy thousand new Otomi allies, having secured the region and shored up his political alliances.[6]

Behind the crumbling and tenuous walls of Tenochtitlán, the eighth day of Cuauhtémoc's proclamation came and went, and still the Spaniards lived. Still the brigantines sliced ceaselessly across the lake waters, making a constant patrol. These facts undermined the emperor's credibility, and soon large numbers of superstitious and fickle allies returned from the hills to once again support Cortés.

Just at that time a Spanish messenger from the eastern coast brought highly agreeable news. A Spanish supply ship had recently arrived at Vera Cruz, one belonging to Juan Ponce de León. Ponce de León had recently been defeated by natives off the coast of Florida, Cortés learned, while trying to land (near what is now the Charlotte Harbor Estuary), in his second attempt to discover the mythical Fountain of Youth. One ship, carrying a mortally wounded Ponce de León, returned to Cuba; the other continued around the gulf and made land at Villa Rica. That was a great windfall for Cortés, since the ship contained large quantities of gunpowder and crossbows, as well as a number of Spanish fighting men and some horses.*[7]

---

*Juan Ponce de León's first attempt to find the Fountain of Youth was made in 1512, during which voyage he failed to make landing. The wounds he suffered during this second attempt (including being struck by a poisoned arrow) were so extensive that he died not long after his return to Cuba, in late July 1521.

The gunpowder was crucial. Stores were extremely low, to the point that Cortés had recently dispatched an emergency team under Francisco de Montano (one of the Narváez conscripts) to the summit of Popocatépetl to obtain sulfur for fabricating gunpowder. Five bold Spaniards ascended the great volcano, and after casting lots for the "privilege," Montano was lowered by rope chain multiple times some four hundred feet into the mouth of the smoldering caldera, until he had harvested enough sulfur to make gunpowder for the crossbows and artillery, an amount that lasted until the end of the siege.[8]

Buttressed by these recent reinforcements, his Spanish soldiers rested and somewhat recovered, Cortés and his captains noticed something curious and intriguing. With each passing night, the Aztecs appeared to be less and less successful at digging up and unearthing the gaps, until by mid-July they had ceased these efforts altogether, and all the breaches now remained filled in permanently. At first Cortés believed this might be yet another Aztec ruse, but the arrival of two starving and delirious Aztecs told him that Cuauhtémoc's and the Aztec people's situation was most dire. These men said that the Aztecs were dying from starvation and thirst; that the dead bodies of their countrymen were being piled inside houses to conceal the extent of their losses; and that they were now too few and too weak to work through the night. Cuauhtémoc had even resorted to disguising women in men's garb to make them appear as able warriors.[9]

Compounding the Aztecs' already grave situation, Alvarado's forces had recently reached and destroyed the only remaining water source left to the city's inhabitants, a saline spring that was hardly sufficient and its salinity too high. After that spring was destroyed, the Aztec people were reduced to drinking the highly brackish lake water. Aztec accounts attest to the severity of their predicament, stating

> There was no fresh water to drink, only stagnant water and the brine of the lake, and many people died of dysentery. The only food was lizards, swallows, corncobs and the salt

grasses of the lake. The people ate water lilies and chewed on deerhides and pieces of leather. They roasted and seared whatever they could find and then ate it. They ate the bitterest weeds; they even ate dirt.[10]

Cortés decided to see whether the Aztecs, if they were indeed desperate and vulnerable, would agree to a settlement: if Cuauhtémoc would simply surrender, then Cortés would not destroy the city and slaughter whatever inhabitants remained. A few exchanges took place at this time, and Cortés released three captured Aztecs warriors to try to negotiate a peace. Cuauhtémoc stalled and postured (and even consulted his captains and priests), but in the end he was too proud and too committed to surrender. He would make no deals with this Spaniard Cortés. The Aztecs would fight to the death.

Cortés had mixed emotions and uncertainty about his next move. "I did not know," he said, "by what means we might relieve ourselves of all these dangers and hardships, yet avoid destroying them and their city which was indeed the most beautiful thing in the world."[11] Tired of the protracted siege and concerned with the condition of his own men, Cortés now made the fateful decision that he had hoped somehow to avoid. He would reduce Tenochtitlán to rubble. "My plan," he reported, "was to raze to the ground all the houses on both sides of the streets along which we advanced, so that we should move not a step without leaving everything behind us in ruins."[12] He called on his allied leaders to enlist from the surrounding hills and towns all the farm laborers they could muster, and those should come with their *coas* (digging tools like shovels) and prepare to utterly destroy the famed city. Using the laborers and field workers to flatten buildings and permanently fill in all the causeways, canals, and ditches, Cortés had also availed himself of a great many allied warriors, for they were no longer required in the destruction work.[13]

In conjunction with the demolition, Cortés stepped up his offensive and orchestrated a series of concerted raids that lasted through the final days of July 1521. The razing of buildings provided wider and more level avenues for the horses to run, and Cortés employed the cavalry now to great advantage, though near the market the Aztecs had placed giant boulders and walled off some streets to prevent the horses from entering. Despite these defensive tactics, the Spaniards ratcheted up the pressure, and Cortés now had nearly 150,000 allied warriors fighting alongside his own highly skilled and experienced divisions.[14] The brigantines continued to pound Aztec positions around the north end of the city with constant cannon and artillery fire, and to make amphibious landings of stealthy Spanish troops. After a few days of such surges, the remaining Aztec force had cordoned itself off at the Tlatelolco marketplace, the last stronghold of their empire.

Cortés called once more upon his trusted captain Sandoval to bring fifteen horses from Alvarado's camp, and adding them to his own cavalry Cortés mounted a force of forty horsemen for a planned ambush, hoping to draw out as many of the elite Aztec warriors as he could. He sent ten riders ahead to capture the attention of the enemy; then, while Aztecs on rooftops and behind large barricades were engaging them, the remaining thirty followed after, hiding behind houses and walls near the square. The ten horsemen at the front did their job, attracting attention and battling for a time before galloping away in a feigned retreat. The ruse worked. A very large Aztec contingent pursued the retreating horses, which led back to the open square. There Cortés gave the order to attack, and the thirty hidden cavalrymen rode from their hiding positions and ambushed the Aztecs savagely, killing a great number and dispersing the rest.[15]

At precisely the same time, Alvarado and his troops were assaulting the marketplace from their position and encountering surprisingly fierce fighting considering the wretched physical and psychological condition of the Aztecs. The vengeful Tlaxcalans fought and pillaged with increasing vigor, razing and burning Cuauhtémoc's palace. In the last days of July, Cortés looked up to see smoke rising in thick plumes from the pyramid temple in Tlatelolco. It was Alvarado's signal that the great marketplace had been taken. Thereafter Cortés and Alvarado were able to join forces and make coordinated forays against the stubborn holdouts. Francisco de Montano, who had recently returned from the summit of Popocatépetl, and a soldier named Gutierre de Badajoz, placed Cortés's flag at the top of the temple to signal victory there.[16]

For several days the Spaniards and their allies made similar raids, during which the Tlaxcalans were particularly ruthless, killing women and children indiscriminately, despite protestations by Cortés. The captain-general ascended the steps of the high pyramid to gain a view over the whole city and discovered there the decapitated heads of many of his Spanish brethren impaled and displayed on skull racks, as well as the heads of numerous Tlaxcalans, the Aztecs' arch-enemies. Cortés stood at the edge so that the entire city could see him, perhaps hoping the sight of him rather than their own priests, or Cuauhtémoc, would convince the Aztecs at last to give up. Nearly ninety percent of the city was now in his possession.[17] But still the proud and tenacious Cuauhtémoc refused to submit. Despite the appearance of utter dominance for Cortés, pockets of elite Aztec fighting corps remained, brave eagle and jaguar warriors, men who would much sooner die than surrender.

To further illustrate his positional advantage (both tactically and symbolically), Cortés moved his military headquarters to the Amaxac district, setting up a crimson-canopied tent on a prominent rooftop where he could survey the battlefield and orchestrate maneuvers.[18] He noted that large number of the enemy had taken refuge on adjacent rooftops, atop stilt houses near the lakeshore, making them impossible targets for the cavalry and difficult ones for his infantry. They were, however, somewhat exposed to brigantine fire from the water—and in fact this area had a lagoon where most of the remaining Aztec war canoes were moored.

In the first days of August, worried about now-dwindling gunpowder stores and wondering how to conclude a siege that had now gone on for nearly three months, Cortés was approached by a man named Soltelo, a soldier who had served in

Italy under Gonzalo de Córdova. Soltelo claimed to be knowledgeable in the fabrication of war machines and suggested that Cortés manufacture a catapult with which they might bombard the final Aztec redoubt, thereby saving gunpowder and potentially subduing the enemy. At this point Cortés was willing to try anything, so he ordered Diego Hernández, a clever builder who had made wheeled carts back in Cempoala and then assisted Martín López with the brigantines, to construct the elaborate catapult.[19] He hoped that the machine could terrorize the Aztecs into submission.

After just a few days of construction, the catapult was ready and was brought to a specially manufactured launching platform on top of a pyramid, where they positioned it for dramatic firing. The war machine was a complete failure. The great stones they loaded into its sling fell out before they were launched, dropping inconsequentially to the ground below. Try as they might, the carpenters and shipbuilders could not make it work, and in the end Cortés ordered it dismantled and hidden. During construction Cortés and his captains had threatened the Aztecs, saying that this godlike machine (which the Aztecs themselves called "the Wooden Sling") would annihilate them all. He was embarrassed—even a bit sheepish—by the failure. "We were obliged," he admitted, "to conceal the failure of the catapult by saying that we had been moved by compassion to spare them."[20]

During the four days of the construction of the catapult, the Aztec populace had continued to suffer horrendous hardship of famine and dehydration, perishing in such great numbers that a stench rose in the air as the bodies of the unfortunate were piled in houses or thrown into the lake. Emaciated women and children huddled along the streets, gaunt and exhausted, unable to offer resistance.[21] And neither were the Aztec warriors any match for the better-fed and -watered Spaniards and their allies. During two days' fighting—which by now could really only be accurately described as slaughter— Cortés claimed to have killed and imprisoned more than fifty thousand people, warriors and women and children. The

Tlaxcalans annihilated with an ancient vengeance, a kind of hatred and vitriol that shocked even Cortés, who said of his allied killing machine, "No race, however savage, has ever practiced such fierce and unnatural cruelty as the natives of these parts."*22 But despite this claim of compassion (which rings as a bit disingenuous coming from the Butcher of Cholula), Cortés unquestionably benefited from the services of these allies he called "savages."

. Cortés made a few final attempts to meet with the Aztec emperor, who could clearly see that his empire was in its final days. But these parlays never materialized. Once Cortés was told that Cuauhtémoc wished to speak with him from across a canal, but at the appointed time Cortés was informed that the leader was too sick to come. Another rendezvous was planned to take place at the marketplace, but Cortés waited many hours and the emperor never showed up.23 The captain-general, weary of the siege and of these failed correspondences, had one final exchange with some emissaries of Cuauhtémoc. These Aztec generals gorged themselves on the Spaniards' food offerings, then left with food for their leader, which was presumably meant as a powerful enticement to a man ruling over a starving people. But still Cuauhtémoc refused to come, sending the generals back with only a pile of meager cotton garments. Despite their bitter famine, to the end the Aztecs refused to consume the flesh of their own people (the practice was reserved only for religious rituals); Bernal Díaz noted that "the Mexicans did not eat the flesh of their own people, only that of our men and our Tlascalan allies whom they had captured."24

The Spaniards had nothing left to do but continue the wholesale ransacking and guerrilla-style street fighting, and for these duties Cortés relied in great part on the enthusiastic

---

*The Spanish chroniclers are consistent in saying that twelve thousand people were killed or captured on one day, and a staggering forty thousand on another. Most of these people were unarmed or reduced to throwing stones.

Tlaxcalans. Cuauhtémoc could certainly see that the end was near; it was only a matter of how it would unfold. It must have pained him beyond words to see his once-proud people penned into the small quarter the survivors now occupied, the houses nearby smoldering rubble, others filled with the dead and the nearly dead. The air grew thick with obsidian-colored smoke, while the streets were riddled with crying children and wailing women beating their empty hands against what few walls remained.[25]

In a last-ditch effort to combat what appeared inevitable, Cuauhtémoc sent forth one of his greatest individual warriors, bedecking him in the feather garb of the Quetzal Owl, the armor and regalia of former Aztec ruler Ahuitzotl. He flew forth wielding obsidian-tipped spears and arrows, flanked by four attendants. His brilliant green quetzal feathers spanned out, making him seem larger than life. His plumage gleamed and shimmered as he leaped into battle. The Quetzal Owl warrior fought bravely, driving scores of enemies back through intimidation and power. He ascended a rooftop, fired arrows upon the invaders, then leaped from the roof and was gone.[26]

On the evening of August 12, 1521, according to Aztec sources, one last omen appeared. Perhaps it was finally the sign that the emperor Montezuma had been waiting for, come too late:

> At nightfall it began to rain ... Suddenly the omen appeared, blazing like a great bonfire in the sky. It wheeled in enormous spirals like a whirlwind and gave off a shower of sparks and red-hot coals ... It also made loud noises, rumbling and hissing like a metal tube placed over a fire. It hovered for awhile above Coyonacazco. From there it moved out into the middle of the lake where it suddenly disappeared. No one cried out when this omen came into view: the people knew what it meant and they watched in silence.[27]

The end of the Aztec empire was upon them. The wheeling blood-colored whirlwind came to be referred to as "the

Final Omen." In shock and terror the Aztecs realized that their civilization was—both literally and figuratively—being consumed by their enemy and by the lake itself. Their gods, it seemed, had forsaken them.

Cuauhtémoc had no intention of being taken alive, and after consulting with his priests, the next morning he agreed to flee the city by water rather than face certain annihilation.[28] Perhaps he believed he still had a chance to rally some kind of defense if allies could be summoned from across the water. Perhaps he even still clung to a kernel of faith in the oracle of Huitzilopochtli, which had predicted that the Aztecs would find salvation on the eightieth day of the siege, now in its seventy-fifth day. Cuauhtémoc was loaded into a war canoe along with Tetlepanquetzal, the king of Tacuba, another soldier, and a boatman. As quietly as they could, they paddled away from the smoking and flattened island capital.

From his rooftop tent, Cortés had planned what he hoped would be a combined final attack featuring multiple operations: cavalry, infantry, and a sustained naval bombardment. Cortés would direct land divisions under Alvarado and Olid, essentially herding any resistant Aztec forces backward through crumbling Tlatelolco to the very edge of the lake, where most civilians were already huddled. Sandoval would captain a brigantine launch and attack at the same place from the water, firing on any exposed or fleeing canoes in the lagoon and at the people onshore. Cortés instructed his captains and soldiers to find Cuauhtémoc and take him alive if at all possible, "for once that had been done the war would cease."[29] So on August 13, 1521—the day of St. Hippolytus, the patron saint of horses—the Spaniards marched and sailed and rode against the last vestiges of Aztec resistance, which was now little more than knots of emaciated warriors.

Though he had personally wrought this carnage with his sustained and skillful siege, Cortés could hardly believe what he witnessed. "The people of the city had to walk upon their dead while others swam or drowned in the waters of that wide lake where they had their canoes; indeed, so great was their suffering that it was beyond our understanding how they could endure it."[30] As the Spaniards approached, women and children poured forth from the mostly destroyed houses, fleeing in panic and despair. In the frantic press of humanity many were trampled while others attempted to escape into the lake, where many floundered and drowned. In the streets Cortés and his men and horses came across such numbers of dead that they had no choice but to walk over and upon them.

The brigantines encircled the reedy lagoon and engaged a small fleet of war canoes, but these showed no spirit for fighting, and as there were fewer than fifty of them and no match for the large Spanish boats, they gave up. One canoe was spotted escaping, its small crew paddling furiously, and a brigantine captain named Garci Holguín pursued it under sail and oar, ordering his crossbowmen to level on it and fire when in range. Seeing that they were aimed upon, the occupants of the canoe raised their hands and called out for the Spaniards not to shoot, for aboard the canoe was Cuauhtémoc, lord of the Aztecs.[31]

Garci Holguín was thrilled to have made the capture, but immediately Sandoval came alongside in a brigantine and, as he outranked Holguín, ordered that the prisoner be handed over for him to bring in. A vigorous argument ensued between the two, and Cortés demanded that Cuauhtémoc be brought before him immediately, without further discussion; he added that the emperor must be treated with respect and dignity and that no harm should come to him. Despite the two captains' entreaties, it was ultimately Cortés who took credit for the capture of Cuauhtémoc, adding the Aztec emperor to his escutcheon.[32] He prepared the rooftop canopy for the official meeting between conqueror and conquered, carpeting the terrace floor with crimson cloth and laying out opulent foodstuffs on tables, offerings befitting an emperor.

Cortés made sure that Malinche was at his side to translate. The emperor was brought before the captain-general, the Aztec king appearing wan and haggard. Bernal Díaz remembered that "Cuauhtémoc was very delicate, both in body and in features. His face was long but cheerful, and when his eyes dwelt on you they seemed more grave than gentle, and did not waver." He was anything but cheerful as he stood before his captor, gesturing toward the dagger at his waist. "Ah, captain," Cuauhtémoc is said to have implored, "I have already done everything in my power to defend my kingdom and free it from your hands. And since my fortune has not been favorable, take my life, which would be very just. And this will put an end to the Méxican Kingdom, since you have destroyed my city and killed my vassals."[33]

Cortés, through Malinche and Aguilar, offered some soft assurances, adding that he wished that Cuauhtémoc had surrendered earlier, for he could have avoided much bloodshed and destruction. Cortés suggested that the emperor should eat and rest, and later they could discuss the terms of the surrender of the city. At Cuauhtémoc's' request, Cortés had his wife — Montezuma's youngest daughter — brought to him, and they were quartered together and guarded. After the capture Cortés and most of his captains retired to their camps away from Tlatelolco, needing a respite from the stench of the dead, which rose from the streets in a foul, miasmatic vapor, causing them nausea and headaches.[34] The day of the city's capture would be documented as August 13, 1521. The war was officially over.

At the meeting the next day Cortés wasted little time before inquiring about the gold. The event had an initial air of formality to it: Cuauhtémoc was allowed to dress in ornate (if soiled) quetzal feathers, his remaining nobles beside him in flowery cloaks. But after very brief initial courtesies, Cortés got down to business, demanding the gold lost during La Noche Triste and the rest of the empire's treasure. Cuauhtémoc, apparently prepared for this question, had some of his nobles and priests bring forth various hidden stores with which they had attempted to escape in their canoes — there were golden banners and armbands and helmets and disks — but the amount hardly impressed Cortés. "Is this all the gold that was kept in Mexico?" Cortés demanded. "Get it all out, for it is all needed."[35] Cuauhtémoc and his men discussed things among themselves, suggesting that perhaps the rest was taken by common people, or hidden under the skirts of women, or thrown into the lake. Whatever the case, Cortés was halfheartedly ensured that any remaining gold would be sought after and, if found, brought before him.

Humbled, humiliated, and not even granted his wish to die, Cuauhtémoc now only asked that, as the conditions in his former city were so riddled with disease and famine, the people be allowed to leave, to depart the city for the healthier towns along the lake, where they might take refuge and begin to heal. Cortés consented to the request, figuring a general exodus would aid in commencing the much-needed purification of the city. Fires were lit to begin the burning of the dead, and the timbers and flames could be heard spitting and crackling, for there was no longer the sound of drums, or conch shells, or flutes. Now there was only the plaintive wailing of a defeated people as they began to come out of hiding, emaciated and dressed only in rags. According to Bernal Díaz, "For three whole days and nights they never ceased streaming out, and all three causeways were crowded with men, women, and children so thin, sallow, dirty, and stinking that it was pitiful to see them."[36]

Though they had been instructed not to harass or hinder the unfortunate Aztecs in their departure from the city, many Spanish soldiers, greedy for the lost gold, waylaid the destitute stragglers, violently body-searching them. They looked everywhere, including inside their noses, even within their genital cavities, hoping to find gold nuggets but often finding only jadestones or other gems.[37] In the end the Spanish captains and soldiers found very little, and they watched with pity as the ragged train of Aztec survivors staggered from their home of Tenochtitlán, sickly and expiring children carried on their fathers' backs, lank warriors bleeding and covered with wounds and weals, the famished women limping and forlorn. The healthiest and best-looking of the women and the younger men were culled out and branded on the face "with the King's iron"[38] and taken as slaves.

Cortés left Juan Rodríguez de Villafuerte in command of a force of some three hundred Spaniards to oversee the initial cleanup of the city, and then departed with the rest of his men for Coyoacán, where he planned to convene with all his forces from Tacuba and Tepeyac to celebrate with a victory banquet. Great stores of wine were sent for in Villa Rica, where another Spanish ship had recently arrived, and a bunch of pigs were herded from the eastern coast as well. On the evening of the party, so many people arrived that there was not enough room to seat everyone, so that only the captains and favored soldiers were seated at the tables. Some Spanish women had come recently from Cuba as well, and they, along with native slave and servant women, helped to prepare the feast. After seventy-five days of constant fighting, the Spaniards took their reveling seriously, and they drank flagons of wine as fast as it could be brought to them. Soon the makeshift banquet room was awash in screaming and disorder, with men dancing on the tables, fighting, and dragging women away to copulate in the wide open. According to a chronicler who was present, "So many discreditable things occurred, indeed, that it would have been better if the banquet had never been held."[39]

At sunrise the next morning, Cortés awoke with a throbbing hangover and apologized to Father Olmedo, promising to gather the debauched Spaniards for a proper mass, at which he and all of his men would kneel and pray and ask their God for forgiveness. Looking through the blood-orange haze that lay low across the lake waters, seeing the smoke from the funeral pyres curling like vaporous black serpents over the burning and demolished city, Cortés must have wondered if there existed enough forgiveness to accommodate what they had done.

The Shadows of Smoke

A *rain of darts falls on the earth*
Flowers of many hues wilt under the dark cloud
And the heavens in anguish bellow.

AZTEC POEM, CANTARES MEXICANOS

TENOCHTITLÁN, THE ONCE-GREAT CRADLE of the Aztec nation, smoldered for months. Cortés went about his business and administration, contemplating the implications of having finally taken the city for the crown, for his men, and perhaps above all for himself. He must have felt a great deal of personal pride at having stayed a course laid out a few years earlier, a course from which he had not turned back since the day he ordered the ships scuttled on the coast at Vera Cruz. It must have all seemed like some vaguely remembered dream. But if he may have mused romantically in his own mind, in his correspondence on his military and political achievement he was matter-of-fact, saying only, "On the day that Cuauhtémoc was captured and the city taken, we gathered up all the spoils we could find and returned to our camp, giving thanks to Our Lord for such a favor and the much desired victory which He had granted us."[1]

As it turned out, "the spoils" to which Cortés referred, the great hoard of Montezuma's treasure that he had hoped to uncover and on which he had staked his own life and those of his men, amounted to much less than they had dreamed of. While preparing for the expedition back in Cuba in early 1519, Cortés had lured many of his original fighting men with the promise of bounty, and he had sustained their spirits along the way—through defeat, near-death, and the death of their comrades in arms—with offers of great riches. Now, seeing his disgruntled and wounded men and under pressure from the king's treasurer Alderete, Cortés had Cuauhtémoc brought forth and demanded for the last time that more gold be produced.

The stoic emperor, bereft of all dignity, would say nothing, so officers ordered him to be tortured. (Cortés's personal involvement in the actual order is unclear.) Spaniards lashed the last emperor of the Aztecs to a pole, poured oil over his feet, and then lit them on fire. The flesh crackled and bubbled, yet still Cuauhtémoc would admit nothing of consequence—though he is said to have attempted to hang himself to avoid further torture and indignity. When the king of Tacuba was brought alongside and tortured in similar fashion, Cuauhtémoc eventually revealed that his deities had warned him of the impending fall of the city and that all remaining treasure should be thrown deep into the lake where the enemies could not pilfer it.[2] The severe torture left the king of Tacuba dead, and though Cortés himself eventually stopped the torture of Cuauhtémoc, the emperor's feet were so badly mangled that he limped for the remainder of his life. Cortés had him hanged from a pochote tree a few years later for allegedly orchestrating a rebellion and assassination attempt of Cortés during the late 1523 Honduras expedition. With him were also executed the lords Cohuanacoah of Texcoco and Tetlepanquetzal of Tacuba, finalizing the demise of the Triple Alliance, the formal triumvirate buttressing the Aztec empire.[*][3]

Cortés sent a team of divers to scour the lake bottom, but very little was recovered. Allied Tlaxcalans were allowed to

---

*Cuauhtémoc, the last (eleventh) emperor of the Aztecs, is revered in modern Mexico much more highly than is Montezuma. Cuauhtémoc remains a national hero, a symbol of resistance, of pride and honor, a leader who fought until the very end. Montezuma's legacy is much more complex, controversial, and enigmatic.

search and pillage the city for treasure, and many found small quantities of gold, precious stones, and iridescent tail-feather mantels of the quetzal bird. They seemed satisfied with the plunder and returned to their villages with stories of vanquishing their ancient enemies. Some even carried the dismembered limbs of slain Aztecs with them.[4]

But the Spanish soldiers were less than pleased with their paltry shares of the spoils. Searches around the palace ruins and ponds brought forth a few significant finds, including a great golden disk similar to the gift from Montezuma that Cortés had sent to Spain in the first "treasure ship," as well as a handsome jade head, but it was hardly enough to raise the value of their collective shares.[5] A general discord surfaced among common soldiers and officers alike, all of whom waited impatiently for the gold to be melted down, weighed, and distributed according to Spanish law. Unconfirmed rumors went around that Cortés had hidden an immense cache of personal plunder—a literal room filled with gold—which the captain-general would claim later.

There was in fact a remarkable (and except for the contents of the original treasure ship, unprecedented) array of jewels and finery, of a magnitude and quality never witnessed by Europeans before. According to Cortés's secretary López de Gomara, the king's fifth included

> shields of wickerwork covered with tiger skins and lined with feathers, with bosses and rims of gold; many pearls, some as large as hazelnuts...a fine emerald as large as the palm of one's hand, square, pointed like a pyramid...many coronets, earrings, finger rings, lip rings, and other jewels for men and women, and several idols and blowguns of gold and silver.[6]

Also included for the king's pleasure and fascination were giant bones discovered in Coyoacán, as well as three live jaguars, one of which broke loose from its cage while en route aboard the ship, scratching a half dozen men before leaping to its death overboard. A second jaguar escaped and had to be killed to avoid an identical fiasco. So in addition to the gold currency allotted in his royal fifth, the king was to receive plenty of curiosities and antiquities of the very kind that had tantalized him initially, enough that he had taken the first load in August 1520 on an exhibition tour in Brussels. These created quite a stir among the nobility, the aristocracy, and even among famed artists like the German Albrecht Dürer, who saw the display at the Brussels residence of the Holy Roman emperor and was absolutely awestruck. Dürer later recalled:

> I saw the things which have been brought to the King from the new land of gold, a sun of all gold a whole fathom broad, and a moon all of silver of the same size, also two rooms of the armor of the people there, with all manner of wondrous weapons, harness, spears, wonderful shields, extraordinary clothing, beds and all manner of wonderful objects of human use, much better worth seeing than prodigies...All the days of my life I have seen nothing that touches my heart so much as these things, for I saw amongst them wonderful works of art, and I marveled at the subtle ingenuity of men in foreign lands. Indeed I cannot express my feelings about what I saw there.[7]

In choosing these current treasures as part of the royal fifth, Cortés certainly hoped to further impress the king, from whom he still, at the time of the conquest, had no official sanction. But the immediate problem was how to appease his men, who clamored and grumbled for their shares.

Despite the opulent and majestic appearance of the treasure, the reality was grim, as the remaining tally had to be split many ways, starting with Cortés's own fifth. After the king and Cortés were paid, and a few under-the-table payments were made to special captains—men close to Cortés—there remained so little to distribute among the soldiers that the amount suggested came to an insulting 160 pesos per man, at a time when the cost of a crossbow alone, or a serviceable battle sword, was fifty or sixty pesos.

A few captains—Alvarado and Olid among them—suggested

that since the shares were so minuscule, they ought to be reserved for those who were "maimed and lame and blind, or had lost an eye or their hearing, and others who were crippled...or had been burnt by gunpowder."[8] An uproar began among the men, shouting and fighting, and mutiny appeared imminent. In the end, Cortés used the same powers of persuasion, diplomacy, and promises that had convinced these men to follow him so many times before. Pointing out the ruins of the capital, he reminded the men that they now possessed this land from which all the gold they sought had come, and they now controlled all the gold and silver mines as well. If they would only remain patient, true to Cortés and to their king, then each and every one of them would be granted their fair share—a plot of land and the laborers to work it. Eventually, as he had told them, they would all profit—it was only a matter of time.

To keep some men appeased—especially the captains—Cortés immediately planned expeditions of further conquest and settlement, the fruits of which (if successful) would ostensibly go straight into the captains' personal coffers. That was the promise, anyway. Pedro de Alvarado was sent west to the Pacific coast, while Cristóbal de Olid, sent to subdue intractable Tarascans, was stationed in the new vassal Michoacán. Gonzalo de Sandoval, Cortés's constant captain, was dispatched to the Gulf Coast, to found a town near Tuxtepec southeast of Vera Cruz. (Many loyal and trusted comrades-in-arms did in fact eventually receive generous payments from Cortés—in the form of *encomiendas*, which offered land, status, and material wealth—for Cortés had personally appropriated vast mineral holdings and armies of Indians to work the mines.)[*9]

---

*Cortés was initially against the *encomienda* system, which was essentially a euphemism for slavery in which a number of the conquered population (sometimes in the hundreds) were distributed as laborers to work the newly appropriated land of a designated landholder (conquistadors, primarily, and in the case of México, some high-ranking indigenous chiefs and officials who had converted to Christianity). In lieu of making cash payments to his officers, men who had fought gallantly beside him, Cortés could see no alternative but to offer *encomiendas* as payment for their years of services rendered. The first of these *encomiendas* were parceled out as early as April 1522.

The potential mutiny quelled, Cortés turned his attention to other pressing matters, including rebuilding a new México City where the great Tenochtitlán had stood for nearly two hundred years. Cortés's dream, such as it was, had been realized. He had taken Mexico—at the time the most populated city in the world—for Spain.[10] But the costs—still visible in the rubble of buildings and the exodus of a vanquished people—had been staggering. The most accurate accounts, estimated by native chroniclers in the years directly following the conquest, suggest that more than 200,000 Aztecs fell during the siege of Tenochtitlán, as well as 30,000 Tlaxcalans. Even by the most conservative estimates, the battle for the Aztec empire ranks, in terms of human life, as the costliest single battle in history.[11]

Bernal Díaz remembered the devastation that the Spaniards left in their wake, noting that word spread quickly to the distant provinces. People from afar made pilgrimages to see for themselves, to witness whether Tenochtitlán could really have been utterly razed to the ground. Some brought presents of tribute to Cortés, he recalled, while others simply held their children aloft in their arms, letting them behold the destroyed city, "pointing it out to them in much the same way that we would say: 'Here stood Troy.' "[12]

The Aztecs recalled the end of their city, the demise of their civilization, reflectively and poetically, their memories tinged with loss and futility:

> *Broken spears lie in the roads;*
> *we have torn our hair in grief.*
> *The houses are roofless now, and their walls*
> *are red with blood.*
>
> *Worms are swarming in the streets and plazas,*
> *And the walls are spattered with gore.*
> *The water has turned red, as if it were dyed,*
> *and when we drink it,*
> *it has the taste of brine.*

We have pounded our hands in despair
against the adobe walls,
for our inheritance, our city, is lost and dead.
The shields of our warriors were its defense,
but they could not save it.[13]

In addition to curious pilgrims, leaders and delegates from far-flung provinces, including the powerful province Michoacán directly to the west, came to pay tribute and confer their vassalage to Spain. This development pleased Cortés greatly, for he could now send a few scouts across these lands toward the so-called "Southern Sea" (actually, the Pacific Ocean), the presumed gateway to the Far East, to the Orient, and the route that he believed would lead to "islands rich in gold, pearls, precious stones and spices, and many wonderful and unknown things."[14]

Hernán Cortés, in fact if not legally, now ruled nearly all of Central America, a massive swath of land extending from Vera Cruz on the east coast all the way west, through the jungles and rain forests of the *tierra caliente*, across the volcanic scablands to the Pacific Ocean, and far south, effectively to the boundary of what is now Guatemala.[15] He controlled New Spain, much larger diplomatic and geographical holdings than the island governors of Cuba, Jamaica, and Hispaniola combined. But his self-proclaimed governorship would have to endure one more political threat before he would at last be legally vindicated.

That threat sailed into Villa Rica harbor in December 1521, in the form of two Spanish ships from Hispaniola, one of them bearing an inspector by the name of Cristóbal de Tapia. He came on behalf of Juan de Fonseca, the bishop of Burgos, and bore papers prepared in Spain authorizing him as governor of New Spain. Tapia presented his letters and papers to those in charge at Vera Cruz, but captains there instructed him to present his case (and himself) before Hernán Cortés, who was presently over the mountains in the high country at Coyoacán. Tapia immediately drafted a letter to Cortés, telling him that he came as governor of New Spain, in the king's name, and requested a meeting, either at Vera Cruz or in Coyoacán, whichever would be more convenient for Cortés.

Messengers had informed Cortés of Tapia's arrival long before the letter arrived, and Cortés had already launched into evasive and proactive political action. He knew Cristóbal de Tapia well from his years in Hispaniola and realized he must act decisively and immediately. He instantly dispatched Gonzalo de Sandoval to a small Totonac town on the Vera Cruz coast, instructing him to formally found a city there, complete with judges and representatives, and to name it Medellín (a nice touch, as this was the name of Cortés's hometown in Spain, as well as Sandoval's).[16] Cortés himself formed and officially founded the new municipality of Mexico City, of which he made Pedro de Alvarado *alcalde* and legal spokesperson. Cortés now had handpicked representatives of four complete municipalities, including the previously founded Villa Rica and Segura de la Frontera. Responding calmly and politely to Tapia's request for a meeting, Cortés then sent his henchmen to deal with the political threat in a meeting at Cempoala. His representatives were Cristóbal Corral, battle standard-bearer and now councilman of Segura de la Frontera; Pedro de Alvarado, new magistrate of Mexico City–Tenochtitlán; and Bernardino Vázquez de Tapia, councilman of Villa Rica de la Vera Cruz.[17]

Cortés's men met Cristóbal de Tapia on December 24, 1521, when the two sides presented their cases and their documents. Cortés had cleverly included a document that construed Tapia's arrival as a threat equal to that of Narváez (who was, incidentally, still a prisoner on the coast) and that pointed out that Cortés could not possibly abandon the capital region and its governorship, for fear of Aztec rebellion. (Tapia could not have known it at the time, but this claim was hardly genuine.) Cortés's delegation listened carefully to Tapia and read the papers with scrutiny, but after four days of deliberation they responded with a formal document denying Cristóbal de Tapia any authority in the region and even countering with claims against Diego Velázquez, Pánfilo de Narváez, and Tapia himself.

The unwanted inspector was offered some gold ingots for his trouble (and ostensibly in exchange for a few horses, one ship, and a few black slaves) and was told that he must return at once to Santo Domingo. Tapia dug in his heels for a few days and claimed he had become too sick to travel. Gonzalo de Sandoval then reportedly told him that he would personally send him home in a dugout canoe if the inspector failed to board the ship at once.[18] Tapia did as he was told. Through shrewd countermeasures Cortés had thwarted another serious political challenge to his power in New Spain.

Cortés, who had referred to Tenochtitlán as "the most beautiful thing in the world,"[19] determined to rebuild the fantastic city he had destroyed, adding that he "always wished the great city to be rebuilt because of its magnificence and marvelous position."[20] There was a strategic rationale for maintaining the location of the capital, for as Cortés had seen firsthand, the island city was extremely defensible. It is also likely that Cortés, in choosing to construct his own Spanish-style city directly on top of the former Aztec marvel, intended to overlay symbolic conquest and eradicate the Aztec monuments and all memory of them. The construction of Mexico City commenced in 1522, using labor from the few surviving Aztecs and Texcocan allies. Cortés enlisted chief architect Alonso García Bravo to draw up plans for the new city and Cortés moved back onto the island to personally oversee the project. Ironically, one of Montezuma's surviving sons, Don Pedro Montezuma, administered the reconstruction of a section of the city. Before long hundreds of thousands of residents from the Valley of Mexico were employed in the rebuilding project.[21]

Cortés, as if to add insult to injury and death, placed his own palace—complete with Castilian-style towers—directly on top of the former Palace of Montezuma. His Spanish architects erected Christian churches where the great Aztec temples and pyramids had formerly stood. The indigenous laborers from the valley and beyond could see the changes immediately. The orderly canals fell to disuse, replaced by new ones poorly placed or dug; the distribution of saline and fresh water, controlled by the elaborate dike system, languished, so that the waters grew brackish and gave off a foul odor; and the lakes began to evaporate and shrink. Native workers used, for the first time in their lives, wheeled tools—carts and wheelbarrows and pulleys—as well as draft animals, previously unknown to them.[22]

These were primarily physical changes and shifts; the spiritual alterations to the Aztec civilization would arrive soon, in the form of Dominican and mendicant friars (mostly from Hispaniola) charged with converting the natives to Christianity, a process that began in the years immediately following the conquest and that persisted for more than half a century.[23] This "conversion" was thorough and possessed a political underpinning, because even if some of the well-intended friars believed they were saving souls, they were in fact (unwittingly or not) annihilating a culture and spiritual system to pave the way for Spain's colonization in these newly conquered lands, and colonization required religious unification. In only one generation, virtually all vestiges of the Aztec religion—temples, idols, shrines, pyramids—were reduced to rubble and memory. Perhaps even more devastating to Aztec religious culture and thought, annihilated too were the keepers of the knowledge, the Aztec teachers and priests.[*24]

---

*Despite the quick and categorical extinction of religion, however, one important and marvelous irony resulted from the arrival and tenure of the friars—they essentially saved the Nahuatl language. Two highly educated and highly trained Franciscan friars—Andrés de Olmos and Alonso de Molina—spent decades working with remaining Nahuatl speakers of Mexico, first learning their language and then compiling magnificent (and massive) volumes of grammar, pronunciation, idiomatic expression, and vocabulary. Following them, Fray Bernardino de Sahagún and numerous Nahuatl speakers spent nearly forty years compiling a monumental volume—an encyclopedia—of every conceivable aspect of preconquest Nahua life. This archival text has come to be known as the Florentine Codex. See James Lockhart, *The Nahuas After the Conquest: A Social and Cultural History of the Indians of Central Mexico, Sixteenth Through Eighteenth Centuries* (Stanford, Calif., 1992), 5–6. Also see Ignacio Bernal, in Fray Diego Duran, *The History of the Indies of New Spain* (Norman, Okla., 1994), 565–77.

With the rebuilding of the city under way, in May 1522 Cortés completed the third of his letters to the emperor-king, in which he not only related the details of the siege and ultimate conquest of Tenochtitlán but also took pains to reconfirm his own legal position in the region, since he still had no official word from Spain regarding his activities for the past three years. He dispatched, along with a ship containing his letters and legal documents, another treasure ship containing the spoils won for Spain. In addition to the king's fifth of gold, which amounted to 37,000 pesos, he included a vast array of exotic marvels from the Americas: live animals, intricate masks with golden ears and precious stones for teeth, gold goblets, and place settings.[25] All was placed aboard ships that set sail on May 22, 1522. Aboard one was the king's treasurer, Julián de Alderete.

These treasure ships never made it to Spain. Somewhere beyond the Azores, near Cape St. Vincent, French pirates (having heard stories of the wonders coming from the Americas as a result of the exhibition in August 1520 in Brussels) led by corsair Jean Florin attacked, seized the ships and the treasure and caravels, and sailed them directly to France, where the booty (including over five hundred pounds of gold dust and seven hundred pounds of pearls) was delivered to King Francis I. Alderete died mysteriously en route, either from poisoning or from eating tainted food. Cortés's letters and correspondences (including a detailed inventory of the treasure) made it safely to Spain on a different ship, but unfortunately paper was all Charles V would receive of the second treasure, the prizes of Tenochtitlán lost to his arch-rival in France.[26]

At precisely the same time—May or June 1522—Malinche, still at Cortés's side and continuing her role of interpreter during the transition of power, bore him the son she had been carrying since the latter part of the conquest. Cortés named the child Martín, after his own father.[27] The palatial house in Coyoacán into which Martín was born included many women. There was Malinche, his mother, of course, but Cortés kept a number of other mistresses, both indigenous women and recently arrived Spanish women from the Indies. Ships now came regularly on the news of Cortés's victory. But it still would have come as a surprise to Cortés when, in August 1522, an exhausted messenger arrived, sent by Sandoval from the coast, saying that a ship had anchored, newly arrived from Cuba, bearing important passengers. Foremost among them was Catalina Suárez Marcaida de Cortés, Cortés's legal spouse.

Catalina (along with her brother Juan, who had previously fought alongside Cortés, and her sister) was transported across the mountains and given a regal entrance to her accommodations at the palace in Coyoacán. Cortés's reunion with Catalina, whom he had not seen for three years, turned out to be tragically star-crossed. Certainly the initial transition would have been awkward, including Catalina's first meeting with Malinche and the baby Martín Cortés that Malinche was nursing. Still, Catalina apparently reclaimed her marital position, and she and Cortés lived for a very brief time as husband and wife.[28]

Shortly after Catalina's arrival, Cortés held a large banquet, with drinking and dining and dancing. Apparently sometime during the party Cortés and Catalina engaged in a loud verbal spat, and Catalina stormed angrily off to bed. Cortés entertained his guests until quite late, then he too retired to his quarters. Sometime deep in the night he called on two of his chief confidants, Diego de Soto and Isidro Moreno, and reported to them the grim news. Catalina was dead. Doctors came immediately and reported that there were bruises about her neck, but they determined in the end that she had perished as the result of an asthmatic attack and a weak heart condition, perhaps triggered by the altitude and stress.

Cortés was accused—by Catalina's maids among others— of strangling his wife to death in a fit of rage. Cortés claimed (and his defenders backed him) that she had died of natural causes, and the bruises on her neck were the marks of his attempts to revive her after her attack. No formal criminal charges were brought against Cortés, though a litany of civil cases were, and his descendants were still paying damages to Catalina's descendants a century later. For Cortés, the tragic and unsavory episode eventually faded into whispers of rumor and speculation.[29]

Late the following year, in September 1523, Cortés finally received documents from the crown, signed by the king himself, officially naming Hernán Cortés captain-general of Mexico, *distributor* and chief justice of New Spain. Cortés had already been operating in those capacities since his arrival, but he was overjoyed by the royal sanction and could hardly contain his emotion when he wrote back to his ruler: "I kiss the Royal feet of Your Caesarean Majesty a hundred thousand times."[30] The verification provided Cortés, perhaps, the highlight of his life. For though he was later officially given the title of Marqués de Valle de Oaxaca and immense landholdings, bureaucracy and legal problems plagued him for the remainder of his life, and he was ultimately forbidden to rule the Mexico that he and his conquistador brethren and native allies had won. He spent much of his last years battling lawsuits and various *residencias*, his time divided between estates and palaces in Mexico and Spain.[31]

Hernán Cortés became immensely wealthy, though he never lost his adventurous spirit. He would go on to discover the peninsula of Baja California in 1536 and to survey the Gulf of California (later named the Sea of Cortés) that separates it from Mexico. Subsequent attempts at conquest in Honduras and Guatemala were failures, as was his last disastrous expedition in Algiers in 1541. Still, he was given a hero's welcome in Spain and was considered and referred to as the Gran Conquistador, the conqueror against whom all others would ultimately be measured. He was bestowed with many honors, even offered knighthood, which he declined although he had earned it. Cortés's expedition to and conquest of Mexico garnered the largest addition of land and treasure to the Spanish empire ever secured by a single individual. Knowing this, Cortés is said (according to Voltaire) to have once brashly remarked to the king, who did not recognize him, "I am the one who gave you more kingdoms than you had towns before."[32]

Despite the partial veracity of the boast, Cortés's final years were passed in relative obscurity. Planning to return once more to Mexico, he fell ill, quickly wrote his last will and testament, made his confession to a priest, and died on December 2, 1547, at the age of sixty-two.

Hernán Cortés left behind a considerable legacy, from off-spring to legends to lore, an entire mythology. He remains—like his arch-enemy Montezuma—enigmatic and misunderstood, sometimes revered, sometimes reviled, always controversial. People suggest that had Cortés not conquered Mexico, someone else surely would have. Given the devastating effects of smallpox on the indigenous population, that is probably true. But the argument misses the point. Hernán Cortés *did* conquer Mexico. Others tried and failed; most barely made it out of their ships; many did not escape alive.

An incredible confluence of circumstances occurred during the period of Cortés's expedition, 1519–21. Looked at through the hindsight of history, this confluence can scarcely be believed. Cortés could certainly not have succeeded in his mission without the brave assistance of hundreds of thousands of allied warriors, bearers, cooks, and workers. Had smallpox not laid to waste a large percentage of the Aztecs' fighting force, perhaps they could have held on.

But in the end it was Cortés, the consummate gambler, who staked great wagers and won. It was Cortés who scuttled his fleet to leave his men only one course of action—to proceed onward over the mountains and through the smoking volcanoes toward the ruling emperor Montezuma. It was Cortés who used guile and bravado and misinformation and politics to secure the indigenous armies necessary to march on the Aztec capital. It was Cortés who imprisoned Montezuma and who realized that his magical island city could be taken only by water. It was Cortés who imagined the building of the brigantines. It was Cortés who learned how to delegate power and authority over hand-selected captains and who wielded that power with the cutting sharpness of Toledo steel. It was Cortés who became, against the greatest odds, a supreme commander of allied forces, pitting Indians against Indians in civil war. For nearly three years he had operated independently, a free agent in a foreign land, with absolutely no justification or sanction from his government, either in the West Indies or across the Atlantic in Spain. In effect, he was a rogue, a rebel, a pirate. Arguments about his relative morality will persist: he was manipulative, duplicitous, and egomaniacal. He was barbarous in his own way, using his religious faith and convictions to justify brutalities including torture, branding, execution, unprovoked massacre, and slavery. But his military, tactical, and political genius remains unquestionable.

Hernán Cortés also left behind vast material wealth and numerous children, among whom was Martín Cortés, first son of the conquest.

The boy's mother, Malinche—or Doña Marina as the Spaniards referred to her—had stayed with Cortés from the moment she was gifted to him by a Tabascan chief in 1519 on the eastern shores of Mexico, through the fall of Tenochtitlán and into the aftermath. As interpreter, guide, and mistress, she had earned a status unprecedented among women of her time and place—some native people even looked upon her as a goddess. She remained close to Cortés after his wife's untimely death and accompanied him as personal interpreter and liaison on his ill-fated expedition to Honduras in 1524, a journey riddled with privation, disease, mutiny, and the death of all but one hundred of his men. During this arduous two-year campaign, at Cortés's urging, Malinche married Juan Jaramillo, a trusted soldier who had served honorably as one of the brigantine captains during the siege of Tenochtitlán. The wedding is said to have been conducted beneath the massive shadow of the looming Orizaba volcano. During this expedition Malinche was also temporarily reunited with her mother, the woman who had sold the young girl to slavery in the first place.[33]

Still she remained, until Cortés returned to Spain for the last time, his trusted interpreter and the mother of his first acknowledged child—the son later legitimized by papal decree and formally knighted. Malinche and Cortés, it can be said, gave birth to the first *mestizo*,[34] the first mixed-blood Mexican-European child. For many Mexicans, with a healthy mixture of controversial emotion, Hernán Cortés and Malinche are considered to this day the mother and father of modern Mexico, symbols of the new order and the new people who rose from the ashes of the fallen Aztec civilization.

Significant Participants in the Conquest

Aguilar, Jerónimo de (1489–1531?) Lost by shipwreck in 1511 during the Córdoba expedition, Aguilar lived as a slave among the Mayan people of the Yucatán until he was discovered and rescued by Hernán Cortés in 1519. He subsequently served as Cortés's interpreter, collaborating with Malinche once she became part of the expedition.

Ahuitzotl ("Water Mammal," "Otter") Eighth Aztec king, ruled 1486–1502.

Alvarado, Pedro de (1485–1541) Participated in the second (Grijalva, 1518) and third (Cortés, 1519) expeditions to Mexico. Impetuous and temperamental, as a captain Alvarado played a major role in the conquest, leading the controversial massacre at the Toxcatl festival. Known for his flaming reddish-blond beard and hair, the Tlaxcalans nicknamed him Tonatiuh, meaning "Sun."

Axayacatl ("Water Face") Sixth Aztec king, ruled 1468–81. Father of Montezuma Xocoyotl, or Montezuma the Younger (Montezuma II).

Barba, Pedro Trusted friend of Cortés who arrived in Mexico on a Narváez resupply ship. He became a captain and head of the crossbowmen during the conquest. He died from wounds suffered during the brigantine battle at the siege of Tenochtitlán.

Cacama King of Texcoco, nephew of Montezuma II (Montezuma Xocoyotl). Imprisoned by Cortés in 1520, he was slain by Spanish captains during the Aztec siege of the Palace of Axayacatl.

Charles V (1500–58) King of Spain, ruled 1516–56, and Holy Roman emperor, ruled 1519–56. It was to Charles V that Cortés wrote his five famous *Letters from Mexico*, explaining and justifying his actions during the expedition.

Coanacoch Brother of Ixtlilxochitl. He became king of Texcoco upon the death of Cacama and led the insurgency against Cortés and the Spaniards.

Córdoba, Francisco Hernández de (died 1517) Captained first expedition to Mexico (under aegis of Diego Velázquez, governor of Cuba) and "discovered" the Yucatán. He suffered fatal wounds during engagements at Champoton and died on his return to Cuba in 1517, still believing that Mexico was an island.

Cortés, Hernán (1485–1547) Ultimately considered the Gran Conquistador, Cortés was an Extremadurian from Medellín, born into a family of lesser nobility. He came to Hispaniola in 1504 and, with Diego Velázquez, conquered Cuba in 1511. He led the third expedition from the West Indies to Mexico in 1519, marching his troops (and Indian allies) from the east coast to the Valley of Mexico. His expedition resulted in the conquest of Mexico.

Cuauhtémoc ("Descending Eagle," died 1525) Son of Ahuitzotl, last (eleventh) Aztec king, ruled 1520–21. A symbol of pride and resistance in modern Mexico and a national hero, he was hanged by Cortés in 1525 for alleged conspiracy against the captain-general.

Cuitláhuac ("Excrement," died 1520) Tenth Aztec king, son of Axayacatl and brother of Montezuma II. He succeeded Montezuma II after his death and ruled for a mere eighty days before dying from smallpox in 1520.

Díaz del Castillo, Bernal (1495–1583) Conquistador and chronicler, he was a member of all three Mexico expeditions (Córdoba 1517, Grijalva 1518, Cortés 1519) and claims to have participated in 119 battles. He began his *True History of the Conquest of New Spain* in 1568 at age seventy-three.

Escalante, Juan de A participant in the Cortés expedition of 1519, he was in charge of the garrison at Villa Rica during the initial march inland to the Valley of Mexico by Cortés and his force.

Grijalva, Juan de (1489?–1527) Nephew of Diego Velázquez, he participated in the conquest of Cuba in 1511 and later led the second (1518) expedition to Mexico.

Ixtlilxochitl A vocal political enemy of Cacama, he became a significant ally of Cortés and ascended to the throne of Texcoco. He led the Texcocan allied army alongside Cortés in the siege and battle of Tenochtitlán, 1521.

Malinche (baptized and called Doña Marina by the Spaniards) A bilingual (Nahuatl and Maya) slave girl given to Cortés by Tabascans at Pontonchan, she became Cortés's chief interpreter, later his mistress, and eventually the mother of his son Martín Cortés. At Cortés's side throughout the conquest, Malinche translated and interpreted all major diplomatic and political negotiations, including the famous historical first conversations between Cortés and Montezuma.

Montezuma Xocoyotl (Montezuma the Younger, 1468?–1520) Son of Axayacatl and ninth Aztec king, ruled 1502–20, at the height of the Aztec empire. He was held captive by Cortés for many months during 1519–20 and ultimately died (either from wounds sustained by own people, or slain by Spanish captains) in 1520.

Narváez, Pánfilo de (1480?–1528) Captained the ill-fated expedition sent by Diego Velázquez, governor of Cuba, charged with capturing Cortés and bringing him back to Cuba. He arrived on the east coast of Mexico in April 1520, with a large force of men, horses, and arms. Cortés vacated Tenochtitlán in May, marched to the coast, and defeated Narváez quickly in a one-sided battle on May 28. During the rout Narváez was blinded in one eye. Narváez later led a disastrous expedition to Florida in 1528, in which he and nearly four hundred Spaniards died. That fatal journey was later chronicled by Alvar Nuñez Cabeza de Vaca, one of only four survivors.

Olid, Cristóbal de Conquistador and captain under Cortés during the third expedition to Mexico, 1519–21. He captained one of the three primary armies during the siege and battle of Tenochtitlán, 1521. He participated in the expedition to Honduras in 1524 and was executed as a rebel in 1525.

Sandoval, Gonzalo de Conquistador and trusted captain under Cortés during the conquest of Mexico, 1519–21. He captained one of the three primary armies in the siege and battle of Tenochtitlán, 1521. After the conquest Sandoval founded towns, squelched rebellions, and remained a constant confidant to Cortés.

Velázquez de Cuéllar, Diego (1465–1524) Initial patron and eventual nemesis of Hernán Cortés. He sailed with Christopher Columbus on his second voyage to the New World, 1493. First governor of Cuba, which he conquered (with Cortés then under him) in 1511. He sanctioned and helped finance the first three Mexico expeditions (Córdoba 1517, Grijalva 1518, Cortés 1519), as well as the disastrous Narváez expedition of 1520, with which he hoped to capture and arrest Cortés.

A Brief Chronology of the Conquest

1300 The Mexica (or Aztecs) settle in Anahuac, the Valley of Mexico.

1325 Tenochtitlán, the civic, religious, and tributary capital of the Aztec empire, is founded.

1492 Christopher Columbus makes landfall in the New World, the West Indies.

1493 Pope Alexander VI issues first papal bull (charter), granting Spain dominion over all lands, undiscovered or discovered, in the New World.

1502 Montezuma II becomes *tlatoani* ("he who speaks"), ninth Aztec king and supreme ruler of Tenochtitlán and the vast Aztec empire.

1511–14 Spaniards conquer Cuba. Diego Velázquez becomes first governor of Cuba and begins expansion plans, including Spanish-backed expeditions to the west, using Cuba as launching point.

1517 Cordóba mounts expedition to Mexico. He lands at Yucatán, is attacked at Campeche, is wounded, and returns to Cuba to die.

1518 Grijalva mounts expedition to Mexico. He lands at Cozumel, then on small islands off the coast of Vera Cruz, where he discovers pyramids and evidence of human sacrifice. He names this place the Isle of Sacrifices.

1519 Cortés mounts expedition to Mexico.

APRIL 21 Spaniards land at San Juan de Ulúa

JUNE 3 — They reach Cempoala; Cortés founds settlement of Villa Rica de la Vera Cruz.

JULY 26 Cortés sends treasure ship and letter to Spain; petitions the crown for recognition as separate colony.

AUGUST 16 Cortés departs Cempoala, heading west toward Montezuma and the Valley of Mexico.

SEPTEMBER 2–20 Spaniards battle the Tlaxcalans.

SEPTEMBER 23 Cortés and his forces enter the city of Tlaxcala.

OCTOBER 10–25 Cortés and his forces enter Cholula, commit the Massacre of Cholula.

NOVEMBER 8 Cortés enters Tenochtitlán and has historic first face-to-face meeting with Montezuma.

NOVEMBER 14 Cortés arrests Montezuma and takes him under his guard, effectively as hostage.

1520

APRIL 20 Pánfilo de Narváez, sent on a punitive expedition under Diego Velázquez to seize and imprison Cortés; lands at Vera Cruz. Charles V receives petition from Cortés.

MAY Cortés leaves Tenochtitlán to march on Narváez. Pedro de Alvarado and Spanish soldiers massacre thousands of Aztec nobles during the Festival of Toxcatl.

MAY 27–28 Cortés reaches Narváez camp at Cempoala, launches night attack, and defeats Narváez, one of whose eyes is stabbed out during the rout.

JUNE 24 Cortés and his men (including most of Narváez's men, horses, and weapons) return to Tenochtitlán.

JUNE 24–29 Spaniards are under siege in Tenochtitlán. Aztecs trap Spaniards in the Palace of Axayacatl. Cuitláhuac is chosen, in secret meetings, to replace the imprisoned Montezuma II as *tlatoani* and Aztec emperor.

JUNE 29 Montezuma is killed, likely from stones thrown by his own people.

JUNE 30 La Noche Triste. Cortés and the Spaniards flee Tenochtitlán at night. Hundreds die during the flight, and nearly all the treasure taken from Montezuma is lost.

JULY 2–10 Spaniards retreat toward Tlaxcala and the Battle of Otumba. Cortés is severely wounded—his skull is fractured and two fingers are mangled.

JULY 11 Spaniards arrive in Tlaxcala and receive welcome and protection.

SEPTEMBER 15 Cuitláhuac officially becomes tenth Aztec king.

OCTOBER–DECEMBER Smallpox plague, "the Great Rash," ravages Tenochtitlán and the Valley of Mexico.

DECEMBER 4 Cuitláhuac dies of smallpox after ruling just eighty days.

DECEMBER 28 Cortés initiates his reconquest of Tenochtitlán. The brigantine-building project is under way.

1521

FEBRUARY Cuauhtémoc becomes *tlatoani*, ruler of Tenochtitlán, the eleventh (and last) Aztec king.

FEBRUARY 18 Cortés arrives back in Texcoco. The brigantine and canal project is well advanced.

APRIL 28 Cortés officially launches brigantines at Lake Texcoco.

MAY 22 Battle for Tenochtitlán begins. Cortés directs a three-pronged naval and amphibious assault, using captains Sandoval, Alvarado, and Olid to lead ground forces.

LATE MAY Spaniards destroy the Chapultepec aqueduct, eliminating the city's freshwater supply.

JUNE 30–EARLY JULY Spaniards suffer heavy losses. More than seventy are captured and sacrificed alive at the Aztec temples.

AUGUST 1 Cuauhtémoc issues a bold proclamation, claiming that within eight days not a single Spaniard will be left alive. Spaniards fight their way to the market at Tlatelolco.

AUGUST 13 Cuauhtémoc is captured while escaping the city in a canoe. Cuauhtémoc is taken before Cortés, to whom he formerly surrenders after asking to be slain. The Aztecs surrender, and the siege and battle of Tenochtitlán ends. The Aztecs have been conquered.

A Note on Nahuatl Language Pronunciation

Nearly all Nahuatl words are accented on the next to last syllable.

Vowels take the usual English sounds: *a, e, i, o,* and *u*. Their corresponding sounds would be "ah," "eh," "ee," "oh," and "oo." The letter *u*, when preceding *a, e, i,* or *o*, is pronounced like the English *w*.

Consonants approximate English, except for the following:

> *x* and *ch* sound like the English *sh*
> *z* sounds like the English *s*
> *tl* has a single sound, as in the English word *atlas*. A Nahuatl example would be *atlatl*.
> *ts* and *tz* also have a single sound

Major Deities of the Aztec Pantheon[1]

Deities of War, Sacrifice, Death, and Blood

The deities in this group required human blood for life, as well as to perpetuate the existence of the earth and the sun. Blood was provided either through self-sacrifice (auto/personal sacrifice in the form of cutting
and piercing with obsidian blades or cactus spines) or through human
sacrifice of captured prisoners, primarily obtained in battle.

Huitzilopochtli "Hummingbird of South." God of war, sacrifice, and
sun. Patron of the Mexica Aztecs.

Mictlantecuhtli "Lord of Mictlan, Place of Death." God of the under-
world, death, and darkness.

Mixcoatl "Cloud Serpent." God of sacrifice, hunting, and war.

Tonatiuh "He Goes Shining Forth." God of the sun.

Deities of Creation, Creativity, and Divine Paternalism

Deities in this group are connected to the origins and creation of the
world and sources of life.

Ometeotl "Two God." Originator and creator-progenitor of the gods.

Tezcatlipoca "Smoking Mirror." God of omnipotent power (sometimes malevolent power). Patron of kings.

Xiuhtecuhtli "Turquoise Lord." God of fire and hearth.

Deities of Rain and Agricultural Fertility

The gods of fertility and rain were the most commonly worshipped of all the gods, revered by Aztec priests and common people alike.

Centeotl "Maize God." God of maize and its harvest.

Ometochtli "Two Rabbit." God of pulque, maguey, and fertility.

Teteoninnan "Mother of Gods." Goddess of earth and fertility. Patroness of curers, midwives, birth.

Xipe Totec "Our Lord with the Flayed Skin." God of agricultural fertility. Patron of goldsmiths.

Other Deities

Quetzalcoatl "Quetzal-Feathered Serpent," "Plumed Serpent." God of creation, fertility, wind. Patron of the priesthood.

Yacatecuhtli "Nose Lord." God of commerce. Patron of merchants.

The Aztec Kings[1]

Acamapichtli ("Reed-Fist") Ruled 1372–91. Founder of royal Aztec lineage.

Huitzilíhuitl ("Hummingbird Feather") Ruled 1391–1415. Son of Acamapichtli.

Chimalpopoca ("Smoking Shield") Ruled 1415–26. Son of Huitzilíhuitl.

Itzcóatl ("Obsidian Serpent") Ruled 1426–40. Son of Acamapichtli.

Montezuma I Ilhuicamina ("Angry Lord," "Pierces the Sky with an Arrow") Ruled 1440–68. Son of Huitzilíhuitl.

Axayacatl ("Water Mask" or "Water Face") Ruled 1468–81. Son of Montezuma I.

Tízoc ("Bled One") Ruled 1481–86. Brother of Axayacatl.

Ahuitzotl ("Water Animal") Ruled 1486–1502. Brother of Tízoc.

Montezuma Xocoyotl (or Xocoyotzin), Montezuma II ("Frowned like a Lord," "The Younger") Ruled 1502–20. Son of Axayacatl. Great-grandson of Montezuma I.

Cuitláhuac ("Excrement") Ruled only eighty days in 1520. Brother of Montezuma II.

Cuauhtémoc ("Descends like an Eagle") Ruled 1520–21. Son of Ahuitzotl.

NOTES

Introduction

1. Francisco López de Gómara, *Cortés: The Life of the Conqueror by His Secretary*, tr. and ed. Lesley Byrd Simpson (Berkeley and Los Angeles, Calif., 1964), 8.
2. Overviews of the early life of Hernán Cortés (for which there is significantly less information than for his later life) can be found in the following: Gómara, *Cortés*, 7–10; Hernán Cortés, *Letters from Mexico*, tr. and ed. Anthony Pagden (New Haven, Conn., 2001), xxxix–xliii; William H. Prescott, *History of the Conquest of Mexico* (New York, 2001), 170–73; and Dennis Wepman, *Hernán Cortés* (New York, 1986), 13–21.
3. Details of Montezuma's upbringing, education, and life as emperor are thoroughly treated in the excellent C. A. Burland, *Montezuma: Lord of the Aztecs* (New York, 1973), 41–61, 83–143. Also useful is Peter G. Tsouras, *Montezuma: Warlord of the Aztecs* (Washington, D.C., 2005), 3–33. A fascinating overview of the ruling and organizational structure of Aztec government is Susan D. Gillespie, *The Aztec Kings: The Construction of Rulership in Mexica History* (Tucson, Ariz., 1989). Also see Maurice Collis, *Cortés and Montezuma* (New York, 1954), 40–52. For the complex Aztec cosmovision, see David Carrasco and Eduardo Matos Moctezuma, *Moctezuma's Mexico: Visions of the Aztec World* (Boulder, Colo., 2003), 3–38. Also Jane S. Day, *Aztec: The World of Moctezuma* (Denver, Colo., 1992), 41–56.
4. Montezuma's self-deification, appearance, and behavior are described in R. C. Padden, *The Hummingbird and the Hawk* (Columbus, Ohio, 1967), 80–82, 165.
5. The cities of Texcoco and Tacuba have the frequently used alternative

spellings (and in the case of Tacuba, names) Tetzcoco and Tlaco-pan. A thorough treatment of the Triple Alliance is Pedro Carrasco, *The Tenochca Empire of Ancient Mexico: The Triple Alliance of Tenochtitlán, Tetzcoco, and Tlacopan* (Norman, Okla., 1999).

6. Tzvetan Todorov, *The Conquest of America* (New York, 1984), 4.
7. Cortés, *Letters*, 261–63, 491n. This large figure of over 200,000 includes death by smallpox. Burland, *Montezuma*, cites "a quarter of a million Aztecs died" (249–51). John Pohl and Charles M. Robinson III, *Aztecs and Conquistadors: The Spanish Invasion and the Collapse of the Aztec Empire* (Oxford, U.K., 2005), 150, and Charles C. Mann, *1491: New Revelations of the Americas Before Columbus* (New York, 2005), 129, both cite a more conservative estimate of 100,000 dead during the siege.
8. Richard Townsend, *The Aztecs* (London, 1992), 208.

Chapter 1

1. For the arrival on Cozumel, see Cortés, *Letters*, 11–17, and Bernal Díaz del Castillo, *The Conquest of New Spain*, trans. J. M. Cohen, (New York, 1963), 57–61. See also Prescott, *History*, 194–97; Hugh Thomas, *Conquest: Montezuma, Cortés, and the Fall of Old Mexico* (New York, 1993), 158–64; Richard Lee Marks, *Cortés: The Great Adventurer and the Fate of Aztec Mexico* (New York, 1993), 40–44.
2. Quoted in Thomas, *Conquest*, 158; Díaz, *New Spain*, trans. Cohen, 58.
3. Díaz, *New Spain*, trans. Cohen, 58.
4. C. Harvey Gardiner, *Naval Power in the Conquest of Mexico* (Austin, Tex., 1956), 17–21; Prescott, *History*, 191; Marks, *Cortés*, 42.
5. The muster is chronicled in Gómara, *Cortés*, 21–29; Díaz, *New Spain*, trans. Cohen, 58–59; and Marks, 41–42. For Spanish weaponry and armor, see Pohl and Robinson, *Aztecs and Conquistadors*, 33–50.
6. Gómara, *Cortés*, 28–29.
7. Andrés de Tapia, in *The Conquistadors*, ed. and trans. Patricia de Fuentes (New York, 1963), 20. Also in Díaz, *New Spain*, trans. Cohen, 61–62; Prescott, *History*, 195; Thomas, *Conquest*, 159; Marks, *Cortés*, 43.
8. Quoted in Díaz, *New Spain*, trans. Cohen, 62; also see Gómara, *Cortés*, 28–33.
9. The episode is chronicled by Cortés, *Letters*, 18; Díaz, *New*

Spain, trans. Cohen, 62; Gómara, *Cortés*, 28; Tapia, in Fuentes, *Conquistadors*, 21; Prescott, *History*, 197–98; Thomas, *Conquest*, 159–60; Marks, *Cortés*, 43–44.

10. Díaz, *New Spain*, trans. Cohen, 63.
11. Ibid., 59.
12. Tapia, in Fuentes, *Conquistadors*, 20; Gómara, *Cortés*, 30–31; Cortés, *Letters*, 17; Díaz, *New Spain*, trans. Cohen, 63–64.
13. The amazing saga of Aguilar and Guerrero is reported variously in Cortés, *Letters*, 17,19, 453n (an extensive note by Anthony Pagden); Gómara, *Cortés*, 28–32; Díaz, *New Spain*, trans. Cohen, 63–64; Peter O. Koch, *Aztecs, Conquistadors, and the Making of Mexican Culture* (North Carolina and London, 2006), 28–31; Hammond Innes, *The Conquistadors* (New York, 1969), 50–52.
14. Cortés, *Letters*, 17; Tapia, in Fuentes, *Conquistadors*, 21; Gómara, *Cortés*, 31–32; Díaz, *New Spain*, trans. Cohen, 64–65; Prescott, *History*, 199–200.

Chapter 2

1. Díaz, *New Spain*, trans. Cohen, 67.
2. This episode is recounted in numerous places, including a detailed account in John Grier Varner and Jeannette Johnson Varner, *Dogs of the Conquest* (Norman, Okla., 1983), 61–63.
3. Cortés, *Letters*, 19–20; Díaz, *New Spain*, trans. Cohen, 68–69, 68n; Gómara, *Cortés*, 40; Innes, *Conquistadors*, 50–51, map on 40–41.
4. Cortés, *Letters*, 19–20; the history of the *requerimiento* is fully explained in 453–454n. See also Díaz, *New Spain*, trans. Cohen, 69–70; Tapia, in Fuentes, *Conquistadors*, 22–23; Gómara, *Cortés*, 38–39; Prescott, *History*, 201–2.
5. Quoted in Díaz, *New Spain*, trans. Cohen, 71. Prescott's translation is "Strike at the chief!" Prescott, *History*, 202. See also Cortés, *Letters*, 21–22; Gómara, *Cortés*, 38–42.
6. Prescott, *History*, 203; Gómara, *Cortés*, 42; Díaz, *New Spain*, trans. Cohen, 71.
7. Díaz, *New Spain*, trans. Cohen, 71; Prescott, *History*, 203; Cortés, *Letters*, 19–20.
8. Díaz, *New Spain*, trans. Cohen, 70–71, 71n; Thomas, *Conquest*, 167; Prescott, *History*, 203–4; Marks, *Cortés*, 48–49.
9. Díaz, *New Spain*, trans. Cohen, 72; Prescott, *History*, 204; Salvadore

de Madariaga, *Hernán Cortés: Conqueror of Mexico* (Coral Gables, Fla., 1942), 114–15; John Eoghan Kelly, *Pedro de Alvarado: Conquistador* (Princeton, N.J., 1932), 11, 22.

10. Quoted in Díaz, *New Spain*, trans. Cohen, 72; Cortés, *Letters*, 20–21; Gómara, *Cortés*, 45–46.

11. Díaz, *New Spain*, trans. Cohen, 73–74; Prescott, *History*, 204–5; Gómara, *Cortés*, 45–47. Díaz claims there were 24,000 Tabascans, while Gómara says 40,000.

12. See R. B. Cunninghame Graham, *Horses of the Conquest* (Long Riders' Guild Press, 2004), 15–20. Also see Robert M. Denhardt, *The Horse of the Americas* (Norman, Okla., 1947), 5–11, 53–65. Also J. Frank Dobie, *The Mustangs* (Edison, N.J., 1934), 3–9, 21–24. For further reading on the history of the horse and its reintroduction to North America, see Sylvia Loch, *The Royal Horse of Europe* (London, 1986); and Paulo Gonzaga, *The History of the Horse*, vols. 1 and 2 (London, 2004).

13. For a discussion of Mexican armor and weaponry, see Pohl and Robinson, *Aztecs and Conquistadors*, 56–91. Díaz, *New Spain*, trans. Cohen, 75. Also of interest is Ross Hassig, *War and Society in Ancient Mesoamerica* (Berkeley, Calif., 1992), 135–64.

14. The Battle of Cintla, which took place on March 25, 1519, and its aftermath are recounted in Díaz, *New Spain*, trans. Cohen, 74–84; Gómara, *Cortés*, 45–47; Prescott, *History*, 206–8; Cortés, *Letters*, 20–22; Innes, *Conquistadors*, 51–55; Koch, *Aztecs*, 126–28; John Manchip White, *Cortés and the Downfall of the Aztec Empire* (Worcester and London, 1970), 167–69; and Thomas, *Conquest*, 169–70.

15. Díaz, *New Spain*, trans. Cohen, 76.

16. The ploy with the mare and stallion is recorded variously, including in Díaz, *New Spain*, trans. Cohen, 79–80; Innes, *Conquistadors*, 55; Madariaga, *Cortés*, 115–16.

17. Prescott, *History*, 209; Innes, *Conquistadors*, 55; Díaz, *New Spain*, 82.

18. Díaz, *New Spain*, trans. Cohen, 81–82; Gómara, *Cortés*, 56–58; Tapia, in Fuentes, *Conquistadors*, 24; Innes, *Conquistadors*, 55–56; Prescott, *History*, 213–15. Also see Matthew Restall, *Seven Myths of the Spanish Conquest* (Oxford, U.K., 2003), 77–99. For a fascinating study of the life and mythology surrounding the historical figure of Malinche, see Anna Lanyon, *Malinche's Conquest* (New South Wales, 1999). Also very interesting is Frances Karttunen, *Between Worlds: Interpreters, Guides, and Survivors* (New Brunswick, N.J., 1994), 1–23.

Finally, see Francis Karttunen's "Rethinking Malinche," in Susan Schroeder, Stephanie Wood, and Robert Haskett, *Indian Women of Early Mexico* (Norman, Okla., and London, 1997), 290–312.

Chapter 3

1. Díaz, *New Spain*, trans. Cohen, 88–90; Gómara, *Cortés*, 54–55; Cortés, *Letters*, 23–24; Prescott, *History*, 212–14; Thomas, *Conquest*, 175–76.
2. Though it is imprecise (actually pronounced something akin to "Mock-tey-coo-schoma," and commonly now spelled Motecuhzoma, I have opted for the more commonly used term Montezuma.
3. Díaz, *New Spain*, trans. Cohen, 89; Gómara, *Cortés*, 55; Cortés, *Letters*, 23; Koch, *Aztecs*, 130; Thomas, *Conquest*, 176.
4. Gómara, *Cortés*, 56; Thomas, *Conquest*, 176–77; Koch, *Aztecs*, 131.
5. Díaz, *New Spain*, trans. Cohen, 89–90; Gómara, *Cortés*, 56; Koch, *Aztecs*, 131; Marks, *Cortés*, 58.
6. Quoted in Díaz, *New Spain*, trans. Cohen, 90.
7. Ibid., 91. These "books" told the story of the people, and were similar to the ones made later, after the conquest, by friars, including Bernardino de Sahagún, which are now referred to as the "codices." The so-called Florentine Codex (also referred to as the Codice Florentino) was prepared by Dominican friar Bernadino de Sahagún under the title *The General History of the Things of New Spain*. Written over a time span of nearly forty years (approximately 1540–77), Sahagún's work was monumental in scope, translated from Nahuatl Indians who were present before, during, and after the conquest. The thirteen-volume work records all aspects of Aztec life and culture in one of the most remarkable and ambitious ethnological studies ever attempted. The English-language gold standard of this text is Bernardino de Sahugún, *The General History of the Things of New Spain*, 13 vols, trans. Charles E. Dibble and Arthur J. O. Anderson (Salt Lake City, 1950–82).
8. Sahagún quoted in Varner and Varner, *Dogs*, 61–63. Also Gómara, *Cortés*, 57; Díaz, *New Spain*, trans. Cohen, 91. The helmet reference is also in Inga Clendinnen, *Aztecs* (Cambridge, U.K., 1991), 268; and Koch, *Aztecs*, 131–32.
9. Díaz, *New Spain*, trans. Cohen, 94, 94n; Marks, *Cortés*, 58–59, 101; Thomas, *Conquest*, 177–79; Prescott, *History*, 604n. See also Innes, *Conquistadors*, 60.

10. Quoted in Gómara, *Cortés*, 58; Díaz, *New Spain*, trans. Cohen, 91–92; Koch, *Aztecs*, 131–32; Marks, *Cortés*, 58–61; Thomas, *Conquest*, 177–78; Prescott, *History*, 219–20.

11. Díaz, *New Spain*, trans. Cohen, 85–87; Gómara, *Cortés*, 56–58; Prescott, *History*, 214–15; Thomas, *Conquest*, 171–73. A fascinating and informative account of her life and role in the conquest of Mexico is Lanyon, *Malinche's Conquest*. Also of interest is Mary Louise Pratt, " 'Yo Soy La Malinche': Chicana Writers and the Poetics of Ethnonationalism," *Callaloo* 16:4 (1993), 859–73.

12. Some translations use the phrase "as big as a cartwheel." Díaz, *New Spain*, trans. Cohen, 93; Innes, *Conquistadors*, 60.

13. Díaz, *New Spain*, trans. Cohen, 93; Gómara, *Cortés*, 59. The itemized list of these gifts, in detail, appears in Cortés, *Letters*, 40–46; Koch, *Aztecs*, 149–51; Prescott, *History*, 230.

14. Quoted in Prescott, *History*, 232. Also a nearly identical quote in Díaz, *New Spain*, trans. Cohen, 94.

15. Díaz, *New Spain*, trans. Cohen, 94–95; Thomas, *Conquest*, 199; Prescott, *History*, 233; Koch, *Aztecs*, 151.

16. Miguel León-Portilla, *The Broken Spears: The Aztec Account of the Conquest of Mexico* (Boston, 1992), 30.

17. Ibid., 14–15.

18. For explanations of the complex calendar systems see Michael E. Smith, *The Aztecs* (Malden, Mass., 2003), 246–50; and Jacques Soustelle, *Daily Life of the Aztecs* (London, 1961), 109–11, 246–47. Also see the monumental work by Fray Diego Duran, *Book of Gods and Rites of the Ancient Calendar*, trans. and ed. Fernando Horcasitas and Doris Heyden (Norman, Okla., 1971).

19. The myth of Quetzalcoatl, including the argument that the myth was apocryphal, is discussed thoroughly in H. B. Nicholson, *Topiltzin Quetzalcoatl: The Once and Future Lord of the Toltecs* (Boulder, Colo., 2001). For this reference see especially 32–33. See also Carrasco and Moctezuma, *Moctezuma's Mexico* 143–47. Also very informative are David Carrasco, *Quetzalcoatl and the Irony of Empire* (Chicago, 1982), 30–32, 180–204; John Bierhorst, *Cantares Mexicanos* (Stanford, Calif., 1985), 479–80; James Lockhart, *We People Here: Nahuatl Accounts of the Conquest of Mexico*, vol. I (Berkeley, Calif., 1993), 18–22; Koch, *Conquistadors*, 103–4; Marks, *Cortés*, 74. Lyrical and highly readable is Rudolfo A. Anaya, *Lord of the Dawn: The Legend of Quetzalcoatl* (Albuquerque, N.M., 1987).

Also of interest is Gillespie, *Aztec Kings*, 123–72, 179–85. Finally, see Souselle, *Daily Life*.

20. Quoted in Díaz, *New Spain*, trans. Cohen, 95.
21. Ibid., 101–3; Gómara, *Cortés*, 65–69; Thomas, *Conquest*, 199–202; Prescott, *History*, 238–41; Koch, 151–52; Marks, *Cortés*, 65–66; Jorge Gurria Lacroix, *Itinerary of Hernán Cortés* (Mexico, 1973), 77.
22. Díaz, *New Spain*, trans. Cohen, 103–4; Prescott, *History*, 241; Marks, *Cortés*, 65.
23. Cortés, *Letters*, 30; Díaz, *New Spain*, trans. Cohen, 98; Prescott, *History*, 237; Koch, *Aztecs*, 153; Marks, *Cortés*, 68.
24. Prescott, *History*, 243.
25. Lacroix, *Itinerary*, 82.
26. Díaz, *New Spain*, trans. Cohen, 104; Prescott, *History*, 244; Pohl and Robinson, *Aztecs*, 103; Marks, *Cortés*, 68.
27. Díaz, *New Spain*, trans. Cohen, 107–8; Prescott, *History*, 249; Koch, *Conquistadors*, 154.
28. Díaz, *New Spain*, trans. Cohen, 108–10; Prescott, *History*, 247–49; Thomas, *Conquest*, 208–9; Koch, *Conquistadors*, 154. For further details on taxes paid the Aztecs by tribute states and cities, see Fray Diego Duran, *History of the Indies of New Spain* (Norman, Okla., 1994), 202–07. Also interesting is Ross Hassig, *Trade, Tribute, and Transportation: The Sixteenth Century Political Economy of the Valley of Mexico* (Norman, Okla., 1985), 103–10. Finally see Charles Gibson, "Structure of the Aztec Empire," *Handbook of Middle American Indians*, vol. 15 (1975), 322–400.
29. Díaz, *New Spain*, trans. Cohen, 110; Thomas, *Conquest*, 207–10; Koch, *Aztecs*, 154–55; Marks, *Cortés*, 73.

Chapter 4

1. Díaz, *New Spain*, trans. Cohen, 110–11; Tapia, in Fuentes, *Conquistadors*, 25; Gómara, *Cortés*, 76; Thomas, *Conquest*, 209; Lacroix, *Itinerary*, 85–86.
2. Díaz, *New Spain*, trans. Cohen, 111–13; Gómara, *Cortés*, 77–79; Ross Hassig, *Mexico and the Spanish Conquest* (Norman, Okla., 2006), 71–73.
3. Díaz, *New Spain*, trans. Cohen, 112–13; Gómara, *Cortés*, 77–79; Prescott, *History*, 250–51; Koch, *Aztecs*, 156–57.

4. Díaz, *New Spain*, trans. Cohen, 114.
5. Thomas, *Conquest*, 205–11; Hassig, *Mexico*, 73; Prescott, *History*, 239–40.
6. Díaz, *New Spain*, trans. Cohen, 116.
7. Ibid., 120–21; Prescott, *History*, 254–55; Koch, *Aztecs*, 157–58. There is confusion over the thief's name—some sources say Mora (Díaz), but more say Morla, which I have chosen.
8. Díaz, *New Spain*, trans. Cohen, 119–21; Gómara, *Cortés*, 82–83; Koch, *Aztecs*, 157–59; Pohl and Robinson, *Aztecs*, 103; Thomas, *Conquest*, 212–13. Duran, *Indies*, trans. Heyden, 283n, 524n, confirms the practice of prostitution.
9. Díaz, *New Spain*, trans. Cohen, 123; Prescott, *History*, 255–57.
10. Marks, *Cortés*, 78–79; Duran, *Indies*, trans. Heyden, 230, 486n. (Aztec priests also painted their bodies completely black).
11. Díaz, *New Spain*, trans. Cohen, 124–125; Prescott, *History*, 257–58; Thomas, *Conquest*, 213.
12. Díaz, *New Spain*, trans. Cohen, 123; Bernal Díaz del Castillo, *The Discovery and Conquest of Mexico, 1517–1521*, ed. and trans. A. P. Maudslay (New York, 1928), 163–65; Marks, *Cortés*, 78–79; Thomas, *Conquest*, 213–14.
13. Thomas, *Conquest*, 216–18; Innes, *Conquistadors*, 65.
14. Ibid., 220, 691n.
15. Díaz, *New Spain*, trans. Cohen, 126–27; Prescott, *History*, 258–59; Tapia, in Fuentes, *Conquistadors*, 28; Thomas, *Conquest*, 215; Hassig, *Mexico*, 76.
16. Quoted in Díaz, *New Spain*, trans. Cohen, 129; Gómara, *Cortés*, 89; Koch, *Aztecs*, 161; Lacroix, *Itinerary*, 88; Prescott, *History*, 264. Not all the punishments were carried out as originally specified by Cortés. He may have been bluffing, knowing he would need the men.
17. Díaz, *New Spain*, trans. Cohen, 130–31; Gómara, *Cortés*, 90–91; Gardiner, *Naval Power*, 28–32; Prescott, *History*, 266–68; Thomas, *Conquest*, 222–26; Koch, *Aztecs*, 162; Marks, *Cortés*, 85.
18. Quoted variously in Thomas, *Conquest*, 223. Also quoted in Michael Wood, *Conquistadors* (Berkeley, Calif., 2000), 48; and Paul Schneider, *Brutal Journey: The Epic Story of the First Crossing of North America* (New York, 2006), 115.

Chapter 5

1. Thomas, *Conquest*, 227. See also Mann, *1491*, 19, 222–23.
2. Pohl and Robinson, *Aztecs*, 43–45, 71–72.
3. Bernardino de Sahagún, *The Conquest of New Spain*, trans. and ed. Howard F. Cline and S. L. Cline (Salt Lake City, 1989), 73. Thomas, *Conquest*, 227. Varner and Varner, *Dogs*, 63–65. The numbers of the troops and the porters varies considerably among the sources, with Prescott citing a thousand porters; Thomas says 800, Díaz says 200, and Gómara 300. Similar discrepancies exist in the Spanish troop numbers, with 300 to 400 the average and most consistent.
4. Quoted in Prescott, *History*, 283; also see Thomas, *Conquest*, 228–29.
5. Prescott, *History*, 284. Duran, *Indies*, trans. Heyden, 10–11n, 207n.
6. Prescott, *History*, 243, 243n. See also Hubert Howe Bancroft, *History of Mexico* (New York, 1914), 232–33.
7. Díaz, *New Spain*, trans. Cohen, 135. Prescott, *History*, 285.
8. The itinerary of this fabled march toward Tlaxcala and Tenochtitlán is recorded in the following: Lacroix, *Itinerary*, 91–103; Díaz, *New Spain*, trans. Cohen, 134–39; Gómara, *Cortés*, 94–97; Prescott, *History*, 284–89; Thomas, *Conquest*, 232–34; Hassig, *Mexico*, 78; Madariaga, *Cortés*, 167–70.
9. Duran, *Indies*, trans. Heyden, 190; David Carrasco, *City of Sacrifice: The Aztec Empire and the Role of Violence in Civilization* (Boston, 1999), 75–76, 121–22; and Dirk R. Van Turenhout, *The Aztecs: New Perspectives* (Santa Barbara, Calif., 2005), 190. The Festival of Toxcatl is described in depth, with respect to the Aztecs in particular, in Chapter 12. Also see Clendinnen, *Aztecs*, 104–10.
10. Quoted in Beatrice Berler, *The Conquest of Mexico: A Modern Rendering of William Prescott's History* (San Antonio, Tex., 1998), 31.
11. Díaz, *New Spain*, trans. Cohen, 136; Gómara, *Cortés*, 96–97; Berler, *Conquest*, 31.
12. Berler, *Conquest*, 31; Soustelle, *Daily Life*, 155–57. Henry J. Bruman, *Alcohol in Ancient Mexico* (Salt Lake City, 2000), 61–82.
13. Díaz, *New Spain*, trans. Cohen, 137; Thomas, *Conquest*, 234–35; Gómara, *Cortés*, 95–96.
14. Koch, *Aztecs*, 165; Thomas, *Conquest*, 237; Lacroix, *Itinerary*, 103–6; Gómara, *Cortés*, 96–98; Díaz, *New Spain*, trans. Cohen, 138, 139.

15. Quoted in Díaz, *New Spain*, trans. Cohen, 141. Also quoted in Koch, *Aztecs*, 166.
16. Madariaga, *Cortés*, 173; Díaz, *New Spain*, trans. Cohen, 141.
17. The journey through the *tierra caliente* into the mountains and the battle with the Tlaxcalans are drawn from firsthand accounts in Gómara, *Cortés*, 100–23; and Díaz, *New Spain*, trans. Cohen, 140–65. Also see Prescott, *History*, 284–324; Berler, *Conquest*, 27–35; and Collis, *Cortés*, 78–95.
18. Ross Hassig, *Aztec Warfare* (Norman, Okla., 1988), 41–43. Hassig primarily describes Aztec practices here. According to the sources, the different tribes' face and body paint colors differed, as did their significance.
19. Ibid., 42. Also George C. Vaillant, *Aztecs of Mexico: Origin, Rise, and Fall of the Aztec Nation* (New York, 1941), 215–23.
20. Hassig, *Warfare*, 41–47. See also Pohl and Robinson, *Aztecs*, 61, 64–68.
21. Díaz, *New Spain*, trans. Cohen, 143–44; Prescott, *History*, 304; Marks, *Cortés*, 91–92; Koch, *Aztecs*, 166–67.
22. Koch, *Aztecs*, 167; Thomas, *Conquest*, 242.
23. Hassig, *Warfare*, 53, 89, 96; Hassig, *War and Society*, 152, 253n. Also Smith, *Aztecs*, 155.
24. Hassig, *Warfare*, 96.
25. Díaz, *New Spain*, trans. Cohen, 144; Gómara, *Cortés*, 100–3; Koch, *Aztecs*, 168; Pohl and Robinson, *Aztecs*, 106.
26. Quoted in Wood, *Conquistadors*, 49.
27. Quoted in Díaz, *New Spain*, trans. Cohen, 147; Koch, *Aztecs*, 170–71.
28. Quoted in Thomas, *Conquest*, 244.
29. Díaz, *New Spain*, trans. Cohen, 149.
30. The political alignment and structure of Tlaxcala is outlined in Charles Gibson, *Tlaxcala in the Sixteenth Century* (New Haven, Conn., 1952), 15–27. Also Marks, *Cortés*, 95–100.
31. Díaz, *New Spain*, trans. Cohen, 151.
32. Prescott, *History*, 321–22; Díaz, *New Spain*, trans. Cohen, 151–52; Marks, *Cortés*, 101–2; Berler, *Conquest*, 39–40.
33. Quoted in Díaz, *New Spain*, trans. Cohen, 161.
34. Díaz, *New Spain*, trans. Cohen, 163; Marks, *Cortés*, 99; Koch, *Aztecs*, 173.
35. The entire battle with the Tlaxcalans is recorded variously in Díaz,

New Spain, trans. Cohen, 140–65; Gómara, *Cortés*, 94–116; Prescott, *History*, 295–335; Thomas, *Conquest*, 227–250; Koch, *Aztecs*, 163–76; Marks, *Cortés*, 85–103. Also detailed and fascinating is Gibson, *Tlaxcala*, 15–27.

Chapter 6

1. Cortés, *Letters*, 67.
2. Díaz, *New Spain*, trans. Cohen, 180. The importance of this aqueduct is also noted in Duran, *Indies*, trans. Heyden, 66–68. Also see Van Tuerenhout, *Aztecs*, 42; and Smith, *Aztecs*, 69.
3. See Hassig, *Mexico*, 37–38, 43, 91; Smith, *Aztecs*, 171, 307n; Pohl and Robinson, *Aztecs*, 62–63. On Montezuma's comment, see Tapia, in Fuentes, *Conquistadors*, 33, 217n.
4. Charles S. Braden, *Religious Aspects in the Conquest of Mexico* (Durham, N.C., 1930), 100–02.
5. Ibid., 76–81.
6. There is some discrepancy as to the date. A number of sources (Koch, Thomas) cite October 12 rather than October 10.
7. For the importance of Quetzalcoatl and its relationship to Cholula, see Nicholson, *Topiltzin*, 93–95. Also see Neil Baldwin, *Legends of the Plumed Serpent: Biography of a Mexican God* (New York, 1998), 37–41.
8. Thomas, *Conquest*, 257; Marks, *Cortés*, 109–10.
9. Pohl and Robinson, *Aztecs*, 103, 108; Thomas, *Conquest*, 258; T. R. Fehrenbach, *Fire and Blood: A History of Mexico* (New York, 1995), 29–30. Anaya, in *Lord of the Dawn*, calls it the "largest single structure in the New World" (151).
10. Its close rival Teotihuacán had been abandoned, so now fewer people in total ventured there each year.
11. Cortés, *Letters*, 75.
12. Tapia, in Fuentes, *Conquistadors*, 34.
13. On the zoo animals, see Gómara, *Cortés*, 126; Thomas, *Conquest*, 259; Koch, *Aztecs*, 179–80.
14. Koch, *Aztecs*, 177, 179–80; Fehrenbach, *Fire*, 130. Note that the Spanish and Aztec versions of the "Massacre of Cholula" differ considerably. No mention of an Aztec plot exists in Aztec accounts, which claim that the massacre was entirely unprovoked. This seems

rather doubtful, though, given Cortés's genuine attempts, in all cases but Cholula, at diplomacy and confederacy rather than unprovoked attack. For a fascinating theoretical explanation devoted to the military and political rationale for the massacre, see Hassig, *Mexico*, 94–102.

15. Cortés, *Letters*, 73; Díaz, *New Spain*, trans. Cohen, 196–97; Gómara, *Cortés*, 126–27; Tapia, in Fuentes, *Conquistadors*, 34–35; Prescott, *History*, 356–58; Padden, *Hummingbird and Hawk*, 160–62; Thomas, *Conquest*, 260; Marks, *Cortés*, 111. Hassig, *Mexico*, argues that "Malinche's Discovery" is an elaborate justification for the massacre (97–98).

16. Diego Muñoz Camargo, from *Historia de Tlaxcala*, in León-Portilla, *Broken Spears*, 47–48.

17. Gómara, *Cortés*, 133; Thomas, *Conquest*, 264; Koch, *Aztecs*, 185–86.

18. The Massacre of Cholula is variously chronicled in Cortés, *Letters*, 73–74, 465–66n; Díaz, *New Spain*, trans. Cohen, 194–207; Gómara, *Cortés*, 126–34; Prescott, *History*, 361–74; Thomas, *Conquest*, 256–64; Pohl and Robinson, *Aztecs*, 108–9; Koch, *Aztecs*, 178–86; Marks, *Cortés*, 108–15; Burr Cartwright Brundage, *A Rain of Darts: The Mexica Aztecs* (Austin, Tex., and London, 1972), 258–63; and Padden, *Hummingbird and Hawk*, 158–62. For indigenous accounts and alternative interpretations of the events, see Tapia, in Fuentes, *Conquistadors*, 33–36; León-Portilla, *Broken Spears*, 47–49; Stuart B. Schwartz, *Victors and Vanquished: Spanish and Nahua Views of the Conquest of Mexico* (Boston and New York, 2000), 103, 114–19; Bernardino de Sahagún, *The War of Conquest: How It Was Waged Here in Mexico: The Aztecs' Own Story*, trans. Arthur J. O. Anderson and Charles E. Dibble (Salt Lake City, 1978), 23–24; Laurette Séjourné, *Burning Water: Thought and Religion in Ancient Mexico* (New York, 1956), 2. For revisionist approaches, see Restall, *Seven Myths*, 25, 112, 168n; Hassig, *Mexico*, 94–99; and Inga Clendinnen, "Fierce and Unnatural Cruelty," in *New World Encounters*, ed. Stephen Greenblatt (Berkeley, Calif., 1993), 12–47.

Chapter 7

1. Prescott, *History*, 376; Marks, *Cortés*, 115–16.

2. Nicholson, *Topiltzin*, 29–30; Thomas, *Conquest*, 267; Cortés, *Letters*, 77, 466n. The climb up Popocatépetl is recorded variously

in Prescott, *History*, 377–80; Pohl and Robinson, *Aztecs*, 109–11; Díaz, *New Spain*, trans. Cohen, 182–83 (though Díaz places the account in the wrong spot, while they are still in Cholula); Marks, *Cortés*, 116–17; Koch, *Aztecs*, 186–88; Thomas, *Conquest*, 265–68. The mountains are now locally (and affectionately) referred to as Popo and Izta. See also R. J. Secor, *Mexico's Volcanoes* (Seattle, Wash., 2001) and G. W. Heil, *Ecology and Man in Mexico's Central Volcanoes Area* (Dordrecht, Netherlands, 2003).

3. Cortés, *Letters*, 77–78; Díaz, *New Spain*, trans. Cohen, 182–83; Madariaga, *Cortés*, 218–21; Prescott, *History*, 376–79; Marks, *Cortés*, 117; Thomas, *Conquest*, 266.

4. Quoted in Thomas, *Conquest*, 266; Díaz, *New Spain*, trans. Cohen, 182.

5. Jean Descola, *The Conquistadors* (New York, 1957), 174–77.

6. Prescott, *History*, 381; Thomas, *Conquest*, 268; Koch, *Aztecs*, 189; Marks, *Cortés*, 119; Pohl and Robinson, *Aztecs*, 110–11.

7. Cortés, *Letters*, 80–81, 466n; Prescott, *History*, 383.

8. Codex Florentino, in León-Portilla, *Broken Spears*, 34.

9. Quoted in Thomas, *Conquest*, 269; Wood, *Conquistadors*, 52.

10. Díaz, *New Spain*, trans. Cohen, 213; Cortés, *Letters*, 81.

11. Cortés, *Letters*, 82.

12. Díaz, *New Spain*, trans. Cohen, 214.

13. Quoted in Wood, *Conquistadors*, 53.

14. Cortés, *Letters*, 83; Díaz, *New Spain*, trans. Cohen, 214; Gómara, *Cortés*, 137–38.

15. Díaz, *New Spain*, trans. Cohen, 216.

16. Hassig, *Mexico*, 152; Van Tuerenhout, *Aztecs*, 105–6; Hassig, *Trade, Tribute*, 47–53; Day, *Aztec*, 12–17; Vaillant, *Aztecs of Mexico*, 125–26.

17. Sahagún, *War of Conquest*, 23. Another translation is found in Lockhart, *We People Here*, vol. 1, 96–97.

18. Mann, *1491*, 112–33; Smith, *Aztecs*, 1–55; Townsend, *Aztecs*, 44–71; Marks, *Cortés*, 9–10.

19. Hassig, *Mexico*, 101–102, 213n. Also see John E. Kicza, *The Peoples and Civilizations of the Americas Before Contact* (Washington, D.C.), 22.

20. The historic meeting between Cortés and Montezuma is variously (and not altogether consistently) recorded. See Cortés, *Letters*, 84–85; Gómara, *Cortés*, 138–40; Díaz, *New Spain*, trans. Cohen, 216–19; Prescott, *History*, 395–96; Sahagún, *War of Conquest*, 68–9; León-Portillo, *Broken Spears*, 62–63; Tapia, in Fuentes, *Conquis-*

tadors, 38; Fray Drego Duran, *The Aztecs: The History of the Indies of New Spain,* trans. Doris Heyden and Fernando Horcasitas (New York, 1964), 289–93; Koch, *Aztecs,* 194–201; Marks, *Cortés,* 125–27; Restall, *Seven Myths,* 77–82; Pohl and Robinson, *Aztecs,* 114; Wood, *Conquistadors,* 56–64.

21. Cortés, *Letters,* 85; Díaz, *New Spain,* trans. Cohen, 219.
22. Brundage, *Rain of Darts,* 266; Koch, *Aztecs,* 195; Thomas, *Conquest,* 279.
23. León-Portillo, *Broken Spears,* 64–65; Sahagún, *War of Conquest,* 68–69. The conversations between Cortés and Montezuma are the subject of much interpretation and controversy. Interestingly, even the Aztec versions record language that suggests that Montezuma alluded to the Quetzalcoatl myth. For further analyses, see Wood, *Conquistadors,* 56–64; Thomas, *Conquest,* 280–85; Brundage, *Rain of Darts,* 266–69; Nicholson, *Topiltzin,* 85–87. Also compelling is Baldwin, *Legends,* 96–112.
24. Gómara, *Cortés,* 168; Koch, *Aztecs,* 196.
25. León-Portilla, *Broken Spears,* 66; Wood, *Conquistadors,* 57.
26. Quoted in Wood, *Conquistadors,* 61; Sahagún, *War of Conquest,* 33. Other Aztec versions of this speech, very similar in tenor and detail, include León-Portilla, *Broken Spears,* 64; Florentine Codex, 16. Some modern scholars, including Francis J. Brooks, are highly skeptical of the accuracy of the conversation, pointing out the unlikelihood of such clean communication and translation, especially considering the multiple languages involved and the circumstances of formal speeches. See Francis J. Brooks, "Motecuzoma Xocoyotl, Hernán Cortés, and Bernal Díaz del Castillo: The Construction of an Arrest," in *Hispanic American Historical Review* 75:2 (1995), 149–83.
27. Quoted in Wood, *Conquistadors,* 2. Similar version in Sahagún, *War of Conquest,* 34.
28. Thomas, *Conquest,* 285, Wood, *Conquistadors,* 64. The historically unprecedented meeting of the Spanish and Aztec empires and the various versions and interpretations of the initial discourse between Cortés and Montezuma are recorded in Díaz, *New Spain,* trans. Cohen, 220–26; Gómara, *Cortés,* 138–44; Tapia, in Fuentes, *Conquistadors,* 38–39; Prescott, *History,* 392–409; Berler, *Conquest,* 52–57; Innes, *Conquistadors,* 128–38; and Wood, *Conquistadors,* 56–62, 64. For Aztec accounts, see León-Portillo, 56–65. For interesting commentary on the Aztec calendar and this meeting, see

Brundage, *Rain of Darts*, 133–35. Gillespie, *Aztec Kings*, discusses the possibility that Cortés's references to Quetzalcoatl are apocryphal (179–185). Also compelling in dealing with the complexities of communication and miscommunication is Restall, *Seven Myths*, 77–82. Finally, for a fantastic and critical analysis of the rhetorical complexities of interpreting the discourse between Cortés and Montezuma, see Glen Carman, *Rhetorical Conquests: Cortés, Gómara, and Renaissance Imperialism* (West Lafayette, Ind., 2006), 113–71.

29. Quoted in Wood, *Conquistadors*, 64, and Thomas, *Conquest*, 285.

Chapter 8

1. Soustelle, *Daily Life*, 120–62. See also Smith, *Aztecs*, 135–46; Townsend, *Aztecs*, 156–91; Thomas, *Conquest*, 286.
2. Gómara, *Cortés*, 148–49; Díaz, *New Spain*, trans. Cohen, 221; Thomas, *Conquest*, 294–95; Prescott, *History*, 404. The skilled craftsmanship is also outlined in Vaillant, *Aztecs of Mexico*, 139–54.
3. Díaz, *New Spain*, trans. Cohen, 222; Prescott, *History*, 405–6.
4. Quoted in Díaz, *New Spain*, trans. Cohen, 223.
5. Smith, *Aztecs*, 220–21; Carrasco, *City of Sacrifice*, 66–87 and 196–97; Marks, *Cortés*, 131–33; Mann, *1491*, 120; Collis, *Cortés*, 47–49.
6. Cortés, *Letters*, 109–10; Díaz, *New Spain*, trans. Cohen, 225; Gómara, *Cortés*, 144, 148–49; Soustelle, *Daily Life*, 120–27; Mathilde Helly and Rémi Courgeon, *Montezuma and the Aztecs* (New York, 1996), 23; Van Tuerenhout, *Aztecs*, 247. The number of women ranges from 1,000 to 3,000. Collis, *Cortés*, 130–33.
7. Gómara, *Cortés*, 150–53; Díaz, *New Spain*, trans. Cohen, 228–29; Smith, *Aztecs*, 254–56.
8. Gómara, *Cortés*, 160–63; Prescott, *History*, 439–45; Thomas, *Conquest*, 297–98; Collis, *Cortés*, 131; Vaillant, *Aztecs of Mexico*, 234–38.
9. Cortés quoted in Gómara, *Cortés*, 162. The market is also described by Díaz, *New Spain*, trans. Cohen, 225–34. Also see Van Tuerenhout, *Aztecs*, 83–89; Smith, *Aztecs*, 106–110.
10. Gómara, *Cortés*, 161.
11. Ibid., 167. Arguments over the number of human sacrifice victims continue to this day, but there appears to be no doubt that the practice

took place on a very large scale in Tenochtitlán. Recent and ongoing archaeological work in Tenochtitlán and nearby Teotihuacán continues to add to the evidence. For a fascinating study, see Carrasco, *City of Sacrifice*, 2–3, 81–85. Also see Mann, *1491*, 120–21.

12. Carrasco, *City of Sacrifice*, 2–3. See also Roberta H. Markman and Peter T. Markman, *The Flayed God: The Mesoamerican Mythological Tradition* (San Francisco, 1992), 174–79, 206–7; Van Tuerenhout, *Aztecs*, 186–91.

13. *Codex Mendoza* (Fribourg, 1978), 113; Helly, and Courgeon, *Montezuma*, 45; S. Jeffery K. Wilkerson, "And Then They Were Sacrificed: The Ritual Ballgame of Northeastern Mesoamerica Through Time and Space," in Vernon L. Scarborough and David R. Wilcox, eds., *The Mesoamerican Ballgame* (Tucson, Ariz., 1991), 45; Soustelle, *Daily Life*, 22–23, 159–60. Finally see Theodore Stern, *The Rubber-Ball Games of the Americas* (New York, 1948), 46–74.

14. Díaz, *New Spain*, trans. Cohen, 234; Prescott, *History*, 445; Thomas, *Conquest*, 299–300.

15. Thomas, *Conquest*, 299. On ritual bloodletting and other autosacrifice of priests, see Carrasco, *City of Sacrifice*, 181, 185. Also see Cecilia Klein, "The Ideology of Autosacrifice at the Templo Mayor," in *The Aztec Templo Mayor*, ed. Elizabeth Boone (Washington, D.C., 1987), 293–395.

16. Díaz, *New Spain*, trans. Cohen, 234; Gómara, *Cortés*, 166–67. Duran quoted in Thomas, *Conquest*, 301; Prescott, *History*, 447–48.

17. Quoted in Díaz, *New Spain*, trans. Cohen, 237.

18. Quoted in Díaz, *New Spain*, trans. Cohen, 237; Miguel León-Portilla, *Aztec Thought and Culture: A Story of the Ancient Nahuatl Mind* (Norman, Okla., 1963), 162–63; Carrasco, *City of Sacrifice*, 3; Padden, *Hummingbird and Hawk*, 171–73.

Chapter 9

1. Díaz, *New Spain*, trans. Cohen, 242; also quoted in Prescott, *History*, 452.

2. León-Portillo, *Broken Spears*, 68.

3. Díaz, *New Spain*, trans. Cohen, 243–44; Prescott, *History*, 444–58; Gómara, *Cortés*, 176–78; Thomas, *Conquest*, 304–5.

4. Cortés, *Letters*, 88.

5. Quoted in Díaz, *New Spain*, trans. Cohen, 246.
6. Quoted in Thomas, *Conquest*, 306; Koch, *Aztecs*, 205; Díaz, *New Spain*, trans. Cohen, 246; Prescott, *History*, 460.
7. Quoted in Díaz, *New Spain*, trans. Cohen, 246. Also quoted in Prescott, *History*, 460–61.
8. Brooks, "Motecuzoma," 149–83. Brooks makes a concerted and fascinating (if at times far-reaching and highly speculative) case that the initial "arrest" of Montezuma by Cortés in November 1519 was more an elaborate "construction" than an actual arrest, arguing also that the actual imprisonment did not take place until April 1520. The entire sequence of the seizure is also recorded by Prescott, *History*, 456–68.
9. Brooks, "Motecuzoma," 149–57.
10. Gómara, *Cortés*, 176–77; Díaz, *New Spain*, trans. Cohen, 248.
11. Gómara, *Cortés*, 178–79; Díaz, *New Spain*, trans. Cohen, 249; Prescott, *History*, 464–65.
12. Díaz, *New Spain*, trans. Cohen, 249; Cortés, *Letters*, 90–91.
13. Díaz, *New Spain*, trans. Cohen, 249; Cortés, *Letters*, 91.

Chapter 10

1. Cortés, *Letters*, 91; Díaz, *New Spain*, trans. Cohen, 256–57; Prescott, *History*, 467–79.
2. Helly and Courgeon, *Montezuma*, 44; Scarborough and Wilcox, *Mesoamerican Ballgame* (Tucson, Ariz., 1991), vii; Smith, *Aztecs*, 232–33; Stern, *Rubber-ball Games*.
3. Díaz, *New Spain*, trans. Cohen, 252–53; Helly and Courgeon, *Montezuma*, 44; Prescott, *History*, 471.
4. Gardiner, *Naval Power*, 62–72; Díaz, *New Spain*, trans. Cohen, 251–52; Madariaga, *Cortés*, 264, 297; Innes, *Conquistadors*, 156.
5. Díaz, *New Spain*, trans. Cohen, 254–57; Prescott, *History*, 473–75; Thomas, *Conquest*, 314–15.
6. Cortés, *Letters*, 91.
7. Gardiner, *Naval Power*, 71.
8. Prescott, *History*, 393; Thomas, *Conquest*, 315, 711n (86). See Oscar Apenes, "The Primitive Salt Production of Lake Texcoco," *Thenos* 9, no. 1 (25–40), 1944. Also see Mark Kurlansky, *Salt: A World History* (New York, 2002), 202–4.

9. Cortés, *Letters*, 92–95; Gómara, *Cortés*, 179–82; Díaz, *New Spain*, trans. Cohen, 265–69.

10. Quoted in Díaz, *New Spain*, trans. Cohen, 268.

11. Cortés, *Letters*, 92–96. Díaz, *New Spain*, trans. Cohen, 265–69; Gómara, *Cortés*, 179–82; Thomas, *Conquest*, 318–20; Koch, *Aztecs*, 210.

12. Cortés, *Letters*, 96–98; Gómara, *Cortés*, 182–84; Díaz, *New Spain*, trans. Cohen, 257–64; Pohl and Robinson, *Aztecs*, 121, 125; Prescott, *History*, 476–79; Hassig, *Mexico*, 105–107.

13. Quoted in Díaz, *New Spain*, trans. Cohen, 264.

14. Díaz, *New Spain*, trans. Cohen, 264. The speech is also variously recorded in Gómara, *Cortés*, 184–86; Cortés, *Letters*, 98–99; Prescott, *History*, 480–82. Thomas, *Conquest*, 324–25, points out that though the precise wording of the speech has been questioned, there were at least six other conquistadors present who confirmed, under oath, the nature, tenor, and content of Montezuma's speech that day.

15. Cortés, *Letters*, 99–101; Gómara, *Cortés*, 186–87; Prescott, *History*, 482–84; Koch, *Aztecs*, 210–11.

16. Cortés, *Letters*, 99–101, 108–9. Also quoted in Thomas, *Conquest*, 303; Díaz, *New Spain*, trans. Cohen, 271–73; Prescott, *History*, 482–83; Innes, *Conquistadors*, 151–53; White, *Cortés*, 210–212.

17. Cortés, *Letters*, 100; Gómara, *Cortés*, 187; Díaz, *New Spain*, trans. Cohen, 272–73 (Díaz mentions the bribes or secret payments); Prescott, *History*, 484–88; Marks, *Cortés*, 148; Koch, *Aztecs*, 211.

18. Pohl and Robinson, *Aztecs*, 125; Thomas, *Conquest*, 327–28.

19. Díaz, *New Spain*, trans. Cohen, 276–77; Pohl and Robinson, *Aztecs*, 125–26; Thomas, *Conquest*, 328–29.

20. Pohl and Robinson, *Aztecs*, 126; Díaz, *New Spain*, trans. Cohen, 278–79.

21. Díaz, *New Spain*, trans. Cohen, 281; Gómara, *Cortés*, 192–93; Thomas, *Conquest*, 332–34; Prescott, *History*, 492–94; Pohl and Robinson, *Aztecs*, 126; Koch, *Aztecs*, 212–13.

Chapter 11

1. Díaz quoted in Thomas, *Conquest*, 358.

2. Hassig, *Mexico*, 107. See also Gardiner, *Naval Power*, 76–79.

3. Cortés quoted in Thomas, *Conquest*, 368, 723n; Kelly, *Alvarado*, 62–64.

4. Thomas, *Conquest*, 360–62; Innes, *Conquistadors*, 158. Marks, *Cortés*, 153–54; Kelly, *Alvarado*, 63–66.

5. Cortés, *Letters*, 118–22; Gómara, *Cortés*, 192–98; Díaz, *New Spain*, trans. Cohen, 281–83; Prescott, *History*, 494–503; C. Harvey Gardiner, *The Constant Captain: Gonzalo de Sandoval* (Carbondale, Ill., 1961), 37–42.

6. Gardiner, *Constant Captain*, 40–41; Thomas, *Conquest*, 366–67.

7. Gómara, *Cortés*, 196–97; Prescott, *History*, 501–2; Díaz, *New Spain*, trans. Cohen, 282; Collis, *Cortés*, 167; Innes, *Conquistadors*, 156–58.

8. Cortés, *Letters*, 114–16, 473n; Gardiner, *Constant Captain*, 41–44.

9. Paul Schneider, *Brutal Journey* (New York, 2006), 7–8.

10. Prescott, *History*, 509; Thomas, *Conquest*, 370.

11. Cortés, *Letters*, 122; Thomas, *Conquest*, 371; Díaz, *Discovery*, 366; Prescott, *History*, 510–11.

12. Prescott, *History*, 512.

13. Ibid., 510–15.

14. Cortés quoted ibid., 514. Also Cortés, *Letters*, 123–24.

15. Gómara, *Cortés*, 194–96; Cortés, *Letters*, 124–25; Díaz, *Discovery*, 375–76.

16. Quoted in Schneider, *Brutal*, 7.

17. Ibid., 8–9; Díaz, *Discovery*, 388 (citing the number as three thousand pesos); Gardiner, *Constant Captain*, 45.

18. Díaz, *Discovery*, 388–89; Gómara, *Cortés*, 198–200; Prescott, *History*, 516–18; Madariaga, *Cortés*, 316–18.

19. Quoted in Prescott, *History*, 518 and footnote 11.

20. Cortés, *Letters*, 125; Prescott, *History*, 518–19; Thomas, *Conquest*, 376–77.

21. Cortés, *Letters*, 125–26; Prescott, *History*, 519.

22. Díaz, *Discovery*, 390; Prescott, *History*, 519; Madariaga, *Cortés*, 317–18.

23. Gómara, *Cortés*, 203.

24. Díaz, *Discovery*, 391.

25. Schneider, *Brutal*, 10; Thomas, *Conquest*, 379.

26. Schneider, *Brutal*, 10–11; Thomas, *Conquest*, 379.

27. Díaz, *Discovery*, 390–93; Gómara, *Cortés*, 203–4; Cortés, *Letters*, 26–27; Prescott, *History*, 522–24.

28. Tapia, in Fuentes, *Conquistadors*, 47.

29. Thomas, *Conquest*, 381.

30. Díaz, *Discovery*, 392.

31. See Alvar Nuñez Cabeza de Vaca's chronicle of the Narváez expedition in the following: Alvar Nuñez Cabeza de Vaca, *Chronicle of the Narváez Expedition*, trans. Fanny Bandelier, rev. Horold Augenbraum (New York, 2002); John Upton Terrell, *Journey into Darkness* (New York, 1962); David A. Howard, *Conquistador in Chains: Cabeza de Vaca and the Indians of the Americas* (Tuscaloosa and London, 1997). Also see Schneider, *Brutal.*
32. Thomas, *Conquest*, 380–381; Prescott, *History*, 530–31. For troop numbers, see Hassig, *Mexico*, 111.

Chapter 12

1. Thomas, *Conquest*, 384, 727n (note 7).
2. The Feast of Toxcatl is described at length in Duran, *Book of the Gods*, chap. 4. See also Smith, *Aztecs*, 229–230; Guilhem Oliver, "The Hidden King and the Broken Flutes," in Eloise Quiñones Keber, *Representing Aztec Ritual: Performance, Text, and Image in the Work of Sahagún* (Boulder, Colo., 2002), 107–27. The Festival of Toxcatl and sacrifice of Tezcatlipoca are also discussed in detail in Carrasco, *City of Sacrifice*, 117–21, 126–29, 132–37. Carrasco points out that the final sacrifice of the *ixiptla* took place at the ceremonial center Chalco, fifteen miles south of Tenochtitlán. Also see Clendinnen, *Aztecs*, 104–10, 147–48.
3. Marks, *Cortés*, 162–63; Koch, *Aztecs*, 230.
4. Quoted in León-Portilla, *Broken Spears*, 72. The elaborate construction and dress of the statue of Huitzilopochtli during the Festival of Toxcatl is also found in Duran, *Book of the Gods*, chap. 4.
5. León-Portilla, *Broken Spears*, 72–73; Duran, *Book of the Gods*, chap. 4; Carrasco, *City of Sacrifice*, 129–33.
6. Thomas, *Conquest*, 385, 728n. On the matter of the torturing, Alvarado remains silent, though the tortures are recorded in the later *Residencia against Alvarado*, and by Juan Alvarez and Valzquez de Tapia. Koch, *Aztecs*, 231; Kelly, *Alvarado*, 238–40.
7. León-Portilla, *Broken Spears*, 74.
8. Descriptions of the ceremonial costumes appear in *Codex Mendoza*, (Fribourg 1978), 78–120; Gómara, *Cortés*, 206–7; Thomas, *Conquest*, 388, 728n; Koch, *Aztecs*, 231; Carrasco, *City of Sacrifice*, 132–35.
9. For an interesting discussion of synesthesia as it pertains to this ritual, see Carrasco, *City of Sacrifice*, 121–23, 157–58.
10. The command *"Mueran!"* is cited in the Codex Aubin and also

quoted in Thomas, *Conquest*, 389; Duran, *Indies*, trans. Heyden, 536–37.

11. Pohl and Robinson, *Aztecs*, 132.
12. Quoted in León-Portilla, *Broken Spears*, 76. Anthony Pagden, in his notes to Cortés, *Letters*, 477–78n, points out the difficulty in explaining either the rationale or the exact details of the massacre, so varied and conflicting are the sources. Many sources do concur that Alvarado heard rumors of a potential uprising, and what he saw on the streets further distressed him, propelling him into action. Hassig, *Mexico*, suggests that Cortés himself ordered the massacre (10), instructing Alvarado to perpetrate it in his absence, but this seems highly unlikely, with Cortés knowing how thinly stretched his forces would be and uncertain what would happen to him and his men in the battle with Narváez.
13. From the Codex Aubin, in Schwartz, *Victors*, 164.
14. Gómara, *Cortés*, 208; White, *Cortés*, 220.
15. León-Portilla, *Broken Spears*, 76–77. From Codex Ramirez and Codex Aubin. Also in Lockhart, *We People Here*, 132–36.
16. Marks, *Cortés*, 163; Hassig, *Mexico*, 109–11; Brundage, *Rain of Darts*, 273. Numbers of the slain range widely, from two thousand to ten thousand. Duran, *Indies*, trans. Heyden, 536–37, cites the larger number.
17. León-Portilla, *Broken Spears*, 77. The elaborate nature of funeral rites for fallen warriors is treated at length in Duran, *Indies*, trans. Heyden, 149–52, 283–90.
18. Padden, *Hummingbird and Hawk*, 196; Thomas, *Conquest*, 391, 729n, 790n; Camilo Polavieja, *Hernán Cortés, Copias de Documentos* (Seville, 1889), 280–81.
19. Quoted in León-Portilla, *Broken Spears*, 77–78; Lockhart, *We People Here*, 138.
20. Prescott, *History*, 540; Hassig, *Mexico*, 111, 215n; Thomas, *Conquest*, 392–93; Koch, *Aztecs*, 234.

Chapter 13

1. Díaz, *Discovery*, 398; Cortés, *Letters*, 475n. Thomas names the two captains of these expeditions as Velázquez de León and Rodrigo Rangel.
2. Prescott, *History*, 531–32; Susan Toby Evans, *Ancient Mexico and Central America* (New York, 2004), 45–61.

3. Hassig, *Mexico*, 111; Gardiner, *Constant Captain*, 46–48.

4. Cortés, *Letters*, 128.

5. Marks, *Cortés*, 165; Thomas, *Conquest*, 395.

6. Cortés, *Letters*, 128–29; Gardiner, *Constant Captain*, 48.

7. Clendinnen, *Aztecs*, 29–30; Alfonso Caso, *The Aztecs: People of the Sun* (Norman, Okla., 1958), 41–51.

8. Cortés, *Letters*, 130.

9. Díaz, *New Spain*, trans. Cohen, 285–86. Also in Díaz, *Discovery*, 402–4.

10. Quoted in Díaz, *New Spain*, trans. Cohen, 286; and in Díaz, *Discovery*, 404.

11. Thomas, *Conquest*, 396–97.

12. Quoted in Díaz, *New Spain*, trans. Cohen, 286, and Díaz, *Discovery*, 406.

13. Quoted in Díaz, *New Spain*, trans. Cohen, 287; Díaz, *Discovery*, 406; Innes, *Conquistadors*, 162–63.

14. Padden, *Hummingbird and Hawk*, 199; Brundage, *Rain of Darts*, 274.

15. Prescott, *History*, 542–43; Koch, *Aztecs*, 236.

16. Wood, *Conquistadors*, 73; Schwartz, *Victors*, 157; Brundage, *Rain of Darts*, 275; Prescott, *History*, 543. Hassig, *Mexico*, suggests that Cuitláhuac would not officially be anointed king until about September 15, 1520, but from this moment on (until his death) Cuitláhuac assumed the role of Aztec *tlatoani* or emperor.

17. Cortés, *Letters*, 130.

18. Ibid.; Prescott, *History*, 552.

19. Díaz, *Discovery*, 407; Cortés, *Letters*, 130.

20. Cortés, *Letters*, 130; Díaz, *New Spain*, trans. Cohen, 288; Hassig, *Mexico*, 112; Thomas, *Conquest*, 399.

21. Díaz, *Discovery*, 409.

22. Cortés, *Letters*, 131.

23. Koch, *Aztecs*, 241.

24. Cortés, *Letters*, 132; Díaz, *New Spain*, trans. Cohen, 290; Prescott, *History*, 573–74; Jose López-Portillo, *They Are Coming: The Conquest of Mexico*, trans. Beatrice Berler (Denton, Tex., 1992), 257–58; Hassig, *Mexico*, 112.

25. Prescott, *History*, 574–75; Marks, *Cortés*, 167; López-Portillo, *They Are Coming*, 258.

26. Quoted in Díaz, *New Spain*, trans. Cohen, 293. Also in Díaz,

Discovery, 415; Gómara, *Cortés*, 212; Prescott, *History*, 561. Cortés, *Letters*, claims that Montezuma asked him if he could speak to the people (132), but this sounds unlikely, given the circumstances. Even his first biographer, Gómara, who wrote much of the history from Cortés's and the Spaniards' point of view, says that "Cortés begged Montezuma to go up on the roof and command his men to cease fighting and go away." Gómara, *Cortés*, 212.

27. Quoted in Prescott, *History*, 561.
28. Quoted in Díaz, *Discovery*, 415; Díaz, *New Spain*, trans. Cohen, 293.
29. Quoted in Thomas, *Conquest*, 402.
30. Cortés, *Letters*, 132; Díaz, *New Spain*, trans. Cohen, 294; Gómara, *Cortés*, 212; Burland, *Montezuma*, 231–33; Tsouras, *Montezuma*, 80–85. There are two distinct and opposite versions of Montezuma's death, as described in the footnote on page 182 of this text. Nearly all the Spanish chroniclers are consistent in supporting Cortés's story that Montezuma was stoned on the roof and died from his wounds. Both Bernal Díaz and Vázquez de Tapia, who were present, agree that the emperor had been shielded, and that likely the Aztecs below did not recognize Montezuma and were hurling stones at the Spanish soldiers. Díaz (in *New Spain*, trans. Cohen, 294; and *Discovery*, 416) asserts that Montezuma refused food and medical help and succumbed to his wounds. The chronicler Antonio de Herrera supports this version. Bernal Díaz claims that he, Cortés, and many of the other soldiers wept at Montezuma's passing, adding that "there was no man among us who knew him and was intimate with him who did not bemoan him as though he were our own father" (*Discovery*, 416). While such sentiment certainly smacks of exaggeration, they had spent over half a year in intimate contact with the ruler, and it is reasonable to assume that they had developed an affinity for him. Of all the Spanish versions, that of Díaz sounds the most credible. See also Cortés, *Letters*, 475–76n.

The Aztec accounts almost universally suggest that Montezuma survived the stoning, recovered briefly, and was stabbed to death (or alternately garrotted) just before the Spaniards fled on La Noche Triste. Duran, *Indies*, trans. Heyden, claims that Montezuma was discovered, stabbed to death five times in the chest (545). A few other native accounts support the stabbing version: both the Codex Ramirez and Ixtlilxochitl claim that Montezuma was stabbed or impaled by swords. Fray Bernardino de Sahagún posits the garrotting account. Thomas, *Conquest*, calls the Aztec version of the murder by the conquistadors "improbable" (404).

Equal mystery and controversy surround the fate of Montezuma's body. Cortés claims, "I told two of the Indians who were captive to carry him out on their shoulders to the people. What they did with him I do not know; only that the war did not stop because of it, but grew more fierce and pitiless each day." Cortés, *Letters*, 132. Díaz, writing many years after the conquest and without much of a political ax to grind, supports Cortés, saying, "Cortés ordered six Mexicans, all important men... to carry him out on their shoulders and hand him over to the Mexican captains." Díaz, *New Spain*, trans. Cohen, 295.

Aztec accounts argue that Montezuma's body was found, alongside the slain bodies of Cacama and Itzquauhtzin (who were, in fact, executed—the Spaniards do not deny this), deposited outside the palace near a canal at a place known as Teoayoc. All were subsequently cremated. See Sahagún in Schwartz, *Victors*, 177–78; López-Portillo, *They Are Coming*, 260; Cortés, *Letters*, 478n.

31. Quoted in Brundage, *Rain of Darts*, 276. For more on the enigmatic Montezuma II's death, see Duran, *Indies*, trans. Heyden, 544–45. For comprehensive studies of his life and rule, see Burland, *Montezuma*; and Tsouras, *Montezuma*.

Chapter 14

1. Sahagún, *Conquest of New Spain*, 82. Cortés, Gómara, and Díaz all state that they stormed the Great Temple, but the closer proximity of the Temple of Yopico and its direct overview of the Palace of Axayacatl, and therefore its use as a command post, makes it the much more likely candidate.

2. Cortés, *Letters*, 133.

3. Ibid., 133–34; Thomas, *Conquest*, 403, 731n.

4. Díaz, *Discovery*, 413.

5. Cortés, *Letters*, 134–35.

6. Díaz, *New Spain*, trans. Cohen, 297; Gómara, *Cortés*, 219.

7. Cortés, *Letters*, 137–38; Díaz, *Discovery*, 420; López-Portillo, *They Are Coming*, 263–64.

8. Quoted in Prescott, *History*, 588, 588n.

9. Díaz, *Discovery*, 421.

10. Gómara, *Cortés*, 220; Prescott, *History*, 589; López-Portillo, *They Are Coming*, 263.
11. Cortés, *Letters*, 138; Gómara, *Cortés*, 220.
12. Florentine Codex, xii, 24; Camargo, *Tlaxcola*, 220; León-Portilla, *Broken Spears*, 84–85. Cortés, *Letters*, mentions that before he reached the second gap in the causeway guards raised a shout, sending Aztec troops in pursuit (138).
13. Quoted in León-Portilla, *Broken Spears*, 85.
14. Nigel Davies, *The Aztecs* (New York, 1974), 269–70; Díaz, *New Spain*, trans. Cohen, 297–99.
15. Díaz, *New Spain*, trans. Cohen, 298–99.
16. León-Portilla, *Broken Spears*, 85–87.
17. Gómara, *Cortés*, 220–21; Díaz, *New Spain*, trans. Cohen, 300; Marks, *Cortés*, 171.
18. Pohl and Robinson, *Aztecs*, 139. The number of lost varies among sources. See the table provided in Prescott, *History*, 600. See also Gardiner, *Naval Power*, 86–88. Hassig, *Mexico*, offers an interesting speculative conspiracy theory, suggesting that Cortés actually intentionally left the Narváez men in the rear, since they had proved ineffectual soldiers and were expendable (116–17). While Cortés was clearly unimpressed by the performance of his Narváez conscripts, it seems implausible that he would intentionally sacrifice nearly one-third of his Spanish fighting force, whose weapons, armor, and manpower he would also lose. Hassig makes the case that the lone woman on the causeway who cried for help seems unlikely, since she would hardly be drawing water there, as claimed, in the middle of the night. Many other accounts (including Cortés, *Letters*, 138) make no mention of the woman, saying only that guards "raised a shout."
19. Gómara, *Cortés*, 221; López-Portillo, *They Are Coming*, 268. The tree is among the longest-living in the world, averaging about five hundred years, but some in Oaxaca are as old as two thousand years.
20. Díaz, *New Spain*, trans. Cohen, 301.
21. Kelly, *Alvarado*, 90, 94; Innes, *Conquistdors*, 175; Prescott, *History*, 596–97.
22. Quoted in Thomas, *Conquest*, 412, 735n; Gardiner, *Naval Conquest*, 89; C. Harvey Gardiner, *Martín López: Conquistador Citizen of Mexico* (Lexington, Mass., 1958), 35.
23. León-Portilla, *Broken Spears*, 88; López-Portillo, *They Are Coming*, 269.
24. León-Portilla, *Broken Spears*, 88; Lockhart, *We People Here*, 160.
25. López-Portilla, *They Are Coming*, 269.

26. Ibid., 270. Lockhart, *We People Here*, 156–60, from Book 12 of the Florentine Codex.

27. López-Portillo, *They Are Coming*, 270; Carrasco, *City of Sacrifice*, 23, 83–84. Carrasco describes the importance of prisoners as sacrificial victims as well as the symbolic significance of skulls and skull racks.

28. Carrasco, *City of Sacrifice*, 164–87. Carrasco's chapter "Cosmic Jaws" offers a truly fascinating interpretation of the mythological and cosmological bases for cannibalism prevalent in Aztec religious ceremony, pointing out the preponderance of "jaws, mouths, tongues, eating gestures, and the rituals of using the mouth to eat human beings and, in the case of at least one god, the sins of human beings" (168).

29. Cortés, *Letters*, 140; Gómara, *Cortés*, 222–23; López-Portillo, *They Are Coming*, 270; Prescott, *History*, 597–98.

30. Cortés, *Letters*, 140; Gómara, *Cortés*, 223.

31. Carrasco, *City of Sacrifice*, 71, 76–77; Keber, *Representing Aztec Ritual*, 57, 59, 100, 120; Gillespie, *Aztec Kings*, 203; David Carrasco and Edwardo Matos Moctezuma, *Moctezuma's Mexico: Visions of the Aztec World* (Boulder, Colo., 2003), 62, 156; Thomas, *Conquest*, 29.

32. Cortés, *Letters*, 141; Gómara, *Cortés*, 224.

33. Quoted in López-Portillo, *They Are Coming*, 271; Duran, *Indies*, trans. Heyden, 305–6. The importance of Cihuacoatl (Snake or Serpent Woman) is dealt with in detail in Duran, *Book of the Gods*, 210–20. For a strong and detailed description of the military garb worn by accomplished and elite Aztec warriors, see Hassig, *Aztec Warfare*, 37–47.

34. Cortés, *Letters*, 142.

35. Quoted in Díaz, *Discovery*, 427.

36. Cortés, *Letters*, 142.

37. Kelly, *Alvarado*, 24–25, 95–98, 117–118n; Collis, *Cortés*, 202–3.

38. Hassig, *Mexico*, 119.

39. Díaz, *New Spain*, trans. Cohen, 304.

40. Ibid.; Prescott, *History*, 616; Vaillant, *Aztecs of Mexico*, 253–54.

41. Anonymous Conqueror, in Fuentes, *Conquistadors*, 168; Hassig, *Aztec Warfare*, 58; Pohl and Robinson, *Aztecs*, 141; López-Portillo, *They Are Coming*, 271–73.

42. Cortés, *Letters*, 144, 480n. Prescott, *History*, 622 and footnote. In his letter to the king Cortés claimed to have lost two fingers in the battle,

but other chroniclers say that while his hand was "maimed," he retained all digits. As for his head injuries, we have physical evidence: Cortés's skull (along with the rest of his skeleton) is archived in the Hospital de Jesús in Mexico City, discovered there in a crypt by archaeologists in 1946, along with legal documents confirming that the bones were his. The skull bears severe fractures on the left side, consistent with his own claims and those of other chroniclers. See Cortés, *Letters*, 144, 480n; Marks, *Cortés*, 175–76.

Chapter 15

1. Prescott, *History*, 622; Marks, *Cortés*, 187.
2. Díaz, *Discovery*, 433.
3. Sahagún, in *Conquest of New Spain*, 101; Díaz, *Discovery*, 434–35; López-Portillo, *They Are Coming*, 276–77;
4. Quoted in Prescott, *History*, 621.
5. Hassig, *Mexico*, 122. Gibson, *Tlaxcala*, 159–60.
6. Thomas, *Conquest*, 428, 737n; Marks, *Cortés*, 188. Gibson, *Tlaxcala*, 10, 104–5, 158–61. For the most part Spain honored its legal agreement with Tlaxcala for nearly three hundred years, but although the Tlaxcalans no longer had to pay tribute to Tenochtitlán, they were obligated, as vassals of Spain, to make payments to the crown.
7. Díaz, *Discovery*, 433–34; Díaz, *New Spain*, trans. Cohen, 308.
8. Díaz, *Discovery*, 434; Díaz, *New Spain*, trans. Cohen, 308
9. Cortés, *Letters*, 143–44.
10. Quoted in Gómara, *Cortés*, 228.
11. Ibid. 227–28; Prescott, *History*, 624.
12. Quoted in Thomas, *Conquest*, 432.
13. Ibid. 432, 738n.
14. Quoted in Gómara, *Cortés*, 228.
15. Quoted in Prescott, *History*, 192; Berler, *Conquest of Mexico*, 14.
16. Quoted in Gómara, *Cortés*, 229.
17. Ibid., 229.
18. Ibid., 230.
19. Ibid., 229. Cortés would shortly begin using the term "New Spain" in letters to the king.
20. Cortés, *Letters*, 145. Cortés did not coin this phrase, but he used it more than once. It was, at the time, in relatively common usage, also

rendered as "Fortune favors the brave." Sometimes attributed to Virgil, from *The Aeneid.*

21. Quoted in Gómara, *Cortés*, 230.

22. Cortés, *Letters*, 145.

23. Hassig, *Mexico*, 123.

24. Cortés, *Letters*, 145–46; Gómara, *Cortés*, 231; Díaz, *Discovery*, 438; Prescott, *History*, 632–33.

25. Cortés, *Letters*, 146.

26. Ibid., 146; Gómara, *Cortés*, 231–32; Díaz, *New Spain*, 308.

27. Cores, *Letters*, 146.

28. Díaz, *Discovery*, 439; Prescott, *History*, 634; Souselle, *Daily Life*, 73.

29. Varner and Varner, *Dogs*, 68.

30. Cortés, *Letters*, 146; Gómara, *Cortés*, 232.

31. Cortés, *Letters*, 146, 480–81n. Pagden, in his note on 480–81, points out that Cortés here overstates the term *cannibals*, and that most of the consumption of human flesh was symbolic and ritualistic. See also Carrasco, *City of Sacrifice*, 164–68. Marvin Harris makes the controversial case that the Aztec diet lacked protein and that cannibalism compensated for this deficiency. See Marvin Harris, *Cannibals and Kings* (New York, 1978), 147–66.

32. Thomas, *Conquest*, 437 and 739n; J.M.G. Le Clezio, *The Mexican Dream: Or, The Interrupted Thought of Amerindian Civilizations* (Chicago and London, 1993), 10–20.

33. Quoted in Thomas, *Conquest*, 442; Gardiner, *Naval Power*, 98, 100–1; Gardiner, *Martín López*, 37–39.

Chapter 16

1. Díaz, *Discovery*, 440; Díaz, *New Spain*, trans. Cohen, 309.

2. Quoted in Díaz, *Discovery*, 440.

3. Díaz, *Discovery*, 440; López-Pórtillo, *They Are Coming*, 281; Hassig, *Mexico*, 128; Prescott, *History*, 641.

4. Díaz, *Discovery*, 440–41.

5. Cortés, *Letters*, 157.

6. Ibid., 157–58; Díaz, *Discovery*, 442–43; Gardiner, *Naval Power*, 107; Prescott, *History*, 642.

7. Díaz, *Discovery*, 443–44; Gardiner, *Naval Power*, 108; Thomas, *Conquest*, 447–48.

8. Díaz, *Discovery*, 443; Díaz, *New Spain*, trans. Cohen, 309; López-Pórtillo, *They Are Coming*, 282.

9. Gardiner, *Naval Power*, 108; Thomas, *Conquest*, 448; Marks, *Cortés*, 196.
10. Mann, *1491*, 92–93; Crosby, *Columbian*, 47; William H. McNeill, *Plagues and Peoples* (New York, 1976), 206–7.
11. Mann, *1491*, 93; Duran, *Aztecs*, 323; Crosby, *Columbian*, 48–49. A few reports indicate that additional Cuban servants aboard Narváez's ships were infected, but all indications point to the Narváez expedition as the source of the disease in New Spain proper. See David Noble Cook, *Born to Die: Disease and the New World Conquest, 1492–1650* (Cambridge, Mass., 1998), 64–70.
12. Quoted in Crosby, *Columbian*, 48–49.
13. León-Portilla, *Broken Spears*, 92–93; Aztec Accounts, Florentine Codex, in Lockhart, *We People Here*, 182–83; Schwartz, *Victors*, 188–90.
14. Clendinnen, *Aztecs*, 270; Brundage, *Rain of Darts*, 279.
15. Soustelle, *Daily Life*, 196–98; Restall, *Seven Myths*, 140–42; Cook, *Born to Die*, 62–67.
16. Soustelle, *Daily Life*, 130; Van Tuerenhout, *Aztecs*, 137 and 216; Bernard R. Ortiz de Montellano, *Aztec Medicine, Health, and Nutrition* (New Brunswick, N.J., and London, 1991), 163–164.
17. Florentine Codex, in Lockhart, *We People Here*, 182.
18. Quoted in León-Portilla, *Broken Spears*, 93. On the devastation of the disease and its implications in the region, see also Robert V. Hine and John Mack Faragher, *The American West: A New Interpretive History* (New Haven, Conn., and London, 2000), 25–27.
19. Francisco de Aguilar quoted in Fuentes, *Conquistadors*, 159.
20. McNeill, *Plagues*, 207–8. See also Robert McCaa, "Spanish and Nahuatl Views on Smallpox and Demographic Catastrophe in Mexico," *Journal of Interdisciplinary History* 25 (1995), 397–431.
21. Cortés, *Letters*, 154–55; Hassig, *Mexico*, 129–130; Thomas, *Conquest*, 446.
22. Prescott, *History*, 643–44.
23. Ibid., 644; Thomas, *Conquest*, 440.
24. Cortés, *Letters*, 157.
25. Ibid., 158, 482n. Pagden notes that Grijalva was actually the first to coin this phrase.
26. Ibid., 159.
27. Díaz, *Discovery*, 448–49; Díaz, *New Spain*, trans. Cohen, 311; Gómara, *Cortés*, 237; Prescott, *History*, 644–46.

28. Díaz, *Discovery*, 448; Prescott, *History*, 641.
29. Díaz, *Discovery*, 444.
30. Ibid., 446.
31. Ibid., 449; Cortés, *Letters*, 164; Gómara, *Cortés*, 237; Prescott, *History*, 646; Thomas, *Conquest*, 450.
32. Cortés, *Letters*, 164; Gómara, *Cortés*, 237.
33. Prescott, *History*, 646.
34. Ibid., 446; Cortés, *Letters*, 165; Gómara, *Cortés*, 238; Díaz, *Discovery*, 450.
35. Díaz, *Discovery*, 450; Prescott, *History*, 646.
36. Cortés, *Letters*, 165; Gómara, *Cortés*, 238.
37. Quoted in Gardiner, *Naval Power*, 103.

Chapter 17

1. Quoted in Prescott, *History*, 649, 649–50n. Prescott borrows from Sahagún, *General History*.
2. Codex Ramirez, 145.
3. Quoted in Díaz, *New Spain*, trans. Cohen, 309.
4. Gómara, *Cortés*, 239.
5. Ibid., 239; Hassig, *Mexico*, 172.
6. Cortés, *Letters*, 166; Gómara, *Cortés*, 239.
7. Díaz, *Discovery*, 552; Díaz, *New Spain*, trans. Cohen, 311. Gómara, *Cortés*, 243, says that there were twenty thousand Tlaxcalans.
8. Quoted in Gómara, *Cortés*, 241; Cortés, *Letters*, 166, 482n.
9. Gómara, *Cortés*, 241.
10. This phrase, "laugh or cry," was uttered by Bartolomé de las Casas in *History of the Indies of Spain*, trans. and ed. Andree Collard (New York, 1971).
11. Cortés, *Letters*, 166.
12. Quoted in Thomas, *Conquest*, 456; Prescott, *History*, 654. Prescott's translation, though slightly different, retains the flavor: "The principal motive . . . is the desire to wean the natives from their gloomy idolatry, and to impart to them the knowledge of the purer faith; and next, to recover for his master, the emperor, the dominions which of right belong to him."
13. Prescott, *History*, 655. These provisions or ordinances of conduct are also in Gardiner, *The Constant Captain*, 68–70.

14. Quoted in Prescott, *History*, 655.
15. Cortés, *Letters*, 167.
16. Ibid., 168; Prescott, *History*, 658; Díaz, *New Spain*, trans. Cohen, 312.
17. Cortés, *Letters*, 168.
18. Ibid., 169. Smoke signals were commonly used to warn nearby towns and cities that war was engaged or that an enemy was marching. See Hassig, *Aztec Warfare*, 95–96, 292n.
19. Gómara, *Cortés*, 244.
20. Díaz, *Discovery*, 453; Díaz, *New Spain*, trans. Cohen, 312–13; Gómara, *Cortés*, 244.
21. Thomas, *Conquest*, 458, 744n; Fernando de Alva Ixtlilxochitl, *Ally of Cortés: Account 13: Of the Coming of the Spaniards and the Beginning of Evangelical Law*, trans. and ed. Douglass K. Ballentine (El Paso, Tex., 1969), 10–15, 272–73; Hassig, *Mexico*, 136; *Duran, Indies*, 550. Duran points out the long-standing relationship that developed between Cortés and Ixtlilxochitl.
22. Cortés, *Letters*, 170; Gómara, *Cortés*, 244.
23. Cortés, *Letters*, 172; Díaz, *New Spain*, trans. Cohen, 315.
24. Thomas, *Conquest*, 459, 744n; Ixtlilxochitl, *Ally*, 12–15.
25. Hassig, *Mexico*, 136–37; Jerome A. Offner, *Law and Politics in Aztec Texcoco* (London, 1983), 239–40; Padden, *Hummingbird and Hawk*, 209–10. Hassig suggests, interestingly, that Tecocol's sudden death was "convenient and suspicious," which makes sense, given the usefulness of having Ixtlilxochitl installed for political purposes (though Cortés could simply have assisted in installing Ixtlilxochitl in the first place).
26. Smith, *Aztecs*, 143–45; Van Tuerenhout, *Aztecs*, 144 and 202; Esther Pasztory, *Aztec Art* (New York, 1983), 202–3.
27. Cortés, *Letters*, 172; Gómara, *Cortés*, 245.

Chapter 18

1. As usual, the number of members of the expeditions that went around the lake varies considerably. Hassig, *Mexico*, 138, cites seven thousand, while other sources suggest only half that many. Ixtlilxochitl, *Ally*, claims there were six thousand (13–14), but they weren't exclusively Tlaxcalans—there were Texcocan warriors as well. Other

chroniclers place the number lower, in the three-to-four-thousand range. Cortés, *Letters*, says there were "three or four thousand of our Indian allies" (174).

2. Cortés, *Letters*, 82–83, 174; Nigel Davies, *The Aztecs* (New York, 1973), 254.

3. Cortés, *Letters*, 175; Ixtlilxochitl, *Ally*, 13.

4. Cortés, *Letters*, 175.

5. Ibid., 177; Díaz, *New Spain*, trans. Cohen, 320–21; Ixtlilxochitl, *Ally*, 16; Hassig, *Aztec Warfare*, 248–49.

6. Díaz, *New Spain*, trans. Cohen, 322; Hassig, *Mexico*, 141.

7. Ixtlilxochitl, *Ally*, 16–17; Gómara, *Cortés*, 247–48.

8. Díaz, *New Spain*, trans. Cohen, 322; Cortés, *Letters*, 179.

9. Quoted in Díaz, *Discovery*, 467; Gardiner, *Constant Captain*, 75–76.

10. Díaz, *Discovery*, 467; Cortés, *Letters*, 184; Prescott, *History*, 686–87.

11. Gardiner, *Naval Power*, 115–16; Hassig, *Mexico*, 142.

12. Gardiner, *Naval Power*, 116–17; Gardiner, *Martín López*, 42–43; Gardiner, *Constant Captain*, 76–78; Prescott, *History*, 687. The number of members of the caravan varies—some sources claim that as many as fifty thousand Tlaxcalans participated in carrying the brigantines from Tlaxcala to Texcoco, a distance of over fifty miles.

13. López-Portillo, *They Are Coming*, 293.

14. Quoted in Díaz, *Discovery*, 469; Cortés, *Letters*, 186.

15. Gardiner, *Naval Power*, 125–27; Hubert Howe Bancroft, *History of Mexico*, vol. 1 (San Francisco, 1883–88), 581; Ixtlilxochitl, *Ally*, 15; López-Portillo, *They Are Coming*, 293.

16. Cortés, *Letters*, 186–87; Hassig, *Mexico*, 142.

17. Cortés, *Letters*, 187.

18. Díaz, *Discovery*, 473; Prescott, *History*, 692.

19. Díaz, *Discovery*, 473.

20. Cortés, *Letters*, 187.

21. Ibid.

22. Quoted in Cortés, *Letters*, 188.

23. Ibid.

24. Díaz, *Discovery*, 476.

25. Quoted in Cortés, *Letters*, 188; Gómara, *Cortés*, 253.

26. Prescott, *History*, 704; Gardiner, *Naval Power*, 119–20; Marks, *Cortés*, 213; Thomas, *Conquest*, 469–71.

27. Thomas, *Conquest*, 471–72; Duran, *Indies*, trans. Heyden, 17n.

28. Díaz, *Discovery*, 512–14; Prescott, *History*, 726–27; López-Portillo, *They Are Coming*, 300–1.
29. Díaz, *Discovery*, 514.
30. Cortés, *Letters*, 278; Díaz, *Discovery*, 514–15; López-Portillo, *They Are Coming*, 300–1; Thomas, *Conquest*, 469; Cortés, *Letters*, 497–98n.
31. Gómara, *Cortés*, 262.
32. Ibid., 261–62; Prescott, *History*, 703; Gardiner, *Naval Power*, 121–25; Ixtlilxochitl, *Ally*, 15–16; Marks, *Cortés*, 223–24.

Chapter 19

1. Díaz, *Discovery*, 478; Gómara, *Cortés*, 254; Prescott, *History*, 698–99. For Prescott's overall version of the entire military encirclement of the region, see 691–724.
2. Cortés, *Letters*, 190.
3. Ibid., 191; Gardiner, *Constant Captain*, 78–79. Gómara, *Cortés*, 254; Prescott, *History*, 702.
4. Quoted in Díaz, *Discovery*, 486.
5. Cortés, *Letters*, 193.
6. Díaz, *Discovery*, says twenty thousand, but Cortés, *Letters*, 193, and Gómara, *Cortés*, 256, both cite the higher number of forty thousand. In any case, the growing number of allies would certainly have concerned Cuauhtémoc greatly.
7. Cortés, *Letters*, 194; Díaz, *Discovery*, 488.
8. Cortés, *Letters*, 194; this was most likely the town of Tlaycapan.
9. Díaz, *Discovery*, 489–90; Díaz, *New Spain*, trans. Cohen, 334–35; Cortés, *Letters*, 194–95; Prescott, *History*, 707.
10. Díaz, *New Spain*, trans. Cohen, 336.
11. Gómara, *Cortés*, 257–58; Díaz, *Discovery*, 492.
12. Cortés, *Letters*, 196.
13. Ibid.
14. Duran, *Indies*, trans. Heyden, 205n, 244–45, 244n.
15. Cortés, *Letters*, 197.
16. Díaz, *Discovery*, 497.
17. Gómara, *Cortés*, 258–59; Cortés, *Letters*, 198; Díaz, *New Spain*, trans. Cohen, 339; Prescott, *History*, 711–12; López-Portillo, *They Are Coming*, 294–95.
18. Díaz, *Discovery*, 497.

19. Madariaga, *Cortés*, 369; Davies, *Aztecs*, 272.
20. Díaz, *Discovery*, 500.
21. Duran, *Indies*, trans. Heyden, 44–45n, 236–37.
22. Hassig, *Mexico*, 144–45; Thomas, *Conquest*, 479.
23. Díaz, *Discovery*, 501.
24. Ibid., 510; López-Portillo, *They Are Coming*, 297; Cortés, *Letters*, 486n; Marks, *Cortés*, 221; Prescott, *History*, 718. Díaz, *Discovery*, says that the limbs were sent to the provinces by Cuauhtemoc as a warning to those who had sided with the Spaniards (507–8).
25. Cortés, *Letters*, 200.
26. Ibid., 202.
27. Ibid., 486n.
28. Díaz, *New Spain*, trans. Cohen, 348; Prescott, *History*, 722; Thomas, *Conquest*, 481; López-Portillo, *They Are Coming*, 298.

Chapter 20

1. Hassig, *Aztec Warfare*, 241. Aztec canoe design is discussed in Gardiner, *Naval Power*, 55–57. Also see Van Tuerenhout, *Aztecs*, 88, 94–95.
2. Padden, *Hummingbird and Hawk*, 211–12.
3. Soustelle, *Daily Life*, 140–41; Smith, *Aztecs*, 166–68.
4. Hassig, *Aztec Warfare*, 238; Ixtlilxochitl, *Ally*, 24.
5. For a discussion of the structure and organization of Aztec military order, including jaguar and eagle warriors, see Hassig, *War and Society*, 82–85, 142; Hassig, *Aztec Warfare*, 37–47.
6. Thomas, *Conquest*, 487–88; Duran, *Book of the Gods*, 19, 164. Pantitlán, place of whirlpool and water rituals, is also discussed in Keber, *Aztec Ritual*, 88, 182.
7. Cortés, *Letters*, 206.
8. Díaz, *New Spain*, trans. Cohen, 353.
9. Gardiner, *Naval Power*, 127–33. Gardiner does an admirable job of re-creating the precise size and appearance of the brigantines, based on lake levels, intended usage, Martín López's comments, and comparable Spanish craft of the day. Gardiner, *Martín López*, 42–46. The send-off is also chronicled in Francisco Cervantes de Salazar, *Cronica de la Nueva España* (Madrid, 1914), 600–1.
10. The exact time estimates for the project are difficult to determine

and depend on whether one includes initial planning phases or adheres strictly to the physical construction phase. For an interesting discussion, see Gardiner, *Naval Power*, 128, 128n.

11. Cortés, *Letters*, 206–7. Most scholars and other chroniclers (Díaz, Gómara, Hassig) generally concur on these numbers.

12. Interestingly, Ixtlilxochitl, *Ally* (an account that carries a noticeable indigenous bias), places the number of allies at 200,000 (22), while some European chroniclers lean toward 500,000.

13. Quoted in Díaz, *Discovery*, 520.

14. Hassig, *Mexico*, 149; Thomas, *Conquest*, 491. A detailed discussion on the incident may be found in Ross Hassig, "Xicotencatl: Rethinking an Indigenous Mexican Hero," *Estudios de Cultura Nahuatl* 32 (2001), 29–49. The accounts conflict on the precise details; a number of sources (including Bernal Díaz) suggest that the delegation sent to retrieve Xicotenga hanged him on the spot where they overtook him rather than bringing him back to Texcoco. No sources dispute the fact that he was hanged. Hassig makes the interesting (and controversial) case that Cortés had Xicotenga the Younger branded as a traitor and hanged as an act of political expedience.

15. Díaz, *Discovery*, 524; Prescott, *History*, 738.

16. Díaz, *Discovery*, 526.

17. Cortés, *Letters*, 209.

18. Marks, *Cortés*, 228; López-Portillo, *They Are Coming*, 308–09.

19. Cortés, *Letters*, 211.

20. Ibid.

21. Ibid., 212.

22. Ibid.

23. Ixtlilxochitl, *Ally*, 27; Gardiner, *Naval Power*, 164–65.

24. Quoted in Cortés, *Letters*, 212; Thomas, *Conquest*, 496. Thomas attributes the comment to Sandoval at Iztapalapa, but actually Cortés doesn't specifically say which person made the comment, alluding rather to "the garrison at Coyoacán." Those at the garrison could better see the action on the water, he wrote, which if true would suggest that the comment more likely came from Olid.

25. Cortés, *Letters*, 213–14; Marks, *Cortés*, 232; López-Portillo, *They Are Coming*, 311.

26. Cortés, *Letters*, 214; Díaz, *Discovery*, 532.

Chapter 21

1. Cortés, *Letters*, 215; Gómara, *Cortés*, 269; Marks, *Cortés*, 233.
2. Hassig, *Mexico*, 156–57.
3. Cortés, *Letters*, 214.
4. Ibid., 216.
5. Gómara, *Cortés*, 270; Thomas, *Conquest*, 500; López-Portillo, *They Are Coming*, 313.
6. Florentine Codex, Book 12, in Lockhart, *We People Here*, 193–94.
7. Cortés, *Letters*, 217; Thomas, *Conquest*, 500; Marks, *Cortés*, 235.
8. Lockhart, *We People Here*, 194–95; Cortés, *Letters*, 218; León-Portilla, *Broken Spears*, 99.
9. Quoted in Léon-Portilla, *Broken Spears*, 99.
10. Ibid.; Lockhart, *We People Here*, 195–96; Cortés, *Letters*, 219.
11. Cortés, *Letters*, 220.
12. Díaz, *New Spain*, trans. Cohen, 364.
13. Ibid., 365.
14. Ibid.; Thomas, *Conquest*, 501; Prescott, *History*, 751–52.
15. Marks, *Cortés*, 234; Thomas, *Conquest*, 501; Ixtlilxochitl, *Ally*, 35.
16. Cortés, *Letters*, 222.
17. Ibid., 222–23.
18. Ibid., 223; Gómara, *Cortés*, 274–75; Prescott, *History*, 753–54.
19. López-Portillo, *They Are Coming*, 315. Padden, *Hummingbird and Hawk*, 213–16; Duran, *Indies*, trans. Heyden and Horcacitas, 312.
20. Kelly, *Alvarado*, 43, 94; Thomas, *Conquest*, 504.
21. Díaz, *Discovery*, 549.
22. Ibid., 550; López-Portillo, *They Are Coming*, 318–21; Pohl and Robinson, *Aztecs*, 145.
23. Díaz, *New Spain*, trans. Cohen, 372.
24. Cortés, *Letters*, 235.
25. Gardiner, *Naval Power*, 181; López-Portillo, *They Are Coming*, 327.
26. Gardiner, *Naval Power*, 181; Kelly, *Alvarado*, 109; Hassig, *Mexico*, 160–61.
27. Cortés, *Letters*, 235; Gardiner, *Constant Captain*, 89–90.
28. Cortés, *Letters*, 234.
29. Ixtlilxochitl, *Ally*, 38–39; López-Portillo, *They Are Coming*, 322–23.
30. Cortés, *Letters*, 236.
31. Ibid., 236–37; Gómara, *Cortés*, 280; Prescott, *History*, 764–65.
32. Cortés, *Letters*, 237.
33. Ibid., 238; Díaz, *New Spain*, trans. Cohen, 379; Gómara, *Cortés*, 280–81.

34. Cortés, *Letters*, 238–39.
35. Díaz, *New Spain*, trans. Cohen, 380. Ixtlilxochitl, *Ally*, claims that it was actually his ancestor (and namesake) Ixtlilxochitl who severed the arms of the Aztecs who·had seized and were absconding with Cortés (39–41). Most other sources confirm Díaz on this point.
36. Quoted in Cortés, *Letters*, 239.
37. Cortés egregiously underestimates the number of Spaniards who died that day, writing to his king that thirty-five to forty were slain and twenty wounded. He claims that a thousand allies perished, likely another understatement given the immediate subsequent attrition by allied forces. In addition, he mentions the loss of a number of crossbows, harquebuses, and one small field gun. For an itemized list of more likely numbers, see Cortés, *Letters*, 489n. Most sources place the count closer to sixty Spaniards dead (the greatest number by sacrifice), as well as eight horses and two cannons lost—plus thousands of allies.
38. Quoted in Díaz, *Discovery*, 561–62.
39. Ibid., 569; Díaz, *New Spain*, trans. Cohen, 387. The Florentine Codex also records this spectacle; Lockhart, *We People Here*, 210–18. Also interesting is León-Portilla, *Broken Spears*, 104–9.
40. Cortés, *Letters*, 241; Duran, *Indies*, trans. Heyden and Horcasitas, 314; Carrasco, *City of Sacrifice*, 50–51, 87.

Chapter 22

1. Marks, *Cortés*, 243–44; León-Portilla, *Broken Spears*, 104, 107.
2. López-Portillo, *They Are Coming*, 330–31; Marks, *Cortés*, 244; Cortés, *Letters*, 246; Gómara, *Cortés*, 282–83.
3. Cortés, *Letters*, 242; Gómara, *Cortés*, 283; Prescott, *History*, 780.
4. Gardiner, *Constant Captain*, 93; Cortés, *Letters*, 242; Gómara, *Cortés*, 283.
5. The reference to the "roasted babies" is found in Cortés, *Letters*, 245; Gómara, *Cortés*, 284; Marks, *Cortés*, 247.
6. Ixtlilxochitl, *Ally*, 42–44; Gardiner, *Constant Captain*, 93–95; Hassig, *Mexico*, 166–68.
7. Cortés, *Letters*, 247, 490n; Prescott, *History*, 781; Thomas, *Conquest*, 516 and 752n.
8. Prescott, *History*, 379; Cortés, *Letters*, 279, 325; Thomas, *Conquest*, 516.
9. Gómara, *Cortés*, 287; Prescott, *History*, 783; Thomas, *Con-*

quest, 516. Women disguised as warriors are described in Duran, *Indies*, 555.

10. Florentine Codex, in Lockhart, *We People Here*, 218; León-Portilla, *Broken Spears*, 107–9; Thomas, *Conquest*, 516; Kelly, *Alvarado*, 114–15.

11. Cortés, *Letters*, 248.

12. Ibid.

13. Ixtlilxochitl, *Ally*, 43–44; Hassig, *Mexico*, 169.

14. As we have seen, the estimates vary considerably. The figure 150,000 is actually conservative.

15. Gardiner, *Constant Captain*, 95–96; Cortés, *Letters*, 251–52; Kelly, *Alvarado*, 114–15; Díaz, *New Spain*, trans. Cohen, 398–99.

16. Thomas, *Conquest*, 518; Prescott, *History*, 790–91; Díaz, *Discovery*, 578.

17. Cortés, *Letters*, 256.

18. Lockhart, *We People Here*, 242–43. The tent is also referred to as "red" and "varicolored."

19. Prescott, *History*, 794–95; Cortés, *Letters*, 256–57, 490–91n; Thomas, *Conquest*, 520; Díaz, *Discovery*, 587–88.

20. Cortés, *Letters*, 257.

21. Sahagún, *War of Conquest*, 79; Marks, *Cortés*, 246; Kelly, *Alvarado*, 115.

22. Cortés, *Letters*, 262–63.

23. Díaz, *New Spain*, trans. Cohen, 400.

24. Ibid., 407.

25. From Aztec accounts, including "Epic Description of the Beseiged City" in León-Portilla, *Broken Spears*, 137–38; and "The Fall of Tenochtitlán," of Cantares Mexicanas, in Schwartz, *Victors*, 212–13. Finally, see Bancroft, *History of Mexico*, 192.

26. León-Portilla, *Broken Spears*, 112–13; Lockhart, *We People Here*, 241; Clendinnen, *Aztecs*, 271–72.

27. Florentine Codex, in Lockhart, *We People Here*, 242–43. Also in León-Portilla, *The Broken Spears*, 116.

28. López-Portillo, *They Are Coming*, 349; Duran, *Indies*, trans. Heyden and Hornacitas, 316; Clendinnen, *Aztecs*, 272.

29. Cortés, *Letters*, 263.

30. Ibid., 263.

31. Ibid., 264; Díaz, *New Spain*, trans. Cohen, 402; Pohl and Robinson, *Aztecs*, 149; Duran, *Indies*, trans. Heyden, 556.

32. Prescott, *History*, 807, 807n; Díaz, *New Spain*, trans. Cohen, 402–4;

León-Portilla, *Broken Spears*, 123–24; Duran, *Indies*, trans. Heyden, 556.

33. Ixtlilxochitl, *Ally*, 52; Duran, *Indies*, trans. Heyden, 556, 556n. Very similar versions of this speech are found in León-Portilla, *Broken Spears*, 123; Cortés, *Letters*, 264–65; Gómara, *Cortés*, 292.

34. Prescott, *History*, 809; Díaz, *New Spain*, trans. Cohen, 406; León-Portilla, *Broken Spears*, 120.

35. Florentine Codex, in Lockhart, *We People Here*, 252.

36. Díaz, *New Spain*, trans. Cohen, 406.

37. León-Portilla, *Broken Spears*, 118–20; Thomas, *Conquest*, 528; Prescott, *History*, 810–12.

38. Gómara, *Cortés*, 293; León-Portilla, *Broken Spears*, 120.

39. Díaz, *New Spain*, trans. Cohen, 407; López-Portillo, *They Are Coming*, 356–57.

Epilogue

1. Cortés, *Letters*, 265.

2. Gómara, *Cortés*, 295–96; Díaz, *New Spain*, trans. Cohen, 408–10; Thomas, *Conquest*, 546, 758–59n; López-Portillo, *They Are Coming*, 358–60. There is general agreement among the sources that the tortures occurred directly after the fall of the city, which makes sense, as Cortés and his men were still searching for the lost treasure of Montezuma.

3. Cortés, *Letters*, 492–93n. Versions of Cuauhtémoc's death are in 518n; Clendinnen, *Aztecs*, 273; Gillespie, *Aztec Kings*, 228.

4. Marks, *Cortés*, 268.

5. Prescott, *History*, 830.

6. Gómara, *Cortés*, 296–97.

7. Quoted in Wood, *Conquistadors*, 15–16; Thomas, *Conquest*, 536, 755n.

8. Díaz, *New Spain*, trans. Cohen, 410.

9. For detailed discussions of the *encomienda* system, see Lesley Byrd Simpson, *The Encomienda in New Spain: Forced Native Labor in the Spanish Colonies, 1492–1550* (Berkeley, Calif., 1950); Charles Gibson, *The Aztecs under Spanish Rule: A History of the Indians of the Valley of Mexico, 1519–1810* (Stanford, Calif., 1964), 58–97; and Ida Altman, "Spanish Society in Mexico City After the Conquest," *Hispanic American Historical Review* 71:3 (1991), 413–45;

Robert Himmerich y Valencia, *The Encomenderos of New Spain, 1521–1555* (Austin, Tex., 1991).

10. Pratt, " 'Yo soy,' " 859. On population, see also John E. Kicza, *The Peoples and Civilizations of the Americas Before Contact* (Washington, D.C., 1998), 22.

11. Cortés, *Letters*, 261–63, 491n. This large figure of over 200,000 includes death by smallpox. Burland, *Montezuma*, cites the dead at "nearly a quarter of a million" (249–50). Pohl and Robinson, *Aztecs*, 150, and Mann, *1491*, 129, both cite a more conservative estimate of 100,000 dead during the siege.

12. Díaz, *New Spain*, trans. Cohen, 413.

13. Quoted in Clendinnen, *Aztecs*, 272; Léon-Portilla, *Broken Spears*, 137–38.

14. Cortés, *Letters*, 267; Gómara, *Cortés*, 298; Innes, *Conquistadors*, 194.

15. Innes, *Conquistadors*, 194; White, *Cortés*, 266–68. Also see Henry Kamen, *Spain's Road to Empire: The Making of a World Power, 1492–1763* (London and New York, 2002), xiv–xv.

16. Gardiner, *Constant Captain*, 104–5; Marvin E. Butterfield, *Jerónimo de Aguilar, Conquistador* (Tuscaloosa, Ala., 1955), 48.

17. Gardiner, *Constant Captain*, 105; Gómara, *Cortés*, 303–4; Prescott, *History*, 836.

18. Gardiner, *Constant Captain*, 105–8; Thomas, *Conquest*, 550–53; Marks, *Cortés*, 270–72; Cortés, *Letters*, 496–97n.

19. Quoted in Wood, *Conquistadors*, 53.

20. Cortés, *Letters*, 321, 495–96n.

21. As usual, the numbers vary considerably. Ixtlilxochitl reports that as many as 400,000 indigenous people from the Valley of Mexico and beyond assisted in the rebuilding during the first years after the conquest. See also Thomas, *Conquest*, 562; Pohl and Robinson, *Aztecs*, 155; Prescott, *History*, 833, 839, 843. Rebuilding is also discussed in Gómara, *Cortés*, 323–25.

22. Burland, *Montezuma*, 251–54; Gómara, *Cortés*, 323–25; Thomas, *Conquest*, 562–63; Pohl and Robinson, *Aztecs*, 155. Also see Felipe Solis, *The Aztec Empire* (New York, 2004), 347.

23. Duran, *Indies*, trans. Heyden, 560–61, 568. A useful and comprehensive overview of this system of conversion is offered in Gibson, *Under Spanish Rule*, 98–135. Also see Ronald Wright, *Stolen Continents: The Americas Through Indian Eyes Since 1492* (New York, 1992), 143–60. Finally see David E. Stannard, *American*

Holocaust: Columbus and the Conquest of the New World (New York, 1992), 216–21.

24. Hassig, *Mexico*, 184–85. Also see the fascinating and comprehensive (nearly five hundred pages) study by James Lockhart, *The Nahuas After the Conquest: A Social and Cultural History of the Indians of Central Mexico, Sixteenth Through Eighteenth Centuries* (Stanford, Calif., 1992), 202–10, 442–46.

25. Gómara, *Cortés*, 297.

26. Pohl and Robinson, *Aztecs*, 139, 155; Thomas, *Conquest*, 568–69; Cortés, *Letters*, 509–10n; Marks, *Cortés*, 277.

27. Anna Lanyon, *The New World of Martín Cortés* (Cambridge, Mass., 2003), ix, 4; Prescott, *History*, 214, 868, 906.

28. Lanyon, *Martín Cortés*, ix, 4; Marks, *Cortés*, 274–75.

29. Prescott, *History*, 891n; Pohl and Robinson, *Aztecs*, 159; Wood, *Conquistadors*, 100–1; Thomas, *Conquest*, 579–82, 635; Marks, *Cortés*, 274–75; Madariaga, *Cortés*, 415–17.

30. Cortés, *Letters*, 302.

31. Pohl and Robinson, *Aztecs*, 159; Wood, *Conquistadors*, 101.

32. Quoted in Prescott, *History*, 900n; Marks, *Cortés*, 332.

33. Lanyon, *Malinche's Conquest*, 144–53; Cortés, *Letters*, 464–65n; Díaz, *New Spain*, trans. Cohen, 85–87; Prescott, *History*, 867. Also very useful is Frances Karttunen, *Between Worlds: Interpreters, Guides, and Survivors* (New Brunswick, N.J., 1994), 1–23, 305–7. Finally see Frances Karttunen, "Rethinking Malinche," in Susan Schroeder, Stephanie Wood, and Robert Haskett, *Indian Women of Early Mexico* (Norman, Okla., 1997), 291–312.

34. Lanyon, *Martín Cortés*, xi. Lanyon points out that the term *mestizo* is not to be used pejoratively or derogatorily but rather connotes a blending or fusing of peoples and cultures.

Appendix D

1. This list of principal Aztec deities is adapted from a number of sources, including H. B. Nicholson, "Religion in Pre-Hispanic Central Mexico," in *Archeology of Northern Mesoamerica*, part 1, edited by Gordon F. Ekholm and Ignacio Bernal, 395–446; and *Handbook of Middle American Indians*, vol. 10 (Austin, 1971). Also in Smith, *Aztecs*, 200–1, and Van Tuerenhout, *Aztecs*, 180.

Appendix E

1. For more detailed information on the Aztec kings and the imperial Aztec lineage, see Gillespie, *Aztec Kings*, 3–24; Van Tuerenhout, *Aztecs*, 38–46; Smith, *Aztecs*, 43–55.

A NOTE ON THE TEXT
AND THE SOURCES

Conquistador is concerned primarily (although certainly not exclusively) with the events directly leading up to and directly following the expedition to Mexico led by Hernán Cortés, 1519–21. For those interested in further reading and inquiry, especially regarding the remainder of Cortés's life and the aftermath of the conquest, numerous works are listed below and in the extensive bibliography that follows, works which have either been cited, quoted directly, or used as reference.

Winston Churchill's famous witticism "History is written by the victors" is all too apt when it comes to the firsthand accounts chronicling the conquest of Mexico. In the aftermath of the conquest, adding dreadful insult to what was already devastating injury, the Spanish conquistadors destroyed nearly all of the native books. As a result, native firsthand accounts—though incredibly rich, lyrical, and informative—are few. Additionally, nearly all the native chronicles are in fact postconquest reconstructions that rely on, or are based upon, those lost original preconquest documents.

Still, a number of extremely important native sources were vital to *Conquistador*. The Aztec codices (a number of which appear early in the bibliography that follows) are particularly important. They are books written (or in many cases, drawn) by pre-Columbian and Spanish colonial–era Aztecs, and they provide some of the best existing primary source material pertaining to Aztec life and culture. Foremost among them is the so-called Florentine Codex (also referred to as the Codice Florentino), prepared by Dominican friar Fray Bernardino de Sahagún under the title *The General History of the Things of New Spain*. Written over a time span of nearly forty years (approximately 1540–77), Sahagún's work was monumental in scope, translated from Nahua

Indians who were present before, during, and after the conquest. The thirteen-volume work records all aspects of Aztec life and culture in one of the most remarkable and ambitious ethnological studies ever attempted. The English-language gold standard of this text is Bernardino de Sahagún, *The General History of the Things of New Spain*, 13 vols., translated by Charles E. Dibble and Arthur J. O. Anderson (Salt Lake City, 1950–82), and Book 12, *Conquest of New Spain 1585 Revision*, translated by Howard F. Cline (Salt Lake City, 1989). A comprehensive study of the life of Sahagún is the rich and readable Miguel León-Portilla, *Bernardino de Sahagún: First Anthropologist* (Norman, Oklahoma, 2002).

Another friar to embark on work similar to that of Sahagún was Fray Diego Duran, who came to Mexico as a small child and grew up speaking both his native Spanish and Nahuatl. In 1581 he completed his work, which is available now as *The History of the Indies of New Spain*, translated by Doris Heyden (Norman, Okla., and London, 1994). Duran based much of his work on the lost so-called Crónica X, a document of unknown authorship said to have influenced many subsequent codices.

As important as any of the native sources (and the earliest, written directly after the fall of Tenochtitlán, 1524–28) is the *Anales de Tlatelolco*. The first-ever ethnographic work transcribing the Nahuatl language into Latin characters, the *Anales de Tlatelolco* is housed in Paris at the Bibliothèque Nationale de France. A delightfully readable (and heartbreaking) version of the work is available in English in the form of *The Broken Spears: The Aztec Account of the Conquest of Mexico*, edited by Miguel León-Portilla (Boston, 1990). The text is also referred to in Spanish as it was first published in 1959: *Visión de los Vencidos* (Vision of the Vanquished).

A last crucial early Aztec source is the *Crónica Mexicana* (Mexico City, 1944) or, alternatively, *Crónica Mexicoyotl* (Mexico City, 1949), written by Hernando Alvarado Tezozómoc, the grandson of Montezuma II. Tezozómoc interviewed his own parents as well as individuals who had been alive before the conquest in compiling his work, which he wrote in 1598.

A number of Spanish conquistadors recorded their accounts of the events before, during, and after the conquest. Hernán Cortés penned five letters to Charles V during, and directly following, his expeditions. By far the best, most comprehensive, and most meticulously annotated collection is *Letters from Mexico*, edited and translated by Anthony

Pagden (New Haven, Conn., 2001). Cortés recorded a tremendous amount of detail during his historic conquest of Mexico (1519–21), including daily life in the Aztec capital, the palaces and buildings of Montezuma, and the living conditions, religious practices, and cultural mores of the people from the Yucatán coast all the way to the Valley of Mexico. It is important, however, to read Cortés's letters with a healthy dose of critical circumspection, bearing in mind that they are highly political, in effect long justifications for actions that might even be construed as treasonous. Still, his observations and recordings of life in Mexico during the period are among the finest, most detailed, and most fascinating in existence. The 2001 Yale Nota Bene edition, edited by Anthony Pagden, is the version relied upon in *Conquistador*, and Pagden's nearly one hundred pages of extensive notes provide a comprehensive and rich resource for further research and study of all the events related to the conquest and its central figures.

A close relative of Cortés's letters is the "biography" written by Cortés's chaplain and secretary, Francisco López de Gómara. Written in 1552 and based very closely on Cortés's letters, personal recollections, and conversations, the work appears now as *Cortés: The Life of the Conqueror by His Secretary*, edited and translated by Lesley Byrd Simpson (Berkeley, Calif., 1964). Gómara's work employs a number of revisions to Cortés's letters.

The best and most readable of all the Spanish accounts is certainly the memoir of participant conquistador Bernal Díaz del Castillo, a man who was present at all three expeditions to Mexico and claims to have participated in 119 battles. In 1568, at over seventy years old, he undertook to write his memoirs, his *True History of the Conquest of New Spain*. In part written to take Gómara to task on a number of details where Cortés seemed to be garnering undue credit, Díaz's work lay neglected and unpublished until 1632, when it was discovered in a private library and published in Madrid. Though written some fifty years after the stirring events it describes, the work of Bernal Díaz del Castillo remains among the most important extant firsthand accounts of the conquistadors, and it is so reliable as to have been borrowed from liberally by famed historian William H. Prescott in his groundbreaking *The History of the Conquest of Mexico* (New York, 2001). Nearly every other scholar and writer since Prescott has leaned heavily on Bernal Díaz, in part because his writing is so detailed, descriptive, and dramatic, but also because—at least compared with other chroniclers like Cortés and Gómara—Díaz is the least politically motivated. Díaz, writing near the end of his life, had virtually nothing to gain by fabrication, and although he comes across as a proud Spaniard imbued with a sense of mission and duty, he appears to be trying to provide an accurate account of the events, and not to justify them. In a vigorous writing style Díaz conveys the wonder and awe felt by the conquistadors as they encountered the people of Mexico for the first time. A number of versions exist (including useful and modernized abridged versions). Quoted and relied on in *Conquistador* are two versions: *The Discovery and Conquest of Mexico, 1517–1521*, translated by Alfred Percival Maudslay (New York, 1928); and *The Conquest of New Spain*, translated by J.M. Cohen, abridged ed. (New York, 1963).

A handful of other accounts by conquistadors were written during and after the conquest, and these are compiled together in an excellent book by Patricia de Fuentes called *The Conquistadors: First-person Accounts of the Conquest of Mexico* (Norman, Okla., 1993). The collection includes the work of Pedro de Alvarado, Andrés de Tapia, Juan Díaz, and the notorious Anonymous Conquistador, among others.

Of the histories, one must inevitably begin with William H. Prescott's monumental *The History of the Conquest of Mexico* (1843; New York, 2001). Originally published in 1843, the three-volume tome was then regarded as a masterpiece, and it remains one to this day. Epic in scope and stunning in its scholarship, Prescott's nearly one-thousand-page history was the English-speaking audience's first foray into Mesoamerica, and his work remains the standard by which all others (*Conquistador* included) must ultimately be judged. His massive treatise suffers from stereotypical notions and language that are products of its age, and the tone and point of view are decidedly pro-Spanish, so it is important to employ critical circumspection (as I have tried to do) when assessing Prescott's observations and conclusions. But in re-creating the stunning detail and sheer epic drama of the events (as he also did in his 1847 *History of the Conquest of Peru*), Prescott is unequaled.

In 1993 the British historian Hugh Thomas published *Conquest: Montezuma, Cortés, and the Fall of Old Mexico*, which is nearly as bold and comprehensive (and almost as long) as Prescott's work. Thomas provides a thorough and vibrant modern telling, utilizing a great deal of contemporary research that was not available to Prescott. The result is a riveting account, impressive in sweep and detail. Thomas's *Conquest* offers the most authoritative contemporary overview of the conquest of Mexico, and *Conquistador* has benefited tremendously from the historian's impressive scholarship.

Military aspects of the conquest of Mexico are treated thoroughly by the fine scholar Ross Hassig, particularly from the standpoint of Aztec warfare: philosophy, technique, practice, weaponry, and dress. Hassig is the unrivaled expert in the field, and all of his books are highly recommended. Noteworthy are *Mexico and the Spanish Conquest* (Norman, Okla., 2006), *Aztec Warfare: Imperial Expansion and Political Control* (Norman, Okla., 1988), and *Trade, Tribute, and Transportation: The Sixteenth-Century Political Economy of the Valley of Mexico* (Norman, Okla., 1985).

Books on the history of the Aztec people (also referred to as the Mexica) are numerous and varied, both in approach and in quality. The best recent overviews are: John Pohl and Charles M. Robinson III, *Aztecs and Conquistadors: The Spanish Invasion and the Collapse of the Aztec Empire* (London and New York, 2005); Dirk R. Van Tuerenhout, *The Aztecs: New Perspectives* (Santa Barbara, 2005); Michael E. Smith, *The Aztecs* (Malden, Mass., 2003); Richard F. Townsend, *The Aztecs* (London, 2003); and finally the stunning and visually amazing coffee-table art book *The Aztec Empire*, curated by Felipe Solis for the Solomon R. Guggenheim Museum (New York, 2004).

Works devoted to the enigmatic emperor Montezuma II, so inextricably connected to the fall of Mexico, are scarce. Two very good ones are Peter G. Tsouras, *Montezuma: Warlord of the Aztecs* (Washington, D.C., 2005); and the full-length biography by C. A. Burland, *Montezuma: Lord of the Aztecs* (New York, 1973).

Aztec thought and religion and the complex aspects of the Aztec spiritual realm play a significant role in the history of the conquest, and there are many fine books devoted to the subject. Of particular interest are Miguel León-Portilla, *Aztec Thought and Culture* (Norman, Okla., 1963); Inga Clendinnen, *The Aztecs* (New York, 1991); Neil Baldwin, *Legends of the Plumed Serpent: Biography of a Mexican God* (New York, 1998); Roberta H. Markman and Peter T. Markman, *The Flayed God: The Mythology of Mesoamerica* (San Francisco, 1993). For a detailed and fascinating account of the practice of human sacrifice in the Aztec world, see David Carrasco, *City of Sacrifice: The Aztec Empire and the Role of Violence in Civilization* (Boston, 1999). Finally, on the importance of the Templo Mayor as a religious center, see Eduardo Matos Moctezuma, *Life and Death in the Templo Mayor* (Boulder, Colo., 1995).

BIBLIOGRAPHY

Primary Sources

Firsthand Accounts by Spanish Conquistadors and Chroniclers

Acosta, Joseph de. *Historia natural y moral de las Indias*. Seville, Spain, 1590; Mexico, 1962.

——. *Natural and Moral History of the Indies*. Edited by Jane E. Mangan. Translated by Frances López-Morillas. Durham, N.C., 2002.

Aguilar, Fray Francisco de. *Relación breve de la conquista de la Nueva España*. Spain, 1954.

Alarcón, Hernando Ruíz de. *Treatise on the Heathen Superstitions That Today Live Among the Indians Native to This New Spain, 1629*. Translated and edited by J. Richard Andrews and Ross Hassig. Norman, Okla., 1984.

Alvarado, Pedro de. *An Account of the Conquest of Guatemala in 1524*. Edited by Sedley J. Mackie. New York, 1924.

Arber, Edward. *The First Three English Books on America, 1511–1555: Being Chiefly Translations, Compilations, et cetera by Richard Eden, From the Writings, Maps, et cetera of Pietro Martire of Anghiera, Sebastian Münster, and Sebastian Cabot*. Birmingham, U.K., 1971.

Cabeza de Vaca, Alvar Nuñez. *Relación*. Translated by Martin A. Favata and José B. Fernandez. Houston, Tex., 1993.

Camargo, Diego Muñoz. *Historia de Tlaxcala*. Mexico, 1892.

Córdoba, Francisco Hernández de. *The Discovery of the Yucatán.* Translated by Henry R. Wagner. Pasadena, Calif., 1942.

Cortés, Hernán. *Cartas de relación de la conquista de México.* Madrid, 1970.

——. *Letters from Mexico.* Translated by Anthony Pagden. New Haven, Conn., and London, 2001.

Díaz, Juan. *Itinerario de Juan de Grijalva.* In *Crónicas de la Conquista.* Mexico, 1950.

Díaz del Castillo, Bernal. *The Discovery and Conquest of Mexico, 1517–1521.* Translated by A. P. Maudslay. New York and London, 1928.

——. *The Conquest of New Spain.* Translated by J. M. Cohen. New York, 1963.

Duran, Fray Diego. *The Aztecs: The History of the Indies of New Spain.* Translated by Doris Heyden and Fernando Horcasitas. New York, 1964.

——. *Book of the Gods and Rites and The Ancient Calendar.* Translated and edited by Fernando Horcasitas and Doris Heyden. Norman, Okla., 1971.

——. *History of the Indies of New Spain.* Translated by Doris Heyden. Norman, Okla., and London, 1994.

Fuentes, Patricia de, ed. *The Conquistadors: First Person Accounts of the Conquest of Mexico.* New York, 1963.

Gómara, Francisco López de. *Historia de la conquista de Mexico.* 2 vols. Mexico, 1943.

——. *Cortés: The Life of the Conqueror by His Secretary.* Translated and edited by Lesley Byrd Simpson. Berkeley and Los Angeles, "1964.

Grijalva, Juan de. *The Discovery of New Spain in 1518.* Edited and translated by Henry Raup Wagner. Pasadena, Calif., 1942.

Herrera, Antonio de. *Historia general de los hechos de los Castellanos en las isles y tierra firme de el Mar Oceano.* 1601–1615. 10 vols., Madrid, 1944–47.

Ixtlilxochitl, Fernando de Alva. *Ally of Cortés: Account 13: Of the Coming of the Spaniards and the Beginning of the Evangelical Law.* Translated by Douglass K. Ballentine. El Paso, Tex., 1969.

Las Casas, Bartolomé de. *History of the Indies of New Spain.* Translated and edited by Andree Collard. New York, 1971.

Lockhart, James. *We People Here: Nahuatl Accounts of the Conquest of Mexico,* vol 1. Berkeley, Calif., 1993.

Sahagún, Bernardino de. *The Conquest of New Spain.* Translated by Howard F. Cline. Edited by S. L. Cline. Salt Lake City, 1989.

———. *The War of Conquest: How It Was Waged Here in Mexico: The Aztecs' Own Story.* Rendered into modern English by Arthur J. O. Anderson and Charles E. Dibble. Salt Lake City, 1978.

Salazar, Francisco Cervantes de. *Crónica de Nueva España.* Madrid, 1914.

Saville, Marshall H. *Narrative of Some of the Things of New Spain and of the Great City of Temestitan Mexico, Written by the Anonymous Conqueror, a Companion of Hernán Cortás.* Boston, 1978.

Tapia, Andrés de. *Relación de Andrés de Tapia.* Published in *Crónicas de la Conquista,* ed. Garcia Icazbalceta. University of Mexico, 1950.

The Codices and Aztec Sources

Aubin Codex. Edited by Charles E. Dibble. Mexico, 1963.

Codex Borgia. Full Color Restoration of the Ancient Mexican Manuscript. Gisele Díaz and Alan Rogers, with introduction and commentary by Bruce E. Byland. New York, 1993.

Codex Chimalpopoca: History and Mythology of the Aztecs. Translated from the Nahuatl by John Bierhorst. Tucson, 1992.

Codex Florentine. Also know as Bernardino de Sahugún, *General History of the Things of New Spain.* 13 vols. Translated by Charles E. Dibble and Arthur J. O. Anderson. Salt Lake City, 1950–82.

Codex Mendoza. Commentaries by Kurt Miller. Fribourg, 1978.

Codex Ramirez. Edited by Jose M. Vigil. Mexico, 1878.

Crónica Mexicana. Edited by Alvarado F. Tezozomoc. Mexico City, 1944.

Crónica Mexicayotl. Edited by Alvarado F. Tezozomoc. Spanish version by Adrian León. Mexico City, 1949.

Books and Articles

Almazán, Marco A. "Hernán Cortés: Virtù vs. Fortuna." *Journal of American Culture* 20:2 (1997): 131–38.

Altamirano, Juan Carlos. *The Spanish Horse Under the Bourbon Kings.* Málaga, Spain, 2004.

——. *History and Origins of the Spanish Horse.* Málaga, Spain, 2002.

——. *The Royal Stables of Cordoba.* Málaga, Spain, 2001.

Altman, Ida. "Spanish Society in Mexico City After the Conquest." *Hispanic American Historical Review* 71:3 (1991): 413–45.

Anawalt, Patricia Rieff. *Indian Clothing Before Cortés: Mesoamerian Costumes from the Codices* (Norman, Okla., 1981).

——. "Understanding Aztec Human Sacrifice." *Archaeology* 35:5 (1982): 38–45.

——. "Riddle of the Emperor's Cloak." *Archaeology* 46:3 (1993): 30–36.

Anaya, Rudolfo A. *Lord of the Dawn: The Legend of Quetzalcoatl.* Albuquerque, N.M., 1987.

Anderson, Arthur J. O., Frances Berdan, and James Lockhart. *Beyond the Codices: The Nahua View of Colonial Mexico.* Berkeley, 1976.

Anderson, Arthur J. O. and Charles E. Dibble. *The War of Conquest: How It Was Waged Here in Mexico.* Salt Lake City, 1978.

Andrews, J. Richard. *Introduction to Classical Nahuatl.* Austin, Tex., 1975.

Apenes, Oscar. "The Primitive Salt Production of Lake Texcoco," *Thenos* 9:1 (1944) 25–40.

Armillas, Pedro. "Mesoamerican Fortifications." *Antiquity* 25 (1951): 77–86.

——. "Gardens on Swamps." *Science* 174 (1971): 653–61.

Baldwin, Neil. *Legends of the Plumed Serpent: Biography of a Mexican God.* New York, 1998.

Bancroft, Hubert Howe. *History of Mexico.* New York, 1914.

Benitez, Fernando. *In the Footsteps of Cortés.* New York, 1952.

Berdan, Frances. *The Aztecs of Central Mexico: An Imperial Society.* New York, 1982.

Berler, Beatrice. *The Conquest of Mexico: A Modern Rendering of William H. Prescott's History.* San Antonio, 1988.

Bierhorst, John, trans. *Cantares Mexicanos: Songs of the Aztecs.* Stanford, Calif., 1985.

——. *Four Masterworks of American Indian Literature: Quetzalcoatl, the Ritual of Condolence, Cuceb, the Night Chant.* New York, 1974.

——. *A Nahuatl-English Dictionary in Concordance to "Cantares Mexicanos," with an Analytic Transcription and Grammatical Notes.* Stanford, Calif., 1985.

Birney, Hoffman. *Brothers of Doom: The Story of the Pizarros of Peru.* New York, 1942.

Bishop, Morris. *The Odyssey of Cabeza de Vaca.* New York and London, 1933.

Boone, Elizabeth. *The Aztec Templo Mayor.* Washington, D.C., 1987.

Boorstin, Daniel. *The Discoverers.* New York, 1983.

Boyd-Bowman, Peter. "Negro Slaves in Early Colonial Mexico." *Americas* 26:2 (1969): 134–51.

Braden, Charles S. *Religious Aspects of the Conquest of Mexico.* Durham, N.C., 1930.

Brading, David. *The First America: The Spanish Monarchy, Creole Patriots, and the Liberal State, 1492–1867.* Cambridge, 1991.

Brereton, J. M. *The Horse in War.* New York, 1976.

Broda, Johanna, David Carrasco, and Eduardo Moctezuma. *The Great Temple of Tenochtitlan: Center and Periphery in the Aztec World.* Berkeley, Calif., 1988.

Brooks, Francis J. "Motecuzoma Xocoyotl, Hernán Cortés, and Bernal Díaz Castillo: The Construction of an Arrest." *Hispanic American Historical Review* 75:2 (1995): 149–83.

Bruman, Henry. *Alcohol in Ancient Mexico.* Salt Lake City, 2000.

Brundage, Burr Cartwright. *A Rain of Darts: The Mexica Aztecs.* Austin, Tex., and London, 1972.

——. *The Phoenix of the Western World: Quetzalcoatl and the Sky Religion.* Norman, Okla., 1981.

Burkhart, Louise M. *The Slippery Earth: Nahua-Christian Moral Dialogue in Sixteenth-Century Mexico.* Tucson, Ariz., 1989.

Burland, C. A. *Montezuma: Lord of the Aztecs.* New York, 1973.

——. *Magic Books from Mexico.* Viking Penguin, 1953.

——. *Art and Life in Ancient Mexico.* Oxford, 1947.

Butterfield, Marvin E. *Jerónimo de Aguilar, Conquistador.* Tuscaloosa, Ala., 1955.

Carman, Glen. *Rhetorical Conquests: Cortés, Gomara, and Renaissance Imperialism.* West Lafayette, Ind., 2006.

Carrasco, David. *City of Sacrifice: The Aztec Empire and the Role of Violence in Civilization.* Boston, 1999.

——. *Quetzalcoatl and the Irony of Empire: Myths and Prophecies in the Aztec Tradition.* Chicago and London, 1982.

Carrasco, David, and Eduardo Matos Moctezuma. *Moctezuma's Mexico: Visions of the Aztec World.* Boulder, Colo., 2003.

Carrasco, Pedro. *The Tenochca Empire of Ancient Mexico: The Triple Alliance of Tenochtitlán, Tetzcoco, and Tlacopan.* Norman, Okla., 1999.

Caso, Alfonso. *The Aztecs: People of the Sun.* Norman, Okla., 1958.

——. *The Religion of the Aztecs.* Mexico City, 1937.

Castilo-Feliu, Guillermo. *Xicotencatl: An Anonymous Historical Novel About the Events Leading Up to the Conquest of the Aztec Empire.* Austin, Tex., 1999.

Cisneros, José, and John O. West. *Riders Across the Centuries: Horsemen of the Spanish Borderlands.* El Paso, Tex., 1984.

Clendinnen, Inga. *Aztecs: An Interpretation.* New York, 1991.

———. *Ambivalent Conquests: Maya and Spaniard in Yucatán, 1517–1570.* New York, 2003.

———. "'Fierce and Unnatural Cruelty': Cortés and the Conquest of Mexico." In Stephen Greenblatt, *New World Encounters.* Berkeley, Calif., 1993.

Cocker, Mark. *Rivers of Blood, Rivers of Gold: Europe's Conquest of Indigenous Peoples.* New York, 1998.

Coe, Michael D. *Mexico: From the Olmecs to the Aztecs.* London, 1994.

Coe, Sophie D. *America's First Cuisines.* Austin, Tex., 1994.

Coe, Sophie D., and Michael D. Coe. *The True History of Chocolate.* London, 1996.

Collis, Maurice. *Cortés and Montezuma.* New York, 1954.

Cook, Noble David. *Born to Die: Disease and New World Conquest, 1492–1650.* New York and London, 1998.

Cook, Sherburne F., and Lesley Byrd Simpson. *The Population of Central Mexico in the Sixteenth Century.* Berkeley, Calif., 1948.

Crosby, Alfred W., Jr. *The Columbian Exchange: Biological and Cultural Consequences of 1492.* Westport, Conn., 2003.

Cypress, Sandra Messenger. *La Malinche in Mexican Literature: From History to Myth.* Austin, Tex., 1991.

Davies, Nigel. *The Aztecs: A History.* Norman, Okla., 1980.

Day, Jane S. *Aztec: The World of Moctezuma.* Denver, Colo., 1992.

Denhardt, Robert M. *The Horse of the Americas.* Norman, Okla., 1975.

Descola, Jean. *The Conquistadors.* Translated by Malcolm Barnes. New York, 1957.

Diamond, Jared. *Guns, Germs, and Steel: The Fates of Human Societies.* New York, 1997.

Díaz, Juan. *Itinerario de Juan de Grijalva. From Cronicas de la Conquista.* Mexico, 1950.

Dobie, Frank J. *The Mustangs.* Edison, N.J., 1952.

Durand-Forest, J. de. *The Native Sources and the History of the Valley of Mexico.* BAR International Series 204. London, 1984.

Elliot, J. H. *Spain and Its World, 1500–1700: Selected Essays.* New Haven, Conn., 1989.

Evans, Susan Toby. *Ancient Mexico and Central America: Archeology and Culture History.* New York and London, 2004.

——. "The Productivity of Maguey Terrace Agriculture in Central Mexico During the Aztec Period." In *Gardens of Prehistory: The Archeology of Settlement Agriculture in Greater Mesoamerica.* Edited by Thomas W. Killion. Tuscaloosa, Ala., 1992.

——. "Aztec Palaces." In *Palaces of the Ancient New World.* Edited by Susan Toby Evans and Joanna Pillsbury. Washington, D.C., 1999.

Fagan, Brian M. *Kingdoms of Gold, Kingdoms of Jade: The Americas Before Columbus.* New York, 1991.

——. *The Aztecs.* New York, 1984.

Fehrenbach, T. R. *Fire and Blood: A History of Mexico.* New York, 1995.

Florescano, Enrique, and Lysa Hochroth, trans. *The Myth of Quetzalcoatl.* Baltimore, 1999.

——. *Memory, Myth, and Time in Mexico: From the Aztecs to Independence.* Austin, Tex., 1994.

Gardiner, C. Harvey. *The Constant Captain: Gonzalo Sandoval.* Carbondale, Ill., 1961.

——. *Martín López. Conquistador Citizen of Mexico.* Lexington, Kentucky, 1958.

——. *Naval Power in the Conquest of Mexico.* Austin, Tex., 1956.

Gibson, Charles. *Spain in America.* New York, 1967.

———. "The Aztec Aristocracy in Colonial Mexico." *Comparative Studies in Society and History,* 2 (1960): 169–96.

———. *The Aztecs Under Spanish Rule.* Stanford, Calif., 1964.

———. "Structure of the Aztec Empire." In *Handbook of Middle American Indians,* vol. 15 (1975): 322–400.

———. *Tlaxcala in the Sixteenth Century.* Stanford, Calif., 1952.

Gillespie, Susan D. *The Aztec Kings: The Construction of Rulership in Mexica History.* Tucson, Ariz., 1989.

Gonzaga, Paulo Gaviao. *A History of the Horse,* vol. 1: *The Iberian Horse from Ice Age to Antiquity.* London, 2004.

Grafton, Anthony. *New World, Ancient Texts: The Power of Tradition and the Shock of Discovery.* Cambridge, Mass., 1992.

Graham, R. B. Cunninghame. *Horses of the Conquest: A Study of the Steeds of the Spanish Conquistadors.* Long Riders, 2004.

Greenblatt, Stephen. *New World Encounters.* Berkeley, Calif., 1993.

———. *Marvelous Possessions: The Wonder of the New World.* Chicago, 1991.

Griffiths, Nicholas, and Fernando Cervantes. *Spiritual Encounters: Interactions between Christianity and Native Religions in Colonial America.* Birmingham, U.K., 1999.

Gruzinski, Serge. *The Conquest of Mexico: The Incorporation of Indian Societies into the Western World, 16th–18th Centuries.* Cambridge, U.K., 1993.

Guilmartin, John Francis. *Changing Technology and Mediterranian Warfare at Sea in the Sixteenth Century.* Princeton, N.J., 1971.

———. "The Logistics of Warfare at Sea in the Sixteenth Century: The Spanish Perspective." In *Feeding Mars: Logistics in Western Warfare from the Middle Ages to the Present.* Edited by John A. Lynn. Boulder, Colo., 1993.

Hamnett, Brian. *A Concise History of Mexico.* Cambridge, Mass., 1999.

Harner, M. "The Ecological Basis for Aztec Sacrifice." *American Ethnologist* 4 (1977): 117–35.

Harris, Marvin. *Cannibals and Kings: The Origins of Cultures*. New York, 1977.

Harris, Max. *Aztecs, Moors, and Christians: Festivals of Reconquest in Mexico and Spain*. Austin, Tex., 2000.

Hassig, Ross. *Mexico and the Spanish Conquest*. Norman, Okla., 2006.

———. *Trade, Tribute, and Transportation: The Sixteenth-Century Political Economy in the Valley of Mexico*. Norman, Okla., 1985.

———. *Aztec Warfare: Imperial Expansion and Political Control*. Norman, Okla., 1988.

———. *War and Society in Ancient Mesoamerica*. Berkeley, Calif., 1992.

———. *Time, History, and Belief in Aztec and Colonial Mexico*. Austin, Tex., 2001.

Heath, Ian. *The Armies of the Aztec and Inca Empires, Other Native Peoples of the Americas, and the Conquistadores 1450–1608*. Nottingham, U.K., 1999.

Heil, Gerrit W., Roland Bobbink, and Nuri Trigo Boix. *Ecology and Man in Mexico's Central Volcanoes Area*. Dordrecht, Netherlands, 2003.

Held, Robert. *The Age of Firearms: A Pictorial History from the Invention of Gunpowder to the Advent of the Modern Breechloader*. Chicago, 1970.

Helly, Mathilde, and Rémi Courgeon. *Montezuma and the Aztecs*. New York, 1996.

Helps, Arthur. *The Life of Hernando Cortés*. 2 vols. London, 1894.

Hemming, John. *The Conquest of the Incas*. New York, 1970.

———. *The Search for El Dorado*. London, 1978.

Henty, G. A. *By Right of Conquest, or, With Cortez in Mexico*. New York, 1890.

Hicks, Frederic. "Gift and Tribute: Relations of Dependency in Aztec Mexico." In *Early State Economics*. Edited by Henri J.M. Claessen and Pieter van de Velde. New Brunswick, N.J., 1991.

Highwater, Jamake. *Arts of the Indian Americas: Leaves from the Sacred Tree.* New York, 1983.

——. *The Primal Mind: Vision and Reality in Indian America.* New York, 1981.

——. *The Sun, He Dies.* New York, 1980.

Hine, Robert V., and John Mack Faragher. *The American West: A New Interpretive History.* New Haven, Conn., 2000.

Holmer, Rick. *The Aztec Book of Destiny.* Booksurge, North Charleston, S.C., 2005.

Howard, David A. *Conquistador in Chains: Cabeza de Vaca and the Indians of the Americas.* Tuscaloosa, Ala., 1977.

Howard, Robert West. *The Horse in America.* Chicago and New York, 1965.

Innes, Hammond. *The Conquistadors.* New York, 1969.

Isaac, Barry. "Aztec Warfare: Goals and Battlefield Comportment." *Ethnology* 22:2 (1983): 121–31.

Johnson, John J. "The Introduction of the Horse into the Western Hemisphere." *Hispanic American Historical Review* 23:4 (1943): 587–610.

Johnson, William Weber. *Heroic Mexico: The Violent Emergence of a Modern Nation.* New York, 1968.

Johnson, Willis Fletcher. *The History of Cuba.* New York, 1920.

Jones, Archer. *The Art of War in the Western World.* Urbana, Ill., 1987.

Kamen, Henry. *Spain's Road to Empire: The Making of a World Power, 1492–1763.* New York and London, 2002.

Kandell, Jonathan. *La Capital: The Biography of Mexico City.* New York, 1989.

Karttunen, Frances. *Between Worlds: Interpreters, Guides, and Survivors.* New Brunswick, N.J., 1994.

——. "Interpreters Snatched from the Shore: The Successful and the Others." In *The Language Encounter in the Americas, 1492–1800.* Edited by Edward G. Gray and Norman Fiering. New York, 2000.

Kay, Almere Read. *Time and Sacrifice in the Aztec Cosmos.* Bloomington, Ind., 2005.

Keen, Benjamin. *The Aztec Image in Western Thought.* New Brunswick, N.J., 1971.

Kellogg, Susan. *Law and the Transformation of Aztec Culture.* Norman, Okla., 2005.

Kelly, John Eoghan. *Pedro de Alvarado, Conquistador.* Princeton, N.J., 1932.

Kicza, John E. *The Peoples and Civilizations of the Americas Before Contact.* Washington, D.C., 1998.

———. "A Comparison of Indian and Spanish Accounts of the Conquest of Mexico." In *Five Centuries of Mexican History.* Edited by Virginia and Jaime E. Rodriquez O. Irvine, Calif., 1992.

Kirkpatrick, F. A. *The Spanish Conquistadors.* London, 1934.

Klein, Cecilia. "The Ideology of Autosacrifice at the Templo Mayor." In *The Aztec Templo Mayor.* Edited by Elizabeth Boone, Washington, D.C., 1987.

Knight, Alan. *Mexico: From the Beginning to the Spanish Conquest.* New York and London, 2002.

Koch, Peter O. *The Aztecs, the Conquistadors, and the Making of Mexican Culture.* North Carolina and London, 2006.

Kurlansky, Mark. *Salt: A World History.* New York, 2002.

Lacroix, Jorge Gurria. *Itinerary of Hernán Cortés.* Mexico, 1973.

Lanyon, Anna. *The New World of Martín Cortés.* Cambridge, Mass., 2003.

———. *Malinche's Conquest.* New South Wales, 1999.

Le Clezio, J. M. G. *The Mexican Dream: Or the Interrupted Thought of Amerindian Civilizations.* Chicago and London, 1993.

León-Portilla, Miguel. *The Broken Spears: The Aztec Account of the Conquest of Mexico.* Boston, 1992.

———. *Aztec Thought and Culture: A Study of the Ancient Nahuatl Mind.* Norman, Okla., 1963.

———. *Pre-Columbian Literatures of Mexico*. Norman, Okla., 1969.

———. *Native Mesoamerican Spirituality*. Ramsey, N.J., 1980.

———. *The Aztec Image of Self and Society*. Salt Lake City, 1992.

———. *Bernardino de Sahagún: First Anthropologist*. Norman, Okla., 2002.

Levin, David. *History as Romantic Art: Bancroft, Prescott, Motley, and Parkman*. New York, 1967.

Linne, Sigvald. "Hunting and Fishing in the Valley of Mexico in the Middle of the 16th Century." *Ethnos* (Stockholm) 2 (1937): 56–64.

Loch, Sylvia. *The Royal Horse of Europe: The Story of the Andalusian and Lusitano*. London, 1986.

———. *The Nahuas After the Conquest: A Social and Cultural History of the Indians of Central Mexico, Sixteenth Through Eighteenth Centuries*. Stanford, Calif., 1992.

———. "Sightings: Initial Nahua Reactions to Spanish Culture." In *Implicit Understandings: Observing, Reporting, and Reflecting on the Encounters between Europeans and Other Peoples in the Early Modern Era*. Edited by Stuart B. Schwartz. Cambridge: Cambridge University Press, 1994.

López Austin, Alfredo. *The Human Body and Ideology: Concepts of the Ancient Nahuas*. Translated by Thelma Ortiz de Montellano and Bernard Ortiz de Montellano. 2 vols. Salt Lake City, 1980.

López-Portillo, José. *They Are Coming: The Conquest of Mexico*. Denton, Tex., 1992.

Madariaga, Salvador de. *Hernán Cortés: Conqueror of Mexico*. Coral Gables, Fla., 1942.

Mann, Charles C. *1491: New Revelations of the Americas Before Columbus*. New York, 2005.

Markman, Roberta H., and Peter T. Markman. *The Flayed God: The Mesoamerican Mythological Tradition*. New York, 1992.

Marks, Richard Lee. *Cortés: The Great Adventurer and the Fate of Aztec Mexico*. New York, 1993.

Maynard, Theodore. *De Soto and the Conquistadores*. New York, 1930.

McCaa, Robert. "Spanish and Nahuatl Views on Smallpox and Demographic Catastrophe in Mexico." *Journal of Interdisciplinary History* 25 (1995): 397–431.

McNeill, William H. *Plagues and Peoples*. New York, 1976.

McPheeters, D. W. "An Unknown Early Seventeenth-Century Codex of the Cronica Mexicana of Hernando Alvarado Tezozomoc." *Hispanic American Historical Review* 34:4 (1954): 506–12.

Meyer, Michael C., William H. Sherman, and Susan M. Deeds. *The Course of Mexican History*. Oxford, 2002.

Meyer, Michael C., and Williman H. Beezley. *The Oxford History of Mexico*. New York, 2000.

Moctezuma, Eduardo Matos. *Life and Death in the Templo Mayor*. Boulder, Colo., 1995.

Montellano, Bernard R. Ortiz de. *Aztec Medicine, Health, and Nutrition*. New Brunswick, N.J., and London, 1990.

Montfort, Fernando Carrizosa, and Ximena Chavez Balderas. *Great Temple of Tenochtitlán: Aztec Empire Sacred Precinct and Museum*. Translated by David B. Castledine. Mexico, 2003.

Morison, Samuel Eliot. *Admiral of the Ocean Sea: A Life of Christopher Columbus*. Boston, 1944.

Mundy, Barbara E. *Mapping of New Spain: Cartography and the Maps of the Relaciones Geograficas*. Chicago, 1996.

Nicholson, H. B. *Topiltzin Quetzalcoatl: The Once and Future Lord of the Toltecs*. Boulder, Colo., 2001.

Offner, Jerome A. *Law and Politics in Aztec Texcoco*. London, 1983.

——. "Aztec Legal Process: The Case of Texcoco." In *The Art and Iconography of Late Post-Classic Central Mexico*. Edited by Elizabeth Hill Boone. Washington, D.C., 1982.

Oliver, Guilhem. "The Hidden King and the Broken Flutes." In *Representing Aztec Ritual: Performance, Text, and Image in the Work of Sahagún*. Edited by Eloise Quiñones Keber. Boulder, Colo., 2002.

Oman, Sir Charles. *A History of War in the Sixteenth Century*. London, 1937.

Padden, R. C. *The Hummingbird and the Hawk: Conquest and Sovereignty in the Valley of Mexico, 1503–1541*. Columbus, Ohio, 1967.

Pagden, Anthony. *The Fall of Natural Man: The American Indian and the Origins of Comparative Ethnology*. Cambridge, Mass., 1982.

——. *Lords of All the World: Ideologies of Empire in Spain, Britain, and France*. New Haven, Conn., and London, 1995.

Paiewonsky, Michael. *Conquest of Eden: 1493–1515*. Rome and Chicago, 1991.

Parker, Geoffrey. "The Political World of Charles V." In *Charles V and His Time, 1500–1558*. Edited by Hugo Soly. Antwerp, Belgium, 1999.

Parry, J. H. *The Spanish Seaborne Empire*. New York, 1974.

Pasztory, Esther. *Aztec Art*. New York, 1983.

Peterson, David A., and Z. D. Green. "The Spanish Arrival and the Massacre at Cholula." *Notas Mesoamericanas* 10 (1987): 203–23.

Pohl, John, and Charles M. Robinson, III. *Aztecs and Conquistadors: The Spanish Invasion and the Collapse of the Aztec Empire*. Oxford, U.K., 2005.

——. *Aztec, Mixtec, and Zapotec Armies*. Oxford, U.K., 1991.

Polavieja, General Camilo, *Hernán Cortés, Copias de Documentos*, Seville, 1889.

Powell, Philip W. *Soldiers, Indians, and Silver: The Northward Advance of New Spain, 1550–1600*. Berkeley and Los Angeles, 1952.

Pratt, Mary Louise. "'Yo Soy La Malinche': Chicana Writers and the Poetics of Ethnonationalism." *Callaloo* 16:4 (1993): 859–73.

Prescott, William H. *History of the Conquest of Mexico*. New York, 2001.

——. *The World of the Aztecs*. Minerva, S.A. Geneva, 1970.

Pupo-Walker, Enrique, and Frances M. López-Morillas. *Castaways: The Narrative of Alvar Núñez Cabeza de Vaca*. Berkeley, Calif., 1993.

Ramsey, John Fraser. *Spain: The Rise of the First World Power*. Tuscaloosa, Ala., 1973.

Restall, Matthew. *Seven Myths of the Spanish Conquest.* New York, 2003.

Rout, Leslie B., Jr. *The African Experience in Spanish America.* London, 1969.

Saville, Marshall H. *Narrative of Some of the Things of New Spain and of the Great City of Temestitan Mexico, Written by the Anonymous Conqueror, a Companion of Hernan Cortés.* Boston, 1978.

——. *The Goldsmith's Art in Ancient Mexico.* Indian Notes and Monographs. New York, 1920.

——. *The Wood-Carver's Art in Ancient Mexico.* New York, 1925.

——. *Tizoc, Great Lord of the Aztecs 1481–1486.* New York, 1929.

Scarborough, Vernon L., and David R. Wilcox. *The Mesoamerican Ballgame.* Tucson, Ariz., 1991.

Schneider, Paul. *Brutal Journey: The Epic Story of the First Crossing of North America.* New York, 2006.

Schroeder, Susan, Stephanie Wood, and Robert Haskett. *Indian Women of Early Mexico.* Norman, Okla., and London, 1997.

Schwartz, Stuart B. *Victors and Vanquished: Spanish and Nahua Views of the Conquest of Mexico.* Boston and New York, 2000.

Séjourné, Laurette. *Burning Water. Thought and Religion in Ancient Mexico.* New York, 1956.

Sellnow, Les. *The Journey of the Western Horse: From the Spanish Conquest to the Silver Screen.* Lexington, Kentucky, 2003.

Sensing, Welton Jerry. "The Policies of Hernán Cortés as Described in His Letters." Ph.D. thesis, University of Illinois, Urbana, 1954.

Shorris, Earl. *The Life and Times of Mexico.* New York, 2004.

Simmons, Marc. *The Last Conquistador: Juan de Onate and the Settling of the Far Southwest.* Norman, Okla., 1991.

Simpson, Lesley Byrd. *The Encomienda in New Spain: Forced Native Labor in the Spanish Colonies, 1492–1550.* Berkeley, Calif., 1929.

Smith, Michael E. *The Aztecs.* Malden, Mass., 2003.

Solis, Felipe. *The Aztec Empire.* New York, 2004.

———. *Mexica: National Museum of Anthropology.* Mexico, 2004.

Soustelle, Jacques. *The Daily Life of the Aztecs on the Eve of the Spanish Conquest.* London, 1961.

Sowell, Thomas. *Conquests and Cultures: An International History.* New York, 1998.

Stannard, David E. *American Holocaust: Columbus and the Conquest of the New World.* New York, 1992.

Stern, Steve J. "Paradigms of Conquest: History, Historiography, and Politics." *Journal of Latin American Studies* 24 (1992): 1–34.

Stern, Theodore. *Rubber-ball Games of the Americas.* New York, 1950.

Stuart, Gene S. *The Mighty Aztecs.* Washington, D.C., 1981.

Talty, Stephan. *Empire of Blue Water: Captain Morgan's Great Pirate Army, the Epic Battle for the Americas, and the Catastrophe that Ended the Outlaw's Bloody Reign.* New York, 2007.

Terrell, John Upton. *Journey into Darkness.* New York, 1962.

Thomas, Hugh. *Conquest: Montezuma, Cortés, and the Fall of Old Mexico.* New York, 1993.

———. *Who's Who of the Conquistadors.* London, 2000.

Todorov, Tzvetan. *The Conquest of America: The Question of the Other.* New York, 1984.

Tompkins, Ptolemy. *This Tree Grows Out of Hell: Mesoamerica and the Search for the Magical Body.* New York, 1990.

Townsend, Camilla. "Burying the White Gods: New Perspectives on the Conquest of Mexico." *American Historical Review* 108 (2003): 659–87.

Townsend, Richard. *The Aztecs.* London, 1992.

Tozzer, Alfred M. *Landa's Relación de Las Cosas de Yucatán: A Translation.* Peabody, Mass., 1941.

Trexler, Richard C. *Sex and Conquest: Gendered Violence, Political Order, and the European Conquest of the Americas.* Ithaca, N.Y., 1995.

Tsouras, Peter G. *Montezuma: Warlord of the Aztecs.* Washington, D.C., 2005.

Valencia, Robert Himmerich y. *The Encomenderos of New Spain,* *1521–1555.* Austin, Tex., 1991.

Valliant, George C. *Aztecs of Mexico: Origin, Rise, and Fall of the Aztec Nation.* New York, 1941.

Van Tuerenhout, Dirk R. *The Aztecs: New Perspectives.* Santa Barbara, Calif., 2005.

Van Zantwijk, R. *The Aztec Arrangement: The Social History of Pre-Spanish Mexico.* Norman, Okla., 1985.

Varner, John Grier, and Jeannette Johnson Varner. *Dogs of the Conquest.* Norman, Okla., 1983.

Von Hagen, Victor W. *The Aztec: Man and Tribe.* New York, 1964.

Wagner, H. R. "The Discovery of the Yucatán by Francisco Hernandez de Cordoba." *Geographical Review* 6:5 (1918).

———. *Spanish Voyages to the Northwest Coast of America.* California Historical Society Special Publication No. 4. San Francisco, 1929.

———. "Peter Martyr and His Works." *Proceedings of the American Antiquarian Society* 56 (1946): 239–288.

Wasserman, Martin. "Montezuma's Passivity: An Alternative View Without Postconquest Distortions of a Myth." *Masterkey* 57:3 (July–September 1983): 85–93.

Weatherford, Jack. *The History of Money.* New York, 1997.

Weber, David J. *New Spain's Far Northern Frontier: Essays on Spain in the American West, 1540–1821.* Albuquerque, N.M., 1979.

Wepman, Dennis. *Hernán Cortés.* New York, 1986.

Werner, Louis. "Equine Allies in the New World." *Americas* 53:4 (2001): 24–30.

Wild, Peter. *Alvar Nuñez Cabeza de Vaca.* Boise, Id., 1991.

White, John Manchip. *Cortés and the Downfall of the Aztec Empire: A Study in a Conflict of Cultures.* Worcester, Mass., and London, 1970.

Wolf, Eric R. *Sons of the Shaking Earth.* Chicago, 1959.

———. *Europe and the People without History.* Berkeley, Calif., 1982.

———. *The Valley of Mexico: Studies in Pre-Hispanic Ecology and Society.* Albuquerque, N.M., 1976.

Wood, Michael. *Conquistadors.* Berkeley, Calif., 2000.

Wright, R. R. "Negro Companions of the Spanish Explorers." *American Anthropologist* 4:2 (1902): 217–28.

Wright, Ronald. *Stolen Continents: The Americas Through Indian Eyes Since 1492.* New York, 1992.

Xenophon. *The Art of Horsemanship.* Translated by M. H. Morgan. London, 2004.

PHOTO CREDITS:

ACKNOWLEDGMENTS

Authors never write books alone, even if it often feels as if we do. As usual, I first have to thank my writing family, the Free Range Writers: Kim Barnes, Jane Varley, Lisa Norris, and Collin Hughes. They keep the fire stoked, the cabin warm, and the music going. Thanks, always, to my literary agent Scott Waxman, who suggested I see a man about a horse, and that man ended up being Hernán Cortés. Scott's imagination is sweeping and boundless, his ability to see his way to the good story uncanny. Thanks also to foreign rights agent Farley Chase, whose hard work has ensured that *Conquistador* will reach readers in numerous languages.

I'm deeply grateful to my intrepid first readers, compadres John Larkin and Kim Barnes, for their careful proofing and surveillance of the text. Thanks, John, for the humor and scathing honesty, and thank you, Kim, for your profound ability to see the larger narratives.

In June 2006 I took a lengthy research trip during which I followed the route of the conquistadors from where they landed on the Gulf Coast at San Juan de Ulúa, over the mountains and across the plains to Mexico City. Many people assisted me during my journey, making it among the best, most educational experiences of my life. Thanks to the Museo de Antropología, Xalapa, for the wonderful tour and detailed explanations of stunning pre-Columbian works, particularly the awe-inspiring Olmec heads. Thanks also to Veracruz University in Xalapa.

In Cholula, big embraces go out to Rodrigo Moctezuma and the amazing crew at Jazzatlán. I will always remember their kindness and enthusiasm for my project, and their suggestions for the music of Mexico. Rodrigo gave me a personal tour from Cholula to the Pass of Cortés in his Volkswagen van, a trip that was as informative as it was adventurous.

In Mexico City and environs, the attentive and knowledgeable curators and guides at the Museo Templo Mayor, Teotihuacán, and the Museo Nacionale de Antropolgía took excellent care of me and thoroughly answered my many questions.

Throughout the process of writing *Conquistador*, the folks at Random House/Bantam Dell have been fantastic to work with. My editor John Flicker brought his considerable expertise and vision to bear on the book at every stage, from conception to polished manuscript. His eye is sharp and his ear keen, and he understands the delicate balance of narrative pacing and historical accuracy. I look forward to working on more books with him.

The Washington State University libraries were instrumental in my research, especially everyone in Interlibrary Loans, and at Holland New Library. Their organization, knowledge, and timely retrieval of my innumerable requests made my work smooth and efficient.

Edward Whitley at Bridgeman Art Library offered invaluable assistance and expertise in my image search, and I certainly owe him a debt of gratitude for his expedient work and correspondence with me.

Finally, thanks to my wonderful family, extended and immediate. To my children Logan and Hunter, who endure my late nights, deadlines, and travel junkets, and to my partner, friend, and spouse Camie, who continues to support me: you allow me to live the life I always dreamed of.

INDEX

BUDDY LEVY is also the author of *River of Darkness, American Legend: The Real-Life Adventures of David Crockett,* and *Echoes on Rimrock: In Pursuit of the Chukar Partridge.* As a freelance journalist he has covered adventure sports and lifestyle around the world. He is clinical associate professor of English at Washington State University, and lives in northern Idaho with his wife, Camie, and two children.